GREEK TO ME

GREEK TO ME
Learning New Testament Greek through Memory Visualization

J. Lyle Story

Cullen I K Story

Illustrated by
Peter Allen Miller

HarperSanFrancisco
A Division of HarperCollins*Publishers*

LIBRARY OF CONGRESS CATALOG CARD NUMBER: 79–1769

INTERNATIONAL STANDARD BOOK NUMBER: 0–06–067705–8

93   94   95   96   97   RRD(H)   21   20   19   18   17   16   15   14   13

Contents

Acknowledgments

The Biblical readings which accompany the various lessons are based on standard texts of the Greek Bible. The Old Testament readings are adapted from the Septua- ginta, ed. A. Rahlfs, Vols. I and II (third ed., 1949), used by permission of the Deutsche Bibelstiftung of Stuttgart. The specific portions used - in order of appearance in our grammar - are taken from 2 Kingdoms 9 (= 2 Samuel 9), 4 Kingdoms 6 (= 2 Kings 6), Job 1, 3 King- doms 22 (= 1 Kings 22), 1 Kingdoms 16 (= 1 Samuel 16), Genesis 37, Genesis 41-45, 4 Kingdoms 7 (= 2 Kings 7), Jonah 1-4, 4 Kingdoms 22-23 (= 2 Kings 22-23). New Test- ament readings are adapted from The Greek New Testament, United Bible Societies (third ed., 1975), used by per- mission of the copyright owner. The particular portions used - in order of appearance in our grammar - are taken from Matthew 22:1-10, Luke 19:1-10, John 11:1-45, John 6:1-69, Acts 13:1-13; 15:36-41, 2 Timothy 4:11, John 12, 13-17, Acts 10:1-48, Acts 16:1-34. In addition, numerous individual texts of The Greek New Testament have been produced - used by permission - to illustrate specific points of grammar. Vocabulary definitions - in abbrevi- ated form - are based on A Greek-English Lexicon of the New Testament and Other Early Christian Literature, by Bauer-Arndt-Gingrich, The University of Chicago Press (1955), used by permission of the copyright owner.

Furthermore, we acknowledge that Professor Bruce M. Metzger has kindly given permission for the use of the word-frequency lists in his work, Lexical Aids for Students of New Testament Greek, Princeton, N.J. (1965) upon which the vocabulary of our grammar is based.

One reading (Lesson 12-C) is from The Second Apology of Justin Martyr, chapter two, adapted from the text of G. Krüger, Die Apologieen Justins des Märtyrers (Tübingen und Leipzig, Verlag von J.C.B. Mohr, 1904), pp. 60-62. And, one other reading (Lesson 19), comes from The Martyrdom of Polycarp, adapted from the text of Gebhardt, Harnack, and Zahn, Patrum Apostolicorum Opera (Lipsiae, J.C. Hinrichs, 1900), pp. 119-127.

The photograph of one page of Papyrus 46 is re- produced by permission of the Trustees of the Chester Beatty Library and Gallery of Oriental Art. The plate includes I Corinthians 8:1-3. The words to the Greek hymn (found in Lesson 10) are adapted from the text of I Timothy 3:16 and set to a traditional French tune. We are indebted to the Reverend Aristides Varrias of Salonika, Greece, and to Mr. Robert Bernard of Lawrence- ville, New Jersey for valuable suggestions pertaining to the Greek readings which accompany the lessons.

We are especially indebted to Peter Allen Miller for his excellent art work and lay-out, to Beth Visbal for her accurate typing, and to the many students who have encouraged and supported us in the development of our work. We also thank Ed Hartnell for his art work at the early stages.

Our work is dedicated with appreciation to those many students of New Testament Greek from whom — in the past — we have learned so much, and to those students of New Testament Greek from whom — today and tomorrow — we will learn even more.

ὅπου πλείων κόπος, πολὺ κέρδος

"Where there is more toil, there is much gain."
Ignatius to Polycarp
(ca: AD 108)

About This Book...

The grammar which follows has emerged from our desire to see Greek become a useful and exciting tool for New Testament study and personal growth. It has been our growing concern that for many students in seminaries and Bible colleges, as well as self-taught students, Greek is the language of never-ending endings as well as being the impossible requirement of an inflexible curriculum. Our grammar aims to encourage and motivate students to learn both the grammar and vocabulary of koine Greek in a creative and productive way. The approach is new, yet it has been tried and tested with several hundred students and the response has been well worth the effort. We think that you will not only enjoy the new approach but profit from it.

Before beginning with the grammar itself, our approach needs some explanation. Obviously, much of our learning process associates what is known with what is unknown. For example, a grade school student, Joey, learns a new sport unknown to him, i.e. softball. He is confused not only by an unfamiliar ball and bat, but also by rules concerning strikes, balls, outs, and bases. However, if Joey knows how to play kickball, then he will learn the game of softball with surprising ease. He learns to relate the known to the unknown, so much so that the unknown becomes a part of his life. In language, the learning process is complicated by the fact that the relationship between the unknown and known is not apparent or made clear. As a result, students become victims of the painful "rote" method and are often tempted to throw in the sponge. If, however, a bridge can be built between the unknown and known, new interest will be aroused and the learning process will be enhanced.

For instance, observe the Greek vocabulary word, ἐγείρω. It is pronounced e gei row, and it means, "I raise up." By itself, the word with its meaning represent the unknown or the intangible. However, we can adopt and/or adapt ENGLISH SUBSTITUTE WORDS, that is the known, visualize the picture, and relate the Greek word to its meaning, namely relate the unknown to the known.

ἐγείρω - I raise up

"I RAISE UP AN EGG ARROW"

What you see is a young would-be Robin Hood who says, "I raise up an egg-arrow" (ἐγείρω - I raise up). Look well at the egg-shaped arrow. You will not soon forget the picture because of its ridiculous character. Very simply, we have taken the unknown (ἐγείρω - I raise up), related it to the known (raising up an egg-arrow), and through an absurd picture we have learned the unknown and locked it in our memory bank for ready reference and use.

Therefore, throughout our grammar you will find substitute words to aid in the mastery of the entire Greek grammar. Not only will individual words and endings be learned by association words, but many concepts can and will be LINKED together. Memory experts recommend the use of SUBSTITUTE WORDS and a LINK SYSTEM. In this way, the Greek grammar with its endings will be visualized and remembered, both for initial and long-term retention.

One important suggestion -- learn the vocabulary of a lesson before trying to read or translate the exercises which go with that lesson. You will save much time and avoid the frustration of turning pages endlessly to find the meanings of Greek words which need to be mastered first. In a later edition, individual vocabulary pictures may be printed separately.

You will be introduced to the vocabulary and idiom (usage) of New Testament Greek, learning almost 600 words, the vast majority of which occur in the New Testament 25 times or more. The exercises will use each word at least two or three times, many words being used more frequently. The illustrations and stories are adapted from, and incorporate the style and idiom of, Biblical narratives drawn either from the Greek Old Testament (the Septuagint) or from the Greek New Testament. One reading, "The Martyrdom of Polycarp," is adapted from an authentic account (ca. A.D. 155) found in the Apostolic Fathers. One other reading from the same period is patterned after a story in Justin Martyr's Second Apology.

As the grammar goes forth our hope and prayer is that you will have an exciting experience with the Greek Bible, and thereby grow into the likeness of the Savior. We desire that Greek become an effective tool for the student and teacher of God's Word.

Cullen I K Story

J. Lyle Story

An Introduction to the Greek Alphabet

Welcome to the exciting world of New Testament Greek. You are in for quite an experience. Greek is important for understanding and interpreting the message of the New Testament. You will study the common (koine) Greek, the language which is the melting pot of the ancient Greek dialects. Koine Greek became the means by which the writers of the New Testament communicated the Gospel message to the Mediterranean world.

Alphabet

As you can surmise, we start with the Greek alphabet. There are twenty four letters in the Greek alphabet. It will be important for you to learn the names of the letters, the form of the small letters, and the English equivalent and pronunciation of each. The small letters are the most important to learn and should be learned first, then, later the capital letters. There is no clear way of knowing how Greek was pronounced in ancient times. The pronunciation of the alphabet and diphthongs, in this grammar, follows the pronunciation accepted in numerous grammars.

The Greek Alphabet

small letters	CAPITAL LETTERS	Names of letters	English Pronunciation
α	Α	alpha	a as in far
β	Β	beta	b
γ[1]	Γ	gamma	g (hard) as in get
δ	Δ	delta	d
ε	Ε	epsilon	e as in get
ζ	Ζ	zeta	z (initial) as in zoo dz (medial) as in adz
η	Η	eta	e as in obey
ϑ	Θ	theta	th as in think
ι	Ι	iota	i (short) as in pit i (long) as in machine
κ	Κ	kappa	k
λ	Λ	lambda	l
μ	Μ	mu	m
ν	Ν	nu	n
ξ	Ξ	xi	x as in box
ο	Ο	omicron	o as in not
π	Π	pi	p
ρ	Ρ	rho	r
σ,ς[2]	Σ	sigma	s
τ	Τ	tau	t
υ	Υ	upsilon	u as in put
φ	Φ	phi	ph as in phone
χ	Χ	chi	ch as in German "ach"
ψ	Ψ	psi	ps (initial) as in psalms ps (medial or final) as in lips
ω	Ω	omega	o as in ode

---

[1] Before γ, κ, χ, or ξ, the γ is pronounced similar to an "n," (ἄγγελος).

[2] The form σ is used at the beginning of a word or within it, the form ς at the very end (ἐσθίω, λόγος).

Vowels

The vowels are as follows:

ε and ο, always short

η and ω, always long

α, ι, υ either short or long

All diphthongs are long except final "οι" and final "αι." The letter "ι" is often written below the letters α, η, ω (ᾳ, ῃ, ῳ), and is called iota subscript. It does not affect the pronunciation of the letters under which it appears.

Diphthongs

In English, the letters "o" and "u" are found together in the word "couch," forming a new sound, different in quality from either vowel pronounced by itself. The combination of "ou" is called a diphthong. The Greek language also has diphthongs, quite similar to those found in English.

αι as ai in aisle - καί
αυ as au in Faust - αὐτός
ει as ei in weight - ἐγείρω
ευ as eu in feud - εὐθύς

ηυ as eu in feud - προσηυχόμην
οι as oi in oil - λόγοις
ου as ou in youth - ἀκούω
υι as ui in suite - υἱός

Syllables

At this point you may wonder how to pronounce words. This principle may help you. EVERY SYLLABLE MUST CONTAIN A VOWEL OR A DIPHTHONG. Therefore, each word will have as many syllables as it has vowels and/or diphthongs. Observe the following examples:

λαμ-βάν-ο-μεν - four vowels = four syllables
ἄν-θρω-πος   - three vowels = three syllables
υἱ-έ   - one diphthong, one vowel = two syllables

Breathing Signs

You may have noticed in the alphabet that there is no letter "h." In the word ἁμαρτάνω the "h" sound appears as an inverted apostrophe, i.e. the first syllable is pronounced as "ha." The sign is called a rough breathing (ʽ). The smooth breathing (ʼ) which appears as an apostrophe, is seen in the word ἔχω, which does not have the "h" sound. A word which begins with a vowel or diphthong must have either a rough (ʽ) or smooth (ʼ) breathing sign, which is shown to you as the word appears in the vocabulary.

Practice

Write the small letters of the alphabet several times until you are very familiar with them.

αβγδεζηθικλμν ξοπρσ-ςτυφχψω

Identify the letters, the breathing marks, and pronounce the words:

χριστός   ἐκκλησία   ἄνθρωπος   ἁμαρτία   χαρίζομαι   ζωή

λόγος   φωνή   κοινή   χάρις   μαρτυρία   βίος

Enrichment

As you observe the first and last letters of the Greek alphabet (α and ω), you may recall the claim of the risen Jesus, Ἐγώ εἰμι τὸ ἄλφα καὶ τὸ ὦ, "I am the Alpha and the Omega." The claim is found in Rev. 1:8; 21:6; 22:13.

Many of you have seen engravings or signs bearing the capital letters ΙΧΘΥΣ, which spell the Greek word for "fish." Among early Christians, the five letters of the word were used as an acrostic to give expression to faith in Christ as follows:

Ι   = Ἰησοῦς = Jesus

Χ   = Χριστός = Christ

Θ   = θεοῦ   = of God

Υ   = Υἱός   = Son

Σ   = Σωτήρ   = Savior

i.e. Jesus Christ, Son of God, Savior

Chapter 1

<u>Vocabulary</u>

1. αἴρω — I take up, take away, lift up
2. ἀκούω — I hear (acoustic)[1]
3. ἀμαρτάνω — I sin
4. ἀνοίγω — I open
5. ἀποκτείνω — I kill
6. βάλλω — I throw (<u>b</u>allistic)
7. βαπτίζω — I baptize (baptize)
8. βλέπω — I see
9. γινώσκω — I know (gnostic)
10. γράφω — I write (graph)
11. διδάσκω — I teach (didactic)
12. διώκω — I pursue, persecute
13. δοξάζω — I glorify (<u>doxo</u>logy)
14. ἐγείρω — I raise up
15. ἐσθίω — I eat
16. εὑρίσκω — I find (eureka, "I have found it")
17. ἔχω — I have, hold
18. θεραπεύω — I heal (therapeutic)
19. κρίνω — I judge (critic)
20. λαμβάνω — I take, receive
21. λέγω — I say, speak (dia<u>lect</u>)
22. λύω — I loose, destroy
23. πέμπω — I send

---

[1]English derivatives or cognate words are listed in parentheses. They play an important role in the student's retention of Greek vocabulary.

IN THIS LESSON YOU WILL:

. . . learn the fundamentals of the verb system

. . . identify and translate simple Greek verbs

Hi! My name is Lu (λύω) and "I loose" and "destroy" things.

We will become great friends because I will help you to memorize the never-ending endings of the verb system.

The Verb

Each word in the vocabulary is a verb. A verb is an action word or a state of being. As an action word the verb among other things can:

1. State a fact - He threw the frisbee.

2. Give a command - Throw the frisbee!

3. Ask a question - Who threw the frisbee?

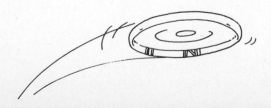

Foundational Concepts

Vera Verb

Hi! My name is Vera Verb. I will help you to learn the different parts of the verb that you will need to know. You will parse me. To parse means to <u>pick apart</u> or to identify a word fully. From the very beginning you must train yourself to parse me correctly since I appear in different forms. In lesson one, you will see many pictures. Pictures are essential to the learning process since we remember what we see far more than what we only read.

Now, look carefully at how I am parsed. I am picked apart from top to bottom. Examine the different parts <u>slowly</u>.

T.   Have you ever seen <u>tense</u> tears?   (Tense)

V.   Have you heard a <u>voice</u> with electrical amps? (Voice)

M.   Have you seen a <u>mu-mu</u> dress, or . . .   (Mood)

P.   A <u>purse</u> with . . .   (Person)

N.   <u>Numbers</u>?   (Number)

Look at my picture again and then close your eyes and see if you can remember the different parts of the verb which I represent.

TVMPN. What does this formula mean? Examine each part.

Tense

Describes Time & Type of action. The <u>tense</u> (tense) <u>clock</u> (time) <u>types</u> (type). Tense describes (1) Time of action (past, present, future) and (2) Type of action (momentary or continuous).

<u>TENSE</u> = <u>TIME</u> & <u>TYPE</u> of action.

1. λύω   Present = Present   Continuous
    I loose or I am loosing.
2. ἔλυον   Imperfect = Past   Continuous
    I was loosing.
3. ἔλυσα   Aorist = Past   Point (momentary)
    I loosed. (Gk. Past)

Voice

Relates the Subject to the Verb. Does the subject perform the action or receive the action of the main verb?

1. <u>Active</u> - I loose.
    Subject (I) does the action.
2. <u>Middle</u> - I baptize for myself.
    Subject (I) does the action "for myself."
3. <u>Passive</u> - I am being baptized.
    Subject (I) receives the action - is acted upon.

In English, we are accustomed to the Active and Passive voices. Greek contains a Middle voice as well in which the subject performs the action out of personal interest or advantage.

11

Mood

Expresses HOW something is said. Mood suggests the word "moody." Vera's mu-mu dress tells <u>how</u> good a mood she is in. Mood may express some definite fact, something probable, a command, or a remote wish. Greek has four moods.

1. <u>Indicative</u>

"I loose the <u>Indicator</u>"
Fact.

2. <u>Subjunctive</u>

"I may loose the <u>Subjunk</u>"
Probability.

3. <u>Imperative</u>

"<u>Imp-pear</u>! Loose!"
Command.

4. <u>Optative</u>

"I may loose the <u>Octopus</u>
who wishes to be loosed."
Remote Possibility.

Person

There are three persons. One hand of the purse points
to I (1st person), another to YOU (2nd person), and the
third to the grandmother, SHE (3rd person).

			Singular	Plural
1.	1st person	-	I	We
2.	2nd person	-	You	You
3.	3rd person	-	He, She, It	They

Number

Singular or Plural. Is the subject one or more than one?

A. Singular - I loose.

B. Plural   - We loose.

There you have the overview! Now, look back over Vera
Verb for the TVMPN and the different meanings of those
parts as you pick Vera Verb apart.

Concepts Applied

Consider how these concepts are applied to the . . .

Present Active Indicative of λύω (first principal part).

1. λύ ω   - I loose, I am loosing
2. λύ εις - You loose, you are loosing.
3. λύ ει   - He (she,it) looses, he is loosing.

(1) λύ ομεν - We loose, we are loosing.
(2) λύ ετε - You loose, you are loosing.
(3) λύ ουσι - They loose, they are loosing.

Observations

1. You will see that the stem λύ occurs in each form and that the personal endings are joined directly to the stem. Every verb has a built-in subject dependent upon the personal ending. The endings change according to Person and Number. This change is called Inflection. In the above chart, the endings are separated for easy identification.

2. Tense = Time and Type of action. The present tense = present time and continuous type of action whether simple (I loose) or progressive (I am loosing). Examples:

   A. I loose the dog every day and take him for a walk (simple).
   B. I am loosing the dog right now (progressive).

3. The third person plural may have a final ν called "movable nu." Thus, βάλλουσι - "they throw" or βάλλουσιν - "they throw." Compare "a horse," "an elephant."

4. In Greek there are three types of accents and the presence of any accent over a syllable indicates where the stress falls (for accent rules, see p. 314):

   Acute (´)
   Grave (`)
   Circumflex (˜)

5. The word λύομεν is parsed as follows: Present Active Indicative 1st plural of the verb λύω. The translation of λύομεν is, "we loose."

Memory Aid

Look at the following picture:

Lu is holding a <u>present</u> (present tense) and he <u>actively</u> (active voice) <u>looses</u> the <u>indicator</u> (indicative mood). He is standing in an <u>oasis</u> with an <u>omelette</u> <u>oozing</u> out of the pan. The words oasis (-ω, -εις, -ει) and omelette oozing (-ομεν, -ετε, -ουσι) will help you to remember the personal endings, singular and plural.

Practice

Now see if you can recall Vera Verb! List her different parts and review the meaning of each.

What does parsing mean?

For the following verbs, divide the stem from its ending and parse.

	T V M P N	Vocabulary Form	Translation of Given Form
1. λύομεν			
2. βαπτίζετε			
3. ἔχουσι(ν)			
4. διώκει			
5. πέμπετε			
6. λαμβάνεις			

<u>KEY</u>:

1. Present Active Indicative 1st Plural λύω - We loose
2. P A I 2 P βαπτίζω - You baptize.   3. P A I 3 P ἔχω - They have.   4. P A I 3 S διώκω - he, she, it persecutes.
5. P A I 2 P πέμπω - You send.   6. P A I 2 S λαμβάνω You take, receive.

15

Enrichment

Remember that the word "tense" suggests both time and
type of action. The present tense is used of present
time and has a continuous type of action. Look at the
following sentence:

πᾶς ὁ ἐν αὐτῷ μένων οὐχ ἁμαρτάνει - I John 3:6 -
Everyone in him abiding does not sin (present and continuous). With the use of the present tense John does
not say that a Christian never sins (cf. I John 1:8,10).
Rather by the present tense, he describes the life-style
of one who abides in Christ. He does not practice sin.

By a series of present tenses John the Evangelist
describes the excitement of Mary Magdalene and the disciples at the empty tomb - John 20:1-3. Mary Magdalene
comes . . . βλέπει τὸν λίθον (the stone). . . τρέχει
(τρέχω - I run) . . . λέγει αὐτοῖς (to them) . . . the
other disciple βλέπει the linen garments.

Hence, the present tense (historical present) may
give, at times, a vivid and dramatic quality to the
narrative.

Assignment

Greek to English: <u>Pronounce</u> - <u>Parse</u> - <u>Translate</u>.

1. γράφουσι, πέμπει, κρίνετε, λέγεις.
2. διώκομεν, ἐγείρουσι, βαπτίζεις, εὑρίσκετε.
3. βάλλουσιν, ἀποκτείνομεν, δοξάζει, ἁμαρτάνετε.
4. βλέπεις, γινώσκομεν, ἀνοίγετε, δοξάζουσιν.
5. λαμβάνει, διδάσκετε, ἔχομεν, ἀκούεις.

Chapter 2

<u>Vocabulary</u>

1. ἄγγελος, -ου, ὁ[1] — angel, messenger (angel)

2. ἀγρός, -οῦ,[2] ὁ — field (<u>agrar</u>ian)

3. ἀδελφός, -οῦ, ὁ — brother (Phila<u>delphia</u>)

4. ἄνθρωπος, -ου, ὁ — man (<u>anthropo</u>logy)

5. ἄρτος, -ου, ὁ — bread, loaf (pl. = "bread" or "loaves")

6. βιβλίον, -ου, τό[1] — book (Bible)

7. διδάσκαλος, -ου, ὁ — teacher (<u>didac</u>tic)

8. δοῦλος, -ου, ὁ — slave

9. δῶρον, -ου, τό — gift

10. ἔργον, -ου, τό — work (<u>energy</u>)

11. θάνατος, -ου, ὁ — death (<u>thanatopsis</u> = a view of death)

12. θεός, -οῦ, ὁ — God (<u>theo</u>logy)

13. ἱερόν, -οῦ, τό — temple (<u>hier</u>arch)

14. ἱμάτιον, -ου, τό — garment

15. καί — and

16. καρπός, -οῦ, ὁ — fruit (sing. or pl. = "fruit")

17. κόσμος, -ου, ὁ — world (<u>cosmic</u>)

18. λαός, -οῦ, ὁ — people (<u>lai</u>ty)

19. λόγος, -ου, ὁ — word (<u>theo</u>logy)

20. νόμος, -ου, ὁ — law (metro<u>nome</u>)

21. οἶκος, -ου, ὁ — house, home (ec<u>o</u>nomy)

22. πλοῖον, -ου, τό — boat

23. πρόσωπον, -ου, τό — face

24. τέκνον, -ου, τό — child

25. υἱός, -οῦ, ὁ — son

[1]The form ὁ is the masculine definite article, τό the neuter definite article. The article is included to show the gender of the noun.

[2]This is the genitive case, the "of" case which will be explained in what follows.

The Noun

IN THIS LESSON YOU WILL:

    . . . learn the meaning of the word "declension,"

    . . . understand the second declension,

    . . . meet the Noun Clown,

    . . . learn the meaning and use of "case" and

    . . . meet five pairs of new friends who will help
        you to master the "cases."

Foundational Concepts

In the last lesson you met Vera Verb. You discovered how to parse verbs and you also learned the present active indicative endings of the verb λύω. Now you will meet the NOUN which forms the other major building block of Greek grammar.

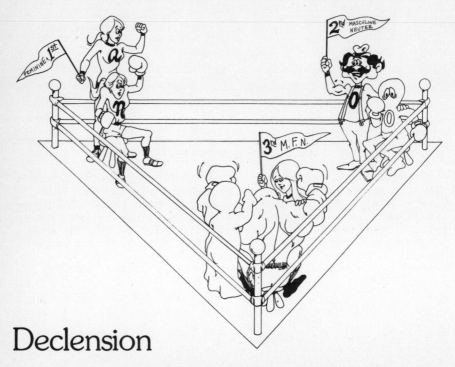

Declension

The above picture represents the word "declension." A declension is a cluster of nouns, similar in form, to fingers when clenched together. The three corner boxing ring shows three "clenchings" or declensions.

18

In group #1, women <u>clench</u> their fists representing the feminine nouns of the <u>first</u> declension. The common letters on their jerseys are "α" and "η."

In corner #2 the masculine and neuter (ghost) nouns stand together showing a common letter "o."

And last -- but not least -- masculine, feminine, and neuter nouns occupy the third corner of the ring, i.e. the third declension whose common features you will meet later.

Parsing Nouns

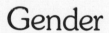

Hi! My name is Noun Clown. Just as Vera Verb helped you to parse (pick apart) verbs that you met in Lesson One, so I will help you to parse nouns. By parsing nouns correctly, you will then be ready to translate them. Just as you visualized Vera, so look at me from top to bottom.

I have three main features:

<u>G</u> -- grinder teeth   (gender)
<u>N</u> -- a number on my chest (number)
<u>C</u> -- a suit-case   (case)

Gender

The grinder teeth are impressive. "Grinder" reminds you of the word "gender." In the boxing ring you saw three genders: masculine, feminine, and neuter. Every Greek noun has a gender. When you memorize a noun you learn its gender which is always constant. For example, a feminine noun is always feminine just as a masculine noun is always masculine and a neuter noun, always neuter. Now you are about to meet the masculine and neuter nouns of the second declension. Look again at the boxing ring. The common letter of the second declension is "o."

Number

The second part of the noun you will need to know is its "number." For example, did the football team win one <u>game</u> or many <u>games</u>? The word "number" indicates whether the noun is singular or plural.

Case

"Case" suggests the role which the noun plays in the sentence.

Alfred
John Joey
Ball to hit

Joey
Ball to Alfred
hit John

Alfred hit John's
Ball to Joey

Suppose that young Joey is sending a secret message to his friend Danny in the tree. From the jumbled code which you see, how can you tell whose ball it is? Is it Joey's, Alfred's, or John's? Who hits the ball? Even their father is puzzled. How can he make sense out of the jumble of words which he hears? Questions, therefore, must be raised, e.g.,

Who hits the ball   (subjective)?

Whose ball is hit   (possessive)?

To whom is the ball hit   (indirect object)?

What is hit   (direct object)?

Who is addressed   (direct address)?

Determining a "case" is similar to decoding a message.

The code in English is determined: (1) by word order (the subject normally precedes the verb; the direct object usually follows the verb), (2) by the use of prepositions (to John), and (3) by using the possessive idea ("Alfred's" or "of Alfred"). The code secret in Greek, however, is found in <u>case endings</u>. The ending of a noun changes to show a different relationship.

The closest equivalent to "case" in English lies in its pronouns:

who (subject)

who<u>se</u> (possession)

who<u>m</u> (indirect object, i.e., <u>To</u> who<u>m</u> did you give the book?)

who<u>m</u> (direct object, i.e., Who<u>m</u> did you see?).

The underlined letters show the "inflection" of the pronoun "who" into different "cases."

Cases

In Greek there are five clearly defined cases which you will now learn to associate with five pairs of persons. In the following lessons, these very persons will help you learn the endings for the entire noun system. In the simple Greek sentences which follow, the underlined Greek words illustrate the various cases.

Norbert and Nora Nominative

NOMINATIVE SUBJET

They point us to the subject of a sentence. They both appear to be intelligent persons who can think and act as they ride a sub-jet (subject).

ἄνθρωπος λύει

λύει ἄνθρωπος

A man looses

Gerard and Geraldine Genitive

They form the case of possession or of definition, the "of" case. As suggested by the heart, Gerard and Geraldine are in "love" reminding you of the word "of."

A brother of
a man looses.

ἀδελφὸς ἀνθρώπου λύει

A man's brother looses.

Demetrius and Demetria Dative

They represent the case of the indirect object, the "to" case. They are young ball players. To be precise, they are catchers. One throws a ball "to" a catcher. Also notice their big "eyes" which remind you of the letter "i" or "ι" so typical of the dative case. In addition to the preposition "to," other prepositions used with the dative case are in, with, by and for.

ἀδελφὸς γράφει ἀνθρώπῳ - A brother writes to a man.

22

Armitage and Amelia Accusative

They point us to the direct object found in the accusative case. It is the "completing" case, since it often completes the meaning of a sentence by supplying the direct object. Armitage, as prosecuting attorney, has just completed his case at City Hall where he has "accused" the mayor of graft.

ἀδελφὸς λύει ἄνθρωπον - A brother looses a man.

Victor and Victoria Vocative

They personify the case of direct address, the "calling" case. Victor appears to demand respect, even to be addressed as "sir." Generally, the vocative case is easily identified by its position in the sentence and sometimes by the word "ὦ" which precedes it as in "O Theophilus" (Acts 1:1).

(ὦ) ἄνθρωπε, λύεις - (O) man, you are loosing.

Quick Review

Review briefly your five pairs of friends and the meaning of their respective cases.
Before you look at the Greek endings, decode the following English sentences. Note the abbreviations for the Greek cases.

1. arrow   shot   John
    (acc)   (nom)

2. fly   pilots   jets
            (nom)   (acc)

3. climb   hikers   mountains   government   June
                (nom)   (acc)   (gen)   (dat)

4. John   Sally   letter   sends   father   he
    (nom)   (voc)   (acc)   (dat)   (gen)

5. four   minutes   mile   Andy   ran
    (dat)   (dat)   (acc)   (nom)

6. watch   Jim   was   clocked   he
    (dat)   (gen)   (nom)

KEY

1. John shot an arrow. 2. Pilots fly jets. 3. Hikers climb the government's mountains in June. 4. O, Sally, John sends a letter to his father. 5. Andy ran a mile in four minutes. 6. He was clocked by Jim's watch.

Concepts Applied

GREEK CASE ENDINGS

Observe below the endings for the masculine and neuter nouns of the second declension. Note how the nouns are inflected, i.e., changes occur in their various endings. Each ending is normally joined to its stem even though, below, endings and stems are separated for easy identification. At this point, do not be concerned about memorizing the endings. You will learn them in Lesson Three and learn how to remember them. Your concern now is to understand how these charts, called paradigms, work. Study them carefully.

THE DECLENSION OF THE MASCULINE NOUN ἄνθρωπος:

	S			P	
N	ἄνθρωπ ος	- a man	(N)	ἄνθρωπ οι	- men
G	ἀνθρώπ ου	- of a man	(G)	ἀνθρώπ ων	- of men
D	ἀνθρώπ ῳ	- to, for a man	(D)	ἀνθρώπ οις	- to, for men
A	ἄνθρωπ ον	- a man	(A)	ἀνθρώπ ους	- men
V	ἄνθρωπ ε	- O man	(V)	ἄνθρωπ οι	- O men

THE DECLENSION OF THE NEUTER NOUN δῶρον:

	S			P	
N	δῶρ ον	- gift	(N)	δῶρ α	- gifts
G	δώρ ου	- of a gift	(G)	δώρ ων	- of gifts
D	δώρ ῳ	- to, for a gift	(D)	δώρ οις	- to, for gifts
A	δῶρ ον	- gift	(A)	δῶρ α	- gifts
V	δῶρ ον	- O gift	(V)	δῶρ α	- O gifts

Refer to the Appendix for detailed rules of accents.

Before going any further, review the parsing procedure related to the Noun Clown (gender, number, case =
GNC). Then, parse and translate the following:

		G N C	Translation
1.	ἄνθρωπος		
2.	ἄνθρωποι		
3.	λόγον		
4.	νόμους		
5.	ἱερῷ		
6.	τέκνα		

KEY

1. MSN - a man. 2. MPN or MPV - men, O men. 3. MSA -
a word. 4. MPA - laws. 5. NSD - to a temple. 6. NPN,
NPA, or NPV - children, children, O children.

Practice

Do you recall the Noun Clown? See if you can list his different parts and review the meaning of each.

Parse each noun and verb and translate:

1. ἀδελφὸς γινώσκει τέκνον.

2. διδάσκαλον γινώσκετε.

3. ἄγγελοι θεοῦ ἀκούουσι νόμον.

4. λέγει ἀπόστολος λόγον ἀνθρώπῳ.

5. ἔχουσι ἄνθρωποι νόμους.

KEY

1. A brother knows a child. 2. You know a teacher. 3. Messengers of God hear a law. 4. An apostle speaks a word to a man. 5. Men have laws.

Enrichment

In a single sentence of Galatians, the words δοῦλος and υἱός appear together in an illuminating way. The word δοῦλος generally connotes a bondslave, one whose will is tied up in the will of a lord or master. Paul, for example, boldly calls himself a bondslave of Jesus Christ, Παῦλος δοῦλος Ἰησοῦ Χριστοῦ (Rom. 1:1), and thereby claims his own will to be irrevocably bound to the will of his Lord.

Nevertheless, he is not only a δοῦλος but a υἱός as well, one who is free to serve the Father as a son. The two words stand in sharp contrast. The word δοῦλος suggests the ideas of servitude, slavish fear, and unquestioning obedience, while υἱός embraces the concepts of freedom as well as the fellowship and inheritance that are found in a family. Paul well realizes the contrast between the two when he writes,"so that no longer are you a δοῦλος but a υἱός." (Gal. 4:7)

26

Assignment

1. δοῦλος ἐσθίει ἄρτον καὶ διδάσκουσι ἄνθρωποι δούλους.

2. ἀνοίγομεν βιβλία καὶ ἀκούομεν λόγους θεοῦ.

3. βλέπετε ἀνθρώπους καὶ ἀγγέλους.

4. τέκνα βάλλουσι ἄρτον δούλοις.

5. βαπτίζουσι διδάσκαλοι ἀδελφούς, καὶ διδάσκουσι υἱούς.

6. ἔχω ἱμάτια καὶ ἔχετε πλοῖα καὶ ἀγροὺς καὶ οἴκους.

7. βλέπουσι ἄγγελοι θεοῦ πρόσωπον.

8. κρίνει θεὸς ἔργα ἀνθρώπων καὶ πέμπει δῶρα δούλοις.

9. γράφεις λαῷ καὶ πέμπομεν ἱμάτια ἀνθρώποις καὶ τέκνοις.

10. εὑρίσκω ἀγρὸν καὶ λαμβάνω δῶρα καρποῦ καὶ ἄρτου.

11. ἀνοίγετε ἱερὰ καὶ βλέπετε ἱμάτια καὶ δῶρα.

12. ἀποκτείνουσι ἄνθρωποι ἀδελφοὺς διδασκάλων.

13. διδάσκαλε, αἴρεις ἄρτον καὶ καρποὺς καὶ πέμπω
    βιβλία ἱεροῖς καὶ γράφω λόγους υἱοῖς.

14. λέγουσι λόγους θανάτου τέκνοις.

Chapter 3

1. ἀγαθός (masc.), ἀγαθή (fem.), ἀγαθόν (neut.) - good
2. ἀγορά, -ᾶς, ἡ[1]   - market place
3. ἀγοράζω   - I buy
4. ἀλήθεια, -ας, ἡ   - truth
5. ἁμαρτία, -ας, ἡ   - sin (cf. ἁμαρτάνω)
6. ἀρχή, -ῆς, ἡ   - beginning (archetype)
7. βασιλεία, -ας, ἡ   - kingdom (basilica)
8. γραφή, -ῆς, ἡ   - writing, scripture (grammar, graph, graphic)
9. δίκαιος, -α, -ον   - righteous
10. δόξα, -ης, ἡ   - glory (doxology)
11. εἰρήνη, -ης, ἡ   - peace (irenic)
12. ἐκκλησία, -ας, ἡ   - church (ecclesiastic)
13. ἐντολή, -ῆς, ἡ   - commandment
14. ἐξουσία, -ας, ἡ   - authority
15. ἔρημος, -ου, ἡ   - desert (hermit)
16. ἔσχατος, -η, -ον   - last (eschatology)
17. ζωή, -ῆς, ἡ   - life (zoology)
18. θύρα, -ας, ἡ   - door
19. καθαρίζω   - I cleanse (catharsis)
20. καθαρός, -ά, -όν   - clean (catharsis)
21. κακός, -ή, -όν   - evil (cacogenics = dysgenics, opposite of eugenics)
22. καλός, -ή, -όν   - good, beautiful (kaleidoscope, callisthenics)
23. καρδία, -ας, ἡ   - heart (cardiac)
24. κώμη, -ης, ἡ   - village
25. μαθητής, -οῦ, ὁ   - disciple
26. μικρός, -ά, -όν   - small (microbe, microphone)
27. νεκρός, -ά, -όν   - dead (necrology)
28. ὁδός, -οῦ, ἡ   - way, road, path (exodus)
29. παραβολή, -ῆς, ἡ   - parable
30. πιστός, -ή, -όν   - faithful
31. πονηρός, -ά, -όν   - evil
32. προφήτης, -ου, ὁ   - prophet
33. πρῶτος, -η, -ον   - first (prototype)
34. χαρά, -ᾶς, ἡ   - joy
35. ὥρα, -ας, ἡ   - hour (horoscope)

---

[1]The form ἡ is the feminine definite article.

IN THIS LESSON YOU WILL:

. . . master the first declension, and review the second declension,

. . . learn the forms and function of the definite article,

. . . learn the forms and functions of the adjective,

. . . meet new friends, and

. . . discover how the noun system is organized.

The task is demanding but with the aid of memory pictures, you will be surprised at how everything holds together.

Foundational Concepts

The meaning of declension is a grouping, a "clenching" together of a cluster of nouns with common endings. In the last lesson you looked at the second declension which contains both masculine and neuter nouns. Now you will see the first declension which contains largely feminine nouns.

Observe the common letter "α" and "η" of the first declension. Look carefully at the chart below.

	S				P		
NV	ὥρ α	δόξ α	γραφ ή	NV	ὥρ αι	δόξ αι	γραφ αί
G	ὥρ ας	δόξ ης	γραφ ῆς	G	ὡρ ῶν	δοξ ῶν	γραφ ῶν
D	ὥρ ᾳ	δόξ ῃ	γραφ ῇ	D	ὥρ αις	δόξ αις	γραφ αῖς
A	ὥρ αν	δόξ αν	γραφ ήν	A	ὥρ ας	δόξ ας	γραφ ᾱς

Observations

1. The plural endings of the three nouns correspond exactly.

2. The singular forms have three patterns:

   a) When the vocabulary form ends in "η" the "η" is retained throughout the singular.

   b) When the vocabulary form ends in "α," the "α" changes to "η" in the genitive and dative singular except when the "α" is preceded by "ε, ι, or ρ." Do you see the "ρ" in the word ὥρα? Because the stem ends in ρ, the "α" is retained in all of the singular forms.

3. It may be helpful to consider the "α" in the singular endings as being equivalent to the "η." In this sense the singular endings agree.

4. For accent rules cf. the Appendix.

NOW LET US HEAR FROM TWO NEW FRIENDS!

Adjective —

A. D. Detective

Hi! My name is A.D. Detective ("adjective"), and I modify nouns. You recognize me in English adjectives such as: smooth, rough, just, and hard. In the vocabulary you see me in the adjectives ἀγαθός which means "good," and δίκαιος which means "righteous." Normally I appear in all three genders.

	MASCULINE	FEMININE	NEUTER
NOMINATIVE	ἀγαθός	ἀγαθή[1]	ἀγαθόν

[1] See the Paradigms for the feminine forms of an adjective whose stem ends in "ρ" (μικρά) or a vowel (δικαία). In essence, the "α" in these forms is maintained throughout the singular.

Article —

Art Icicle

I am glad to meet you. My name is "The" Art Icicle ("Article"), and I make nouns definite, i.e., I sharpen up nouns by the word "the."

While the word "λόγος" means "a word," ὁ λόγος means "the word."

Agreement

Let me ask you a question. If a noun is in the feminine gender, what will the gender be of its modifying adjective? Precisely! It will be feminine. If the noun happens to be singular, what will be the number of its definite article? Singular, of course. Or, if the noun is in the dative case, what will be the case of a modifying adjective? Dative. This leads us to a very important rule.

THE ARTICLE AND ADJECTIVE AGREE WITH THE NOUN WHICH THEY MODIFY IN GENDER, NUMBER, AND CASE (GNC).

Concepts Applied

Keep the above rule in mind and observe the relationship between the endings of the article, adjective, and noun.

ARTICLE

	S				P		
	M	F	N		M	F	N
N	ὁ	ἡ	τό	(N)	οἱ	αἱ	τά
G	τοῦ	τῆς	τοῦ	(G)	τῶν	τῶν	τῶν
D	τῷ	τῇ	τῷ	(D)	τοῖς	ταῖς	τοῖς
A	τόν	τήν	τό	(A)	τούς	τάς	τά

31

ADJECTIVE

	S				P		
	M	**F**	**N**		**M**	**F**	**N**
N	ἀγαθ ός[1]	ἀγαθ ή[1]	ἀγαθ όν[1]	N	ἀγαθ οί	ἀγαθ αί	ἀγαθ ά
G	ἀγαθ οῦ	ἀγαθ ῆς	ἀγαθ οῦ	G	ἀγαθ ῶν	ἀγαθ ῶν	ἀγαθ ῶν
D	ἀγαθ ῷ	ἀγαθ ῇ	ἀγαθ ῷ	D	ἀγαθ οῖς	ἀγαθ αῖς	ἀγαθ οῖς
A	ἀγαθ όν	ἀγαθ ήν	ἀγαθ όν	A	ἀγαθ ούς	ἀγαθ άς	ἀγαθ ά
V	ἀγαθ έ						

NOUN

	S				P		
	M	**F**	**N**		**M**	**F**	**N**
N	ἄνθρωπ ος	γραφ ή	δῶρ ον	N	ἄνθρωπ οι	γραφ αί	δῶρ α
G	ἀνθρώπ ου	γραφ ῆς	δώρ ου	G	ἀνθρώπ ων	γραφ ῶν	δώρ ων
D	ἀνθρώπ ῳ	γραφ ῇ	δώρ ῳ	D	ἀνθρώπ οις	γραφ αῖς	δώρ οις
A	ἄνθρωπ ον	γραφ ήν	δῶρ ον	A	ἀνθρώπ ους	γραφ άς	δῶρ α
V	ἄνθρωπ ε	γραφ ή	δῶρ ον	V	ἄνθρωπ οι	γραφ αί	δῶρ α

[1]In its use, ἀγαθ ός is written ἀγαθός. The paradigms herein given show the ending of each form separated from its stem to enable you to distinguish stem and ending clearly.

Observations

1. Observe the relationship between the endings in the masculine, singular, accusative (M.S.A.) and apply the rule of agreement to find the GNC of the adjective, and noun (M.S.A.). Now find the article, adjective, and noun that correspond with the feminine singular genitive (F.S.G.) of the noun γραφή. They are the circled forms in the second column - τῆς ἀγαθῆς γραφῆς.

2. Note that the endings for the article, adjective, and noun are generally <u>the same</u>. The only exceptions are in the M.S.N. (ὁ ἀγαθὸς ἄνθρωπος) and in the N.S.N. and N.S.A. where in both cases the forms are τὸ ἀγαθὸν δῶρον. You have already learned these forms (ὁ ἄνθρωπος, and τὸ δῶρον). This means that if you learn the endings for the article, <u>you will have learned most of the endings for nouns of the first two declensions and for the adjectives of those nouns as well</u>.

Memory Aids

ART ICICLE - The following eight pictures will help you learn the endings for the article. Thorough knowledge of these endings will help you to master the endings of the adjective and noun as well.

NOMINATIVE - Norbert Nominative is astride a donkey who brays, "ha, hey," to a top (ὁ, ἡ, τό), a strange thing, to be sure. Thus, the question mark. Donkeys normally say, "hee, ha."

	Singular		
	M	F	N
NOMINATIVE	ὁ	ἡ	τό

GENITIVE - Gerard loves stew. And Stu tastes stew (τοῦ, τῆς, τοῦ). Gerard looking on wants some of that stew.

	Singular		
	M	F	N
GENITIVE	τοῦ	τῆς	τοῦ

DATIVE - See yourself throwing a to-tay-to (τῷ τῇ, τῷ) to Demetrius.

	Singular		
	M	F	N
DATIVE	τῷ	τῇ	τῷ

ACCUSATIVE - Imagine
Armitage trying to lift
a <u>ton</u> of <u>tainted</u> <u>tops</u>
(τόν, τήν, τό).

Singular

	M	F	N
ACCUSATIVE	τόν	τήν	τό

NOMINATIVE - Norbert and
Nora (now <u>together</u> representing the <u>plural</u>), the
whiz kids, are at a bridge
party where a book of <u>Hoyle</u>
says, "Hi" to a <u>top</u> (οἱ,
αἱ, τά). It is hard to
imagine.

Plural

	M	F	N
NOMINATIVE	οἱ	αἱ	τά

GENITIVE - Gerard and Geraldine are in love, and what we
see are the <u>tones</u> of love
(τῶν, τῶν, τῶν).

Plural

	M	F	N
GENITIVE	τῶν	τῶν	τῶν

DATIVE - Demetrius and Demetria Dative are now inside playing with <u>toys</u> having <u>ties</u> with more <u>toys</u> (τοῖς, ταῖς, τοῖς).

	Plural		
	M	F	N
DATIVE	τοῖς	ταῖς	τοῖς

ACCUSATIVE - With the sophisticated Armitage and Amelia, you view a ridiculous sight: <u>Twos toss tops</u> (τούς, τάς, τά).

	Plural		
	M	F	N
ACCUSATIVE	τούς	τάς	τά

Practice

Now that you have seen the article, adjective and noun, see if you can parse and translate the following:

	G	N	C	Translation

1. τῆς
2. τῷ
3. ἀνθρώποις
4. ἄρτον
5. οἱ ἀγαθοὶ λόγοι
6. τοῦ πιστοῦ διδασκάλου

KEY

1. F.S.G. - of the. 2. M.S.D., N.S.D. - to the.
3. M.P.D. - to men. 4. M.S.A. - bread. 5. M.P.N. -
the good words. 6. M.S.G. - of the faithful teacher.

Further Application

USE of the adjective

We now see how the adjective is used. It is found in two different positions:

1) <u>ATTRIBUTIVE ADJECTIVE</u> -- In this position, the adjective qualifies the noun by description, i.e., as an "attribute." Observe the sentence -- γινώσκω τὸν ἀγαθὸν λόγον "I know the good word." The <u>article directly precedes the adjective</u>. Its position makes the adjective an attributive adjective. Sometimes the attributive adjective may also function <u>in place of the noun</u>. For example: ὁ ἀγαθὸς γινώσκει τὸν λόγον, "The good (man) knows the word." Compare in English, "<u>The just</u> shall live by faith."

The substitute word for attributive is "tributary." <u>Art Icicle</u> is directly in front of <u>A.D. Detective</u>, floating down the <u>tributary</u>.

2) <u>PREDICATE ADJECTIVE</u> -- In this position the adjective <u>modifies a noun by</u> an affirmation. Observe the sentence, ὁ λόγος ἀγαθός, "the word is good." The English sentence requires "is," a form of the verb "to be," to make the statement complete. The <u>absence of the article</u> immediately before the adjective places the adjective in the <u>predicate</u> position. The sentences ὁ λόγος ἀγαθός, and ἀγαθὸς ὁ λόγος both mean, "The word is good." The key is the absence of the article immediately before the adjective.

The substitute word for predicate is <u>pretty cat</u>. <u>A.D. Detective</u> holds on to the <u>pretty</u> cat, as it is stung <u>by a bee</u>, (verb "to be") while he forcibly ejects <u>Art Icicle</u>.

CON-TEXT

"Con-Text" will generally aid you. When the noun is indefinite (without an article) the adjective may either be attributive or predicate. Context will guide you. If there is no verb you may need to supply one. If there is already a verb, then the sentence may not need another verb, such as the verb "to be." Occasionally it may be difficult to decide whether an adjective is attributive or predicate. For example, ἀγαθὸς λόγος or λόγος ἀγαθός may mean "a good word," or "a word is good." Translate the following sentence: ἀγαθὴν παραβολὴν λέγομεν τῇ κακῇ βασιλείᾳ. Notice the indefinite adjective and noun, ἀγαθὴν παραβολήν. The adjective is to be translated as an attributive adjective since there is already a verb in the sentence. "We speak a good parable to the evil kingdom." Observe the following picture:

The first figure on a skateboard is an ex-con with his stripes and number. He stands for context, so he pulls A.D. in one of two directions when the noun clown is indefinite (dotted lines).

Practice

Translate the following and then check your translation
by the key.

1. ὁ ἀγαθὸς λόγος
2. ὁ λόγος ἀγαθός
3. ἡ ἀγαθὴ γραφή
4. ἡ γραφὴ ἀγαθή
5. τὸ ἀγαθὸν δῶρον
6. τὸ δῶρον ἀγαθόν

KEY

1. the good word. 2. the word is good. 3. the good
writing. 4. the writing is good. 5. the good gift.
6. the gift is good.

Professor Oddity

Professor Oddity majors in
miscellaneous elements of
Greek grammar. You will see
him from time to time teaching some of the famous "exceptions" to the rule. In chapter
three we find:

    1) Feminine nouns with masculine endings. The
words ὁδός - road and ἔρημος - desert are feminine and
take the article "ἡ." But as you can see, their endings correspond to masculine nouns of the second declension. But, since these nouns are feminine, they
take feminine modifiers, such as adjectives and articles.
    2) Masculine nouns with feminine endings. The
words προφήτης - prophet and μαθητής - disciple are
masculine nouns but, generally, their endings follow the
first declension. The exceptions are: (a) the singular
nominative ending, -ης which indicates the agent or
"doer" of the action, (b) the singular genitive ending,
-ου (compare the second declension), and (c) the vocative singular ending in short, -α. Since these nouns
are masculine, they will take masculine adjectives and
articles.

Practice

1. οἱ μαθηταὶ ἀκούουσι τοὺς λόγους τῶν προφητῶν.

2. ἐσθίετε τοὺς ἄρτους.

3. διδάσκομεν τὸν λόγον τοῦ θεοῦ τοῖς ἀγαθοῖς καὶ ταῖς καλαῖς.

4. τοὺς μαθητὰς τῶν προφητῶν λαμβάνουσιν οἱ υἱοί.

5. γράφομεν τὰς ἐντολάς.

6. τὴν φωνὴν ἀκούει. (φωνή = voice).

7. ἡ ἁμαρτία μένει.

8. βλέπομεν τὰ ἔργα τοῦ θεοῦ.

KEY

1. The disciples hear the words of the prophets.
2. You eat the loaves.   3. We teach the word of
God to the good (men) and to the beautiful (women).
4. The sons receive the disciples of the prophets.
5. We write the commandments.   6. He hears the
voice, or she hears the voice.   7. The sin remains.
8. We see the works of God.

Enrichment

The tax collector cries out, "God, be merciful
to me the sinner." He is not merely a sinner in general, but the sinner - more than all others - ὁ ἁμαρτωλός (Luke 18:13).
The article is often used with specific Christian words. Paul writes, "For by grace (lit., "the
grace") are you saved through faith" (Eph. 2:8).
Grace is not an abstract quality, but the grace spe-
cifically demonstrated in God's mercy and love which
makes us alive in Christ (Eph. 2:4,5).

Assignment

διδάσκει[1] ὁ προφήτης τὸν λόγον τοῦ θεοῦ τοῖς πιστοῖς ἀνθρώποις ἐν[2] τῷ ἱερῷ καὶ λέγει·[3] Γινώσκετε,
διδάσκαλοι, ὅτι[4] ἀγαθὸς ὁ νόμος καὶ δίκαιαι αἱ ἐντολαὶ
τῶν γραφῶν καὶ θεραπεύουσι τὰς ἁμαρτίας τοῦ κόσμου.
βλέπετε, τέκνα τοῦ πονηροῦ, τὴν ὁδὸν τῆς ζωῆς. οὐ[5]
δοξάζετε τὸν θεὸν καὶ οὐ[5] βαπτίζετε τοὺς δούλους. οὐ[5]
γινώσκετε τὰ ἀγαθὰ τῆς εἰρήνης ὅτι[4] οὐκ[5] ἀκούετε τὰς
ἀγαθὰς παραβολάς.

καὶ πονηρὲ προφῆτα, ἀγοράζεις τοὺς τῆς ἀγορᾶς
καρποὺς τοὺς καλοὺς καὶ ἐσθίεις καὶ ἔχεις χαρὰν καὶ οὐ
πέμπεις τοὺς καρποὺς ταῖς καλαῖς τῆς κώμης, καὶ διώκεις
τοὺς καλούς.

γινώσκει ὁ θεὸς τὰ ἔργα τῶν πονηρῶν. βλέπει τὰς
ἁμαρτίας τῶν κακῶν καὶ γινώσκει ὅτι[4] οὐ[5] καθαρὰ ἡ
καρδία καὶ ὅτι[4] δικαία ἡ ἐξουσία τῶν μαθητῶν. κακοί,
οὐκ ἀνοίγετε τὰς τῆς ἐκκλησίας θύρας καὶ οὐκ ἀκούουσιν
οἱ πιστοὶ ὅτι καθαρίζει ὁ θεὸς τὰς καρδίας τοῦ λαοῦ καὶ
ὅτι ἐγείρει τοὺς νεκρούς.

γινώσκετε τοὺς τοῦ δικαίου καὶ καλοῦ διδασκάλου
λόγους ὅτι οἱ ἔσχατοι πρῶτοι καὶ οἱ πρῶτοι ἔσχατοι;[3]

ἀκούει ὁ τῆς κώμης λαὸς τοὺς τοῦ προφήτου λόγους;
οὐ.[5] ἀποκτείνουσι τὸν δίκαιον καὶ ἀγαθὸν προφήτην καὶ
βάλλουσι αὐτὸν[6] ἐν τοῖς νεκροῖς.

[1]The present tense in Koine Greek is often found
in narrative, i.e., "historical present." The following uses are from the gospel of Mark, chapter one: They
enter (v.21) . . . he commands, and they obey (v.27)
. . . they speak to him (v.30) . . . they say to him
(v.37) . . . and he says to them (v.38) . . . and a
leper comes to him (v.40). English translation normally expresses the Greek historical present by the
past tense.

[2]ἐν - in, among (with the dative case)

[3]The period above the line stands for a colon or
semi-colon. The sign ; is the question mark (like an
English semi-colon in appearance). The period and
comma in Greek are the same in form and function as in
English.

[4]ὅτι - that, because

[5]οὐ, οὐκ (before smooth breathing) - not, no

[6]αὐτόν - him

Chapter 4

Vocabulary - <u>Note the memory pictures at the end of</u> <u>this lesson to help you remember the prep-</u> <u>ositions</u>.

1. ἄγω — I lead, bring, go (peda<u>gogue</u>)

2. ἀκοή, -ῆς, ἡ — report (<u>acou</u>stics)

3. ἀλλά — but (ἀλλ' usually before a vowel)

4. ἁμαρτωλός, -όν,[1] — sinful, sinner (compare: ἁμαρτάνω, ἁμαρτία)

5. ἀναγινώσκω — I read (compare: γινώσκω)

6. ἀπαγγέλλω — I announce, proclaim (compare: ἄγγελος, "messenger")

7. ἀπό (with gen.) — from (<u>apo</u>gee = furthest point from the earth)

8. ἀποκρίνομαι — I answer (followed by the dative case)

9. ἀποστέλλω — I send (apostle)

10. ἀπόστολος, -ου, ὁ — apostle (apostle)

11. γίνομαι — I become[2] (followed by predicate noun or adjective)

12. διά (with gen.) — through (<u>dia</u>meter)

13. διά (with acc.) — on account of, because of

14. διέρχομαι — I go through

15. εἰς (with acc.) — into, against (<u>eis</u>egesis), unto

16. εἰσέρχομαι — I enter, come into

17. ἐκ (with gen.) — out of (<u>ex</u>odus)

18. ἐκπορεύομαι — I go out

19. ἐν (with dat.) — in (in), among

20. ἐξέρχομαι — I come forth, go forth

21. ἔρχομαι — I come, go

22. θάλασσα, -ης, ἡ — sea

[1]An adjective of two terminations only. The first ending serves for both the masc. and fem. genders, the second for the neuter.

[2]Other meanings are: be born, happen, come about, create, make, and appear.

23.	μένω	- I remain, continue ("re<u>main</u>")[1]
24.	μετά (with gen.)	- with (<u>method</u> - "with a way")
25.	μετά (with acc.)	- after (<u>meta</u>physical)
26.	ὅτι	- because, that
27.	οὐ, οὐκ, οὐχ	- not
28.	οὐρανός, -οῦ, ὁ	- heaven (Uranus)
29.	πορεύομαι	- I go
30.	πρός (with acc.)	- toward, to (<u>pros</u>elyte)
31.	προσφέρω	- I bring to
32.	σῴζω	- I save (creo<u>sote</u>)
33.	ὑπέρ (with gen.)	- in behalf of
34.	ὑπέρ (with acc.)	- above, over, more than
35.	ὑπό (with gen.)	- by
36.	ὑπό (with acc.)	- under (<u>hypo</u>thesis, <u>hypo</u>dermic)
37.	φέρω	- I bring, carry (ferry)
38.	φωνή, -ῆς, ἡ	- voice (<u>phon</u>etic, tele<u>phon</u>e)

---

[1]Similar to γίνομαι, μένω, at times, is
followed by a predicate adjective or a predicate noun. Cf. 2 Tim. 2:13, ἐκεῖνος (that one)
πιστὸς μένει, "that one remains faithful."

IN THIS LESSON YOU WILL:

. . . review the meaning of English prepositions,

. . . discover how Greek prepositions function
with nouns in different cases,

. . . find how Greek prepositions are prefixed to
verbs, thereby forming compound verbs,

. . . observe Lu being loosed (Middle/Passive
Voice),

. . . see Vera face "de opponent" (Deponent Verbs),

. . . learn the negative, and

. . . meet Infant Ivy (Infinitive).

Foundational Concepts

Prepositions

My name is Prep Precision
(Preposition). My slide rule
shows that I am exact, while
my original name "pre-position"
tells you that "I precede"
other words, such as nouns. I
represent precise words such
as "in," "on," "under,"
"through," "by." E.g. the following picture shows a distinct
difference between my position
"on" the plane and "under" the
plane.

<u>on</u> the plane   and   <u>under</u> the plane

The distinction between prepositions is important. Consider the difference in meaning between the phrases "through Christ" (διὰ Χριστοῦ) and "in Christ" (ἐν Χριστῷ), phrases which occur frequently in Paul's writings.

Prepositions and Nouns

A preposition precedes a noun and serves to relate the noun to some other word in a sentence. The noun which follows a preposition may be found in any one of three cases (genitive, dative, or accusative). Look at the final pages of this chapter for memory aids. Have fun!

With some prepositions such as "ἐν," "in" and "ἐκ," "out of," and "εἰς," "into," the noun object is in ONE case only. Other prepositions call for their object in TWO cases or even THREE. The meaning of the prepositional phrase (= preposition + object) will vary according to the case of the noun object. Observe the following examples:

With <u>ONE</u> Case:

     ἐν - with the dative = in
     ἐν ταῖς καρδίαις - in the hearts

     ἐκ - with the genitive = out of
     ἐκ τοῦ οἴκου - out of the house

     ἀπό - with the genitive = from
     ἀπὸ τοῦ οὐρανοῦ - from heaven
            (lit. from the heaven)

With TWO Cases:

διά - with the genitive = through
διὰ τῆς Σαμαρείας - through Samaria (Jn.4:4)

διά - with the accusative = on account of,
   because of
διὰ τὸν λόγον - on account of the word

As you observe, prepositions using only one case pose no problem for translation. But when a preposition is found with two cases or three, its meaning will vary according to the case of the noun which follows.

Examples:

μετά with the genitive = with
μετὰ τῶν ἀδελφῶν - with the brothers

μετά with the accusative = after
μετὰ τὸν ἀπόστολον - after the apostle

ὑπό with the genitive = by (agency)
ὑπὸ τῶν ἀδελφῶν - by the brothers

ὑπό with the accusative = under
ὑπὸ τὸν οἶκον - under the house

Changes in Form

Some prepositions undergo slight changes in form when the following word begins with a vowel. Pronunciation, thereby, becomes smoother. Observe:

ἐκ τοῦ οἴκου - out of the house
ἐξ οἴκου   - out of a house

διὰ τοῦ οἴκου - through the house
δι᾽ οἴκου   - through a house

ἀπὸ τοῦ οἴκου - from the house
ἀπ᾽ οἴκου   - from a house

Note how the omission (elision) of the final vowel of the preposition makes pronunciation easier. And should the next word begin with a rough breathing, the final consonant of certain prepositions absorbs an "h" sound. For example:

ἀφ᾽ ἱεροῦ (ἀφ᾽ for ἀπό) - from a temple

ὑφ᾽ ἁμαρτίαν (ὑφ᾽ for ὑπό) - under sin

μεθ᾽ υἱοῦ (μεθ᾽ for μετά) - with a son

Prepositions and Verbs

Prepositions may be prefixed to verbs and, thereby, enhance their meaning. For example:

ἐκ = out of   and   βάλλω = I throw,

Therefore, ἐκβάλλω = I throw out.

Present Middle/Passive (M/P) Voice

Pause a moment and review the parsing procedure for Vera Verb . . . T V M P N. What do the symbols mean? Now we will change Vera's voice from the Active (Lesson One) to the Middle and Passive Voices.

PRESENT MIDDLE AND PASSIVE INDICATIVE OF λύω

<u>Singular</u>

1. λύ ομαι
(M) I loose for myself
(P) I am being loosed

2. λύ ῃ
(M) You loose for yourself
(P) You are being loosed

3. λύ εται
(M) She looses for herself
    He looses for himself
(P) She is being loosed
    He is being loosed

<u>Plural</u>

1. λυ όμεθα
(M) We loose for ourselves
(P) We are being loosed

2. λύ εσθε
(M) You loose for yourselves
(P) You are being loosed

3. λύ ονται
(M) They loose for themselves
(P) They are being loosed

Observations

1. Like the Present Active Indicative, each form of the P M/P I - Present Middle or the Present Passive - has the verb stem λυ and the personal endings. The present middle and the present passive have the same set of personal endings.

2. The present passive voice means continuous action, "I am <u>being</u> loosed."

3. The passive voice in Greek is far more common than the middle.

4. Each form except the second singular has a thematic (helping) vowel, -ο or -ε. cf. λύο̱μεν and λύε̱τε in the pres. act. indic.

Memory Aid

Observe the following picture:

Lu receives a <u>present</u> and he <u>is being loosed</u> by the <u>indicator</u> (Present Middle/Passive Indicative). As he is being loosed he sees the young lady, Amethyst, and he exclaims, "<u>Oh</u>! <u>My</u>! <u>a tie</u>" (-ομαι, -ῃ, -εται). The lady <u>Amethyst</u> <u>is the</u> <u>untie(r)</u>" (-όμεθα, -εσθε, -ονται).

The underlined words of the quotation will aid you to remember the endings of the present middle and passive indicative.

Now parse the following verbs:

	T V M P N	Vocabulary Form	Translation
1. ἐγειρόμεθα			
2. σώζονται			
3. διώκῃ			

KEY

1. P P I 1 P - ἐγείρω - We are being raised up. (P)
2. P P I 3 P - σώζω - They are being saved. (P)
3. P P I 2 S - διώκω - You are being pursued. (P)

AGENCY AND THE PASSIVE VOICE

Observe the sentence, "I am being taught." Obviously one may ask, "Who does the teaching?" By whom, or by what does the teaching occur? If I receive it, who does it? The question of agency is generally answered in one of two ways:

1. <u>Personal Agency</u> (by a person) is often shown by the use of ὑπό with the genitive case, "by." Thus, ὁ δοῦλος διδάσκεται ὑπὸ τοῦ ἀποστόλου means, "The slave is being taught by the apostle."

2. Impersonal Agency (by an instrument = means) is often expressed by the dative case without any preposition. The sentence διδασκόμεθα τῷ λόγῳ τοῦ ἀποστόλου means, "We are being taught by (i.e., by means of) the word of the apostle."

Deponent Verbs

Look at the following verbs:

ἔρχομαι	- I come	γίνομαι	- I become
πορεύομαι	- I go	ἀποκρίνομαι	- I answer

None of the four verbs has an active form such as λύω. All four verbs have the middle or passive endings, -ομαι, -η, -εται ("Oh my! a tie"), etc. They appear in the vocabulary with the middle/passive endings but they are <u>active</u> in meaning. The picture below of a boxing ring may help you.

When Vera sees "<u>de opponent</u>" she says, "<u>Oh! My!</u>" (-ομαι). "<u>De opponent</u>" lays aside his right-hand glove (<u>active voice</u>) and is prepared to fight Vera with his left hand only, the <u>M/P</u> glove, for, he thinks, "She is a pushover!"

The Negative

The words -- οὐ, οὐκ, οὐχ all mean the same thing, "not."
They simply negate the verb.

οὐ λύω - I do not loose
οὐκ ἔρχομαι - I do not come
οὐχ ἁμαρτάνω - I do not sin

The change in the form of οὐ depends on the letter
that follows. The form is οὐ if it precedes a consonant, οὐκ if it precedes a smooth breathing, οὐχ if a
rough breathing follows. The change facilitates pronunciation.

Present Active Infinitive

λύ ειν   - Active - "to (in order to) loose"

λύ εσθαι - Middle - "to (in order to) loose for
                    oneself"

         Passive - "to (in order to) be loosed"

While a full discussion of infinitives is found in
lesson number fourteen, you will find infinitives in
this lesson and in lessons to come. They often appear
in Greek to express purpose, just as they do in English.
To help you remember the endings, observe the following
picture.

Lu is giving a _present_ to Infant Ivy (present infinitive) standing in the _rain_ (-ειν) with an S-tie (-εσθαι).
Review carefully both the picture and its meaning.

Enrichment

In Romans 11, Paul affirms that God is not obligated to us. That is to say, his favor is not compensation to the deserving but grace to the undeserving. The chapter concludes with an exclamation:

ὅτι ἐξ αὐτοῦ (him) καὶ δι᾽ αὐτοῦ καὶ εἰς αὐτὸν τὰ πάντα (all things). αὐτῷ ἡ δόξα . . . "Because out of (from) him and through him and unto him are all things. To him (be) the glory."

ἐξ αὐτοῦ - out of (from) him. The preposition ἐκ with the genitive suggests that God is the Source or Origin of all things.

δι᾽αὐτοῦ - through him. The preposition διά with the genitive portrays God as the Agency or the Channel through whom all things come to us.

εἰς αὐτόν - unto him. The preposition εἰς with the accusative points to God as the Goal of all things. He is the one to whom all things are directed and the one to whom the glory will redound.

Practice

1. ἐν τῇ ἐκκλησίᾳ.

2. ἐκ τοῦ οἴκου πέμπουσιν οἱ ἀπόστολοι τοὺς δούλους εἰς τὸ ἱερόν.

3. εἰς τὴν ἔρημον.

4. ἐν τῇ ὁδῷ.

5. ἐκ τῆς ἀμαρτίας.

6. διδάσκονται οἱ δοῦλοι ὑπὸ τοῦ θεοῦ.

7. οὐ γίνῃ μαθητὴς τοῦ Χριστοῦ.

8. ἔρχονται οἱ διδάσκαλοι διδάσκειν τοὺς δούλους.

KEY

1. In the church. 2. The apostles send the slaves out of the house into the temple. 3. Into the desert. 4. In the way. 5. Out of sin. 6. The slaves are being taught by God. 7. You do not become a disciple of Christ. 8. The teachers come in order to teach the slaves.

Preposition Memory Aids

The following pictures will help you remember the prepositions for lesson 4 - their meanings and respective cases.

ἀπό with the genitive, "from"

Gerard (gen.) runs <u>from</u> a <u>paw</u> (ἀπό).

διά - with the genitive - "through"
διά - with the accusative - "because, on account of"

Gerard (gen.) dives <u>through</u> a <u>D</u> διά while <u>Armitage</u> (acc.) is holding the <u>D</u> διά on an <u>account</u> (on account of) with <u>bee-gauze</u> (because) wrapped around it.

εἰς with the accusative, "into, unto, against"

An <u>ace</u> (εἰς) flies <u>into</u> <u>Armitage's</u> (acc.) hand giving an advantage <u>against</u> his opponent.

ἐκ with the genitive "out of, from"
Gerard (gen.) emerges <u>out of</u> an <u>egg</u>
(ἐκ) <u>from</u> a long incubation.

ἐν with the dative, "in, among"
<u>Demetrius</u> (dat.) is <u>in</u> (ἐν) and <u>among</u>
the <u>daisies</u> (dative).

μετά with the genitive, "with"
μετά with the accusative,
"after"

<u>Gerard</u> (gen.) is shackled <u>with</u>
<u>metal</u> (μετά) <u>after</u> Armitage
(acc.) turns the metal (μετά)
key.

πρός with the accusative, "to, toward"
<u>Armitage</u> (acc.) is <u>prostrate</u> (πρός)
<u>towards</u> the <u>two</u> (to).

ὑπέρ with the genitive, "on
behalf of"
ὑπέρ with the accusative,
"above, over"

Gerard (gen.) throws a B-half
(behalf) hoop-pear (ὑπέρ) to
Armitage (acc.) playing his
game over the hoop-pear (ὑπέρ).

ὑπό with the genitive, "by means of"
ὑπό with the accusative, "under"

Gerard (gen.) swings by means of the·
hoop (ὑπό) while Armitage (acc.) under
the hoop (ὑπό) is not very charitable.

Assignment
Δαυίδ[1] καί Μεμφιβόσθε[2]

ἀναγινώσκομεν ἐν τοῖς βιβλίοις τῶν βασιλειῶν[3] ὅτι Δαυίδ τοὺς τῆς βασιλείας ἀγγέλους πέμπει πρὸς τὴν Λάδα-βαρ[4] φέρειν Μεμφιβόσθε ἐκ τῆς μικρᾶς κώμης τῆς ἐρήμου τῆς Ἰουδαίας[5]. καὶ οὕτως[6] φέρεται Μεμφιβόσθε εἰς τὸν οἶκον Δαυίδ ἐν Ἱεροσόλυμα[7] ὑπὸ τῶν ἀγγέλων. Μεμφιβόσθε εἰσέρχεται διὰ τῆς θύρας τοῦ οἴκου Δαυίδ καὶ πίπτει[8] πρὸς αὐτὸν καὶ λέγει, Δοξάζω[9] τὸν τοῦ οὐρανοῦ θεὸν διὰ τὴν καρδίαν τὴν ἀγαθὴν Δαυίδ. ἀπαγγέλλω τοῖς διδασκά-λοις τοῦ νόμου ὅτι μένω ἁμαρτωλὸς ἐν τῷ προσώπῳ[10] τοῦ Δαυίδ ὅτι ἐξέρχομαι ἐκ τοῦ οἴκου Σαύλου[11].

ἀλλὰ Δαυίδ ἐγείρει αὐτὸν[12] καὶ ἀποκρίνεται αὐτῷ[13] καὶ λέγει αὐτῷ[13] μετὰ φωνῆς τῆς χαρᾶς· Οὐ ἔργοις καλοῖς, Μεμφιβόσθε, εἰσέρχῃ εἰς τὴν βασιλείαν μου[14], καὶ οὐ διὰ τὴν καρδίαν μου[14] τὴν καλὴν σώζῃ ἀπὸ τῆς κακῆς ζωῆς ἐν Λάδαβαρ, ἀλλὰ διὰ τῆς ἀληθείας τοῦ θεοῦ γίνῃ υἱός μου[14].

καὶ οὕτως[6] μετὰ τοὺς λόγους Δαυίδ, γίνεται Μεμφι-βόσθε υἱὸς μετὰ τῶν υἱῶν Δαυίδ, καὶ μένει ὑπὸ τὴν ἐξουσίαν τῆς βασιλείας ἐν Ἱεροσόλυμα[7].

---

[1] David (indeclinable)

[2] Mephibosheth (indeclinable)

[3] In the Old Testament in Greek (LXX) 1-2 Samuel, 1-2 Kings are called "The books of the Kingdoms."

[4] Lodebar

[5] Judea

[6] οὕτως - thus

[7] Jerusalem (indeclinable)

[8] πίπτω - I fall

[9] Δοξάζω. The first letter of the first word in quotation is capitalized in the grammar. This is also the procedure in certain printed texts of the Greek New Testament.

[10] face = presence

[11] Saul

[12] αὐτόν - him (acc. case)

[13] αὐτῷ - him (dat. case)

[14] μου - my

Chapter 5

1. ἀγάπη, -ης, ἡ — love (agape)
2. ἄλλος, -η, -ο — other, another (compare ἀλλά) N.B. neut. ἄλλο.
3. ἀναβαίνω — I go up (cf. Xenophon's Anabasis)
4. ἀναβλέπω — I look up, regain sight
5. ἀπέρχομαι — I go away
6. ἀπολύω — I release (cf. λύω)
7. αὐτός, -ή, -ό — self, same, he, she, it (automat, automatically)
8. γάρ (post-positive)[1] — for (conj.) - end of Mark 16:8
9. δαιμόνιον, -ου, τό — demon
10. δέ (post-positive)[1] — and, but
11. ἐγώ — I (ego), ἡμεῖς - we
12. εἰμί — I am
13. ἐκβάλλω — I cast out (compare ἐκ, βάλλω)
14. ἐπαγγελία, -ας, ἡ — promise
15. ἔτι — yet, still
16. ἑτοιμάζω — I prepare
17. εὐαγγελίζομαι, -ίζω — I announce good news (evangel) preach (the gospel)[2]
18. εὐαγγέλιον, -ου, τό — gospel (evangel)
19. ἤδη — already
20. κύριος, -ου, ὁ — lord, master
21. οὐδέ — and not, (οὐδέ . . . οὐδέ, "neither . . . nor")
22. οὐκέτι — no more, no longer
23. σύ — you (sing.) ὑμεῖς - you (pl.)
24. τυφλός, -οῦ, ὁ — blind (adjective, often used as a noun)
25. χαίρω — I rejoice (compare χαρά)

---

[1]A post-positive cannot occur first in a sentence or clause. It usually comes second, but it is translated as though it were first.

[2]All NT forms are deponent except two texts in the Revelation. The verb takes the acc. of the thing "proclaimed" and either the dat. or acc. of the persons (or places) to whom the message comes.

IN THIS LESSON YOU WILL:

> . . . Meet Amy (εἰμί = I am),
>
> . . . review the purpose and use of English pronouns,
>
> . . . meet Polly, the Greek pronoun,
>
> . . . learn the use of the personal pronouns and their endings.

Foundational Concepts

Verb "to be"

In Greek as in English, the various forms of the verb "to be" require special attention.

Present Indicative of εἰμί - "I am"

1.	εἰμί	- I am	(1)	ἐσμέν	- we are
2.	εἶ	- you are	(2)	ἐστέ	- you are
3.	ἐστί(ν)	- (s)he is	(3)	εἰσί(ν)	- they are

Observations

1. The movable "ν" occurs with both the 3rd person singular - ἐστί(ν), as well as the 3rd person plural - εἰσί(ν)

2. The verb εἰμί (like γίνομαι) takes the nominative case of a noun (= predicate noun) or of an adjective (= predicate adjective). The brief sentence εἰμί ἀπόστολος means "I am an apostle," while ἐστὲ διδάσκαλοι means "you are teachers."

3. All forms of εἰμί (except εἶ, 2nd sing.) are called enclitic. An enclitic "inclines" to, or depends upon, the preceding word, to which it normally gives its accent. See the appendix for details on the accent of enclitics.

Memory Aid

Look at the picture and analyze it carefully.

Meet our friend Amy (εἰμί), as she carries a <u>present</u> that happens to be an <u>indicator</u> (indicative). On her vacation she is accompanied by <u>Norbert</u> (nominative case) for a visit with her aunt and <u>uncle</u> during the summer. She greets them at the gate with the words, "<u>I am Amy A. Esty</u>" (εἰμί, εἶ, ἐστί). As you observe her relatives lack culture and refinement and so they reply, "<u>We are Esmen and Este(r) (H)aysee(d)</u>" (ἐσμέν, ἐστέ, εἰσί).

Pronouns

My name is <u>Polly Pro Noun</u>. My cheerleading outfit shows that I am "pro," i.e. for the noun. Pronouns are words used in place of nouns. In Greek, they have two main functions:

1. Pronouns relieve <u>boredom</u>. In the English sentence, "I baptize the disciple and I teach the disciple," the repetition of the noun, disciple, is unnecessary. A pronoun can and should be used in its place and, thus, the sentence should read, "I baptize the disciple and I teach <u>him</u>." Now compare the same sentences in Greek:

βαπτίζω τὸν μαθητὴν καὶ διδάσκω τὸν μαθητήν.

βαπτίζω τὸν μαθητὴν καὶ διδάσκω αὐτόν (him).

The second sentence is the better of the two.

2. Pronouns give <u>Special Emphasis</u> - Pronouns may be used to stress the subject of a verb. Observe the following sentences:

λέγω καὶ γράφεις   - I speak and you write.

ἐγὼ λέγω σὺ δὲ γράφεις - <u>I</u> speak but <u>you</u> write.

The separate Greek pronouns "I" and "you" clearly emphasize the subjects of their respective verbs. At times, these separate pronouns may be omitted from a translation, though their emphasis is still to be understood.

The following pictures will help you learn the endings of the 1st and 2nd personal pronouns.

Personal Pronouns

Personal Pronouns are easily mastered. Similar to the verb, they are found in three persons, singular and plural. Review the section on Person in Lesson One and use the following picture to aid you to remember the personal pronouns in their nominative singular forms.

In the window, Polly <u>Pronoun</u> is selling <u>purses</u> (personal pronouns). Driving by is the little <u>ego</u>-centered person named ἐγώ, identified by his <u>egg</u>-shaped head. With him is <u>Sue</u> (σύ), and they are riding in the <u>autos</u>. The personal pronouns are ἐγώ, σύ, and αὐτός.

From the nominative singular forms, we turn to the full declensions of these three pronouns.

1st & 2nd PERSON - PERSONAL PRONOUNS

1st Person

Singular

N ἐγώ   - I
G ἐμοῦ or μου - of me, my
D ἐμοί or μοι - to, for me
A ἐμέ or με - me

Plural

N ἡμεῖς - we
G ἡμῶν - of us, our
D ἡμῖν - to, for us
A ἡμᾶς - us

2nd Person

Singular

N σύ - you
G σοῦ - of you, your
D σοί - to, for you
A σέ - you

Plural

N ὑμεῖς - you
G ὑμῶν - of you, your
D ὑμῖν - to, for you
A ὑμᾶς - you

Memory Aids

1st Person Singular - Our
friend Ego moos because it is
a moist May. Ego is a golfer
who cannot golf early in the
year, because of rain.   His
only response is to "moo."

1st Person Plural - A hay-ace
that owns an inn called the Vas.
The ownership of the hay-ace
is shown by the deed.

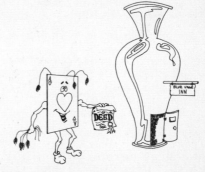

2nd Person Singular - Look at <u>Sue</u>. <u>Sue</u>
<u>Sioux</u> eats <u>soy</u> seeds. This is <u>not</u> the
thing to do on a date with Ego.

2nd Person Plural - Observe the
owl which cries "<u>hoo</u>," as he is
perched on the <u>ace</u> that <u>owns</u>
an <u>inn</u> called the <u>Vas</u>.

Observations

1. The first and second person personal pronouns have no distinction in gender.

2. The plural forms are identical except for the first letter. If you think of the "υ" of the second person as equivalent to "U" or "you," then the distinction between the first and second person is easily remembered.

3. Some singular forms are emphatic, each bearing an accent (ἐμοῦ, ἐμοί, ἐμέ and σοῦ, σοί, σέ). Alternate singular forms - far more common - are enclitics (μου, μοι, με, and σου, σοι, σε). An enclitic loses its accent to the preceding word. (cf. εἰμί and the appendix on enclitics.)

Singular

	Masculine	Feminine	Neuter
N	αὐτός he	αὐτή she	αὐτό it
G	αὐτοῦ of him, his	αὐτῆς of her, her	αὐτοῦ of it, its
D	αὐτῷ to, for him	αὐτῇ to, for her	αὐτῷ to, for it
A	αὐτόν him	αὐτήν her	αὐτό it

Plural

	Masculine	Feminine	Neuter
N	αὐτοί they	αὐταί they	αὐτά they
G	αὐτῶν of them, their	αὐτῶν of them, their	αὐτῶν of them, their
D	αὐτοῖς to, for them	αὐταῖς to, for them	αὐτοῖς to, for them
A	αὐτούς them	αὐτάς them	αὐτά them

Memory Aid

Observe the <u>autos</u>. Art Icicle is close by in the rumble seat since the endings of αὐτός parallel closely the endings of the article.

Practice

1. γινώσκει ὁ ἀπόστολος τὸν <u>δοῦλον</u> καὶ διδάσκει <u>αὐτόν</u>.
2. ἐν <u>αὐτῷ</u> <u>ζωή</u> ἐστιν καὶ λαμβάνομεν <u>αὐτήν</u>.
3. ἡ <u>ἐπαγγελία</u> αὐτοῦ ἐστιν ἀγαθὴ καὶ χαίρομεν ἐν <u>αὐτῇ</u>.
4. ὁ <u>ἄγγελός</u> μου ἔρχεται καὶ λαμβάνω <u>αὐτόν</u>.
5. ἡμῶν ὁ <u>οἶκός</u> ἐστιν καλὸς καὶ διδάσκομεν ἐν <u>αὐτῷ</u>.
6. κρίνετε τὸν <u>ἀπόστολον</u> καὶ οὐ λαμβάνετε τοὺς λόγους <u>αὐτοῦ</u>.

1. The apostle knows the slave and teaches him. 2. In him is life and we receive it. 3. His promise is good and we rejoice in it. 4. My messenger comes and I receive him. 5. Our house is beautiful and we teach in it. 6. You judge the apostle and you do not receive his words.

(In each example the Greek pronoun and its antecedent are underlined to show their relationship and to indicate how boredom is avoided.)

Emphatic and Intensive use

1. Personal pronouns may EMPHASIZE the subject of the VERB.

    A. The nominative forms of the pronouns in all three persons may stress the corresponding <u>personal</u> ending of the verb.

ἐγὼ λέγω - I say   ἡμεῖς λέγομεν - WE say

σὺ λέγεις - YOU say   ὑμεῖς λέγετε - YOU say

αὐτὸς λέγει - HE says   αὐτοὶ λέγουσι - THEY say

> (The nominative form αὐτός with the third person is emphatic at times only. Thus, αὐτὸς λέγει may mean either "<u>He</u> says" or "He says.")

    B. The nominative forms of αὐτός may emphasize the personal ending of the <u>verb</u>.

αὐτὸς ἐγὼ λέγω   - I myself say   - (masc.)

αὐτὴ ἐγὼ λέγω   - I myself say   - (fem.)

αὐτὸς σὺ λέγεις   - You yourself say - (masc.)

αὐτὴ σὺ λέγεις   - You yourself say - (fem.)

αὐτοὶ ἡμεῖς λέγομεν   - We ourselves say - (masc.)

αὐταὶ ἡμεῖς λέγομεν   - We ourselves say - (fem.)

2. Personal pronouns of the third person (αὐτός, αὐτή, αὐτό) may be used idiomatically with NOUNS in an INTENSIVE way. They are found in either the ATTRIBUTIVE or the PREDICATE position.

    A. In the <u>ATTRIBUTIVE</u> position, the word αὐτός means "very, same."

ὁ αὐτὸς διδάσκαλος - the same teacher
                   (or ὁ διδάσκαλος ὁ αὐτός)

τῆς αὐτῆς γραφῆς   - of the same writing
                   (or τῆς γραφῆς τῆς αὐτῆς)

τὸ αὐτὸ τέκνον   - the same child
                   (or τὸ τέκνον τὸ αὐτό)

B. In the <u>PREDICATE</u> position, the word αὐτός
means "self."

αὐτὸς ὁ διδάσκαλος - the teacher himself
    (or ὁ διδάσκαλος αὐτός)

τῆς γραφῆς αὐτῆς   - of the writing itself
    (or αὐτῆς τῆς γραφῆς)

αὐτὸ τὸ τέκνον   - the child himself
    (or τὸ τέκνον αὐτό)

Memory Aids

In one picture you observe
that the αὐτός is scheduled for
<u>intensive</u> care, for, unfortunately,
<u>Ego drove</u> the αὐτός into the
river. Ego escaped but the
αὐτός found himself floating down the <u>very same</u>
<u>tributary</u> (attributive)
which Art Icicle travels.

Small wonder that αὐτός
is in intensive car care.
In the <u>attributive</u> position, i.e. after the
article, the word αὐτός
means very, or same.

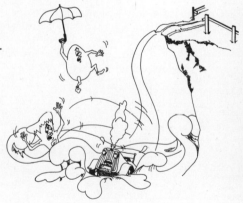

In the same scenario, after intensive
repairs have been made, the <u>elf</u> (self)
drives the <u>pretty cat</u> (predicate) away
in the αὐτός. In the predicate position αὐτός means self.

Practice

1. ὁ διδάσκαλος αὐτός.

2. ὁ αὐτὸς διδάσκαλος.

3. ὁ διδάσκαλός μου.

4. εἰσὶν μαθηταὶ τοῦ αὐτοῦ διδασκάλου.

5. εἰς τὴν αὐτὴν ἐκκλησίαν εἰσερχόμεθα.

6. ἐγώ εἰμι ὁ ἄρτος τῆς ζωῆς.

7. οὐ πορεύονται εἰς τὸν αὐτὸν οἶκον.

8. ἀποκρίνομαι τῷ δούλῳ ἀλλ᾽ ὑμεῖς ἀπέρχεσθε ἀπ᾽ αὐτοῦ.

9. ἡμεῖς αὐτοὶ γινώσκομεν τὸν ἀπόστολον αὐτόν.

10. ἡ αὐτὴ ἐντολὴ διδάσκει ἡμᾶς.

11. βλέπω αὐτῶν τὰ τέκνα καὶ λαμβάνω αὐτά.

12. αὕτη ἐστίν μου ἡ ἐκκλησία. δοξάζω τὸν θεὸν ἐν αὐτῇ.

13. ὑμεῖς αὐταὶ ἀκούετε τὴν φωνὴν αὐτοῦ.

KEY

1. The teacher himself. 2. The same teacher. 3. My
teacher. 4. They are disciples of the same teacher. 5.
We enter the same church. 6. I am the bread of life.
7. They do not go unto the same house. 8. I answer the
slave but <u>you</u> go away from him. 9. We ourselves know
the apostle <u>himself</u>. 10. The same commandment teaches us.
11. I see their children and I receive them. 12. It is
my church. I glorify God in it. 13. You yourselves
(fem.) hear his voice.

Enrichment

Pronouns often enhance the meaning of Scripture. In
Luke 22:58, the pronoun σύ serves to strengthen the
charge made against Peter in the house of the high priest
- καὶ σὺ ἐξ αὐτῶν εἶ, "even you, you are of them." And,
according to John 4:2, in answer to the report that Jesus
made and baptized more disciples than John the Baptist,
the writer inserts Ἰησοῦς <u>αὐτὸς</u> οὐκ ἐβάπτιζεν ἀλλ᾽ οἱ
μαθηταὶ αὐτοῦ, "Jesus <u>himself</u> was not baptizing but his
disciples (were)." Also, in John 3:10, Jesus' answer to
Nicodemus' question may be as much an exclamation as it
is a question, beginning as it does with the emphatic σύ
- σὺ εἶ ὁ διδάσκαλος . . . καὶ . . . οὐ γινώσκεις; "<u>You</u>
are the teacher . . . and . . . you do not know (these
things)?"

Assignment

Ἐλισαῖος[1] καὶ ὁ δοῦλος αὐτοῦ

Ἐν τοῖς βιβλίοις τῶν βασιλειῶν ἔστιν ἀκοὴ περὶ[2] τοῦ προφήτου Ἐλισαίου, τοῦ ἀνθρώπου τοῦ θεοῦ. ἀπαγγέλλει ἡ ἀκοὴ ὅτι ἀπέρχονται ἀπὸ τῆς Ἰουδαίας ὁ προφήτης καὶ ὁ δοῦλος αὐτοῦ. ἀναβαίνουσι δὲ πρὸς τὴν κώμην Δωθαΐμ[3] εὐαγγελίζεσθαι τοῖς πιστοῖς τὴν τῶν γραφῶν ἀλήθειαν καὶ ἑτοιμάζειν τὸν λαὸν ταῖς τοῦ κυρίου ἐπαγγελίαις. καὶ ἰδοὺ[4] ἐν τῇ αὐτῇ κώμῃ ἀπολύονται δοῦλοι καὶ ἀναβλέπουσι τυφλοὶ τῷ λόγῳ τοῦ Ἐλισαίου. ἤδη χαρὰ ἔστιν καὶ ἀγάπη ἐν ταῖς καρδίαις αὐτῶν, διδάσκονται γὰρ ὑπὸ τοῦ προφήτου τὰς ὁδοὺς τὰς δικαίας τοῦ νόμου.

ἐν τῇ αὐτῇ ὥρᾳ ἀκούουσιν πονηροὶ ὅτι ἔστιν Ἐλισαῖος ἐν Δωθαΐμ καὶ λέγουσι, Ἡμεῖς ἐσμεν δοῦλοι τῶν θεῶν ἡμῶν, ὁ δὲ προφήτης δοξάζει ἄλλον θεόν, τὸν τοῦ λαοῦ αὐτοῦ θεόν. καὶ ἀναβαίνουσι αὐτοὶ οἱ πονηροὶ πρὸς Δωθαΐμ ἀποκτείνειν Ἐλισαῖον.

καὶ ἐξέρχεται ὁ δοῦλος τοῦ προφήτου πρὸς τὴν ἀγορὰν ἐν Δωθαΐμ καὶ ἀναβλέπει καὶ ἰδοὺ[4] αὐτοὶ οἱ πονηροὶ ἄνθρωποι, καὶ λέγει πρὸς τὸν τοῦ θεοῦ ἄνθρωπον, Ἡμεῖς ἐσμεν νεκροί, προφῆτα ἀγαθέ, διώκουσι γὰρ ἡμᾶς καὶ[5] πρὸς τὰς θύρας τῆς κώμης ἡμῶν. ἀποκρίνεται δὲ αὐτῷ, Σὺ αὐτὸς εἶ τὸ τέκνον θεοῦ καὶ ἐγώ εἰμι ὁ προφήτης αὐτοῦ. ἀνοίγει αὐτὸς τὰς καρδίας ἡμῶν καὶ ἀναβλέπομεν διὰ τῶν ἐπαγγελιῶν αὐτοῦ. ἐκβάλλει τὰ δαιμόνια ἐκ τῶν καρδιῶν ἡμῶν καὶ οὐκέτι ἐσμὲν τυφλοί, χαίρομεν γὰρ ἐν τῷ θεῷ ἡμῶν καὶ δοξάζομεν αὐτὸν τοῖς πιστοῖς δώροις τῶν καρδιῶν ἡμῶν.

ἐν τῇ ὥρᾳ τῇ αὐτῇ ἀκούει ὁ θεὸς τοῦ προφήτου[6] καὶ σώζει αὐτὸν καὶ τὸν δοῦλον αὐτοῦ ἐκ τῶν πονηρῶν.

---

[1] Ἐλισαῖος = Elisha

[2] concerning

[3] Dothan. N.B. the dieresis above the iota. Compare naïve.

[4] ἰδού - behold

[5] καί - even

[6] The verb ἀκούω takes the genitive of the person.

65

Chapter 6

1. ἀγαπητός, -ή, -όν   - beloved (compare ἀγάπη)
2. ἀντί (with gen.)   - instead of, opposite (antiChrist)
3. ἀπαίρω   - I take away (compare αἴρω)
4. ἀπιστία, -ας, ἡ   - unbelief (see πιστός)
5. δεῖπνον, -ου, τό   - supper
6. δέχομαι   - I receive, welcome
7. διδαχή, -ῆς, ἡ   - teaching (didactic)
8. ἐκεῖ (adverb)   - there
9. ἐκεῖνος, -η, -ο   - that (demonstrative pronoun)
10. ἐκπλήσσομαι   - I am amazed (apoplexy)
11. ἐλπίζω   - I hope
12. ἐμβαίνω   - I embark, step in (see ἀναβαίνω)
13. ἐνδύω   - I put on - Middle = I dress, clothe myself in, put on
14. ἐπί (with gen.)   - upon, in the time of, on
15. ἐπί (with dat.)   - on, against, at
16. ἐπί (with acc.)   - across, upon
17. ἡμέρα, -ας, ἡ   - day (ephemeral)
18. θερισμός, -οῦ, ὁ   - harvest
19. θηρίον, -ου, τό   - beast
20. καθεύδω   - I sleep
21. κατά (with gen.)   - against, down upon (catacomb)
22. κατά (with acc.)   - according to (catalog)
23. καταβαίνω   - I go down (see ἀναβαίνω)
24. νῦν   - now
25. οὗτος, αὕτη, τοῦτο   - this (demonstrative pronoun)
26. παρά (with gen.)   - from
27. παρά (with dat.)   - near, in the presence of
28. παρά (with acc.)   - along, alongside (paradigm)
29. παραλαμβάνω   - I receive from, take along
30. περί (with gen.)   - concerning
31. περί (with acc.)   - around (perimeter, periscope)
32. πρό (with gen.)   - before (provide)
33. πρόβατον, -ου, τό   - sheep
34. προσεύχομαι   - I pray (dat. of person to whom prayer is made)
35. σύν (with dat.)   - with (synopsis, sympathy)

36. συνάγω   - I gather together (synagogue)
37. τόπος, -ου, ὁ   - place (topography) position
38. τότε   - then
39. φυλάσσω   - I guard (prophylaxis)
40. ψυχή, -ης, ἡ   - soul, person, life (psychology)
41. χόρτος, -ου, ὁ   - grass

. . . learn the Imperfect Tense - both its forms and
       meanings,

. . . meet Amy in her "imperfect" form, and

. . . deal with a "demo" salesman who will try to
       sell you a used car (demonstrative pronoun).

Foundational Concepts

Imperfect Tense

In Chapter one you learned a small, but important formula. You learned that the present tense implies present time as well as continuous action ("I loose," or "I am loosing"). Now observe the imperfect tense. Notice the difference between the imperfect and present. Both imply a continuous type of action, but the time of action changes from the present to the past. At times, the word "continuous" may actually depict action that is customary ("used to"), repeated, begun, or merely attempted.

IMPERFECT ACTIVE INDICATIVE OF λύω

Singular	Plural
1. ἔ λυ ον - I was loosing	(1) ἐ λύ ομεν - We were loosing
2. ἔ λυ ες - You were loosing	(2) ἐ λύ ετε - You were loosing
3. ἔ λυ ε(ν)- She was loosing He was loosing	(3) ἔ λυ ον - They were loosing

Observations

1. The imperfect tense has three parts:
   a. Prefixed augment
   b. Verb Stem
   c. Personal Endings

   The Present has only two parts:
   a. Verb stem
   b. Personal endings

2. The endings of the first and second person plural imperfect are the same as their respective forms in the present. The imperfect, however, has an augment.

3. The 1st person singular and 3rd person plural endings are identical. The context is the clue. If there is a plural subject in the sentence, the plural verb form is intended.

4. The movable "ν" occurs in the 3rd person singular, ἔλυε(ν).

Memory Aid

In the past, Lu <u>was loosing</u> an <u>imperfect</u> honest hen on the <u>indicator</u> (imperfect active indicative). He is talking about his <u>continuous</u> past with his psychiatrist <u>P. Hogman</u> (prefixed augment). The <u>honest hen</u> (-ον, -ες, -εν) with <u>omelete on</u> (-ομεν, -ετε, -ον) her hat will help you <u>remember</u> the personal endings. Study the picture until you know the various parts.

	Singular		Plural
1.	ἐ λυ όμην I was loosing for myself. I was being loosed.	(1)	ἐ λυ όμεθα - We were loos- ing for ourselves. We were being loosed.
2.	ἐ λύ ου - You were loosing for yourself. You were being loosed.	(2)	ἐ λύ εσθε - You were loos- ing for yourselves. You were being loosed.
3.	ἐ λύ ετο - She was loosing for herself. He was loosing for him- self. She was being loosed. He was being loosed.	(3)	ἐ λύ οντο - They were loosing for themselves. They were being loosed.

Observations

1. The endings are somewhat similar to the present middle/passive indicative.

2. Deponent verbs in the present tense are also deponent in the imperfect tense.

Memory Aid

Lu's broken glasses will remind you of the imperfect tense. He was imperfect. He was being loosed by the indicator (Imperfect Passive Indicative). He is talking again to his psychiatrist, P. Hogman (prefixed augment), about the time when a main blew a top (-ομην, -ου, -ετο) and Amethyst is the one on top (-ομεθα, -εσθε, -οντο).

Practice

PARSE THE FOLLOWING FORMS:

	T V M P N	Vocabulary Form	Translation
1. ἔβαλλεν			
2. ἐγινώσκομεν			
3. ἔλεγον			
4. ἐδιωκόμεθα			
5. ἐδοξάζοντο			

KEY

1. I A I 3 S   - βάλλω   - He was throwing.
                           She was throwing.
2. I A I 1 P   - γινώσκω - We were knowing
3. I A I 1 S or - λέγω   - I was saying.
      3 P   -   They were saying
4. I P I 1 P   - διώκω   - We were being pursued
5. I P I 3 P   - δοξάζω   - They were being glorified

Prefixed Augment

PREFIXED AUGMENT

    The prefixed augment (P. Hogman) will appear in three ways:

1. Before Consonants as an "ε" (see above).

    ἐβαπτίζομεν

    ἐγινώσκετε

2. Before Vowels, as a lengthened vowel. The augment is lengthened and disguised, as shown in the picture of P. Hogman on stilts - lengthened and disguised.

"α" and "ε" lengthen to "η" -
ἤκουον from ἀκούω
ἤγειρον from ἐγείρω

"αι" lengthens to "ῃ" -
ᾖρον from αἴρω

"ο" lengthens to "ω" -
ὤφειλον from ὀφείλω

3. With Compound Verbs - between preposition and verb stem.

ἐξεβάλλετε from ἐκβάλλω

Practice

PARSE THE FOLLOWING FORMS:

	T V M P N	Vocabulary Form	Translation
1. ἤγειρον			
2. ἤκουε(ν)			
3. ἐξεβαλλόμεθα			
4. ᾖρον			
5. προσηυχόμην			

KEY

1. I A I 1S or - ἐγείρω - I was raising up.
     3 P   They were raising up.
2. I A I 3 S   - ἀκούω - She was hearing.
                            He was hearing
3. I P I 1P   - ἐκβάλλω - We were being cast out.
4. I A I 1S or - αἴρω   - I was taking up, away.
     3 P   They were taking up, away.
5. I Dep. I 1 S - προσεύχομαι - I was praying

IMPERFECT INDICATIVE OF εἰμί

In Chapter five you observed the present tense of εἰμί - "to be," which had forms all its own. The imperfect also has its own unique forms.

Singular		Plural	
1. ἤμην - I was		1. ἤμεν - We were	
2. ἦς - You were		2. ἦτε - You were	
3. ἦν - She was, He was, It was		3. ἦσαν - They were	

Memory Aid

Poor Amy with her wilted ribbon! She does look a bit <u>imperfect</u> (Imperfect tense). She is also holding the well-known <u>indicator</u> (Indicative mood). She is sitting on a <u>main</u> which is led by an <u>ace</u> with a <u>rein</u> (ἤμην, ἦς, ἦν). The rein is also being pulled by <u>A-men</u> who <u>ate a sun</u> (ἦμεν, ἦτε, ἦσαν).

Demonstrative Pronouns

In Chapter five you were introduced to pronouns. You learned that pronouns are words that take the place of nouns. You met the personal pronouns, ἐγώ, σύ and αὐτός and you saw how αὐτός, (also αὐτή and αὐτό) is used to intensify nouns and verbs. Another very common pronoun is the <u>demonstrative</u> pronoun which specifies a particular person or object. The demonstrative pronouns are of two kinds: <u>near</u> and <u>distant</u>. The near demonstratives, as the name denotes, point to someone or something "near," in close proximity. They appear as the singular word "this" and its plural "these." The distant demonstratives, as their name suggests, appear as "that" (singular), or "those" (plural).

NEAR DEMONSTRATIVES - This, These

	Singular				Plural		
	Masc.	Fem.	Neut.		Masc.	Fem.	Neut.
N	οὗτος	αὕτη	τοῦτο	N	οὗτοι	αὗται	ταῦτα
G	τούτου	ταύτης	τούτου	G	τούτων	τούτων	τούτων
D	τούτῳ	ταύτῃ	τούτῳ	D	τούτοις	ταύταις	τούτοις
A	τοῦτον	ταύτην	τοῦτο	A	τούτους	ταύτας	ταῦτα

DISTANT DEMONSTRATIVES - That, Those

	Singular				Plural		
	Masc.	Fem.	Neut.		Masc.	Fem.	Neut.
N	ἐκεῖνος	ἐκείνη	ἐκεῖνο	N	ἐκεῖνοι	ἐκεῖναι	ἐκεῖνα
G	ἐκείνου	ἐκείνης	ἐκείνου	G	ἐκείνων	ἐκείνων	ἐκείνων
D	ἐκείνῳ	ἐκείνῃ	ἐκείνῳ	D	ἐκείνοις	ἐκείναις	ἐκείνοις
A	ἐκεῖνον	ἐκείνην	ἐκεῖνο	A	ἐκείνους	ἐκείνας	ἐκεῖνα

Observations

1. The endings parallel the endings of the personal
pronoun αὐτός and are very similar to the well-known
article.

2. Demonstrative pronouns occur in the predicate
position, yet they are attributive in meaning:

οὗτος ὁ λόγος = this word
ἐκεῖνος ὁ λόγος = that word

3. Demonstrative pronouns may be used alone, i.e.
in place of a noun:

οὗτος - this (man), this one   ἐκεῖνος- that (man), that one
αὕτη - this (woman)   ἐκείνη - that (woman)
τοῦτο - this thing   ἐκεῖνο - that thing
ταῦτα - these things   ἐκεῖνα - those things

Memory Aid

Meet the demo-salesman who is trying to palm off used "demos" (demonstrative). At the left he points to the near demo and says, "This near demo has a hoot owl that goes toot (οὗτος, αὕτη, τοῦτο). Observe the owl on the radiator. Art Icicle in the rumble seat will remind you of the article endings.

In the distance the salesman points to a badly-worn demo and says, "That 'thar' demo needs a cane (εκειν) to get along." Again, observe Art Icicle in the rumble seat. Study the picture and the paradigms noting carefully the meanings and endings of each demonstrative.

Practice

1. ἐν ταῖς ἡμέραις ἐκείναις
2. τοῦτον τὸν λόγον
3. τοῦτο
4. ταῦτα
5. οὗτοι οἱ ἄγγελοι
6. ἐκείνου τοῦ ἀγαθοῦ νόμου

KEY

1. in those days 2. this word (acc. case) 3. this thing 4. these things 5. these messengers 6. of that good law

76

Professor Oddity

An irregularity occurs with the noun in the <u>neuter plural nominative</u>. It can function either with a <u>plural</u> verb or a <u>singular</u> verb. Thus:

τὰ τέκνα ἄγει δῶρα, or
τὰ τέκνα ἄγουσι δῶρα.

Both sentences mean, "the children bring gifts."

Enrichment

As Jesus speaks about the uncertainty of the Day of the Lord (Luke 17:27), four imperfects are used to describe the life of people in Noah's day. Each imperfect helps "paint the picture" of a day-by-day life-style: "They were eating, they were drinking, they were marrying, they were being given in marriage." The other three verbs in the verse are Aorist (past time and point action): "Noah <u>entered</u> the ark, the rains <u>came</u> and <u>destroyed</u> all (except those in the ark)."

The imperfect form ἠλπίζομεν in Luke 24:21, "we were hoping," expresses the constant living hope of the two disciples in Jesus from the time they first knew him, a hope which they assumed was shattered by Jesus' death. And yet, strangely enough, the one to whom they say ἠλπίζομεν, is the risen Jesus himself!

Preposition Memory Aids

Study these pictures. They will help you learn the new prepositions introduced in this chapter.

ἀντί with the genitive, "instead of, opposite"

Gerard (gen.) with an <u>ant-tee</u> (ἀντί) <u>instead of</u> a golf tee, experiences <u>opposite</u> results. What a fiasco!

ἐπί with the genitive, "upon, in the time of, on"
ἐπί with the dative, "on, against, at"
ἐπί with the accusative, "across, upon"

Gerard (gen.) holds <u>a pawn</u> (upon) and a <u>clock</u> (in the time of) as he stands <u>on a pea</u> pod (ἐπί).

Demetrius (dat.) is <u>on a pea pod</u> (ἐπί). He is leaning <u>against a pea</u> and wearing a <u>big hat</u> (at).

Armitage (acc.) is lying <u>across a pea</u> (ἐπί) pod holding <u>a pawn</u> (upon).

κατά with the genitive, "against, down upon"
κατά with the accusative, "according to"

Gerard (gen.) runs against the cat (κατά) falling down upon the floor. Armitage (acc.) plays his accordion (according to) with the cat (κατά).

παρά with the genitive, "from"

A pair of (παρά) parrots from Gerard (gen.).

PRETTY NEAR!

παρά with the dative, "near, in the presence of"

Demetrius (dat.) is "pretty near" safe in the presence of the parrot (παρά).

παρά with the accusative, "alongside"
Armitage (acc.) is trotting alongside the parrots (παρά). It looks like hard work.

περί with the genitive, "concerning"
περί with the accusative, "around"

Gerard (gen.) and Detective Perry (περί) are concerting (concerning) while Perry (περί) marches around Armitage (acc.) with his sousaphone.

πρό with the genitive, "before"

Bravo! Gerard (gen.), you'll be a pro (πρό) before long!

σύν with the dative, "with"
Demetrius (dat.) holds hands with the sun (σύν).

Assignment

τὸ δεῖπνον ὑπὲρ τοῦ ἀγαπητοῦ υἱοῦ

Ἐν ἐκείναις ταῖς ἡμέραις μετὰ τὸν θερισμόν, ὁ πιστὸς διδάσκαλος καταβαίνει πρὸς τὴν κώμην καὶ ἐκεῖ παρὰ τὴν θάλασσαν ἐδίδασκεν τὰ μικρὰ τέκνα περὶ τῆς βασιλείας τῶν οὐρανῶν.[1] τότε ἐν τῷ αὐτῷ τόπῳ συνῆγεν τοὺς μαθητὰς αὐτοῦ καὶ ἔλεγεν πρὸς αὐτοὺς[2] παραβολάς.

πρῶτον[3] ἤκουον τὴν διδαχὴν τοῦ διδασκάλου περὶ τοῦ χόρτου τοῦ ἀγροῦ καὶ περὶ τοῦ καρποῦ τοῦ θερισμοῦ. ἔλεγεν ὅτι ἐνδύει ὁ θεὸς τὸν χόρτον δόξῃ καὶ ὅτι καρποὶ φέρονται ἐν τοῖς ἀγροῖς ὑπὲρ τοῦ λαοῦ ἐν τῷ κόσμῳ. μετὰ τοῦτο ἔλεγεν ὁ διδάσκαλος παραβολὴν περὶ τῶν προβάτων καὶ ἐδίδασκεν ὅτι φυλάσσει ὁ ποιμὴν[4] αὐτὰ ἀπὸ τῶν κακῶν θηρίων τοῦ ἀγροῦ καὶ ὅτι ἐσθίουσιν χόρτον παρὰ τῷ ποιμένι[5] ἐν εἰρήνῃ.

μετὰ ταῦτα συνῆγεν τοὺς μαθητὰς περὶ αὐτὸν καὶ ἐξεπλήσσετο διὰ τὴν ἀπιστίαν αὐτῶν. διὰ τοῦτο ἔλεγεν αὐτοῖς[2] τὴν παραβολὴν ταύτην. ἄνθρωπος πιστὸς ἐν μικρᾷ κώμῃ τῆς Ἰουδαίας εἶχεν[6] υἱὸν ἀγαπητόν. καὶ παρελάμβανεν οὗτος ὁ υἱὸς παρὰ τῆς ψυχῆς τοῦ πατρὸς[7] αὐτοῦ ἀγάπην καὶ δόξαν κατὰ τὸν τόπον αὐτοῦ ἐν τῷ οἴκῳ. καὶ συνῆγεν ὁ πατὴρ[8] αὐτοῦ ἄρτους καὶ καρποὺς ἐτοιμάζειν γάμον[9] ὑπὲρ τοῦ ἀγαπητοῦ υἱοῦ. καὶ γράφει ὁ πατὴρ[8] πρὸς τοὺς καλοὺς καὶ τὰς καλὰς ἐν τῇ κώμῃ αὐτοῦ ἔρχεσθαι καὶ χαίρειν ἐν τῷ γάμῳ[9] τοῦ υἱοῦ καὶ ἀποστέλλει ἀγγέλους καὶ δούλους σὺν τούτοις τοῖς λόγοις φέρειν τὸν λαὸν πρὸς τὸν γάμον[9] τοῦ υἱοῦ.

ἀλλ᾿ οὐκ ἐδέχοντο ἐκεῖνοι οἱ καλοὶ καὶ αἱ καλαὶ ἐκεῖναι τοὺς τοῦ πατρὸς[7] ἀγγέλους καὶ ἐδίωκον αὐτούς. μετὰ ταῦτα ἀπέστελλεν ὁ πατὴρ[8] ἄλλους ἀγγέλους εὑρίσκειν τοὺς ἁμαρτωλοὺς καὶ φέρειν αὐτοὺς πρὸς τὸν γάμον. καὶ οἱ ἁμαρτωλοὶ σὺν χαρᾷ ἐδέχοντο τοὺς ἀγγέλους. μετὰ τοῦτο ἐνδύονται ἱμάτια καθαρὰ καὶ ἀγοράζουσι δῶρα ἀγαθὰ καὶ φέρουσιν αὐτὰ πρὸς τὸν τοῦ πατρὸς[7] υἱὸν χαίρειν ἐν τῷ γάμῳ. καὶ ἐλάμβανεν αὐτοὺς ὁ πατὴρ καὶ ἔλεγεν, Νῦν χαρᾷ χαίρω[10] διὰ τούτους τοὺς ἀδελφούς μου. ἦσαν ἁμαρτωλοί, ἀλλ᾿ ἀπαίρεται ἡ ἁμαρτία αὐτῶν καὶ νῦν εἰσέρχονται εἰς τοῦτον τὸν τόπον χαίρειν μεθ' ἡμῶν καὶ φέρειν ἀγαθὰ δῶρα πρὸς τὸν ἀγαπητὸν υἱόν μου.

καὶ ἤκουον οἱ μαθηταὶ ταύτην τὴν παραβολὴν καὶ ἀπεκρίνοντο τῷ διδασκάλῳ καὶ ἔλεγον, Ἀπαγγέλλεις τοῦτον τὸν λόγον ἡμῖν;

μετὰ ταῦτα ἐνέβαινεν ὁ διδάσκαλος εἰς πλοῖον μετὰ τῶν μαθητῶν καὶ ἐν τῇ ὁδῷ διὰ τῆς θαλάσσης ἐκάθευδεν.

---

[1]ἡ βασιλεία τῶν οὐρανῶν - "The kingdom of heaven," is a phrase peculiar to the gospel of Matthew. The plural word "heavens" is due to Old Testament influence and indicates the breadth or extent of heaven.

[2]The verb λέγω may be followed by the dative case of the person(s) addressed or by πρός with the accusative case of the person(s) addressed.

[3]πρῶτον - neuter, accusative, singular, used as an adverb = in the first place.

[4]ποιμήν - shepherd (nominative case)

[5]ποιμένι - shepherd (dative case)

[6]εἶχεν - imperfect (3rd singular) of ἔχω

[7]πατρός - father (genitive case)

[8]πατήρ - father (nominative case)

[9]γάμος - wedding, banquet, marriage

[10]χαρᾷ χαίρω - I rejoice with joy (compare John 3: 29; James 5:17).

Chapter 7

1. ἀλλήλων, -οις, -ους - one another . . . (cf. ἄλλος)
2. δένδρον, -ου, τό - tree (<u>dendro</u>logy, rhodo<u>dendron</u>)
3. ἑαυτοῦ, -ῷ, -όν - himself (reflexive pronoun masculine, cf. αὑτοῦ)
4. ἐμαυτοῦ, -ῷ, -όν - myself (reflexive pronoun masculine, cf. ἐμοῦ)
5. Ἰησοῦς, -οῦ, -οῦν - Jesus (gen., dative, and voc. have the same form). Compare the vocative in Mark 10:47 Υἱὲ Δαυὶδ Ἰησοῦ, "O Jesus Son of David."
6. καινός, -ή, -όν - new
7. κεφαλή, -ῆς, ἡ - head (<u>cephal</u>ic)
8. κηρύσσω - I preach, proclaim (<u>kerygma</u>)
9. κλάδος, -ου, ὁ - branch
10. κλίνη, -ης, ἡ - bed (in<u>cline</u>, <u>clin</u>ic)
11. κράζω - I cry out
12. κρυπτός, -ή, -όν - hidden (<u>crypt</u>ic), secret
13. λίθος, -ου, ὁ - stone (<u>lith</u>ograph, mono<u>lith</u>)
14. νηστεύω - I fast
15. νόσος, -ου, ἡ - disease, sickness (<u>noso</u>logy)
16. ὁράω - I see (pan<u>ora</u>ma)
17. ὅτε - when
18. οὔπω - not yet
19. οὕτως - thus (compare οὗτος)
20. παλαιός, -ά, -όν - old (<u>palaeo</u>graphy)
21. πετεινόν, -οῦ, τό - bird ("pet")
22. σεαυτοῦ, -ῷ, -όν - yourself (reflexive pronoun masc., compare σέ)
23. στρατιώτης, -ου, ὁ - soldier
24. συνέρχομαι - I come together
25. τελώνης, -ου, ὁ - tax-collector
26. φανερός, -ά, -όν - visible, manifest (theo<u>phany</u>)

IN THIS LESSON YOU WILL:

 . . . meet Lu of the future tense,

 . . . observe the sigma (σ) of the future tense and
          note how, at times, it is transformed,

 . . . learn how to add letters,

 . . . see the future Amy, and

 . . . meet two new types of pronouns.

Foundational Concepts

In this chapter we will look at the future tense.
The time obviously is future, but the type of action is
either momentary or continuous, depending upon the context.

FUTURE ACTIVE INDICATIVE OF λύω (Second Principal Part)

	Singular		Plural

1.	λύ σ ω -
	    I shall loose
		(1)	λύ σ ομεν -
			    We shall loose

2.	λύ σ εις -
	    You will loose
		(2)	λύ σ ετε -
			    You will loose

3.	λύ σ ει -
	    She will loose
	    He will loose
	    It will loose
		(3)	λύ σ ουσι(ν)-
			    They will loose

Observations

1. Whereas the present and imperfect tenses are
built on the first principal part, λύω, the future
tense is built on the second principal part, λύσω.

2. The three parts of the future active are:
   a. the stem
   b. the tense suffix "σ," and
   c. the personal endings of the present
      active indicative.

Memory Aid

Through his <u>binoculars</u> Lu contemplates the <u>future</u> of the indicator. <u>Using</u> the wrench in his hand he <u>will act</u> to loose the <u>indicator</u> (future active indica<u>tive</u>). Observe the sigma sun for the tense suffix and master the personal endings via the <u>oasis</u> (-ω, -εις, -ει), and the omelette oozing (-ομεν, -ετε, -ουσι(ν)) out of the indicator.

FUTURE MIDDLE INDICATIVE OF λύω

Singular

1. λύ σ ομαι -
   I shall loose for myself
2. λύ σ η   -
   You shall loose for yourself
3. λύ σ εται -
   She will loose for herself
   He will loose for himself
   It will loose for itself

Plural

(1) λυ σ όμεθα - We shall
    loose for ourselves
(2) λύ σ εσθε   - You will
    loose for yourselves
(3) λύ σ ονται - They will
    loose for themselves

Observations

1. The voice is middle, not middle/passive
2. The three parts of the future middle are:
   a. stem
   b. tense suffix "σ," and
   c. personal endings of the present middle/passive.

Memory Aid

Lu contemplates the <u>future</u> when <u>he will loose</u> the <u>indicator for himself</u> (<u>future middle indicative</u>). The <u>middle</u> voice is remembered by the <u>medal</u> hanging from the indicator, and the <u>binoculars</u> remind you of the future. Observe the "σ" sun shining above. As Lu watches, he says, "Oh my . . . a . . . a tie (-ομαι, -η, -εται) <u>Amethyst is the untier</u> (-όμεθα, -εσθε, -ονται)."

Practice

	T	V	M	P	N	Vocabulary Form	Translation

1. ἀκούσομεν
2. θεραπεύσουσιν
3. ἀκούσομαι
4. νηστευσόμεθα
5. λύσετε

KEY

1. F A I 1 P - ἀκούω - We shall hear. 2. F A I 3 P - θεραπεύω - They will heal. 3. F M I 1 S - ἀκούω - I shall hear for myself. 4. F M I 1 P - νηστεύω - We shall fast for ourselves. 5. F A I 2 P - λύω - You will loose.

Adding Letters

When the stem of the verb ends in a consonant, the consonant combines with the tense suffix "σ," and follows definite patterns. The suffix is still found in these future forms but it is HIDDEN.

1. LABIALS (formed at the <u>lips</u>)

   π, φ, or β + σ = ψ

Pronounce each letter with the "σ" and you will hear the double consonant, "ψ."

Present	Future
βλέπω	βλέψω
γράφω	γράψω

2. <u>GUTTURALS OR PALATALS</u> (formed in the throat)

   κ, γ, or χ + σ = ξ

Pronounce each letter with the "σ" and you will hear the double consonant, "ξ."

Present	Future
διώκω	διώξω
ἄγω	ἄξω
φυλάσσω	φυλάξω

(Most double sigma stems [-σσω] are palatals in origin.)

3. <u>DENTALS</u> (formed at the teeth). This class of verbs is also called <u>LINGUALS</u> (because of the action of the tongue)

   δ, ϑ, or ζ + σ = σ

Before the <u>sigma</u> (σ) of the future, a dental is assimilated.

Present	Future
βαπτίζω	βαπτίσω
πείϑω	πείσω
δοξάζω	δοξάσω

Practice

Parse and Translate. Note the hidden "σ" in
each of the first four forms.

		T	V	M	P	N	Vocabulary Form	Translation
1.	πέμψετε
2.	γραψόμεθα
3.	διώξουσιν
4.	φυλάξει
5.	βαπτίσεις

KEY

1. F A I 2 P - πέμπω - You will send.   2. F M I 1 P -
γράφω - We shall write for ourselves.   3. F A I 3 P -
διώκω - They will pursue, persecute.   4. F A I 3 S -
φυλάσσω - She will guard, He will guard.   5. F A I 2 S -
βαπτίζω - You will baptize.

Irregular Verbs

   Now you will meet seven irregular verbs, in which
the future form has little or no relation to the present
stem.   Memory aids for the irregular verbs are provided
which bring together the future and present forms.   Before translating the practice sentences learn these
seven irregular forms and their respective vocabulary
forms.   Note that all their future forms are deponent.

άναβήσομαι - I shall go up
άναβαίνω - I go up

<u>On a base</u> (άναβήσομαι) I
<u>shall go up</u> on a rhino
(άναβαίνω) with <u>binoculars</u>
(fut.). It is rough going
on those horns.

γενήσομαι - I shall become
γίνομαι - I become

"This <u>can ace</u> (γενήσομαι)
<u>will become a kin of mine</u>
(γίνομαι)," says the Ace.
Note the <u>binoculars</u> (fut.)

γνώσομαι - I shall know
γινώσκω - I know

A bloodhound with <u>binocu-
lars</u> (fut.) sniffing the
daisies says, "This nose
<u>of mine</u> (γνώσομαι) <u>will
know, you know</u>! (γινώσκω).

89

έλεύσομαι - I shall come
έρχομαι - I come

A baseball player with
binoculars (fut.) <u>will
come elusively</u> (ἐλεύσομαι) and as he arrives
at home says "<u>Here Come
I</u>" (ἔρχομαι).

φάγομαι - I will eat
ἐσθίω - I eat

<u>Fog</u> (φάγομαι) with <u>binocu-
lars</u> (fut.) <u>will eat
aesthetically</u> (ἐσθίω).

λήμψομαι - I shall take,
          receive
λαμβάνω - I take, receive

<u>A lame-slide</u> (λήμψομαι)
<u>will take a lambasting</u>
(<u>λάμβάνω</u>) from the <u>binoc-
ulars</u> (fut.). He hardly
has a chance.

δψομαι - I shall see
ὁράω - I see

"If I <u>hops</u> (δψομαι) you <u>will see</u> and say <u>hurrah</u> (ὁράω). Note the frog's <u>binoculars</u> (fut.).

Practice

1. ἐλεύσονται πρὸς τὸν οἶκον.
2. γενήσεσθε οἱ μαθηταὶ αὐτοῦ.
3. ἀναβησόμεθα πρὸς τὸ ἱερόν.
4. γνώσῃ τὴν ἀλήθειαν.
5. λήμψεται τὴν δόξαν τῆς βασιλείας.
6. φάγονται τὸν ἄρτον.
7. ὀψόμεθα αὐτὸν πρόσωπον πρὸς πρόσωπον.

<u>KEY</u>

1. They will come to the house. 2. You will become his disciples. 3. We shall go up to the temple. 4. You will know the truth. 5. She (He) will receive the glory of the kingdom. 6. They will eat the bread. 7. We shall see him face to face.

Lexicon Use — the Future

Lexicons generally do not list future forms of regular verbs which follow fixed patterns. To look up διώξω you simply relate the word to the present form διώκω and then use the lexicon.

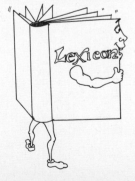

Lexicons will list irregular forms of verbs and indicate their respective present forms. If you meet λήμψομαι and look it up, you will find it listed as the future of λαμβάνω. Then you turn to λαμβάνω to find its present meaning, "I take, receive."

Lexicons will not normally list the future of a compound verb. Should you meet the form παραλήμψομαι, remove the preposition παρά and then look up λήμψομαι. You will discover that λήμψομαι is the future of λαμβάνω. Then restore the preposition and look up παραλαμβάνω and find its meaning, "I receive from, take along."

FUTURE INDICATIVE OF εἰμί

You have been introduced to the present and imperfect tenses of Amy. You have seen her past and her present, and now you will observe her in her future forms.

Singular		Plural	
1. ἔσομαι	- I shall be	(1) ἐσόμεθα	- We shall be
2. ἔσῃ	- You will be	(2) ἔσεσθε	- You will be
3. ἔσται	- She will be	(3) ἔσονται	- They will be
	He will be		
	It will be		

Memory Aid

Here is the Future Amy with her indicator, (Future Indicative of εἰμί). The space helmet and binoculars will remind you of the future. Amy has the letters "εσ" across her jersey and she holds hands with Amethyst who reminds you of the future middle endings. There is one difference only - The third singular of the future of εἰμί is ἔσται (i.e. no thematic vowel). Compare λύσεται. Now, review the endings of the present and imperfect indicative of εἰμί.

92

Practice and Translate

1. ἐσόμεθα σὺν θεῷ.
2. οὕτως δὲ ἔσονται οἱ ἔσχατοι πρῶτοι.
3. οὕτως ἔσται καὶ (also) ἐν ταῖς ἡμέραις τοῦ υἱοῦ τοῦ ἀνθρώπου.
4. πονηροὶ ἦτε, ἀγαθοὶ δὲ ἔσεσθε.
5. ἐν τῷ κόσμῳ ἦν.

KEY

1. We shall be with God. 2. And, thus, the last will be first. 3. Thus it shall be also in the days of the son of man. 4. You were evil, but you will be good. 5. She (He, It) was in the world.

Reflexive Pronouns

Reflexive pronouns refer to a previous subject in a sentence or clause. Observe the following sentences:

ἐγὼ δοξάζω ἐμαυτόν — I glorify myself
δοξάσει αὐτὸν ἐν ἑαυτῷ — He will glorify him in himself
δοξάζετε ἑαυτούς — You glorify yourselves

In the above examples, the pronoun refers directly back to the subject of the sentence in a reflexive fashion.

1. The declension of ἐμαυτοῦ, -ῆς, "of myself," is as follows:

	Singular			Plural	
	Masc.	Fem.		Masc.	Fem.
G	ἐμαυτοῦ	ἐμαυτῆς	G	ἑαυτῶν	ἑαυτῶν
D	ἐμαυτῷ	ἐμαυτῇ	D	ἑαυτοῖς	ἑαυταῖς
A	ἐμαυτόν	ἐμαυτήν	A	ἑαυτούς	ἑαυτάς

2. The declension of σεαυτοῦ, -ῆς, "of yourself," is as follows:

	Singular			Plural	
	Masc.	Fem.		Masc.	Fem.
G	σεαυτοῦ	σεαυτῆς	G	ἑαυτῶν	ἑαυτῶν
D	σεαυτῷ	σεαυτῇ	D	ἑαυτοῖς	ἑαυταῖς
A	σεαυτόν	σεαυτήν	A	ἑαυτούς	ἑαυτάς

3. The declension of ἑαυτοῦ, -ῆς, -οῦ, "of himself," "of herself," and "of itself," follows:

	Singular				Plural		
	Masc.	Fem.	Neut.		Masc.	Fem.	Neut.
G	ἑαυτοῦ	ἑαυτῆς	ἑαυτοῦ	G	ἑαυτῶν	ἑαυτῶν	ἑαυτῶν
D	ἑαυτῷ	ἑαυτῇ	ἑαυτῷ	D	ἑαυτοῖς	ἑαυταῖς	ἑαυτοῖς
A	ἑαυτόν	ἑαυτήν	ἑαυτό	A	ἑαυτούς	ἑαυτάς	ἑαυτά

Observations

1. The reflexive pronouns of the first and second persons singular are formed on the basis of the personal pronoun and the intensive αὐτός (masc.) or αὐτῆς (fem.).

ἐμαυτοῦ = εμ + αυτου - of myself (masc.)
ἐμαυτῆς = εμ + αυτης - of myself (fem.)

σεαυτοῦ = σε + αυτου - of yourself (masc.)
σεαυτῆς = σε + αυτης - of yourself (fem.)

2. Neuter forms of the reflexive pronoun appear in the third person only.

3. The plural forms are the same respectively in each person (1st, 2nd, 3rd). Context will determine the meaning since the pronouns must refer directly to their antecedents.

Reciprocal Pronouns

The reciprocal pronouns have three forms:

Genitive   - ἀλλήλων - of one another
Dative   - ἀλλήλοις - to one another
Accusative - ἀλλήλους - one another

Practice

1. οὐκ ἔχει ζωὴν ἐν ἑαυτῷ.
2. ἔλεγον πρὸς ἀλλήλους (Mark 4:41).
3. ἐγὼ λέγω περὶ ἐμαυτοῦ.
4. ἀπ᾽ ἐμαυτοῦ οὐ λέγω.
5. ὁ γὰρ πατὴρ (father) ἔχει ζωὴν ἐν ἑαυτῷ.

KEY

1. He does not have life in himself. 2. They were saying to one another. 3. I speak concerning myself. 4. From myself I do not speak. 5. For the father has life in himself.

Enrichment

2 Cor. 4:5 - οὐ γὰρ ἑαυτοὺς κηρύσσομεν ἀλλὰ Χριστὸν Ἰησοῦν κύριον, ἑαυτοὺς δὲ δούλους ὑμῶν διὰ Ἰησοῦν.

The verb and the first occurrence of ἑαυτούς are clear - "For we do not proclaim ourselves. But there is no verb with the second occurrence of ἑαυτούς. Possibly Paul intends the verb "reckon," i.e. "(we reckon) ourselves your slaves because of Jesus."

Elsewhere Paul calls himself a δοῦλος Χριστοῦ but it is strange to hear him affirm that he and his companions are δοῦλοι of the church. How do we account for this? Is it perhaps that Paul aims to bridge the widening gap between himself and the church in Corinth?

At times the reflexive pronoun points to God's special concern for the world. He sent "his own Son," τὸν ἑαυτοῦ υἱόν - Rom. 8:3, he demonstrates "his own love toward us," τὴν ἑαυτοῦ ἀγάπην εἰς ἡμᾶς - Rom. 5:8, and he reconciles "us to himself through Christ," ἡμᾶς ἑαυτῷ διὰ Χριστοῦ. And so Paul writes to the Christians at Corinth, οὐκ ἐστὲ ἑαυτῶν, "you are not your own," 1 Cor. 6:19, adding, "You are bought with a price." That is to say, God's own Son and his own love inevitably produce a people who are not "their own," but "his own."

Assignment

<u>'Ιησοῦς διδάσκει μαθητὰς καὶ εὑρίσκει τελώνην</u>

ἀναγινώσκομεν ἐν τῷ εὐαγγελίῳ ὅτι τὰ κρυπτὰ γενήσεται φανερὰ καὶ τὰ παλαιὰ καινά, καὶ ὅτι πέμψει ὁ πατὴρ ὁ ἐν τοῖς οὐρανοῖς[1] ἄρτους καὶ οὐ λίθους πρὸς τὰ τέκνα αὐτοῦ. οὕτως ἐκήρυσσεν ὁ 'Ιησοῦς καὶ ἐν τῷ ἱερῷ καὶ ἐν ταῖς κώμαις ταῖς ἐν Γαλιλαίᾳ. καὶ ἤκουον οἱ πιστοὶ τὴν διδαχὴν αὐτοῦ καὶ ἐξεπλήσσοντο ἐπ' αὐτῇ καὶ ἐφύλασσον αὐτὴν ἐν ἑαυτοῖς. καὶ ἔχαιρον ὅτι ἐξέβαλλεν ὁ κύριος δαιμόνια. ἀλλὰ οἱ στρατιῶται καὶ οἱ κακοὶ τελῶναι οὔπω ἦσαν μαθηταὶ τοῦ 'Ιησοῦ καὶ τοῖς πονηροῖς ἔργοις αὐτῶν ἡμάρτανον εἰς τὸν οὐρανὸν καὶ εἰς τὰς ἑαυτῶν[2] ψυχάς.

διὰ τοῦτο ἐνήστευεν ὁ 'Ιησοῦς καὶ προσηύχετο τῷ θεῷ. ἀλλὰ ἔκραζον οἱ μαθηταὶ καὶ ἔλεγον, 'Ελεύσεται ἡ βασιλεία τοῦ θεοῦ εἰς τοῦτον τὸν κόσμον; παραλήμψονται ἁμαρτωλοὶ παρὰ τοῦ θεοῦ τὸ εὐαγγέλιον καὶ ἕξουσι τὴν εἰρήνην μετ' ἀλλήλων καὶ ὄψονται[3] τὴν τοῦ θεοῦ δόξαν ἐν τῇ ζωῇ ταύτῃ; γινώσκομεν ὅτι προσεύχεται ὁ κύριος καὶ νηστεύει ὑπὲρ ἡμῶν προσφέρειν ἡμᾶς τῷ θεῷ· ἀλλ' ἐσόμεθα οἱ μαθηταὶ αὐτοῦ καὶ αὐτὸς διδάξει ἡμᾶς ἐλπίζειν ἐπὶ τὴν ἀλήθειαν αὐτοῦ; διδάσκει ἡμᾶς ὅτι ἐλπίζει τὰ πετεινὰ[4] τοῦ οὐρανοῦ ἐπὶ τὸν θεὸν καὶ μετ' ἀλλήλων ἐστὶν ἐν τοῖς κλάδοις τῶν δένδρων κἀκεῖ[5] ἐσθίει καὶ καθεύδει, κἀκεῖ[5] φυλάσσεται ὑπὸ τοῦ θεοῦ. οὕτως οὐκ ἀκούσομεν τὴν διδαχὴν αὐτοῦ; οὐκ ἀναβησόμεθα πρὸς αὐτοῦ τὸ ἱερὸν ἐν χαρᾷ καὶ οὐ δοξάσομεν ἐκεῖ τὸν θεόν;

μετὰ ταῦτα ἦγε 'Ιησοῦς τοὺς μαθητὰς παρὰ τὴν θάλασσαν παρὰ κώμῃ τῆς Γαλιλαίας. καὶ ἰδοὺ ἦν ἐκεῖ ἐν τῇ αὐτῇ κώμῃ ἐκείνῃ ἄνθρωπος, τελώνης, ἀλλ' ἦν μικρὸς τῇ ἡλικίᾳ.[6] καὶ ἤλπιζεν βλέπειν τὸν 'Ιησοῦν. καὶ ἔλεγεν ἐν ἑαυτῷ, 'Ιδοὺ ἐγώ εἰμι μικρὸς τῇ ἡλικίᾳ.[6] διὰ τοῦτο ἀναβήσομαι ἐπὶ δένδρον ἐν τῇ ὁδῷ κἀκεῖ[5] ἐλεύσεται ὁ κύριος, καὶ βλέψω αὐτόν. καὶ οὕτως ἀναβαίνει[7] ὁ τελώνης ἐπὶ τὸ δένδρον. τότε ἔρχεται[7] 'Ιησοῦς καὶ οἱ μαθηταὶ αὐτοῦ ἐπὶ τὸν τόπον ὑπὸ τὸ δένδρον ἐκεῖνο καὶ ἀναβλέπει[7] καὶ βλέπει[7] τὸν τελώνην καὶ λέγει[7] αὐτῷ, Ζακχαῖε,[8] καταβήσῃ νῦν ἐκ τοῦ δένδρου καὶ φαγόμεθα ἄρτους ἐν τῷ οἴκῳ

σου. καὶ καταβαίνει Ζακχαῖος ἀπὸ τοῦ δένδρου καὶ
δέχεται τὸν ᾿Ιησοῦν εἰς τὸν οἶκον ἑαυτοῦ.

διὰ τοῦτο ἔκρινον ὁ λαὸς ᾿Ιησοῦν καὶ ἔλεγον, ᾿Ιδοὺ
ἐσθίει οὗτος ὁ ἄνθρωπος μετὰ τελωνῶν καὶ ἁμαρτωλῶν. ἀλλὰ
ἔχαιρεν Ζακχαῖος διὰ τὴν ἀγάπην τοῦ ᾿Ιησοῦ καὶ ἤσθιον
Ζακχαῖος καὶ ᾿Ιησοῦς σὺν ἀλλήλοις καὶ[9] ἄρτον καὶ[9] καρπὸν
ἐν χαρᾷ καὶ εἰρήνῃ.

---

[1]ὁ ἐν τοῖς οὐρανοῖς = who is in heaven

[2]"of themselves" - "their own"

[3]future of ὁράω

[4]Neuter plural subject can take a singular verb

[5]κἀκεῖ is a blending (crasis - κρᾶσις) of two words
καί and ἐκεῖ. The smooth breathing over the α (κἀκεῖ)
shows that the second word of the combination begins
with a vowel.

[6]τῇ ἡλικίᾳ - with respect to stature

[7]Historical present

[8]Ζακχαῖος - Zacchaeus

[9]καί . . . καί . . . = both . . . and

Chapter 8

1. ἁγιάζω — I consecrate, sanctify (<u>Hagio</u>grapha)
2. ἅγιος, -α, -ον — holy (tris<u>agion</u>; "the saints" = οἱ ἅγιοι)
3. ἀδελφή, -ῆς, -ἡ — sister (cf. ἀδελφός)
4. ἀποθνήσκω — I die
5. γῆ, γῆς, ἡ (singular only) — earth, land <u>(geography)</u>
6. δικαιοσύνη, -ης, ἡ — righteousness (compare δίκαιος)
7. ἑπτά — seven (indeclinable, "heptad")
8. εὐθύς — immediately
9. θαυμάζω — I marvel
10. θέλω — I wish, desire
11. ἰσχύω — I am strong
12. παράγω — I pass by (paragon)
13. πείθω — I persuade
14. περιβλέπομαι — I look around (only middle voice in compound form)
15. πίπτω — I fall
16. πιστεύω — I believe (occurs with dative case or with εἰς and accusative), entrust
17. ῥίζα, -ης, ἡ — root (rough breathing over ῥ)
18. Σατανᾶς, -ᾶ, ὁ — Satan (Satan). N.B. the unusual nom. and gen. masc. forms
19. σῖτος, -ου, ὁ — wheat, grain (para<u>site</u>)
20. σκανδαλίζω — I offend, cause to stumble (scandal), middle σκανδαλίζομαι ἐν — I take offense at
21. τρέχω — I run
22. ὑπακούω (foll. by dat.) — I obey (cf. ἀκούω)
23. φεύγω — I flee ("fugitive")
24. φόβος, -ου, ὁ — fear (phobia)
25. φυλακή, -ῆς, ἡ — guard, watch, prison (compare φυλάσσω, <u>prophylaxis</u>)
26. χρεία, -ας, ἡ — need
27. χριστός, -οῦ, ὁ — Christ (Christ)
28. χρόνος, -ου, ὁ — time (<u>chron</u>ology)

Foundational Concepts

The Aorist Tense

The aorist indicative suggests past time. In contrast to the imperfect, the "moving picture" tense, the aorist is the "snapshot" tense. It also suggests decisive action which may happen at a point in time, i.e. "momentary" action (Joe hit the mark), or action which may embrace a period of time, i.e. "comprehensive" action (Lu led the team for two years).

First and Second Aorist Tenses

In English the past tense is formed in two main ways: By adding "ed" and by changing the stem (irregular)

```
I jump . . . I jumped    I rise . . . I rose
I walk . . . I walked     I throw . . I threw
```

In the same way, there are two ways of forming the Greek Past tense. The First Aorist is regular while the Second Aorist is irregular, often showing an internal change. Both First and Second Aorist Tenses express the same meaning = past time and point action. They simply constitute two different patterns that Greek verbs tend to follow.

FIRST AORIST ACTIVE INDICATIVE OF λυω (third principal part)

	SINGULAR			PLURAL	
1.	ἔ λυ σ α	- I loosed	(1) ἐ λύ σ αμεν	- We loosed
2.	ἔ λυ σ ας	- You loosed	(2) ἐ λύ σ ατε	- You loosed
3.	ἔ λυ σε(ν)	- She loosed	(3) ἔ λυ σ αν	- They loosed
		He loosed		
		It loosed		

Observations

1. The first aorist is composed of four parts:

   a. prefixed augment
   b. stem
   c. tense suffix "σ," and
   d. the personal endings

2. The "σα" is a red flag indicating the first aorist. the only place where the "σα" does not appear is the third person singular which has "σε(ν)."

3. Similar to the future, the "σ" may also be "hidden" in the aorist. Compare the following:

  a. LABIALS (π, φ, β)

Present	Future	First Aorist
πέμπω	πέμψω	ἔπεμψα
γράφω	γράψω	ἔγραψα

  b. PALATALS (κ, γ, χ)

Present	Future	First Aorist
διώκω	διώξω	ἐδίωξα
ἀνοίγω	ἀνοίξω	ἤνοιξα

  c. DENTALS (δ, θ, ζ)

Present	Future	First Aorist
πείθω	πείσω	ἔπεισα
δοξάζω	δοξάσω	ἐδόξασα

Memory Aid

Observe Lu as an <u>arrowist</u> with <u>one arrow</u> (First Aorist). He <u>actively loosed the indicator</u> with his <u>arrow</u> (First Aorist Active Indicative). The parts are as follows: P. Hogman (pre-fixed augment), Lu, the "σ" sun, and the endings. Do you see the "<u>α</u>" <u>as-cend</u> (-α, -ας, -ε(ν)) the <u>omelette</u> and get <u>on</u> (-αμεν, -ατε, -αν)?

<u>FIRST AORIST MIDDLE INDICATIVE OF λύω</u> (middle <u>not</u> passive)

Singular	Plural
1. ἐ λυ σ ἁμην - I loosed for myself	(1) ἐ λυ σ ἁμεθα - We loosed for ourselves
2. ἐ λύ σ ω - You loosed for yourself	(2) ἐ λύ σ ασθε - You loosed for yourselves
3. ἐ λύ σ ατο - She loosed for herself, He loosed for himself, It loosed for itself	(3) ἐ λύ σ αντο - They loosed for themselves

Memory Aid

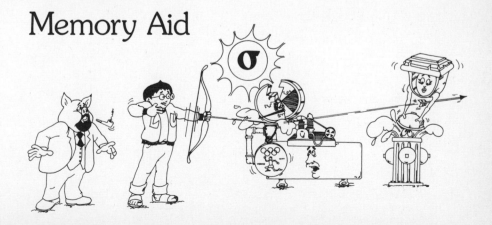

Observe Lu, the finest arrowist of his kind, with his one arrow (first aorist). The indicator with the medal (middle) means he loosed for himself (first aorist middle indicative). The parts are as follows: P. Hogman (prefixed augment) to the left, Lu, and the "σ" sun. The characters are so shocked by Lu's actions that a main blows a top (-αμην, -ω, -ατο) while Amethyst is the one on top (-αμεθα, -ασθε, -αντο).

Practice

Parse & Translate

	T	V	M	P	N	Vocabulary Form	Translation
1. ἔπεμψα							
2. ἐβλέψαμεν							
3. ἠγόρασαν							
4. προσηυξάμην							
5. ἐλύσαντο							

KEY

1. 1A A I 1 S - πέμπω - I sent
2. 1A A I 1 P - βλέπω - We saw
3. 1A A I 3 P - ἀγοράζω - They bought
4. 1A Dep. I 1 S - προσεύχομαι - I prayed
5. 1A M I 3 P - λύω - They loosed for themselves

SECOND AORIST ACTIVE INDICATIVE OF βάλλω

1. ἔ βαλ ον - I threw   1. ἐ βάλ ομεν - We threw
2. ἔ βαλ ες - You threw   2. ἐ βάλ ετε - You threw
3. ἔ βαλ ε(ν) - She threw   3. ἔ βαλ ον   - They threw
                He threw
                It threw

Observations

1. You meet another verb, βάλλω, for a pattern since λύω takes first aorist forms while βάλλω follows the second aorist.

2. You will be pleased to see the exact correspondence in both augment and endings of the second aorist and the imperfect tenses. Be encouraged! But at the same time remember that the second aorist is characterized by an internal change.

For example:

Imperfect	Second Aorist
ἔ βαλλ ον - "I was throwing"	ἔ βαλ ον - "I threw"
ἐ λάμβαν ον	ἔ λαβ ον
ἐ γιν όμην	ἐ γεν όμην

Memory Aid

Instead of Lu the arrowist with one arrow, you see βαλ the arrowist with two arrows (second aorist). At some point in the past, βαλ actively threw his arrows and hit the indicator (second aorist active indicative). From left to right you see P. Hogman (prefixed augment), and then βαλ (stocky βαλ with an internal change), and finally the honest hen (-ον, -ες, -ε(ν)) with an omelette on (-ομεν, -ετε, -ον) her hat, cheering βαλ on for his successful throw.

SECOND AORIST MIDDLE INDICATIVE OF βάλλω

1. ἐ βαλ όμην -
   I threw for myself

2. ἐ βάλ ου -
   You threw for yourself

3. ἐ βάλ ετο -
   She threw for herself
   He threw for himself
   It threw for itself

(1) ἐ βαλ όμεθα-
   We threw for ourselves

(2) ἐ βάλ εσθε -
   You threw for yourselves

(3) ἐ βάλ οντο -
   They threw for themselves

103

Memory Aid

Again you see βαλ the arrowist with two arrows.   He threw his arrow and hit the indicator with the medal (middle).   This represents the second aorist middle indicative.   You see P. Hogman (prefixed augment) observing βαλ (internal change) and then to the right you see a main that blew a top (-όμην, -ου, -ετο) and Amethyst is the one on top (-όμεθα, -εσθε, -οντο).

Professor Oddity

The verbs below are irregular.   Compare the second aorist with the present and you will see little or no relationship between the forms. There is an internal change (e.g. ἔφυγον, 2nd aor. of φεύγω).   The vocabulary pictures below will help you remember the irregular forms, their meanings, and the present tense which corresponds to each.

HERE COME I !

ἦλθον - I came
ἔρχομαι - I come

An L-Thong (ἦλθον) came with the 2 arrows (2nd aorist) saying "Here come I" (ἔρχομαι).

εἶδον - I saw
ὁράω - I see

A don (εἶδον) saw a bull who said, "Hurrah" (ὁράω). Note the strange hat with 2 arrows (2nd aorist).

HURRAH!

LEGGO!

εἶπον - I said
λέγω - I say

The ape on (εἶπον) a swing is having such a time with his 2 arrows (2nd aorist), the tree said, "leggo" (λέγω).

EUREKA!

LAKE HURON

εὗρον - I found
εὑρίσκω - I find

Lake Huron (εὗρον) found 2 arrows (2nd aorist) and said, "Eureka!" (εὑρίσκω)

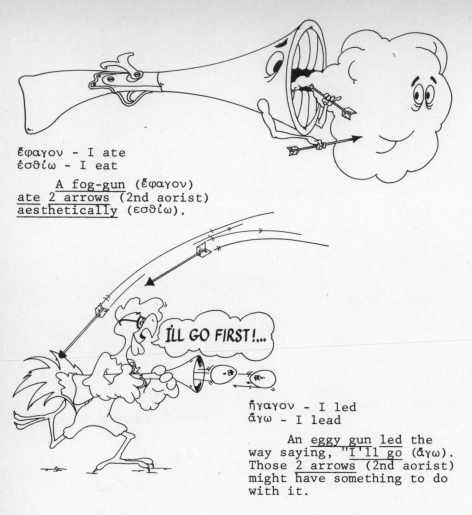

ἔφαγον - I ate
ἐσθίω - I eat

A fog-gun (ἔφαγον)
ate 2 arrows (2nd aorist)
aesthetically (εσθίω).

ἤγαγον - I led
ἄγω - I lead

An eggy gun led the
way saying, "I'll go (ἄγω).
Those 2 arrows (2nd aorist)
might have something to do
with it.

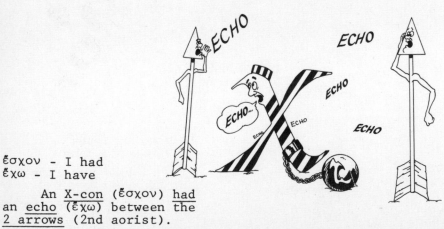

ἔσχον - I had
ἔχω - I have

An X-con (ἔσχον) had
an echo (ἔχω) between the
2 arrows (2nd aorist).

ἔδραμον - I ran
τρέχω - I run

    Ed ran (ἔδραμον) on the tracks (τρέχω) with the 2 arrows (2nd aorist) hot in pursuit.

ἔφυγον - I fled
φεύγω - I flee

    A fool's gun (ἔφυγον) fled from the fugitive (φεύγω). Note the 2 arrows (2nd aorist). Have you ever seen a gun like that?

ἀπέθανον - I died
ἀποθνῄσκω - I die

A Parthenon died at the end of a path where knees go (ἀποθνῄσκω). The knees of those 2 arrow (2nd aorist) supplicants appear a bit sore.

ἔπεσον - I fell
πίπτω - I fall

A peasant (ἔπεσον) fell over a pipe's toe (πίπτω) onto the 2 arrows (2nd aorist).

ἐγενόμην - I became
γίνομαι - I become

A can of mine (ἐγενόμην) became a kin of mine (γίνομαι). How sweet it is. Note the 2 arrows (2nd aorist) piercing the "ε." (The "ε" of the stem differentiates the 2nd aorist from the imperfect).

ἔλαβον - I took, received
λαμβάνω - I take

An L-Bon (ἔλαβον) took and received a lambasting (λαμβάνω) from the 2 arrows (2nd aorist). Injury to Insult!

Practice

Before translating, learn the irregular forms.
Then parse the verbs and translate the sentences:

1. οὗτός ἐστιν ὁ ἄνθρωπος ὑπὲρ οὗ (whom) εἶπον.
2. εἰς τὰ ἴδια (his own) ἦλθεν καὶ οἱ ἴδιοι αὐτὸν οὐκ ἔλαβον.
3. ὁ Πέτρος εἶπεν αὐτῷ, Σὺ εἶ ὁ χριστός.
4. μετὰ ταῦτα ἀπέθανεν ὁ πτωχός (poor).
5. ἐν τῷ κόσμῳ ἦν, καὶ ὁ κόσμος δἰ αὐτοῦ ἐγένετο.

KEY

1. This is the man on behalf of whom I spoke.
2. He came into his own things and his own (people) did not receive him.
3. Peter said to him, "You are the Christ."
4. After these things, the poor (man) died.
5. He was in the world and the world became (came into being) through him.

First Aorist Infinitive

Observe Lu the <u>arrowist</u> with <u>one arrow</u> and little Infant Ivy (first aorist infinitive). As they converse with each other under the "σ" sun, out jumps <u>Sy</u> who says, "I'm <u>Sy</u> (-σαι) with a <u>Sash-tie</u> (-ασθαι) <u>ain't I</u>!" (-θῆναι).

Active	λῦ σαι	- to loose
Middle	λύ σασθαι	- to loose for oneself
Passive	λυ θῆναι	- to be loosed

Second Aorist Infinitive

Note βαλ the <u>arrowist</u> with his internal change and <u>two arrows</u> and little <u>Infant Ivy</u> (second aorist infinitive). They both appear to be rather wet. βαλ says, "I'm βαλ in the <u>rain</u> (-ειν) with an <u>S-tie</u> (-έσθαι), ain't I!" (-ῆναι). Compare the following forms with the forms of the present infinitive.

Active	- βαλεῖν	- to throw
Middle	- βαλέσθαι	- to throw for oneself
Passive	- γραφῆναι	- to be written

Enrichment

In II Corinthians 8:9, Paul writes of Christ that "though being rich, yet for your sakes he became poor." The force of the aorist "(Christ) became poor" stands out very clearly, in contrast to the pres., referring to his state of being, "though being rich." How rich he was . . . and yet he became poor (point action), that we, through his poverty, might become rich.

110

According to John 4:30, as the Samaritan woman reported in the village her remarkable experience with Jesus, the men of the town "went forth and were coming to him," ἐξῆλθον καὶ ἤρχοντο πρὸς αὐτόν (i.e. πρὸς Ἰησοῦν). The two verbs express - successively - decisive and vivid action. The "decisive" verb is ἐξῆλθον, second aorist of ἐξέρχομαι, i.e. "They went forth" while ἤρχοντο is a "vivid" imperfect of ἔρχομαι, i.e. "They were coming toward Jesus." The writer paints a living and memorable scene as the Samaritans - group after group - appeared over the horizon gradually approaching the well of Jacob where Jesus was.

In Mark 12:41-42, the imperfect of βάλλω, i.e. ἔβαλλον occurs referring to the rich who, one after another, placed their gifts in the treasury (imperfect of repeated action). The second aorist of the same verb also occurs, i.e. ἔβαλεν referring to the one decisive act of the poor widow who cast in her gift - her entire living - small though it was. The difference between the tenses contrasts the successive giving of the many rich with the one decisive gift of the poor widow.

Assignment

ἡ ὑπομονή[1] τοῦ Ἰώβ[2]

κατὰ τὰς γραφὰς ἦν Ἰὼβ ἀγαθὸς ἄνθρωπος καὶ δίκαιος. καὶ ἔσχεν ἑπτὰ υἱοὺς καὶ τρεῖς[3] θυγατέρας[4] καὶ πρόβατα καὶ ἀγρούς. καὶ ἐγίνετο[5] ὅτι συνῆγον οἱ υἱοὶ αὐτοῦ τὰς ἀδελφὰς αὐτῶν καὶ ἤσθιον καὶ ἔχαιρον μετ' ἀλλήλων καὶ ἐδόξαζον τὸν θεόν. καὶ ἡγίαζεν Ἰὼβ ἑαυτὸν καὶ προσέφερεν δῶρα ὑπὲρ τῶν τέκνων καὶ ἔπιπτεν ἐπὶ πρόσωπον παρὰ τῷ θεῷ καὶ προσηύχετο περὶ τῶν ψυχῶν τῶν τέκνων αὐτοῦ. οὕτως ὑπήκουσεν Ἰὼβ τῷ κυρίῳ καὶ ἐφύλαξεν τὰς ὁδοὺς αὐτοῦ. ἴσχυσεν[6] γὰρ ἐν τῇ δικαιοσύνῃ τοῦ θεοῦ καὶ οὐκ ἐσκανδαλίσατο ἐν τῇ ἁγίᾳ ἀληθείᾳ αὐτοῦ.

καὶ λέγουσι αἱ γραφαὶ ὅτι ἠθέλησαν οἱ τοῦ θεοῦ ἄγγελοι δοξάζειν αὐτὸν καὶ οὕτως ἦσαν μετ' ἀλλήλων καὶ ἦλθεν μετ' αὐτῶν Σατανᾶς. καὶ περιεβλέψατο περὶ αὐτὸν ὁ κύριος καὶ εἶδεν τὸν Σατανᾶν καὶ εἶπεν αὐτῷ Διὰ τί[7], Σατανᾶ[8], ἠθέλησας ἐλθεῖν[9] πρὸς τοῦτον τὸν τόπον; εἶδές μου τὸν δοῦλον Ἰὼβ ὅτι αὐτός ἐστιν δίκαιος καὶ πιστὸς ἐν τῇ ζωῇ αὐτοῦ; οὐκ ἐθαύμασας ἐπὶ ταῖς ὁδοῖς τούτου τοῦ ἁγίου ὅτι ἔπεισε τὰ τέκνα αὐτοῦ φυγεῖν ἀπὸ τοῦ κακοῦ καὶ ὑπακοῦσαι τοῖς λόγοις μου τοῖς δικαίοις;

καὶ ἀποκρίνεται αὐτῷ Σατανᾶς καὶ λέγει πρὸς αὐτόν, Διὰ τί[7] δοξάζει σε Ἰὼβ καὶ ὑπακούει τῷ λόγῳ σου; εἰ[10] οὐκ ἔστιν ἀγαθὴ ἡ ῥίζα τοῦ δένδρου, οὐ γενήσεται ἀγαθὸς ὁ καρπός. ἰδοὺ ἐφύλαξας τὸν Ἰὼβ ἀπὸ πονηρῶν καὶ νόσων καὶ ἔπεμψας πρὸς αὐτὸν καλά -- καὶ τέκνα καὶ ἀγροὺς καὶ καρποὺς καὶ πρόβατα. ἀλλὰ νῦν εἰ[10] ἀπαίρεις τὰ ἀγαθὰ τοῦ οἴκου αὐτοῦ, καὶ εἰ πέμπεις κατ' αὐτοῦ πονηρὰ καὶ νόσους καὶ εἰ λύσεις τοὺς υἱοὺς καὶ τὰς θυγατέρας[4] αὐτοῦ, καὶ εἰ πέμψεις αὐτὸν εἰς φυλακήν, τότε ἐν τῷ χρόνῳ ἐκείνῳ κράξει ἀπὸ τοῦ φόβου καὶ φεύξεται ἀπὸ σοῦ καὶ θελήσει ἀποθανεῖν. οὐκέτι σὺ ἔσῃ ὁ κύριος αὐτοῦ οὐδὲ αὐτὸς ἔσται ὁ δοῦλός σου, καὶ οὐκέτι πιστεύσει εἰς τὴν ἀγάπην σου. καὶ εἶπεν αὐτῷ ὁ κύριος, Ἰδοὺ αὐτός ἐστιν ἐν τῇ ἐξουσίᾳ σου, ἀλλὰ οὐ λύσεις τὴν ψυχὴν αὐτοῦ. καὶ ἀπῆλθεν Σατανᾶς ἀπὸ τοῦ προσώπου τοῦ κυρίου.

καὶ ἐγένετο ὅτι ἤσθιον οἱ υἱοὶ τοῦ Ἰὼβ καὶ αἱ θυγατέρες[4] αὐτοῦ ἐν τῷ οἴκῳ τοῦ ἀδελφοῦ αὐτῶν τοῦ πρεσβυτέρου[11], καὶ ἦλθεν πνεῦμα μέγα[12] ἐκ τῆς ἐρήμου καὶ ἔλυσεν ἐκεῖνον τὸν οἶκον. καὶ οὕτως ἀπέθανον τὰ τέκνα τοῦ Ἰώβ.

καὶ παρήγαγεν παρὰ τὸν οἶκον δοῦλος τοῦ Ἰὼβ καὶ εἶδεν καὶ ἔπεσεν φόβος ἐπ᾽ αὐτόν. καὶ ἔδραμεν πρὸς τὸν Ἰώβ. καὶ ἤκουσεν τὴν ἀκοὴν τὴν κακὴν παρ᾽ αὐτοῦ περὶ τοῦ θανάτου τῶν τέκνων αὐτοῦ καὶ εὐθὺς ἔπεσεν ἐπὶ τῆς γῆς καὶ ἐδόξασεν τὸν κύριον καὶ εἶπεν, Αὐτὸς γυμνὸς[13] ἐξῆλθον ἐκ μητρός[14] μου, γυμνὸς[13] καὶ ἀπελεύσομαι. ἔπεμψεν πρός με ὁ κύριος τέκνα καὶ ἔλαβεν τέκνα ἀπ᾽ ἐμοῦ. ἐγὼ δοξάσω αὐτὸν καὶ ὑπακούσω ταῖς ἐντολαῖς αὐτοῦ.

---

[1] ὑπομονή - steadfastness, patience (compare James 5:11)

[2] Ἰώβ - Job (indeclinable)

[3] three

[4] θυγατέρας - daughters (accusative case), θυγατέρες (nominative case)

[5] The imperfects in the next two sentences are customary ("would happen . . . would gather together . . . etc.)

[6] The augment in ἴσχυσεν is simply a long ι.

[7] Διὰ τί - why ?

[8] Σατανᾶ - vocative case. It has the same ending as the genitive.

[9] ἐλθεῖν = second aorist active infinitive of ἦλθον (from ἔρχομαι).

[10] εἰ - if (note difference from εἶ = you are)

[11] πρεσβύτερος - elder

[12] πνεῦμα μέγα - a great wind

[13] γυμνός - naked

[14] μήτηρ (genitive μητρός) - mother

Chapter 9

1. δώδεκα (indeclinable) - twelve. Compare the Dodecanese Islands.

2. ἐγγίζω - I come near

3. εἶτα - then

4. ἐπιστρέφω - I turn, turn back

5. θνήσκω - I die (only in perf. act. τέθνηκα, compare ἀποθνήσκω)

6. κελεύω - I command

7. μέν . . . δέ[1] - on the one hand . . . on the other hand

8. ὅτε[2] - when

9. οὖν[1] - therefore, then

10. παιδίον, -ου, -τό - a small child (pediatrics)

11. πάσχω - I suffer (paschal)

12. πειράζω - I tempt, try, put to the test

13. προσέρχομαι (foll. by dat.) - I come to, approach (cf. ἔρχομαι)

14. σπείρω - I sow

15. συναγωγή, -ῆς, ἡ - synagogue (synagogue)

16. σωτηρία, -ας, ἡ - salvation (soteriology)

17. χαρίζομαι - I give freely,[3] forgive (charisma)

18. χώρα, -ας, ἡ - country (chorography = systematic description of a region or regions)

19. ὧδε - here

---

[1]Post-positives.

[2]A particle. "Particle" serves to define small indeclinable words such as οὐ, conjunctions, and prepositions.

[3]With dative of person to whom "it" is freely given and accus. of the thing or person(s) that are freely given.

114

IN THIS LESSON YOU WILL:

    . . . learn the forms and meaning of the perfect tense,

    . . . see Lu "reduplicated," and

    . . . learn some "perfect"ly irregular verbs.

Foundational Concepts

The Perfect Tense

The perfect tense is often called the "long tense," because it frequently covers a long period of time.

An action takes place in the past with results that extend up to, and even include, the present. For example:

a) γέγραπται, "it has been written," or "it is written." The action points to, (1) <u>Past</u> time, i.e. at some point in the past something was put on record, and to, (2) <u>Extended results</u>, i.e. the record still stands. Pilate says, "What I have written, I have written" (John 19:22). The perfect tense - repeated twice - conveys the idea of the permanency of his writing. What he has written remains written, and will not be changed. Clearly the perfect tense is the "long tense."

b) In I John 1:1-3, John says, "That which we have seen and that which we have heard . . . concerns the Word of Life." That is to say, what they had seen and heard is etched forever on their minds and hearts.

<u>FIRST PERFECT ACTIVE INDICATIVE OF λύω</u> (fourth principal part)

	Singular		Plural
1.	λέ λυ κ α I have loosed	(1)	λε λύ κ αμεν We have loosed
2.	λέ λυ κ ας You have loosed	(2)	λε λύ κ ατε You have loosed
3.	λέ λυ κ ε(ν) She has loosed He has loosed It has loosed	(3)	λε λύ κ ασι λέ λυ κ αν They have loosed

Observations

1. The perfect tense is composed of four parts:

   a. an initial reduplication,
   b. stem,
   c. tense suffix "κ," and
   d. personal endings.

2. The personal endings are <u>the</u> <u>same</u> as the first aorist.

3. The 3rd person plural has alternate forms: -κασι and -καν.

Memory Aid

   At the left you will see a <u>perfect parrot</u> next to the loosed <u>indicator</u> (indicative). Lu <u>has loosed</u> (active) the <u>indicator</u>. The results of <u>his</u> action are seen in the broken condition of the indicator (perfect active indicative). From left to right you see Lu in a <u>mirror</u> in which he is "reduplicated," a "κ" kite (tense <u>suffix</u> "κ") and finally the alpha ("α"). The "α" ascends (-α, -ας, -εν) the omelete and gets <u>on</u> saying, "I see" (-αμεν, -ατε, -αν or -ασι). Note the addition of "<u>I see</u>" (third plural). Review the picture thoroughly until each part is clearly visualized in your mind.

Reduplication

Reduplication is formed by:

1. <u>Repeating the initial consonant</u> and placing the "ε" in between.

σέσωκα   - I have saved
               from σώζω
κέκρικα   - I have judged
               from κρίνω
πεπίστευκα - I have believed
               from πιστεύω

2. <u>Repeating the aspirates</u> (φ, θ, χ - "h" sound letters) with corresponding <u>hard letters</u>.

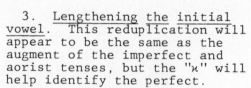

(p ph)πεφύλαχα - I have guarded
      from   φυλάσσω
(t th)τεθεράπευκα - I have healed
      from   θεραπεύω
(k kh)κεχάρισμαι - I have given freely. from χαρίζομαι

3. <u>Lengthening the initial vowel</u>. This reduplication will appear to be the same as the augment of the imperfect and aorist tenses, but the "κ" will help identify the perfect.

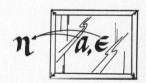

ἤλπικα   - I have hoped
            from ἐλπίζω
ἡτοίμακα - I have prepared
            from ἑτοιμάζω

Dental Perfects

You will recall that since the dental (lingual) stems end in the letters "δ, θ, or ζ," the stem consonant merges into the tense suffix. For example:

σώζω in the future becomes σώσω, and in the aorist, ἔσωσα. Thus in the perfect σώζω becomes σέσωκα = I have saved.

Likewise βαπτίζω (future - βαπτίσω, aorist ἐβάπτισα), in the perfect becomes βεβάπτικα - I have baptized.

Practice

Parse the following

	T	V	M	P	N	Vocabulary Form	Translation

1. βεβαπτίκαμεν
2. κέκραγεν
3. πεπιστεύκατε
4. τεθεράπευκας
5. ἡμάρτηκα

KEY

1. Pf. A I 1 P of βαπτίζω — We have baptized
2. Pf. A I 3 S of κράζω — He, she, has cried out
3. Pf. A I 2 P of πιστεύω — You have believed
4. Pf. A I 2 S of θεραπεύω — You have healed
5. Pf. A I 1 S of ἁμαρτάνω — I have sinned

SECOND PERFECT ACTIVE INDICATIVE OF γράφω

Singular	Plural
1. γέ γραφ α I have written	(1) γε γράφ αμεν We have written
2. γέ γραφ ας You have written	(2) γε γράφ ατε You have written
3. γέ γραφ ε(ν) She has written He has written It has written	(3) γέ γραφ αν γε γράφ ασι They have written

Observation

As you can see, the second perfect is like the first perfect, except that the tense suffix "κ" does not appear.

PERFECT MIDDLE AND PASSIVE INDICATIVE OF λύω — (Fifth principal part - Passive translation alone is given)

Singular	Plural
1. λέ λυ μαι I have been loosed	(1) λε λύ μεθα We have been loosed
2. λέ λυ σαι You have been loosed	(2) λέ λυ σθε You have been loosed
3. λέ λυ ται She has been loosed He has been loosed It has been loosed	(3) λέ λυ νται They have been loosed

Observations

1. The perfect middle/passive has three parts:
   a. reduplication,
   b. stem, and
   c. endings.

2. The endings (except 2nd singular) are like the present middle/passive, but there is no helping vowel such as you observed in λύομαι.

Memory Aid

Lu has been loosed by the indicator. The tables have turned, and Lu finds himself in a hospital. The perfect parrot watches (perfect middle/passive indicative). From left to right we see the mirror (reduplication), then Lu, and finally Amethyst. Lu feels uncomfortable strapped in with "my side tie" (-μαι, -σαι, -ται), but Nurse Amethyst is the untier (-μεθα, -σθε, -νται).

Irregular Perfects

Professor Oddity introduces you to some "perfect"ly irregular verbs. Their perfect forms have little or no relation to their present forms. Again the memory aids below will help you.

ἀκήκοα - I have heard
ἀκούω - I hear

A cake (ἀκήκοα) has heard through acoustical tile (ἀκούω) from the perfect parrot (perfect).

ἐγήγερμαι - I have been raised up

ἐγείρω - I raise up

An egg acre (ἐγήγερμαι) has been raised up by a hand holding an egg arrow (ἐγείρω). The onlooker is the surprised parrot (perfect).

ἐλήλυθα - I have come
ἔρχομαι - I come

An L lying on Lu (ἐλήλυθα) has come saying, "Here come I" (ἔρχομαι). Note the perfect parrot (perfect). Poor Lu!

ἑώρακα - I have seen
ὁράω - I see

A hay oar (ἑώρακα) has seen land and cried, "Hurrah" (ὁράω). The parrot (perfect) is sighting him as well.

ἔγνωκα - I have known
γινώσκω - I know

An egg yolk (ἔγνωκα) has known more than you think - You know! (γινώσκω). The parrot (perfect) seems as surprised as the chef.

εἴληφα - I have received
λαμβάνω - I receive

An elephant (εἴληφα) has received a lambasting (λαμβάνω) from the parrot (perfect). There seems to be no mercy.

121

πέπονθα - I have suffered
πάσχω - I suffer

A pet on the (πέπονθα)
soap box has suffered be-
cause he did not pass go
(πάσχω). Note the parrot
(perfect).

εἴρηκα - I have said
λέγω - I say

An air-rake (εἴρηκα) has
said "leggo" (λέγω) to the
parrot (perfect) who hangs
on for dear life.

γέγονα - I have become
γίνομαι - I become

This fellow says to his
identical mask "A gag on
you (γέγονα) has become a
kin of mine (γίνομαι).
Note the parrot (perfect)
with a gag as well.

122

Practice

Parse the verbs and translate

1. ἀκηκόαμεν τὸν λόγον τοῦ θεοῦ.
2. ταῦτα πέπονθα ἐν τῇ καρδίᾳ μου ὅτι ἡμάρτηκας εἰς ἐμέ.
3. εὑρίσκει Φίλιππος τὸν Ναθαναὴλ καὶ λέγει αὐτῷ, Τὸν Χριστὸν εὑρήκαμεν.
4. κέκριται ὁ πονηρὸς τοῦ κόσμου τούτου.
5. ἐγήγερται ὁ Λάζαρος ἐκ τοῦ μνημείου (tomb).
6. πέποιθεν ἐν τῷ Ἰησοῦ.
7. καὶ ἐν τούτῳ γινώσκομεν ὅτι ἐγνώκαμεν αὐτόν.
8. αὕτη δέ ἐστιν ἡ κρίσις (judgment) ὅτι τὸ φῶς (light) ἐλήλυθεν εἰς τὸν κόσμον.
9. καὶ ἡμεῖς πεπιστεύκαμεν τὴν ἀγάπην ἥν (which) ἔχει ὁ θεὸς ἐν ἡμῖν.
10. ταῦτα ἀκήκοα καὶ κηρύξω αὐτά.

KEY

1. We have heard the word of God. 2. I have suffered these things in my heart because you have sinned against me. 3. Philip finds Nathaniel and says to him, "We have found the Christ." 4. The evil one of this world has been judged. 5. Lazarus has been raised out of the tomb. 6. She, he, has confidence in Jesus. 7. And in this we know that we have known him. 8. And this is the judgment that the light has come into the world. 9. And we have believed the love which God has in us. 10. I have heard these things, and I shall preach them.

Perfect Infinitive

Observe Lu having his tie adjusted by the Infant Ivy with the parrot on the mirror (perfect infinitive). Lu is looking into the mirror (reduplication) and the parrot says, "A nice tie" (-εναι, -σθαι).

Active - λε λυ κ έναι -
     to have loosed

Middle/Passive -
     λε λύ σθαι -
to have loosed for one-self (M)   to have been loosed (P)

Enrichment

Compare John 1:41: εὑρήκαμεν τὸν Μεσσίαν , "We have found the Messiah." Andrew's discovery - fresh and vivid - explains his immediate excitement.

Paul says, πεπίστευμαι τὸ εὐαγγέλιον, "I am entrusted (with) the gospel." The form πεπίστευμαι (the perfect passive of πιστεύω) expresses the permanent responsibility which Paul carried because God at one time entrusted the gospel to him.

The apostle also affirms in Romans 8:38,39: I am persuaded (πέπεισμαι) that nothing in all of creation will be able to separate the Christian from the love of God in Jesus Christ. Paul lived in a <u>state</u> of confidence, fully persuaded of the abiding <u>power</u> of the love of Christ Jesus.

Assignment

'Ιησοῦς παρὰ τῷ μνημείῳ[1] τοῦ Λαζάρου[2]

κατὰ τὸ εὐαγγέλιον τοῦ 'Ιωάννου,[3] ἐν ταῖς ἐσχάταις ἡμέραις τοῦ 'Ιησοῦ ἐπὶ γῆς, ἔπαθεν Λάζαρος[2] νόσον κακὴν καὶ ἀπέθανεν. καὶ εὐθὺς ἔπεμψαν αἱ ἀδελφαὶ τοῦ Λαζάρου ἀγγέλους πρὸς τὸν 'Ιησοῦν περὶ τοῦ ἀγαπητοῦ ἀδελφοῦ αὐτῶν. καὶ ὅτε ἤγγισαν οἱ ἄγγελοι τῷ 'Ιησοῦ ἐθαύμασαν ὅτι εἶπεν ὁ 'Ιησοῦς ὅτι, Οὐκ ἔστιν νεκρὸς ὁ Λάζαρος ἀλλὰ καθεύδει. πορεύσομαι πρὸς αὐτὸν ἐγείρειν αὐτὸν ὅτι ἐλήλυθεν ἡ σωτηρία πρὸς τὸν οἶκον αὐτοῦ.

ὅτε οὖν εἶπεν 'Ιησοῦς ταῦτα περιεβλέψαντο οἱ δώδεκα μαθηταὶ ἀλλήλους καὶ ἐξεπλήσσοντο ἐπὶ τῇ διδαχῇ αὐτοῦ καὶ εἶπον ἐν ἑαυτοῖς, Πειράσει ὁ κύριος ἐπιστρέψαι εἰς τὴν 'Ιουδαίαν[4] χώραν καὶ εἰς τὴν τοῦ Λαζάρου κώμην;

εἶτα ἐγγίζουσιν οἱ δώδεκα τῷ 'Ιησοῦ καὶ λέγουσιν αὐτῷ, Κύριε, νῦν ἔβαλλον[5] οἱ 'Ιουδαῖοι λίθους ἐπὶ σέ, καὶ θέλεις ἐπιστρέψαι ἐκεῖ σπείρειν τὸν λόγον τοῦ θεοῦ ἐν ταῖς συναγωγαῖς καὶ ἀγοραῖς ἐκείνης τῆς χώρας; κατὰ τὸν λόγον σου οὔπω τέθνηκεν ὁ Λάζαρος ἀλλὰ καθεύδει. καὶ διὰ τοῦτο, ἀποκρίνεται ὁ 'Ιησοῦς αὐτοῖς· Τέθνηκεν Λάζαρος, καὶ χαίρω δι' ὑμᾶς ὅτι οὐκ ἤμην ἐκεῖ. πιστεύσετε γὰρ ὅτε ὄψεσθε τὴν τοῦ θεοῦ δόξαν. νῦν πορευσόμεθα πρὸς αὐτὸν καὶ ἐξελεύσεται ὁ ἀδελφὸς ἡμῶν ἐκ τῶν νεκρῶν.

ὅτε οὖν προσελήλυθεν ὁ κύριος τῷ μνημείῳ[1] καὶ οἱ δώδεκα μετ' αὐτοῦ, ἀνέβλεψεν εἰς τοὺς οὐρανοὺς καὶ εἶπεν, Πάτερ,[6] δοξάζω σε ὅτι ἤδη ἀκήκοάς μου.[7] ἀλλὰ προσελήλυθεν ὁ λαὸς ἀπὸ τῆς χώρας τῆς 'Ιουδαίας,[4] καὶ διὰ τοῦτο δοξάζω σε ὅτι γνώσονται ὅτι ἀπέσταλκάς με.

καὶ μετὰ τοῦτο ἔκραξεν ἐν χαρᾷ καὶ ἐκέλευσεν τὸν νεκρὸν οὕτως, Λάζαρε, δεῦρο.[8] καὶ ἐξῆλθεν Λάζαρος ἐκ τοῦ μνημείου.[1] καὶ ὅτε λελύκασι τὰ ἱμάτια τὰ περὶ αὐτόν, ἐδόξασεν τὸν θεόν. καὶ ἐν τῇ ὥρᾳ ἐκείνῃ ἁμαρτωλοὶ καὶ τελῶναι ἐπίστευσαν εἰς 'Ιησοῦν. καὶ ἔπεσον αἱ μὲν[9] ἀδελφαὶ τοῦ Λαζάρου ἐπὶ πρόσωπον παρὰ τῷ 'Ιησοῦ καὶ ἐθαύμασαν καὶ ἔκραξαν, Κύριε, ἐχαρίσω[10] τὴν ζωὴν τῷ ἀδελφῷ ἡμῶν. ἰδοὺ σὺ εἶ ὁ ἅγιος τοῦ θεοῦ καὶ πιστεύομεν

ὅτι θέλεις ἐγείρειν καὶ ἡμᾶς ἐν τῇ ἐσχάτῃ ἡμέρᾳ.   οἱ δὲ[9]
στρατιῶται οἱ τυφλοὶ ἐν καρδίᾳ οὐκ ἐπίστευσαν αὐτῷ ἀλλὰ
ἤθελον ἀποκτείνειν αὐτόν.

[1]μνημεῖον - tomb

[2]Λάζαρος - Lazarus

[3]Ἰωάννης, -ου - John

[4]Ἰουδαῖα - Judea(n)

[5]ἔβαλλον - conative imperfect = "were attempting
to throw"

[6]Πάτερ - vocative of πατήρ "father"

[7]μου - genitive case of person after ἀκούω.

[8]δεῦρο - "come!" (adverb of exhortation)

[9]μὲν . . . δὲ . . . "On the one hand . . . on the
other hand" is an accurate but wooden translation of
μὲν . . . δὲ.   The particle μὲν may be left untranslated
while δὲ = "but"

[10]ἐχαρίσω - First aorist deponent, second singular
of χαρίζομαι, "You freely gave."

126

Chapter 10

1. ἀναλαμβάνω   - I take up (compare λαμβάνω)

2. Γαλιλαία, -ας, ἡ - Galilee (Galilee)

3. ἐγγύς (prep. with - near (cf. ἐγγίζω). Adverb and
   gen. or dative)   preposition.

4. ἕτερος, -α, -ον - other, another (heterodox)

5. ἐχθρός, -οῦ, ὁ - enemy

6. ἕως (prep. w/gen.) - until, as far as

7. ἴδιος, -α, -ον - one's own (idiom)

8. ἱκανός, -ή, -όν - sufficient, fit, worthy

9. Ἰουδαία, -ας, ἡ - Judea (Judea), Judean

10. καθώς   - as, just as

11. καιρός, -οῦ, ὁ - time, opportunity

12. λοιπός, -οῦ, ὁ - remaining, rest

13. μακάριος, -α, -ον - blessed (macarism)

14. μόνον   - alone (adv.), only (monotheism)

15. μόνος, -η, -ον - only (adj.) (monotheism)

16. μυστήριον, -ου, -τό - mystery (mystery)

17. ὀλίγος, -η, ον - few (oligarchy)

18. ὅμοιος, -α, -ον - like, similar (Homoiousian - a
    (with dative)   fourth century church group,
       homeopathy)

19. ὀφθαλμός, -οῦ, ὁ - eye (ophthalmology)

20. ὄχλος, -ου, ὁ - crowd (ochlophobia - fear of a
       crowd)

21. πάλιν   - again (palingenesis, palimpsest)

22. ὡς   - as

IN THIS LESSON YOU WILL:

    . . . meet a young lady named Theta Eta (ϑη),

    . . . learn the Aorist Passive Indicative, and
         the Future Passive Indicative.

Foundational Concepts

In Chapter seven you were introduced to the future <u>active</u> and <u>middle</u>, and Chapter eight to the aorist <u>active</u> and <u>middle</u>, but until now you have <u>met</u> neither the future passive nor the aorist passive. From Chapter one, you will recall that the word <u>voice</u> relates the subject to the verb. The passive voice means that the subject receives the action of the verb. In this lesson we will look at the aorist passive indicative as well as the future passive.

<u>FIRST AORIST PASSIVE INDICATIVE OF λύω</u> - (sixth principal part)

Singular	Plural

1. ἐ λύ ϑη ν
    I was loosed
	(1) ἐ λύ ϑη μεν
	    We were loosed

2. ἐ λύ ϑη ς
    You were loosed
	(2) ἐ λύ ϑη τε
	    You were loosed

3. ἐ λύ ϑη
    She was loosed
    He was loosed
    It was loosed
	(3) ἐ λύ ϑη σαν
	    They were loosed

Observations

1. The first aorist passive indicative is composed of the following:

    a. the prefixed augment,
    b. the verb stem, λυ,
    c. the distinctive ϑη and
    d. the personal endings.

2. The letters ϑη are characteristic of the aorist passive and future passive.

Memory Aid

Look at the <u>one arrow</u> that is <u>passively</u> sleeping against the <u>indicator</u> (first aorist passive indicative). You will see that Lu was <u>loosed</u> (i.e. destroyed) by the <u>indicator</u>. From left to <u>right</u> observe P. <u>Hogman</u> (augment), then Lu's grave, and then the young lady named <u>Theta Eta</u> bringing along her two pets. She has a singular "<u>new</u>" <u>sigma</u> that cost <u>nothing</u> (-ν, -σ, -) and her plural A-men ate a sun (-ημεν, -ητε, -ησαν). Trace the picture through a couple times from beginning to end so that it becomes familiar

<u>FIRST FUTURE PASSIVE INDICATIVE OF λύω</u>

	Singular		Plural
1.	λυ θή σ ομαι	(1)	λυ θη σ όμεθα
	I shall be loosed		We shall be loosed
2.	λυ θή σ η	(2)	λυ θή σ εσθε
	You will be loosed		You will be loosed
3.	λυ θή σ εται	(3)	λυ θή σ ονται
	She will be loosed		They will be loosed
	He will be loosed		
	It will be loosed		

Observations

1. The first future passive indicative is formed by:

   a. the verb stem, λυ,
   b. the characteristic θη,
   c. the tense suffix σ, and
   d. the M/P endings of the present tense.

2. Observe the letters θη and compare them with the first aorist passive. The presence of the augment will indicate the aorist passive while its absence will indicate the future passive.

Memory Aid

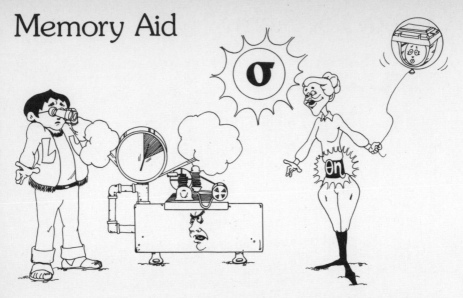

      Lu looks through his binoculars at the indicator (future active indicative), while Theta Eta talks about Lu's <u>future</u> demise when he <u>shall be loosed</u> by the <u>indicator</u> (future passive indicative). The binoculars remind you of the future. From left to right observe Lu with Theta Eta, the sigma (σ) sun and the <u>Amethyst</u> balloon with the tie. Amethyst has appeared in several chapters beginning with chapter four and has helped us learn the M/P endings.

Practice

Parse the following:

	T	V	M	P	N	Vocabulary Form	Translation
1.	ἐπιστεύθην						
2.	ἐθεραπεύθημεν						
3.	ἐπορεύθησαν						
4.	λυθήσονται						
5.	ἀκουσθήσεται						

KEY

1. A P I 1 S – πιστεύω – I was believed, I was entrusted
2. A P I 1 P – θεραπεύω – We were healed
3. A D I 3 P – πορεύομαι – They went
4. F P I 3 P – λύω   – They will be loosed
5. F P I 3 S – ἀκούω   – He, She, It, will be heard

Changes of Stem

When the stem of the verb ends in a consonant, the consonant generally picks up the "h" sound before the ϑη to make pronunciation easier.

Labials - (π, φ, β)

ἐπέμφϑην (from πέμπω) - I was sent
ἐλήμφϑην (from λαμβάνω) - I was taken
(cf. λήμψομαι of the future)

Gutturals - (κ, γ, χ)

ἐδιδάχϑην (from διδάσκω) - I was taught
ἐδιώχϑην (from διώκω) - I was persecuted

Dentals - (δ, ϑ, ζ)

ἐπείσϑην (from πείϑω) - I was persuaded
ἐβαπτίσϑην (from βαπτίζω) - I was baptized

Professor Oddity

The professor introduces you now to certain irregular forms of the aorist passive. Some of the forms which follow resemble their respective present stems. Some, however, are very irregular and need to be learned separately.

βάλλω	- I throw	ἐβλήϑην	- I was thrown
γίνομαι	- I become	ἐγενήϑην	- I became
ἐγείρω	- I raise up	ἠγέρϑην	- I was raised, arose
ὁράω	- I see	ὤφϑην	- I appeared
ἀποστέλλω	- I send	ἀπεστάλην	- I was sent (2Aor/P)
ἀποκτείνω	- I kill	ἀπεκτάνϑην	- I was killed
κρίνω	- I judge	ἐκρίϑην	- I was judged
λέγω (εἶπον)	- I say	ἐρρέϑη	- It was said (3rd Sg)
φέρω	- I bear, carry	ἠνέχϑην	- I was borne, carried

1. ἐ γράφ ην
   I was written
2. ἐ γράφ ης
   You were written
3. ἐ γράφ η
   She was written
   He was written
   It was written

(1) ἐ γράφ ημεν
    We were written
(2) ἐ γράφ ητε
    You were written
(3) ἐ γράφ ησαν
    They were written

Observations

1. The endings are similar to the first aorist passive

2. The "η" alone is the sign of the second aorist passive (cf. the θη of the first aorist passive).

Aorist Middle and Passive of Deponent Verbs

You will remember that deponent verbs in the present tense have middle/passive endings but have active meanings. Some of the deponent verbs in the aorist tens take the middle endings while others take the passive, and still other deponents take both middle and passive. However, the translation is always active.

προσεύχομαι becomes προσηυξάμην (middle) - I prayed
πορεύομαι   becomes ἐπορεύθην (passive) - I went
γίνομαι   becomes ἐγενόμην (2nd aor.mid.) - I became
            ἐγενήθην (1st aor.pass.) - I became

Practice

1. ἐπειράσθη ὑπὸ τοῦ διαβόλου.
2. οὐκ ἀκουσθήσονται οἱ λόγοι ὑμῶν.
3. οἱ λεπροί (lepers)ἐκαθαρίσθησαν ὑπὸ τοῦ Ἰησοῦ.
4. ἐπείσθησαν ὑπ' αὐτοῦ.
5. ἐπορεύθη εἰς ἕτερον τόπον.
6. ἐγερθήσονται οἱ νεκροὶ τῷ λόγῳ τοῦ κυρίου.
7. ἐπιστεύθη ἐν κόσμῳ, ἀνελήμφθη ἐν δόξῃ.
8. ἐσώθην.
9. πεμφθήσονται οἱ ἄνθρωποι ἐν ἐκείνῃ τῇ ἡμέρᾳ.
10. διωχθήσεσθε ὑπὸ τῶν ἁμαρτωλῶν ὅτι ἐγνώκατε με.

KEY

1. She, he, was tempted by the devil. 2. Your words
will not be heard. 3. The lepers were cleansed by Jesus.
4. They were persuaded by him. 5. She, he, went into
another place. 6. The dead will be raised by the word
of the Lord. 7. He was believed in the world, He was
taken up in glory (from 1 Tim. 3:16). 8. I was saved.
9. The men will be sent in that day. 10. You will be
persecuted by the sinners because you have known me.

Enrichment

1 Timothy 3:16

καὶ ὁμολογουμένως μέγα ἐστὶν τὸ τῆς εὐσεβείας μυστήριον·

Ὃς ἐφανερώθη ἐν σαρκί,
ἐδικαιώθη ἐν πνεύματι,
ὤφθη ἀγγέλοις,
ἐκηρύχθη ἐν ἔθνεσιν,
ἐπιστεύθη ἐν κόσμῳ,
ἀνελήμφθη ἐν δόξῃ.

The passage printed at the
side contains an introduction followed by a hymn of
six lines. Each line of
the hymn contains a first
aorist passive verb, each
form underlined for easy
identification. The careful parallelism of the six
strophes shows that the passage was not merely a creedal
confession but quite possibly a hymn. Timothy was ap-
parently in Ephesus as Paul wrote (1 Timothy 1:3). P.C.
Spicq suggests that the introduction, "And great assur-
edly, is the mystery of (our) religion," forms a con-
scious repudiation of the pagan cult-cry that was pre-
valent at Ephesus. Compare Acts 19:34, Μεγάλη ἡ Ἄρτεμις
Ἐφεσίων, "Great is Artemis of (the) Ephesians."[1]

---

[1]Compare P.C. Spicq, Saint Paul, Les Epitres
Pastorales, p. 107.

133

The "hymn" encompasses the entire Christ-event -
from incarnation in the flesh to glorification with the
Father. We commend to you the following adaptation of
the hymn to the music of an old traditional French melody.

1 Timothy 3:16 - Adapted from a traditional French Melody

by C. Story

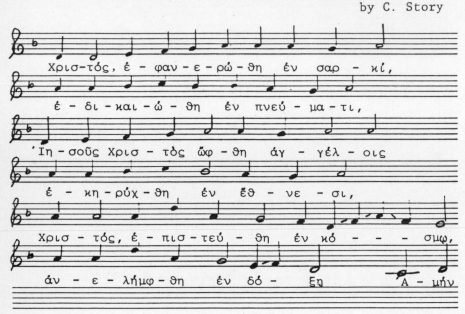

Assignment

Μιχαίας[1] ὁ προφήτης τῆς ἀληθείας

ἐν ταῖς ἡμέραις τῶν τῆς Ἰουδαίας καὶ τοῦ Ἰσραήλ[2] βασιλειῶν, ἐξῆλθον οἱ ἐχθροὶ αὐτῶν ἐκ τῆς ἰδίας χώρας καὶ ἀνέβησαν ἐπὶ τὴν ἀγίαν γῆν ἕως τῶν κωμῶν τῆς Γαλιλαίας. εἶτα ἔπεσεν φόβος ἐπὶ τὸν λαὸν τῆς Ἰουδαίας καὶ τοῦ Ἰσραήλ, καὶ ἐπειράσθησαν ὑπὸ τοῦ Σατανᾶ φυγεῖν ἀπὸ τῆς ἰδίας χώρας καὶ εὑρεῖν εἰρήνην ἐν ἑτέρᾳ γῆ.

συνήχθησαν δὲ προφῆται ὑπὸ τοῦ βασιλέως[3] τοῦ Ἰσραήλ καὶ ἰδοὺ[5] ἔλεγον λόγους οὐ τῆς ἀληθείας οὐδὲ τῆς δικαιοσύνης, ἦσαν γὰρ πονηροὶ προφῆται ὅμοιοι τοῖς προφήταις τοῦ Βάαλ[4]. καὶ ἠνέχθησαν εἰς τὸν βασιλέα[3].

ἐν δὲ τῷ αὐτῷ καιρῷ κατέβη ὁ βασιλεὺς[3] τῆς Ἰουδαίας πρὸς τὸν βασιλέα[3] τοῦ Ἰσραήλ. καὶ εἶπεν αὐτῷ ὁ βασιλεὺς τοῦ Ἰσραήλ, Ἀναβήσῃ μεθ' ἡμῶν ἐπὶ τοὺς ἐχθροὺς ἡμῶν; καὶ ἀπεκρίθη, Καθὼς ἐγὼ οὕτως καὶ σύ, καθὼς ὁ λαός μου ὁ λαός σου, καθὼς οἱ στρατιῶταί μου οἱ στρατιῶταί σου. καὶ ἐχάρη ὁ βασιλεὺς τοῦ Ἰσραήλ ἐν τούτῳ.

καὶ ἰδοὺ[5] ἐκήρυσσον οἱ προφῆται τοῦ βασιλέως Ἰσραήλ ὅτι φυλαχθήσεται ὁ Ἰσραὴλ καὶ σωθήσονται ἐκ τῶν ἐχθρῶν αὐτῶν ὑπὸ τοῦ θεοῦ. ὁ δὲ βασιλεὺς τῆς Ἰουδαίας οὐκ ἐπείσθη οὐδὲ ἐπίστευσεν τοῖς λόγοις τῶν προφητῶν.

καὶ ἐπέστρεψεν πρὸς τὸν βασιλέα τοῦ Ἰσραὴλ καὶ εἶπεν, θέλω ἀκοῦσαι ἱκανὸν λόγον ὅμοιον τοῖς λόγοις τοῦ προφήτου Ἠλίου[6]. ἔστιν οὖν ἔτι ὧδε προφήτης ὅμοιος αὐτῷ; ἀπεκρίθη ὁ βασιλεὺς τοῦ Ἰσραήλ, Ἄνθρωπος ἐν φυλακῇ ἐστιν, ἀλλ' οὐκ ἔπεμψα φέρειν αὐτόν, οὐ γὰρ λέγει περὶ ἐμοῦ καλά, ἀλλὰ κακά. καὶ ἀπεκρίθη ὁ βασιλεὺς τῆς Ἰουδαίας, Διά τί[7] ὁ βασιλεὺς τοῦ Ἰσραὴλ λέγει οὕτως; θέλω ἀκοῦσαι τούτου τοῦ προφήτου.

εἶτα ἀπεστάλη ἄγγελος πρὸς τὴν φυλακὴν καὶ ἠνέχθη Μιχαίας. εἴρηκεν δὲ ὁ ἄγγελος πρὸς Μιχαίαν ἐν φυλακῇ, Μακάριος ὁ κύριος ὁ θεὸς τοῦ Ἰσραήλ· οὐκ ἔσονται οἱ λόγοι σου ὅμοιοι τοῖς λόγοις τῶν προφητῶν τοῦ Ἰσραήλ; ἀπεκρίθη δὲ Μιχαίας, Ἐρῶ[8] μόνον τὸν λόγον κυρίου.

ἤχθη οὖν ὁ Μιχαίας πρὸς τὸν βασιλέα τοῦ Ἰσραήλ[2] καὶ εἶπεν αὐτῷ ὁ βασιλεύς, Εἴρηκέν σοι ὁ κύριος λόγον

135

περὶ ἡμῶν; ἀναβησόμεθα ἐπὶ τοὺς ἐχθροὺς ἡμῶν; καὶ ἐν
πρώτοις[9] ἀπεκρίθη, Ἀναβήσεσθε κατὰ τῶν ἐχθρῶν ὑμῶν καὶ
αὐτοὶ ἀποκτανθήσονται ὑπὸ τῶν στρατιωτῶν σου. ἀλλὰ
εἶπεν πάλιν αὐτῷ ὁ βασιλεύς, Διὰ τί[7] λέγεις μοι μυστήρια;
Διὰ τί οὐ λέγεις λόγους τῆς δικαιοσύνης καὶ τῆς ἀληθείας;
καὶ εἶπεν ὁ προφήτης, Ἑώρακα Ἰσραὴλ μόνον ἐν τῇ ἰδίᾳ
γῇ καὶ ἰδοὺ ἔσονται ὡς πρόβατα χωρὶς[10] ποιμένος.[11] καὶ
οὐκ ἔσται στρατιώτης σὺν ἄλλῳ στρατιώτῃ ἐν τῷ ἀγρῷ, καὶ
φάγονται οἱ ἐχθροὶ τοὺς τοῦ θερισμοῦ ὑμῶν καρποὺς ἐν
χαρᾷ καὶ εἰρήνῃ. καὶ ἐν τῇ αὐτῇ ἡμέρᾳ, ἀποκτανθήσῃ σὺ
αὐτὸς καὶ κριθήσονται οἱ κακοὶ προφῆταί σου, οὔπω γὰρ
ἐκήρυξαν πρὸς ὑμᾶς τὴν ἀλήθειαν. ἐν τούτῳ καὶ δοξασθή-
σεται ὁ κύριος.

καὶ ἐκέλευσεν ὁ βασιλεὺς τοῦ Ἰσραὴλ καὶ πάλιν
ἐβλήθη Μιχαίας εἰς φυλακήν, καὶ ἐπέμφθη πρὸς αὐτὸν
ὀλίγος ἄρτος μόνον. μετ' ὀλίγας δὲ ἡμέρας ἐγένετο κατὰ
τὸν λόγον τοῦ τῆς ἀληθείας προφήτου. ἀπεκτάνθη μὲν ὁ
βασιλεὺς Ἰσραήλ, καὶ ἀπέθανον πολλοὶ[12] τῶν στρατιωτῶν
αὐτοῦ, εἰσῆλθον δὲ οἱ ἐχθροὶ εἰς τὰς λοιπὰς κώμας τῆς
Γαλιλαίας.

---

[1]Μιχαίας - Micaiah

[2]Ἰσραήλ - Israel (indeclinable)

[3]βασιλεύς (nom.) - king. βασιλέως (gen.), βασιλεῖ
(dat.), βασιλέα (acc.)

[4]Βάαλ - Baal

[5]ἰδού - behold

[6]Ἠλίας (genitive - Ἠλίου) - Elijah

[7]διὰ τί - why ?

[8]ἐρῶ - future of λέγω

[9]ἐν πρώτοις - at the first

[10]χωρίς - without

[11]ποιμήν - shepherd (nom.), ποιμένος (gen.)

[12]πολλοί - many

Chapter 11

1. αἷμα, -ματος, τό   - blood (<u>hem</u>oglobin, an<u>emia</u>)
2. αἰών, -ῶνος, ὁ   - age (eon)
   εἰς τὸν αἰῶνα   -forever, always (or εἰς τοὺς αἰῶνας)
3. ἀνήρ, ἀνδρός, ὁ   - man (poly<u>andr</u>ous), husband
4. ἀποκαλύπτω   - I reveal (apocalypse)
5. ἄρχομαι   - I begin (cf. ἀρχή)
6. ἄρχω   - I rule (with gen), rule over (hier<u>archy</u>)
7. ἄρχων, -οντος, ὁ   - ruler (hier<u>archy</u>)
8. βάπτισμα, -ματος, τό - baptism (baptism)
9. βαπτιστής, -οῦ, ὁ   - Baptist
10. γένος, -ους, τό   - race, nation (<u>gen</u>ocide)
11. γράμμα, -ματος, τό - letter, writing (grammar)
12. γυνή, γυναικός, ἡ   - woman (poly<u>gyny</u>), wife
13. ἔθνος, -ους, τό   - nation (ethnic) τὰ ἔθνη = "the Gentiles"
14. ἕκαστος, -η, -ον   - each, every
15. ἐλπίς, ἐλπίδος, ἡ   - hope
16. ἔτος, -ους, τό   - year
17. θέλημα, -ματος, τό - will (θέλω)
18. Ἰουδαῖος, -ου, ὁ   - Jew (Judah)
19. Ἰωάννης, -ου, ὁ   - John (John)
20. κατέρχομαι   - I come down (ἔρχομαι)
21. μετάνοια, -ας, ἡ   - repentance (noetic)
22. μή   - not (with other than indicative mood), lest
23. μήτηρ, μητρός, ἡ   - mother (mother, <u>mater</u>nal)
24. νύξ, νυκτός, ἡ   - night (<u>noc</u>turnal)
25. ὄνομα, -ματος, τό - name (<u>onom</u>atopoeia, an<u>onymous</u>)
26. ὄρος, -ους, τό   - mountain
27. πατήρ, πατρός, ὁ   - father (father, <u>pater</u>nal)
28. πνεῦμα, -ματος, τό - spirit (<u>pneu</u>matic)
29. πούς, ποδός, ὁ   - foot (<u>pod</u>iatrist)
30. ῥῆμα, -ματος, τό   - word ("remark")
31. σάρξ, σαρκός, ἡ   - flesh (<u>sarc</u>ophagus, lit. "flesh-eating)
32. Σίμων, -ωνος, ὁ   - Simon (Simon)

33. σκότος, -ους, τό   - darkness
34. σῶμα, -ματος, τό   - body (psycho<u>somatic</u>)
35. ὑπόδημα, -ματος, τό - sandal
36. χάρις, χάριτος, ἡ - grace (<u>char</u>ismatic, eu<u>charist</u>)
37. χείρ, χειρός, ἡ   - hand ("<u>chiro</u>practor")

    . . . learn the endings of the third declension, and

    . . . review the principal parts of Lu (λύω).

Foundational Concepts

Third Declension

Do you remember the meaning of the word "declension?" It means a "grouping together of nouns with common endings." As you look at the above picture, review the genders in each declension with their common letters. The last grouping or declension of nouns which you meet is the <u>third declension</u>. As you can see, the third declension contains all three genders (masculine, feminine, and neuter), divided into three common patterns:

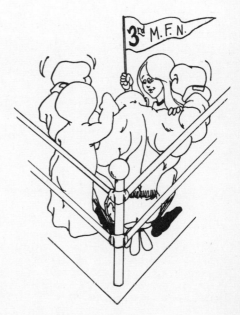

1. Masculine and feminine nouns.

2. Neuter nouns with nominatives ending in "μα."

3. Neuter nouns with nominatives ending in "ος."

1. <u>MASCULINE AND FEMININE NOUNS</u> - Observe the following endings:

	Singular		Plural
N	---	N	-ες
G	-ος	G	-ων
D	-ι	D	-σι(ν), -ξι(ν)
A	-α	A	-ας

Observations

1. The nominative forms end in various ways and must be learned separately.
    ὁ αἰών - αἰῶνος - age
    ἡ μήτηρ - μητρός - mother

2. In the second declension you learned that the important items are:

    a. Nominative singular
    b. Article
    c. Meaning

    but now, in the third declension, you need to learn:

    a. Nominative singular
    b. Genitive singular
    c. Article
    d. Meaning

With the third declension, you will observe the addition of the genitive singular. The reason is that the STEM is found in the genitive case, not the nominative as was true in the first and second declension. This means that as you learn the vocabulary words, you must learn the genitive forms. When you learn the genitive, you are learning the STEM.

Memory Aids

Observe the following pictures and identify the case people for they help you to remember the endings.

NOMINATIVE

Sing.	Pl.
--	ες

Norbert Nominative holds an empty bag while Nora (plural nominative) has the letters "ες" across her jersey. She belongs to the same fraternity as the future Amy. (Chapter seven)

GENITIVE

Sing.	Pl.
ος	ων

Gerard Genitive has a hos (-ος) that he owns (-ων). Geraldine has the deed which shows their joint ownership.

DATIVE

Sing.	Pl.
ι	σι (ν)
	ξι (ν)

Demetrius Dative slides home but he is an easy (-ι, -σι) out, tagged by Demetria. The word easy will remind you of ι - σι, and the alternative ending - ξι.

ACCUSATIVE

Sing.   Pl.

α   ας

Armitage Accusative and his wife Amelia are the kind of persons who frequent museums. He says, "Behold a vas." His words remind you of the singular and plural endings "α" and "ας."

Now review the endings and connect them with the pictures. At this point it may be helpful to see some examples of how the third declension nouns are declined. The plural dative of σάρξ, σαρκός appears with the ending ξι (κ + σι = ξι).

Declension of σάρξ, flesh

Singular	Plural
N σάρξ	N σάρκες
G σαρκός	G σαρκῶν
D σαρκί	D σαρξί(ν)
A σάρκα	A σάρκας

Declension of ἄρχων, ruler

Singular	Plural
N ἄρχων	N ἄρχοντες
G ἄρχοντος	G ἀρχόντων
D ἄρχοντι	D ἄρχουσι(ν)
A ἄρχοντα	A ἄρχοντας

2. Neuter nouns with nominatives ending in -μα.

The second pattern contains <u>neuter</u> nouns with nominatives ending in μα. What case will our stem be found in? The genitive case!

Singular	Plural
NA βάπτισ - μα	NA βάπτισ - ματα
G βάπτισ - ματος	G βάπτισ - μάτων
D βάπτισ - ματι	D βάπτισ - μασι(ν)

Observations

1. The nominative and accusative endings are identical in the singular and plural respectively.

2. The "ος" in the genitive singular and the "ων" in the genitive plural are the same as in pattern 1.

3. The dative case - singular and plural - has the characteristic ending "ι" (-ι and -σι or -ξι).

Memory Aids

NOMINATIVE & ACCUSATIVE

Singular	Plural	
μα	ματα	Norbert and Armitage call for Ma (-μα) because they say, "Nora and Amelia are playing with my top"(-ματα).

GENITIVE

Sing.	Plural
ματος	μάτων

Gerard is crying. He is unable to play his piano because ma tosses out my tones (-ματος, μάτων).

DATIVE

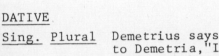

Sing.	Plural
ματι	μασι(ν)

Demetrius says to Demetria, "I can't drink my tea (-ματι) because it is messy (-μασι).

3. Neuter Nouns, Nominative Singular, ending in ος

	Singular		Plural
NA	ἔθνος	NA	ἔθνη
G	ἔθνους	G	ἐθνῶν
D	ἔθνει	D	ἔθνεσι(ν)

Observations

1. The nominative and accusative endings are identical in the singular and plural, respectively.

2. The dative cases have the common "ι."

Memory Aids

<u>Nominative</u> - <u>Sing.</u> <u>Pl.</u>
<u>Accusative</u>
          ος   η

Norbert & Armitage are on
a <u>hos</u> (-ος) while Nora &
Amelia feed the hos <u>hay</u>
(-η).

<u>Genitive</u> - <u>Sing.</u> <u>Pl.</u>
             ους ων

Gerard, in <u>love</u>, oozes
tones of love to Geraldine
(-ους, -ων).

<u>Dative</u> - <u>Sing.</u> <u>Pl.</u>
        ει   εσι

Demetrius is throwing a
ball to Demetria on <u>a</u> <u>S-</u>
sea (-ει, -εσι).

It is important for you to review thoroughly the
above pictures until you feel confident with the new endings. The New Testament contains many third declension
nouns.

Practice

Parse the nouns and translate

		G	N	C	Translation	Vocabulary Form
1.	τὸν αἰῶνα					
2.	ἐν σαρκί					
3.	ἐν ἐλπίδι					
4.	τοῖς ἄρχουσι(ν)					
5.	σώματος					
6.	πνεύματα					
7.	ἄνδρες					
8.	ταῖς γυναιξίν					
9.	τὰ ἔτη					
10.	σκότους					

KEY

1.	MSA	- the age	- ὁ αἰών - αἰῶνος
2.	FSD	- in flesh	- ἡ σάρξ - σαρκός
3.	FSD	- in hope	- ἡ ἐλπίς - ἐλπίδος
4.	MPD	- to the rulers	- ὁ ἄρχων - ἄρχοντος
5.	NSG	- of a body	- τὸ σῶμα - σώματος
6.	NPN,A	- spirits	- τὸ πνεῦμα - πνεύματος
7.	MPN,V	- Men	- ὁ ἀνήρ - ἀνδρός
8.	FPD	- to the women	- ἡ γυνή - γυναικός
9.	NPN,A	- the years	- τὸ ἔτος - ἔτους
10.	NSG	- of darkness	- τὸ σκότος - σκότους

Review of the LU System

You have covered my six principal parts in all voices in the indicative mood. Now see if you can fill in the five remaining parts of the verb πιστεύω.

Present Active	Future Active	Aorist Active	Perfect Active	Perfect Passive	Aorist Passive
λύω	λύσω	ἔλυσα	λέλυκα	λέλυμαι	ἐλύθην
πιστεύω					

(P/A) - πιστεύω - I believe. (F/A) - πιστεύσω - I shall believe. (A/A) - ἐπίστευσα - I believed. (P/A) - πεπίστευκα - I have believed. (Pf/P) - πεπίστευμαι - I have been believed, I am entrusted. (A/P) - ἐπιστεύθην - I was believed, I was entrusted.

Practice

Parse the third declension nouns and translate

1. ἡ δὲ γυνὴ ἔπεσεν πρὸς τοὺς πόδας αὐτοῦ.
2. αὐτός ἐστιν ἐν τῇ σαρκί.
3. χάρις ὑμῖν καὶ εἰρήνη ἀπὸ θεοῦ πατρὸς ἡμῶν καὶ κυρίου Ἰησοῦ Χριστοῦ.
4. χάριτι δὲ θεοῦ εἰμι ὃ (that which) εἰμι
5. ὁ Ἰησοῦς ἔρχεται εἰς τὸν οἶκον τοῦ ἄρχοντος.
6. ἴδετε (behold) τὰς χεῖράς μου καὶ τοὺς πόδας μου ὅτι ἐγώ εἰμι αὐτός.
7. οὐ γάρ ἐστε ὑπὸ νόμον ἀλλ' ὑπὸ χάριν. (irreg. acc. case)
8. οὐκ ἔχουσιν τὸ πνεῦμα τὸ ἅγιον.
9. ἐν ἐκείνῃ τῇ νυκτὶ εἴδετε τὸν ἄρχοντα.
10. ἐγερθήσονται τὰ σώματα τῶν ἁγίων.

1. And the woman fell to his feet. 2. He is in the flesh. 3. Grace to you and peace from God our Father and the Lord Jesus Christ. 4. But by the grace of God I am what I am. 5. Jesus comes into the house of the ruler. 6. Behold my hands and my feet that I am he. 7. For you are not under law but under grace. 8. They do not have the Holy Spirit. 9. In that night you saw the ruler. 10. The bodies of the saints will be raised up.

Enrichment

Romans 8:9 - ὑμεῖς δε οὐκ ἐστὲ ἐν σαρκὶ ἀλλὰ ἐν πνεύματι, εἴπερ (if indeed) πνεῦμα θεοῦ οἰκεῖ (dwells) ἐν ὑμῖν. Two third - declension nouns, σάρξ and πνεῦμα, inform us that Christians live not in the sphere of the flesh but in the Spirit. The demoniac in the synagogue lived in an unclean sphere, ἐν πνεύματι ἀκαθάρτῳ, "in an unclean spirit" (Mark 1:23), but the promise of the Baptist is that Jesus will baptize people in a new sphere, ἐν πνεύματι ἁγίῳ (Mark 1:8 - UBS text). Paul makes it very clear that believers are both in the Spirit and indwelt by the Spirit, very much like the air which surrounds them and yet flows through them.

Assignment

<u>βασιλεὺς[1] καινὸς ἐν Ἰσραήλ</u>

καὶ ἐγένετο ὅτι ἠγέρθη[2] Σαοὺλ[3] βασιλεὺς[1] καὶ ἄρχων
ἐν Ἰσραήλ. ἀλλὰ ἐπέστρεψεν ἀπὸ τοῦ θεοῦ τῶν πατέρων
αὐτοῦ διώκειν τὸ θέλημα τῆς ἑαυτοῦ σαρκός. διὰ τοῦτο
εἶπεν ὁ θεὸς ὅτι, Ἀρθήσεται ἡ βασιλεία ἀπὸ Σαοὺλ
ἡμάρτηκεν γὰρ κατ' ἐμοῦ. καὶ ἦν ἡ χεὶρ τοῦ κυρίου κατ'
αὐτοῦ.

καὶ ἐν τῷ ἔτει τῷ αὐτῷ ἐγένετο τὸ ῥῆμα θεοῦ εἰς τὸν
προφήτην Σαμουήλ,[4] καὶ εἶπεν αὐτῷ, Πέμψω σε εἰς βηθλεὲμ[5]
χρίειν[6] ἐκεῖ ἄρχοντα καινὸν ἐν Ἰσραήλ[7]. καὶ ἔπεσεν
Σαμουὴλ ἐπὶ πρόσωπον καὶ ἔκραξεν Ἐσκανδάλισεν Σαοὺλ τὸν
λαὸν καὶ ἥμαρτεν εἰς οὐρανὸν καὶ εἰς τὸ γένος -- καὶ ἐν
ῥήματι καὶ ἐν ἔργῳ -- ἀλλὰ ἔτι ἐστὶν ὁ χριστὸς καὶ ἄρχει
σου τῆς βασιλείας, ἔγνωκα γὰρ ὅτι ἐστὶν τὸ πνεῦμά σου
ἐπ' αὐτὸν ἀπ' ἀρχῆς. καὶ ἀπεκρίθη αὐτῷ ὁ κύριος·
Ἔφυγεν Σαοὺλ ἀφ' ὁδῶν μου. οὐδὲ γὰρ ἀκήκοέν μου τὰς
ἐντολάς, οὐδὲ ἔγνωκεν μετάνοιαν. διὰ τοῦτο οὐκ ἤγγικεν
ἡ σωτηρία μου εἰς τὸ γένος Ἰσραήλ.

εἶτα ἐπέμφθη Σαμουὴλ εἰς τὰ ὄρη τῆς Ἰουδαίας πρὸς
τὴν μικρὰν κώμην βηθλεέμ.[5] καὶ ὅτε κατήρχετο Σαμουὴλ
εἰς τὴν κώμην ἐγίνετο νύξ, καὶ ἦν σκότος ὑπὲρ τὴν κώμην
ὅμοιον τῷ σκότει ἐν τῇ καρδίᾳ Σαοὺλ.[3]

καὶ ἀπεκαλύφθη τῷ Σαμουὴλ ὅτι εὑρεθήσεται ὁ καινὸς
βασιλεὺς ἐν τοῖς υἱοῖς Ἰεσσαί,[8] εἴρηκεν γὰρ ὁ κύριος,
Ἑώρακα βασιλέα[1] ἐν τοῖς υἱοῖς αὐτοῦ καὶ ἄρξει μου τοῦ
λαοῦ.

καὶ ὅτε ἐγένετο ἡ ἡμέρα, συνήχθησαν οἱ ὄχλοι περὶ
τὸν προφήτην. ἦσαν δὲ ἐκεῖ πατέρες καὶ μητέρες μετὰ τῶν
τέκνων αὐτῶν. ἀκηκόασι γὰρ ὅτι προσελήλυθεν ὁ ἀνὴρ τοῦ
θεοῦ τῇ κώμῃ αὐτῶν καὶ διὰ τοῦτο ἐθαύμασαν. ἤχθησαν δὲ
καὶ οἱ υἱοὶ τοῦ Ἰεσσαί.[8]

ἤρξατο οὖν Σαμουὴλ περιβλέψασθαι εὑρεῖν ἐν τοῖς
υἱοῖς Ἰεσσαὶ τὸν καινὸν ἄρχοντα τὸν ἀγαπητὸν κατὰ τὴν
καρδίαν θεοῦ. καὶ εἶπεν πρὸς τὸν Ἰεσσαί, Εἰρήνη ὑμῖν
καὶ τοῖς τέκνοις ὑμῶν. μετὰ τοῦτο ἡγίασεν τὸν πατέρα
καὶ τοὺς ἑπτὰ υἱοὺς αὐτοῦ. καὶ παρήγαγον οἱ υἱοὶ κατὰ

πρόσωπον[9] Σαμουήλ. ὅτε οὖν Σαμουήλ εἶδεν τὸν Ἐλίαβ[10]
εἶπεν, Μακάριος ὁ θεός. οὗτός ἐστιν ὁ χριστὸς τοῦ
κυρίου. καὶ ἡτοίμασεν χρίειν[6] αὐτόν. ἀπεκρίθη δὲ ὁ
κύριος, Οὐ βλέψεις ἐπὶ τὸ σῶμα αὐτοῦ οὐδὲ ἐπὶ τὸ πρόσωπον
αὐτοῦ· ὅτι οὐχ ὡς βλέψει ἄνθρωπος, ὄψεται ὁ θεός, ὅτι
ἄνθρωπος ὄψεται εἰς πρόσωπον, ὁ δὲ θεὸς ὄψεται εἰς
καρδίαν. καὶ παρήγαγον οἱ ἑπτὰ υἱοὶ ἀπὸ τοῦ πρωτοτόκου[11]
ἕως τοῦ νεωτέρου.[12] καὶ εἶπεν Σαμουήλ, Ἔχεις ἄλλον
υἱόν; καὶ ἀπεκρίθη Ἰεσσαί· Οὐ εἰ μή[13] ὁ νεώτερος,[12]
καὶ παιδίον ἐστί, καὶ φυλάσσει τὰ πρόβατα ἐν τῇ ἐρήμῳ.
καὶ ἤθελεν Σαμουήλ βλέψαι αὐτόν.

διὰ τοῦτο ἀπεστάλη δοῦλος καὶ Δαυίδ[14] ὁ νεώτερος
υἱὸς τοῦ Ἰεσσαί ἤχθη καὶ εἰσῆλθεν εἰς βηθλεέμ. τὸ δὲ
παιδίον ἦν ἐνδεδυμένον[15] ἱμάτια ἀγροῦ καὶ ὑποδήματα οὐκ
αὐτὸς ἔσχεν ἐν τοῖς ποσὶν αὐτοῦ. καὶ εἶπεν ὁ κύριος
πρὸς Σαμουήλ, Οὗτός ἐστιν ὁ χριστός μου. Σαμουήλ δὲ
ἔχρισεν[6] Δαυίδ ἐν τοῖς ἀδελφοῖς αὐτοῦ καὶ ἀπὸ τῆς ὥρας
ἐκείνης ἔπεσεν ἐπὶ Δαυίδ τὸ πνεῦμα τοῦ θεοῦ καὶ ἔμενεν
ἐπ᾿ αὐτὸν εἰς τὸν αἰῶνα.

---

[1] βασιλεύς - king (nom. case), βασιλέα (acc. case).
[2] ἠγέρθη (ἐγείρω) - aorist passive, "was raised up"
or "arose."
[3] Σαούλ - Saul
[4] Σαμουήλ - Samuel
[5] Βηθλεέμ - Bethlehem
[6] χρίειν - to anoint
[7] Ἰσραήλ - Israel
[8] Ἰεσσαί - Jesse
[9] κατὰ πρόσωπον - in the presence of
[10] Ἐλίαβ - Eliab
[11] πρωτότοκος - first-born
[12] νεώτερος - youngest
[13] εἰ μή - except
[14] Δαυίδ - David
[15] ἐνδεδυμένον - wearing

Chapter 12-A

. . . meet Party Zipple (participle),

. . . learn the functions of the present participle,

. . . learn the endings for the present participle, and

. . . see Amy with a sousaphone.

Foundational Concepts

At one time, Vera Verb and A.D. Detective got together under strange circumstances and produced "Little Party Zipple" (participle).

As you can see, a participle is a <u>verbal adjective</u>. Little Party Zipple has characteristics of his father A.D. Detective (adjective) and verbal qualities of his mother, Vera, as well. Thus, in essence, a participle is an adjective, but an adjective with verbal qualities . . . hence, a verbal adjective.

In the examples below, the participles end in "-ing." They are adjectives which modify either a noun or a verb, each participle possessing verbal qualities. Sometimes a participle will emphasize the verbal qualities, at other times, the adjectival qualities. In essence, the participle is a verbal adjective.

Consider the following examples (participles are underlined):

The <u>hiking</u> enthusiast fell.
While <u>hiking</u> up the mountain, I fell.

We saw the <u>swimming</u> instructor.
While <u>swimming</u>, the instructor taught us.

150

Yesterday I saw the <u>canoeing</u>
instructor <u>canoeing</u> at the
beach.

We saw the <u>fishing</u> expert
<u>fishing</u> with a fly.

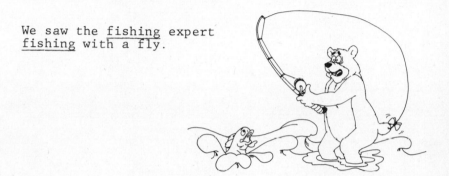

In the expressions "canoeing instructor" and "fishing expert" the participles function essentially as adjectives. But in the expressions "canoeing at the beach"
and "fishing with a fly" the emphasis is verbal. Thus,
the participle is:

   A.   A <u>verbal</u> adjective - it has tense and
        voice (but not mood).

   B.   A verbal <u>adjective</u> - it has gender,
        number, and case.

Use of the Present Participle

If the participle is an adjective, then as an adjective it can be found in both the attributive and predicate positions. You remember how the article was a key to help us in determining the position of the adjective (cf. Lesson three).

The Present Participle in the ATTRIBUTIVE POSITION

    1. Used as an ADJECTIVE

                Just as

ὁ ἀγαθὸς ἄνθρωπος = the good man

                so

ὁ λύων ἄνθρωπος = the loosing man, the man who looses

           And just as

ἡ ἀγαθὴ γυνή = the good woman

                so

ἡ λύουσα γυνή = the loosing woman, the woman who looses.

The attributive participle with the article is conveniently translated by a relative clause, e.g. "the man who looses," "the woman who looses."

    2. Used as a NOUN (SUBSTANTIVE)

              Just as

ὁ ἀγαθός = the good one, the good man

            so

ὁ λύων = the loosing one, the loosing man, the man who looses

          And just as

ἡ ἀγαθή = the good one, the good woman

           so

ἡ λύουσα = the loosing one, the loosing woman, the woman who looses

Memory Aid

As you can see, the floating Party Zipple (participle) is on the tributary (attributive) with Art Icicle (article) directly in front. Observe him with the owl (hoo - who) eating a sandwich (which). Participles in the attributive position are generally introduced by "who" or "which."

Practice

See if you can translate the following. Each participle is parsed for you.

1. ὁ βαπτίζων (Pres.Act.Part. MSN) ἄνθρωπος.
2. ὁ βαπτίζων (Pres.Act.Part. MSN).
3. βλέπω τοὺς λέγοντας (Pres.Act.Part. MPA)
4. τῆς λεγούσης (Pres.Act.Part. FSG)

KEY

1. The man who baptizes. 2. The man who baptizes, or the one who baptizes. 3. I see the men who speak. 4. Of the woman who speaks.

The Present Participle in the PREDICATE POSITION(circumstantial)

The participle in the predicate position is called circumstantial or adverbial. It sets up a circumstance that is related to the main assertion of the sentence. Observe: "While swimming, I caught a cold." The participle "while swimming" is called circumstantial, or adverbial. It sets up a circumstance which is connected with the main assertion of the sentence, "I caught a cold." I know when I caught the cold, (i.e. while swimming). We will see two major divisions of the participle in the predicate position. You meet the present participle now, the aorist participle later.

The action of the present participle coincides with the action of the main verb and is often introduced by the word "while." Observe carefully the following sentences. Single out the main assertion and see how the participle relates to the main verb.

1. κηρύσσει ὁ ἄνθρωπος λύων (Pres.Act.Part. MSN) τὸν δοῦλον.

   The man, while loosing the slave, preaches, or
   While loosing the slave the man preaches.

2. ἡ γυνὴ βλέπει τὸν κύριον λέγουσα (Pres.Act.Part.FSN) ταῦτα ἐν τῷ ἱερῷ
   The woman, while speaking these things in the temple, sees the Lord, or: While speaking these things in the temple, the woman sees the Lord.

Note in the Greek sentences the predicate position of the participle. Observe, also, that it is in the present tense and therefore its action coincides in time with the action of the main verb. The participle is introduced by the word "while." The main assertion of the first sentence is "the man preaches." The circumstantial participle "while loosing" tells us when the preaching occurs. The main assertion in the second sentence is "the woman sees the Lord." The circumstantial participle "while speaking" tells us when she sees the Lord.

154

Memory Aid

Party Zipple (participle) is holding a pretty cat (predicate) while he opens the present (present tense). The participle in the predicate position (present tense) is introduced by the word, "while."

The Present Participle with an INDEFINITE Noun

Earlier (lesson 3) you learned that an adjective modifying an anarthrous noun (= a noun without an article) may be either attributive or predicate. Context is the key. The words ἀγαθὸς ἄνθρωπος can mean either "a good man," or, "a man is good." In the same way ἄνθρωπος πιστεύων ἔρχεται εἰς τὴν ἐκκλησίαν can mean "a trusting man enters the church" (attributive participle) or "while trusting, a man enters the church" (circumstantial participle). Context will usually indicate the meaning.

PRESENT ACTIVE PARTICIPLE OF λύω - "LOOSING"

	Singular				Plural		
	Masc.	Fem.	Neut.		Masc.	Fem.	Neut.
N	λύων	λύουσα	λῦον	N	λύοντες	λύουσαι	λύοντα
G	λύοντος	λυούσης	λύοντος	G	λυόντων	λυουσῶν	λυόντων
D	λύοντι	λυούσῃ	λύοντι	D	λύουσι(ν)	λυούσαις	λύουσι(ν)
A	λύοντα	λύουσαν	λῦον	A	λύοντας	λυούσας	λύοντα

Observations

1. The present participle is formed by:
    a. the present stem, and
    b. endings.

2. The endings follow either the third declension (masc. and neut.) or the first declension (fem.).

Masc.	Fem.	Neut.
Third Declension	First Declension	Third Declension
(3)	(1)	(3)

3. The letters "ντ" are often characteristic of the active participle (masc. and neut.).

Memory Aid

Lu is <u>actively</u> loosing a <u>present</u> from Party Zipple (present active participle) and now <u>owns</u> a <u>sousaphone</u>. The words <u>owns</u> <u>sousaphone</u> will remind you of the singular nominative endings - -ων, -ουσα, -ον - of the masculine, feminine, and neuter genders, respectively.

Practice

Parse the participles. Note the position of
each and then translate the sentences.

1. Attributive - ὁ λύων ἄνθρωπος τὸν δοῦλον κηρύσσει.
2. Attributive (substantive) - ὁ λύων τὸν δοῦλον κηρύσσει.
3. Predicate (circumstantial) - λύων τὸν δοῦλον, κηρύσσει ὁ ἄνθρωπος
4. αἱ πιστεύουσαι εἰς τὸν κύριον σώζονται.
5. γινώσκομεν τὰς λαμβάνουσας τὰ δῶρα.
6. λέγομεν περὶ τοῦ ἐγείροντος τοὺς νεκρούς.
7. βαπτίζοντες τοὺς ἀνθρώπους, ἐχαίρομεν.

KEY

1. P A P M S N - The man who looses the slave preaches.
2. P A P M S N - The man (one) who looses the slave preaches.
3. P A P M S N - While loosing the slave the man preaches.
4. P A P F P N - The women who believe in the Lord are being saved.
5. P A P F P A - We know the women who receive the gifts.
6. P A P M S G - We speak concerning the one who raises the dead.
7. P A P M P N - While baptizing the men, we were rejoicing.

PRESENT PARTICIPLE OF εἰμί - "BEING"

	Singular				Plural		
	Masc.	Fem.	Neut.		Masc.	Fem.	Neut.
N	ὤν	οὖσα	ὄν	N	ὄντες	οὖσαι	ὄντα
G	ὄντος	οὔσης	ὄντος	G	ὄντων	οὐσῶν	ὄντων
D	ὄντι	οὔσῃ	ὄντι	D	οὖσι(ν)	οὔσαις	οὖσι(ν)
A	ὄντα	οὖσαν	ὄν	A	ὄντας	οὔσας	ὄντα

Observations

1. The pattern of the participle of εἰμί follows the 3 - 1 - 3 declension pattern.

2. These forms are also the endings of the present active participle of λύω.

Memory Aid

Amy has a <u>present</u> which "is" from <u>Party Zipple</u> (present participle of εἰμί - translated "being"). The words "now she <u>owns a sousaphone</u> (-ων, -ουσα, -ον) will help you remember the masculine, feminine, and neuter endings. Look at the following example:

ὢν ὁ υἱὸς αὐτοῦ, διδάσκεται ὑπ᾽ αὐτοῦ.
Being his son, he is being taught by him.

PRESENT MIDDLE/PASSIVE PARTICIPLE OF λύω - "BEING LOOSED" (passive)

Singular

	Masc.	Fem.	Neut.
N	λυόμενος	λυομένη	λυόμενον
G	λυομένου	λυομένης	λυομένου
D	λυομένῳ	λυομένη	λυομένῳ
A	λυόμενον	λυομένην	λυόμενον

Plural

	Masc.	Fem.	Neut.
N	λυόμενοι	λυόμεναι	λυόμενα
G	λυομένων	λυομένων	λυομένων
D	λυομένοις	λυομέναις	λυομένοις
A	λυομένους	λυομένας	λυόμενα

Observations

1. The forms are based on the present stem.

2. The pattern of the endings is 2 - 1 - 2 (masc. - fem. - neut.), the pattern of the definite article which you know.

3. A key for the middle/passive forms is found in the letters, "μεν."

158

Memory Aid

Lu and <u>Party Zipple</u> (participle) are both dressed up as <u>presents</u> (present tense) and are "<u>being loosed</u>" (present middle/passive participle). They are being loosed by <u>O-Men</u> (-ομεν) with <u>Art Icicle</u> openers (article). The word O-Men is a helpful clue and Art Icicle will remind you of the article endings.

Practice

Parse the participles. Note the position of each and translate the sentences.

1. Attributive - ὁ λυόμενος δοῦλος χαίρει.
2. Attributive - ὁ λυόμενος χαίρει. (Substantive)
3. Predicate - λυόμενος χαίρει.(Circumstantial)
4. διωκόμενοι ὑπὸ τοῦ ἀνδρός, προσευχόμεθα.
5. αἱ ἐκκλησίαι αἱ διωκόμεναι σώζονται ὑπὸ τοῦ θεοῦ.
6. λέγομεν ταῖς πορευομέναις εἰς τὸν οἶκον.

<u>KEY</u>

1. P M/P P MSN - The slave who is being loosed rejoices.
2. P M/P P MSN - The one who is being loosed rejoices.
3. P M/P P MSN - While being loosed he rejoices.
4. P M/P P MPN - While (we are) being persecuted by the man, we pray.
5. P M/P P FPN - The churches which are being persecuted are being saved by God.
6. P D P FPD - We speak to the women who are going into the house.

Supplementary Participle

A participle can complete the idea of the main verb.

ἦν λύων - He was loosing.

This same thought could be expressed by the imperfect active indicative of λύω.

ἔλυε(ν) - He was loosing

Some New Testament examples are:

Mark 1:4 - ἐγένετο . . . κηρύσσων
He arose . . . preaching

Mark 1:14 - ἦλθεν . . . κηρύσσων
He came . . . preaching

Mark 1:22 - ἦν γὰρ διδάσκων
For he was teaching

Enrichment

In Mark 1:10, the three present participles are instructive. As Jesus goes up (ἀναβαίνων) out of the water, he sees not only the Spirit descending (καταβαῖνον εἰς αὐτόν), but also the heavens, "being split apart" (σχιζομένους). His identity with the human race at his baptism is so significant, says Mark, that all creation is affected.

Assignment

ὁ ἄρτος τῆς ζωῆς

γέγραπται ἐν τῷ εὐαγγελίῳ τοῦ Ἰωάννου ὅτι οἱ ὄχλοι
οἱ ἀκούοντες τὸν λόγον τοῦ Ἰησοῦ ἔσχον χρείαν ἄρτου.
καὶ ἐν τῷ αὐτῷ χρόνῳ ἔφαγον καὶ ἀπῆλθον πρὸς τοὺς ἰδίους
οἴκους σὺν χαρᾷ καὶ εἰρήνῃ ἐν ταῖς καρδίαις αὐτῶν.

καὶ ἐγένετο οὕτως. ἀνέβη ὁ Ἰησοῦς εἰς τὰ ὄρη τῆς
Γαλιλαίας καὶ ἐκεῖ ἦν διδάσκων τοὺς μαθητὰς αὐτοῦ.
αἴρων οὖν τοὺς ὀφθαλμοὺς εἶδεν καὶ ἰδοὺ ἄνδρες καὶ
γυναῖκες ἔρχονται πρὸς αὐτόν. καὶ λέγει πρὸς τοὺς
μαθητὰς ἐκπλησσομένους ἐπὶ τοῖς ὄχλοις· Πόθεν[1] ἀρξόμεθα
ἄρτους εὑρεῖν ἱκανοὺς ὑπὲρ τῶν ὄντων ὧδε; εἶπεν οὕτως
πειράζων αὐτούς, ἤθελεν γὰρ αὐτοῖς ἀποκαλύψαι τὴν χάριν
τοῦ πατρὸς αὐτοῦ. ἀπεκρίθησαν αὐτῷ λέγοντες, Ἐστὶν
παιδίον ὧδε ἔχον ἐν τῇ χειρὶ αὐτοῦ πέντε[2] ἄρτους καὶ δύο[3]
ἰχθύας[4] ἀλλ᾽ οὐχ ἱκανοί εἰσιν τοῖς ὄχλοις τούτοις.

ἐν τῇ ὥρᾳ ἐκείνῃ ἐκέλευσεν Ἰησοῦς τοὺς μαθητὰς καὶ
ἠνέχθησαν οἱ ἄρτοι καὶ οἱ ἰχθύες[4] πρὸς τὸν κύριον. καὶ
ἀναβλέπων εἰς τὸν οὐρανὸν προσηύξατο ὁ κύριος. ἐν τούτῳ
ἐδόξαζεν θεὸν τὸν χαριζόμενον ἀγαθὰ καὶ τοῖς ὑπακούουσιν
αὐτῷ καὶ τοῖς μὴ πιστεύουσιν εἰς αὐτόν. μετὰ τοῦτο
παρέλαβον οἱ μαθηταὶ παρ᾽ αὐτοῦ τοὺς ἄρτους καὶ ἰχθύας[4]
καὶ ἤρξαντο φέρειν ἑκάστῳ ἀνδρὶ καὶ ἑκάστῃ γυναικὶ καὶ
τοῖς τέκνοις αὐτῶν.

καὶ ὡς ἤγγιζεν ἡ νύξ, ἀνέλαβον οἱ μαθηταὶ τὰ κλάσ-
ματα[5] χαίροντες ἐν τῷ ὀνόματι Ἰησοῦ καὶ ἐν τῇ χάριτι τῇ
ἀποκαλυπτομένῃ τοῖς ἁμαρτωλοῖς. καὶ οἱ μὲν ὄχλοι
ἀπῆλθον πρὸς τὰς κώμας ἑαυτῶν, οἱ δὲ μαθηταὶ ἐνέβησαν
εἰς τὸ πλοῖον καὶ διῆλθον διὰ τῆς θαλάσσης. Ἰησοῦς οὖν
μόνος ὤν, ἔπεσεν πρὸς τὸ πρόσωπον καὶ ἐδόξασεν τὸν πατέρα
αὐτοῦ προσευχόμενος αὐτῷ.

καὶ ὅτε γέγονεν ἡ ἡμέρα, οἱ ὄχλοι πάλιν προσερχό-
μενοι εὗρον Ἰησοῦν σὺν τοῖς μαθηταῖς αὐτοῦ καὶ εἶπον,
Πότε[6] ἐλήλυθας ὧδε; καὶ ἀπεκρίθη Ἰησοῦς αὐτοῖς, Ὑμεῖς
χαίρετε ὅτι ἐφάγετε τοὺς ἄρτους ἐν τῷ ὄρει μὴ πιστεύοντες
τοῖς ἁγίοις γράμμασιν. οὐ γινώσκετε ὅτι πέμπει ὑμῖν ὁ
πατήρ μου τὸν ἀληθινὸν[7] ἄρτον τὸν μένοντα εἰς τὸν αἰῶνα;

καὶ θαυμάζοντες περὶ τοῦ ῥήματος αὐτοῦ, ἀπεκρίθησαν,
Κύριε, θέλομεν φαγεῖν τοῦτον τὸν ἄρτον νῦν καὶ εἰς τὸν
αἰῶνα. καὶ περιβλεπόμενος αὐτούς, εἶπεν ὁ Ἰησοῦς· Ἐγώ
εἰμι ὁ ἄρτος τῆς ζωῆς. οἱ ἐρχόμενοι πρός με καὶ πιστεύοντες εἰς ἐμὲ ἕξουσι ζωὴν μετ' ἐμοῦ εἰς τὸν αἰῶνα τῶν
αἰώνων. διὰ τοῦτο οἱ ἐσθίοντες ἐκ τῆς σαρκός μου γνώσονται τὴν ἀλήθειαν τοῦ εὐαγγελίου. καταβέβηκα γὰρ ἐκ τοῦ
οὐρανοῦ φέρειν ζωὴν πρὸς τὸν κόσμον.

καὶ ἀκούοντες ταῦτα ἀπῆλθον οἱ ὄχλοι μὴ ἔχοντες
ἐλπίδα ἐπ' αὐτῷ μηδὲ ῥίζαν ἐν τῇ ἀληθείᾳ. καὶ Ἰησοῦς
ἐπιστρέφων πρὸς τοὺς μετ' αὐτοῦ μένοντας ἔκραξεν, Θέλετε
καὶ ὑμεῖς ἀπελθεῖν; ἀπεκρίθη αὐτῷ Σίμων, Κύριε, οὐκ
ἀπελευσόμεθα ἀπὸ σοῦ· ῥήματα ζωῆς ἔχεις καὶ ἡμεῖς
πεπιστεύκαμεν καὶ ἐγνώκαμεν ὅτι σὺ εἶ ὁ ἅγιος τοῦ θεοῦ.

---

[1]πόθεν - from where?

[2]πέντε - five (indeclinable)

[3]δύο - two

[4]ἰχθύες - (nom.plural), ἰχθύας (acc.pl.) - fish

[5]κλάσματα - broken pieces

[6]Πότε - When?

[7]ἀληθινός - true

Chapter 12-B

IN THIS CHAPTER YOU WILL:

    . . . review the functions of the participle,

    . . . meet the aorist participle in both attributive and predicative positions, and

    . . . see Gerard Genitive salute (genitive absolute).

Review of the Present Participle

In the last chapter, you saw Party Zipple (participle) as a verbal adjective. You observed that at times the participle functions with verbal qualities, at other times with adjectival qualities. Essentially the participle is a verbal adjective, an adjective that has verbal qualities.

Therefore, as an adjective, it has two positions:

1. Attributive,
2. Predicate

You looked at the present participles and observed that the letters "ing" can be used to translate the present participle. You also learned that the present participle in the predicate position is translated with the word "while."

THE PRESENT PARTICIPLE

1. Attributive - ὁ λύων - the loosing one
   - the loosing man
   - the one who looses
   - the man who looses

2. Predicate - λύων τὸν δοῦλον κηρύσσει - while loosing the slave he preaches

Foundational Concepts

The Aorist Participle

The aorist participle like the present occurs in both the attributive and predicate positions.

THE AORIST PARTICIPLE IN THE ATTRIBUTIVE POSITION

1. Used as an <u>adjective</u>:

ὁ λύσας ἄνθρωπος - the man who loosed
ἡ λύσασα γυνή - the woman who loosed
ὁ βλέψας δοῦλος - the slave who saw
ἡ βλέψασα γυνή - the woman who saw

2. Used as a <u>noun</u> (substantive):

ὁ λύσας - the one who loosed, the man who loosed
ἡ βλέψασα - the one who saw, the woman who saw

THE AORIST PARTICIPLE IN THE PREDICATE POSITION (Circumstantial)

1. The idea of the circumstantial participle (aorist).

The participle in the predicate position is called circumstantial or adverbial. It sets up a circumstance that relates to the action of the main verb. "After completing the test, I breathed a sigh of relief." The participle with its object, "after completing the test" forms an adverbial clause. It sets up a circumstance that relates to the main assertion, "I breathed a sigh of relief." I express the time in which I breathed a sigh of relief, i.e. <u>after</u> I completed the test.

In the last lesson you noted how the present participle in the predicate position was translated with the word "while." Its action coincides with the action of the main verb. Now, observe the action of the aorist participle.

2. The use of the circumstantial participle (aorist).

The action of the aorist participle <u>precedes</u> the action of the main verb. The connecting words used to translate the aorist participle are "after, having, after having," or "when." The action in the aorist participle precedes in time the action of the main verb. Observe the following sentences and note carefully the relation between the participle and the main verb.

ὁ ἄνθρωπος λύσας (Aor.Act.Part. MSN) τὸν δοῦλον, ἔβλεψεν τὸν ἀπόστολον - The man, <u>having loosed</u> the slave, saw the apostle.

ἡ γυνὴ λύσασα (Aor.Act.Part. FSN) τὸν δοῦλον, ἔβλεψεν τὸν ἀπόστολον - The woman, <u>having loosed</u> the slave, saw the apostle.

εἰπών (2 Aor.Act.Part. MSN) ταῦτα ἀπῆλθεν - <u>Having said</u> these things, he departed.

Note very carefully the position of the participle. It is found in the predicate position and it is in the aorist tense. Therefore, its action precedes the action of the main verb.

Memory Aid

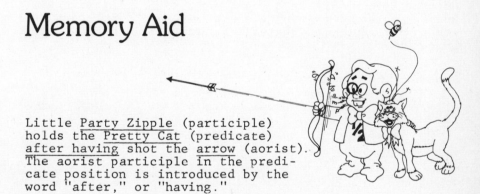

Little <u>Party Zipple</u> (participle) holds the <u>Pretty Cat</u> (predicate) <u>after having</u> shot the <u>arrow</u> (aorist). The aorist participle in the predicate position is introduced by the word "after," or "having."

Practice

1. ἀκούσας (<u>Aor</u>.Act.Part. MSN) ταῦτα ὁ ᾿Ιησοῦς ἐθαύμασεν.
2. διδάσκουσα (<u>Pres</u>.Act. Part. FSN) τὸν δοῦλον, ἔβλεψα τὸν διδάσκαλον.
3. λέγοντες (<u>Pres</u>.Act.Part. MPN) οὖν ὅτι οὐκ ἔχομεν ἁμαρτίαν, οὐ λέγομεν τὴν ἀλήθειαν.
4. εἰποῦσα (<u>2 Aor</u>. Act.Part. FSN) ταῦτα, ἀπέρχεται.

<u>KEY</u>

1. <u>Having heard</u> these things, Jesus marvelled. 2. <u>While teaching</u> the slave, I (fem.) saw the teacher. 3. <u>Therefore, while saying</u> that we do not have sin, we do not speak the truth. 4. <u>After saying</u> these things, she departs.

Party Zipple

You have now had an overview of the participle in its attributive and predicate positions, in the present and aorist tenses. Review again its basic structure and use so that its function is clear.

<u>FIRST AORIST ACTIVE PARTICIPLE OF λύω - "HAVING LOOSED"</u>

Singular

	Masc.	Fem.	Neut.
N	λύσας	λύσασα	λῦσαν
G	λύσαντος	λυσάσης	λύσαντος
D	λύσαντι	λυσάσῃ	λύσαντι
A	λύσαντα	λύσασαν	λῦσαν

Plural

	Masc.	Fem.	Neut.
N	λύσαντες	λύσασαι	λύσαντα
G	λυσάντων	λυσασῶν	λυσάντων
D	λύσασι(ν)	λυσάσαις	λύσασι(ν)
A	λύσαντας	λυσάσας	λύσαντα

Observations

1. Note the 3 - 1 - 3 declension pattern for the active voice. All of the active participles follow this pattern.

2. Observe the familiar "σα." It appears in all forms and is a helpful key for identifying the aorist forms of the participle.

3. Note also the familiar "ντ" of the active voice (masc. and neut.). If you see the participle "λύσαντος," the "σα" and the "ντ" should tell you immediately that it is an aorist active participle. Then you discover that the ending is MSG or NSG.

Memory Aid

Lu is an <u>arrowist</u> with <u>one arrow</u> (first aorist) <u>actively having loosed</u> his <u>sauce</u>. Look at <u>Party Zipple</u> (First Aorist Active Participle). And, do you see the sauce spilled on the ground? The "σ" sun (suffix) is shining above as Lu gives <u>sauce</u> to his <u>sassy son</u> (-σας, -σασα, -σαν). These three words will remind you of the singular nominative endings.

Practice

Parse the participles, note the position of each, and translate the sentences.

1. Attributive - ὁ λύσας ἄνθρωπος τὸν δοῦλον κηρύσσει.
2. Attributive - ὁ λύσας τὸν δοῦλον κηρύσσει.
   (Substantive)
3. Predicate - λύσας τὸν δοῦλον, κηρύσσει.
   (Circumstantial)
4. ἡ ἀκούσασα ταῦτα ἦλθεν εἰς τὸν οἶκον.
5. κηρύξαντες τὸ εὐαγγέλιον, ἀπελευσόμεθα.
6. εἴπομεν περὶ τοῦ σώσαντος ἡμᾶς.

KEY

1. 1A A P MSN - The man (who loosed) the slave preaches.
2. 1A A P MSN - The one (man) who loosed the slave preaches.
3. 1A A P MSN - Having loosed the slave, he preaches.
4. 1A A P FSN - The one (woman) who heard these things came into the house.
5. 1A A P MPN - After preaching the gospel, we shall depart.
6. 1A A P MSG - We spoke concerning the one who saved us.

SECOND AORIST ACTIVE PARTICIPLE OF βάλλω - "HAVING THROWN"

Singular

	Masc.	Fem.	Neut.
N	βαλών	βαλοῦσα	βαλόν
G	βαλόντος	βαλούσης	βαλόντος
D	βαλόντι	βαλούσῃ	βαλόντι
A	βαλόντα	βαλοῦσαν	βαλόν

Plural

	Masc.	Fem.	Neut.
N	βαλόντες	βαλοῦσαι	βαλόντα
G	βαλόντων	βαλουσῶν	βαλόντων
D	βαλοῦσι (ν)	βαλούσαις	βαλοῦσι (ν)
A	βαλόντας	βαλούσας	βαλόντα

Observations

1. The second aorist active participle is formed by:

    a. a stem with internal change, and
    b. endings which are identical with the endings
        of the present active participles.

2. The declensions follow the 3 - 1 - 3 pattern.

3. The letters "ντ" are characteristic of the pattern
    (cf. the present active and first aorist active
    forms).

Memory Aid

βαλ is an arrowist
with two arrows having
actively thrown his arrows
to Party Zipple (second
aorist active participle).
βαλ also owns a sousaphone.
These words will remind
you of the singular nomi-
native endings "ων,
"ουσα," and "ον" of the
masculine, feminine, and
neuter forms. Compare the
picture with the present
active participles.

Practice

Parse the participles, note the position of
each, and translate the sentences.

1. Attributive - ἡ λαβοῦσα γυνὴ τὸν λόγον χαίρει.
2. Attributive - ἡ λαβοῦσα τὸν λόγον χαίρει.
    (Substantive)
3. Predicate - λαβοῦσα τὸν λόγον, χαίρει.
4. λαβόντες ταῦτα, ἐξήλθομεν εἰς τὴν ἔρημον.
5. προσῆλθον τῷ κυρίῳ τῷ ἐλθόντι εἰς τὸ ἱερόν.
6. οἱ ἄγγελοι οἱ πεσόντες ἐκ τοῦ οὐρανοῦ πονηροὶ ἦσαν.

KEY

1. 2A A P FSN - The woman who received the word rejoices.
2. 2A A P FSN - The one (woman) who received the word
              rejoices.
3. 2A A P FSN - Having received the word, she rejoices.
4. 2A A P MPN - Having received these things, we went
              forth into the desert.
5. 2A A P MSD - I, they, approached the Lord who came
              (i.e. had come) into the temple.
6. 2A A P MPN - The angels who fell from heaven were
              evil.

SECOND AORIST MIDDLE PARTICIPLE OF βάλλω - "HAVING THROWN FOR ONESELF"

Singular

	Masc.	Fem.	Neut.
N	βαλόμενος	βαλομένη	βαλόμενον
G	βαλομένου	βαλομένης	βαλομένου
D	βαλομένῳ	βαλομένη	βαλομένῳ
A	βαλόμενον	βαλομένην	βαλόμενον

Plural

	Masc.	Fem.	Neut.
N	βαλόμενοι	βαλόμεναι	βαλόμενα
G	βαλομένων	βαλομένων	βαλομένων
D	βαλομένοις	βαλομέναις	βαλομένοις
A	βαλομένους	βαλομένας	βαλόμενα

Observations

1. The forms show the internal change of the second
   aorist stem.

2. The endings are identical with the endings of the
   present middle/passive participle.

3. The "μεν" is common to all the forms, a characteristic that is shared with the present middle/passive
   participles.

Memory Aid

βαλ "having thrown" his two arrows (2nd aorist) "for himself" surprises Party Zipple. Do you see the medal for the winner (second aorist middle participle)?

βαλ is up against the O-Men (-ομεν) who are armed with Art Icicle arrows (article endings). The picture reminds you of the endings.

Practice

Parse the participles, observe the position of each, and translate the sentences.

1. Attributive - ὁ γενόμενος ἐκεῖ ἐστιν ὁ κύριός μου. (Substantive)
2. εἴδομεν τὰς γυναῖκας τὰς εἰσελθούσας εἰς τὴν ἐκκλησίαν

KEY

1. 2A Dep P MSN - The one who came to be there is my Lord.
2. 2A A P FPA - We saw the women who entered the church.

Singular

	Masc.	Fem.	Neut.
N	λυσάμενος	λυσαμένη	λυσάμενον
G	λυσαμένου	λυσαμένης	λυσαμένου
D	λυσαμένῳ	λυσαμένῃ	λυσαμένῳ
A	λυσάμενον	λυσαμένην	λυσάμενον

Plural

	Masc.	Fem.	Neut.
N	λυσάμενοι	λυσάμεναι	λυσάμενα
G	λυσαμένων	λυσαμένων	λυσαμένων
D	λυσαμένοις	λυσαμέναις	λυσαμένοις
A	λυσαμένους	λυσαμένας	λυσάμενα

Observations

1. The declension pattern is 2 - 1 - 2.

2. The mark of the first aorist - σα - is present in all forms.

3. The "μεν" is common to all forms (compare the present middle/passive and the second aorist middle participles).

Memory Aid

Lu has <u>one arrow</u> (first aorist) having loosed <u>for himself</u> the <u>medal</u> (middle voice). <u>Party Zipple</u> is amazed at Lu's arrow (first aorist middle <u>participle</u>). Above shines the "σ" <u>sun</u> and Lu is up against the <u>O-Men</u> (-ομεν) armed with their <u>article</u> arrows. The picture reminds you of the endings.

Practice

Parse the participles, note the position of each, and translate the sentences.

1. Attributive - ὁ δεξάμενος τὸν δοῦλον κηρύσσει. (Substantive)
2. προσευξάμεναι τῷ κυρίῳ, χαίρομεν.

KEY

1. 1A Dep Part MSN - The one who received the slave preaches.
2. 1A Dep Part FPN - Having prayed to the Lord, we (fem.) rejoice.

SECOND AORIST PASSIVE PARTICIPLE OF γράφω - "HAVING BEEN WRITTEN"

Singular

	Masc.	Fem.	Neut.
N	γραφείς	γραφεῖσα	γραφέν
G	γραφέντος	γραφείσης	γραφέντος
D	γραφέντι	γραφείσῃ	γραφέντι
A	γραφέντα	γραφεῖσαν	γραφέν

Plural

	Masc.	Fem.	Neut.
N	γραφέντες	γραφεῖσαι	γραφέντα
G	γραφέντων	γραφεισῶν	γραφέντων
D	γραφεῖσι(ν)	γραφείσαις	γραφεῖσι(ν)
A	γραφέντας	γραφείσας	γραφέντα

Observation

You need not learn these endings separately since
they are the same as the first aorist passive participles. The one difference is that the letter "ϑ"
does not appear in the second aorist as it does in
the first aorist. Compare the first and second
aorist passive indicative.

FIRST AORIST PASSIVE PARTICIPLE OF λύω - "HAVING BEEN LOOSED"

Singular

	Masc.	Fem.	Neut.
N	λυθείς	λυθεῖσα	λυθέν
G	λυθέντος	λυθείσης	λυθέντος
D	λυθέντι	λυθείσῃ	λυθέντι
A	λυθέντα	λυθεῖσαν	λυθέν

Plural

	Masc.	Fem.	Neut.
N	λυθέντες	λυθεῖσαι	λυθέντα
G	λυθέντων	λυθεισῶν	λυθέντων
D	λυθεῖσι(ν)	λυθείσαις	λυθεῖσι(ν)
A	λυθέντας	λυθείσας	λυθέντα

Observations

1. The pattern of the declension is 3 - 1 - 3. It resembles the patterns of the active voice of the participle.

2. The "ϑ" in all forms reminds you of the "ϑη" of the aorist passive indicative.

Memory Aid

Lu, was loosed and the passive arrow rests in peace against the tomb, to the delight of Party Zipple (first aorist passive participle).

Nearby we see the aces as they saw the hen (-ϑεις, -ϑεισα, -ϑεν). The words will remind you of the singular nominative endings of the three genders.

Practice

1. λυθεὶς ὁ δοῦλος κηρύσσει.
2. πορευθεῖσα πρὸς αὐτούς, ἡ γυνὴ ἐπίστευσεν.
3. εἴπετε ῥήματα ἐλπίδος τοῖς θεραπευθεῖσιν.
4. βληθέντες εἰς φυλακήν, ἐδόξασαν τὸν κύριον.

KEY

1. 1A P P MSN - Having been loosed, the slave preaches.
2. 1A Dep P FSN - After going to them, the woman believed.
3. 1A P P MPD - You spoke words of hope to the ones who
                 were healed.
4. 1A P P MPN - Having been cast into prison, they
                 glorified the Lord.

At this point, review the different patterns. Look carefully at the following keys:

1. The present stem and endings for the present participle.
2. Internal change for the second aorist participle.
3. "σα" for the first aorist participle.
4. "ντ" for active participles.
5. "μεν" for middle or middle/passive voices of the participle.
6. "θ" for first aorist passive participles.

Genitive Absolute

Observe the following sentence: "While the man was loosing the slave, we saw the apostle." There are two different subjects, "man," and "we." The primary subject is "we," and the secondary, "man." The first clause is circumstantial, setting up an occasion for the action of the main verb. This introduces you to a special use of the Greek circumstantial participle.

When a circumstantial participle (predicate position) and its modifying noun or pronoun do not function as the subject or as the main part of the sentence, both the participle and its subject appear in the genitive case - a phenomenon called "genitive absolute."

1. τοῦ ἀνθρώπου λύοντος τὸν δοῦλον, ἐβλέψαμεν τὸν
    ἀπόστολον - While the man was loosing the slave, we
    saw the apostle.

2. τῆς γυναικὸς λυσάσης τὸν δοῦλον, ἐβλέψαμεν τὸν
    ἀπόστολον - After the woman had loosed the slave, we
    saw the apostle.

176

Memory Aid

     Together with little Party Zipple, Gerard Genitive "salutes" (genitive absolute) the <u>Noun Clown</u> and <u>Polly Pronoun</u> as they bid good-bye to Norbert Nominative, and <u>drive</u> the sub-jet. The genitive absolute means that the participle and its subject (noun or pronoun) are in the genitive case.

Enrichment

Interwoven in the structure of Paul's first letter to the Thessalonian church is a series of circumstantial participles which portray vividly the reason why Paul wrote.

(1) <u>The first in the series</u> is found in 1 Thess. 2:17, Ἡμεῖς δέ, ἀδελφοί, ἀπορφανισθέντες ἀφ' ὑμῶν . . . ἐσπουδάσαμεν τὸ πρόσωπον ὑμῶν ἰδεῖν, "But we, brothers because we were 'orphaned' from you . . . endeavored to see your face." The circumstantial participle is a first aorist passive, ἀπ (ὀρφαν) ισθέντες. It occurs only here in the entire New Testament and contains within it our English word 'orphan' (note the part of the Greek form found between the brackets). It expresses at once the wrench which Paul experienced at his forced departure from Thessalonica (cf. Acts 17:5-10) as well as his intense longing to see again the new Christians whom he had won to the faith.

(2) <u>The second in the series</u> is found in 3:1, μηκέτι στέγοντες . . . ἐπέμψαμεν Τιμόθεον, "No longer enduring . . . we sent Timothy." The circumstantial participle, στέγοντες, is present active, as is the singular form of the participle, i.e. στέγων, in 3:5.

(3) <u>**Third in the series**</u> is a group of three circumstantial participles found in 3:6. Two of the three refer to Timothy's return - ἐλθόντος Τιμοθέου . . . καὶ εὐαγγελισαμένου ἡμῖν, "Since Timothy has come . . . and since he has brought good news to us." Both participles are in a genitive absolute construction. The third participle of the three - present active - refers to the Thessalonian Christians, ἐπιποθοῦντες ἡμᾶς ἰδεῖν, "Because (you) are longing to see us." To complete the idea contained in the participles, note that the main verb expressing Paul's "sigh of relief" occurs in 3:7, διὰ τοῦτο παρεκλήθημεν, "Because of this we were encouraged," encouraged to such an extent that at once Paul sends a letter.

In brief, the participles reveal in a lively way the dramatic events which led Paul to write -- his intense longing to see the church (ἀπορφανισθέντες) but his failure to reach the church himself, his inability to bear the news "black-out" (μηκέτι στέγοντες) and thus Timothy is sent, and his unbounding joy at the "gospel" report which Timothy - fresh from Thessalonica - has just announced to him - ἐλθόντος Τιμοθέου . . . καὶ εὐαγγελισαμένου ἡμῖν . . . (ὑμεῖς) ἐπιποθοῦντες ἡμᾶς ἰδεῖν. Yet the participles do more than simply tell why Paul wrote. They imply that Christians need each other for they belong to each other in Christ.

178

Assignment

<u>Μᾶρκος[1] ὁ εὐαγγελίστης[2]</u>

ἀπαγγέλλουσι αἱ γραφαὶ ὅτι συνήρχοντο[3] οἱ πιστεύοντες ἐν τῷ οἴκῳ Μαρίας τῆς μητρὸς Μάρκου, τοῦ γράψαντος τὸ εὐαγγέλιον. καὶ Μᾶρκος ἐν πρώτοις ἦν δοῦλος τοῖς ἀποστόλοις Παύλῳ[4] καὶ βαρναβᾷ[5]. καὶ ἐγένετο ὅτι ἦσαν ἐν Ἀντιοχείᾳ[6] συναχθέντες ἐν τῇ ἐκκλησίᾳ προφῆται καὶ διδάσκαλοι. καὶ ἐν αὐτοῖς εὑρέθησαν Βαρναβᾶς καὶ Σαῦλος[7] ὁ καὶ Παῦλος. καὶ ἰδοὺ προσευχομένων αὐτῶν καὶ δοξαζόντων τὸν θεὸν καὶ νηστευόντων εἶπεν τὸ πνεῦμα τὸ ἅγιον, Ἡγίασα Παῦλον καὶ Βαρναβᾶν εἰς τὸ ἔργον τοῦ εὐαγγελίου. τότε προσευξάμενοι καὶ νηστεύσαντες ἀπέλυσαν οἱ πιστοὶ ἀδελφοὶ τοὺς δύο ἀποστόλους καὶ Μᾶρκος ἦλθεν μετ' αὐτῶν.

γέγραπται δὲ ὅτι πεμφθέντες ὑπὸ τοῦ πνεύματος ἦλθον διὰ τῆς θαλάσσης ἕως Κύπρου[8], κἀκεῖ ἀπήγγελλον τὸν λόγον ἐν ταῖς συναγωγαῖς τῶν Ἰουδαίων. καὶ τῶν ἀποστόλων πειρασάντων εὐαγγελίσασθαι πρὸς τοὺς Ἰουδαίους καὶ τὰ ἔθνη ἐν Κύπρῳ καὶ παθόντων κακὰ καὶ ἐν ἀγορᾷ καὶ ἐν συναγωγῇ, Μᾶρκος ἐγερθεὶς ἔφυγεν καὶ ἐπέστρεψεν εἰς Ἰεροσόλυμα.

Παῦλος καὶ Βαρναβᾶς δὲ κηρύξαντες ἐν ἄλλαις χώραις ἐπέστρεψαν εἰς Ἰεροσόλυμα χαίροντες καὶ δοξάζοντες θεὸν ὅτι ἐδέξαντο τὰ ἔθνη τὸν λόγον κυρίου καὶ τὸ βάπτισμα τοῦ πνεύματος. καὶ Παῦλος πείσας τὴν ἐν Ἰεροσόλυμα ἐκκλησίαν ὅτι οὐκ ἔσχον χρείαν τὰ ἔθνη φυλάξαι τὸν παλαιὸν νόμον τῶν Ἰουδαίων, εἶπεν πρὸς Βαρναβᾶν, Χρείαν ἔχουσιν οἱ ἐν τοῖς ἔθνεσιν ἀδελφοὶ ἡμῶν οἱ πιστεύσαντες τῆς διδαχῆς τοῦ εὐαγγελίου. ἐπιστρέψαντες ὀψόμεθα αὐτοὺς πάλιν καὶ διδάξομεν αὐτοὺς τὰς ὁδοὺς τοῦ κυρίου. καὶ Βαρναβᾶς μὲν ἤθελεν παραλαβεῖν Μᾶρκον, Παῦλος δὲ οὐκ ἠθέλησεν ὅτι ἔφυγεν Μᾶρκος ἀπὸ τοῦ ἔργου. καὶ εὐθὺς ἐσκανδαλίσαντο ἐν ἀλλήλοις. καὶ Βαρναβᾶς μὲν παραλαμβάνων Μᾶρκον ἐπέστρεψεν εἰς Κύπρον. Παῦλος δὲ ἡτοίμασεν εὐαγγελίσασθαι ἄλλην χώραν.

νῦν διὰ ταῦτα, παθόντων τῶν ἀδελφῶν, Παύλου καὶ Μάρκου ἐν ταῖς ἑαυτῶν ψυχαῖς, συνήγαγεν ἡ χάρις τοῦ θεοῦ αὐτούς. ἐν γὰρ ταῖς ἐσχάταις ἡμέραις τῆς ζωῆς τοῦ Παύλου

ἐπὶ γῆς πάσχων ἐν φυλακῇ ἔγραψεν πρὸς Τιμόθεον[9] τὸν υἱὸν
αὐτοῦ ἐν τῷ εὐαγγελίῳ, ἐλπίζων ἰδεῖν αὐτόν, καὶ ὑπὲρ
τοῦτο ἔγραψεν περὶ Μάρκου οὕτως, Ἀναλαβὼν Μᾶρκον
οἴσεις[10] αὐτὸν μετὰ σεαυτοῦ, πιστὸς γάρ ἐστιν καὶ ἔχω
αὐτοῦ χρείαν.

οὕτως ὑμεῖς βλέπετε, οἱ ἀδελφοὶ καὶ αἱ ἀδελφαί μου,
ὅτι γίνεται ἡ χάρις τοῦ θεοῦ φανερὰ καὶ συνάγει μαθητὰς
Ἰησοῦ καὶ καθαρίζει τὰς καρδίας τῶν πιστευόντων εἰς
Χριστόν.

---

[1] Μᾶρκος - Mark

[2] εὐαγγελιστής - evangelist

[3] customary imperfect

[4] Παῦλος - Paul

[5] Βαρναβᾶς - Barnabas

[6] Ἀντιοχεία - Antioch

[7] Σαῦλος - Saul

[8] Κύπρος - Cyprus

[9] Τιμόθεος - Timothy

[10] future of φέρω

Chapter 12-C

IN THIS CHAPTER YOU WILL:

> . . . learn the forms and use of the perfect participle,
>
> . . . review the use of the present and aorist participles, and
>
> . . . observe some special uses of the genitive, dative, and accusative cases.

In the last two chapters you were introduced to the present and aorist participles. Now, you meet the perfect participle.

PERFECT ACTIVE PARTICIPLE OF λύω - "HAVING LOOSED"

Singular

	Masc.	Fem.	Neut.
N	λελυκώς	λελυκυῖα	λελυκός
G	λελυκότος	λελυκυίας	λελυκότος
D	λελυκότι	λελυκυίᾳ	λελυκότι
A	λελυκότα	λελυκυῖαν	λελυκός

Plural

	Masc.	Fem.	Neut.
N	λελυκότες	λελυκυῖαι	λελυκότα
G	λελυκότων	λελυκυιῶν	λελυκότων
D	λελυκόσι (ν)	λελυκυίαις	λελυκόσι (ν)
A	λελυκότας	λελυκυίας	λελυκότα

Observations

1. The reduplication points to the perfect.

2. The characteristic "κ" of the perfect <u>active</u> occurs in all forms.

3. The pattern of the declension is 3 - 1 - 3 (masc. - fem. - neut.).

Memory Aid

Observe Lu, Party Zipple, and the Perfect Parrot (perfect active participle) standing next to the mirror (reduplication). Lu has loosed the coats on the Queen bee-cause it is hot (-κώς, -κυῖα, -κός, the endings for the masculine, feminine, and neuter, nominative singular). Also note the "κ" kite (suffix "κ").

PERFECT MIDDLE/PASSIVE PARTICIPLE OF λύω - "HAVING LOOSED FOR ONESELF," "HAVING BEEN LOOSED"

Singular

	Masc.	Fem.	Neut.
N	λελυμένος	λελυμένη	λελυμένον
G	λελυμένου	λελυμένης	λελυμένου
D	λελυμένῳ	λελυμένῃ	λελυμένῳ
A	λελυμένον	λελυμένην	λελυμένον

Plural

	Masc.	Fem.	Neut.
N	λελυμένοι	λελυμέναι	λελυμένα
G	λελυμένων	λελυμένων	λελυμένων
D	λελυμένοις	λελυμέναις	λελυμένοις
A	λελυμένους	λελυμένας	λελυμένα

Observations

1. The reduplication indicates the perfect tense.

2. The helping vowel of the present middle/passive voice is lost, but the "μεν" of the M/P participle occurs in all forms.

3. The declension pattern is 2 - 1 - 2 (masc. - fem. - neut.)

Memory Aid

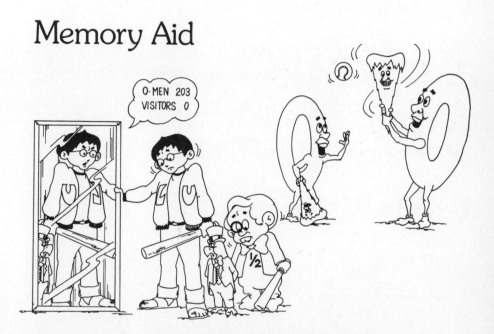

Lu and the Perfect Parrot had been loosed with their friend Party Zipple (perfect middle/passive participle). Lu is looking in the mirror (reduplication) trying to play against the O-Men (-ομεν) with their article bats, but to no avail. The O-Men, armed with article bats, will remind you of the familiar letters "μεν" followed by the endings of the article which you know.

The Meaning of the Perfect Participle

Like the perfect indicative, the perfect participle emphasizes an existing state.

1. John 8:31 - ἔλεγεν οὖν ὁ Ἰησοῦς πρὸς τοὺς πεπιστευκότας αὐτῷ Ἰουδαίους. - Then Jesus was saying to the Jews who had believed on him.

2. John 5:10 - ἔλεγον οὖν οἱ Ἰουδαῖοι τῷ τεθεραπευμένῳ Σάββατόν ἐστιν. Then the Jews were saying to the one who had been healed, "It is (the) Sabbath."

3. John 10:34 - ἀπεκρίθη αὐτοῖς ὁ Ἰησοῦς Οὐκ ἔστιν γεγραμμένον ἐν τῷ νόμῳ ὑμῶν. - Then Jesus answered them, "Is it not written in your law?"

The perfect participle with a form of εἰμί (cf. no. 3 above - ἔστιν γεγραμμένον) is called <u>periphrastic</u> <u>con</u>struction. It emphasizes the existing state.

Review also the keys which help you to parse participles. Review also the attributive and predicate functions of the participle.

Keys to Participles

Tense

Present	= stem + endings
First Aorist	= "σα"
Second Aorist	= stem change
Perfect	= reduplication

Voice

Active	= "ντ"
Middle or M/P	= "μεν"
First Aor. Pass.	= "θ"
Perfect Active	= "κ"
Perfect M/P	= Loss of helping vowel

Endings

Active participles follow: 3 - 1 - 3 declensions
Middle or M/P participles follow: 2 - 1 - 2 declensions
Aorist passive participles follow: 3 - 1 - 3 declensions

Case

Greek cases are often used to express other meanings than the simple meaning presented for each case in lesson two. Observe now these same cases and the variety of their functions. The pictures which follow will help you.

Uses of the Genitive Case

GENITIVE OF TIME = "DURING"

Luke 18:7 - ἡμέρας καὶ νυκτός - during day and night

GENITIVE OF RELATIONSHIP

John 21:2 - οἱ τοῦ Ζεβεδαίου - the ones of Zebedee. The wider context indicates that the οἱ refers to "the sons of" Zebedee.

GENITIVE OF THE ARTICULAR INFINITIVE = PURPOSE

Matthew 13:3 - ἐξῆλθεν ὁ σπείρων τοῦ σπείρειν - The Sower went forth to sow.

Uses of the Dative Case

DATIVE OF TIME

Luke 12:20 - ταύτῃ τῇ νυκτί - This night (more precise than the genitive of time).

DATIVE OF RESPECT

Matthew 5:3 - Μακάριοι οἱ πτωχοὶ τῷ πνεύματι - Blessed are the poor with respect to (their) spirit.

Luke 5:27 - καὶ ἐθεάσατο τελώνην ὀνόματι Λευίν - And he saw a tax-collector, Levi with respect to name (= by name Levi).

DATIVE OF LOCATION (LOCATIVE)

Acts 2:33 - τῇ δεξιᾷ (right hand) τοῦ θεοῦ - At the right hand of God.

Uses of the Accusative Case

ACCUSATIVE OF TIME - IT ANSWERS THE QUESTION, HOW FAR?
OR, HOW LONG?

Luke 2:44 - ἦλθον ἡμέρας ὁδόν - They went a day's journey.

John 4:40 - ἔμεινεν (aor.) δύο ἡμέρας - He remained two
days.

The "accusatives of time" are underlined.

COGNATE ACCUSATIVE (The verbal idea is repeated in the
object)

Matthew 2:10 - ἐχάρησαν χαρὰν μεγάλην - They rejoiced
with great joy.

Memory Aids

The following pictures link together the main uses
of the genitive, dative, and accusative cases which you
have seen in the various lessons. While the pictures
are more involved, a few minutes given to them will enable you to master the different uses of the cases with
ease.

Genitive:

1. Of possession (Chapter Two).
2. Of separation - (Ablative) - ἀπό - "from" (Chapter
   Four).
3. Of time - during which (Chapter Twelve-C).
4. Of comparison (Chapter Twenty-one).
5. Genitive absolute (Chapter Twelve-B).
6. With other prepositions (Chapter Four).
7. Genitive of relationship (Chapter Twelve-C).
8. With the infinitive - Purpose (Chapter Fourteen).

186

Gerard Genitive has a big heart and is in love reminding us of the word "of" (possession). While running from a paw (ἀπό) he looks at his clock during his flight (time - during which). On the raft is a comb-pear (comparison) that salutes (genitive absolute) the Prep-Precision who follows on a relay-ship (relationship) towed along by Infant Ivy's porpoise (infinitive - purpose).

Dative:

1. Of indirect object (Chapter Two).
2. Of instrument - Dative of Means (Chapter Four).
3. Of location (Chapter Twelve-C).
4. With prepositions (Chapter Four).
5. Of time - Precise point in time (Chapter Twelve-C).
6. Of respect (Chapter Twelve-C).

Observe Demetrius Dative with his catcher's glove ("to" case - indirect object) playing by means of his bat instrument (instrumental), having hit a clock (locative) to Prep-Precision (preposition) who stands on a pointed clock (time - point) which evokes respect (respect).

Accusative:

1. Of direct object - completing case (Chapter Two).
2. Of motion - εἰς - into (Chapter Four).
3. Of subject of infinitive (Chapter Fourteen).
4. Of time - how long, how far (Chapter Twelve-C).
5. With prepositions (Chapter Four).
6. Cognate accusative (Chapter Twelve-C).

   H. Armitage (accusative) completes his case
(direct object). You will observe an Ace (εἰς) in
motion into his pocket. He happens to be riding
Infant Ivy's sub-jet (subject of Infinitive) while
looking at his long watch (time - how long). The
chief mechanic on the sub-jet is Prep-Precision (prepositions) aided by his friend Cog-Ant (cognate).
Review now this picture once more until you see all the
parts linked together.

Enrichment

Two New Testament texts illustrate well the use of the perfect participle:

(1) Mark 5:15. The people of Gerasa came forth to see the demoniac whom Jesus healed. The Greek text reads: θεωροῦσιν τὸν δαιμονιζόμενον . . . ἱματισ-μένον, . . . τὸν ἐσχηκότα τὸν λεγιῶνα, "They saw the demoniac . . . clothed, . . . the one who had had the legion."

The underlined words - ἱματισμένον (from ἱματίζω "clothe") and ἐσχηκότα (from ἔχω) - are perfect participles. They depict clearly the new condition ("clothed") which the demoniac came to enjoy and the old state ("he who had had the legion") from which Jesus delivered him.

(2) John 11:44. Jesus raised Lazarus. The text reads: ἐξῆλθεν ὁ τεθνηκὼς δεδεμένος, "He who had died came forth bound." The two perfect participles (τεθνηκώς from θνήσκω "to die" and δεδεμένος from δέω "to bind") point respectively to the former condition of Lazarus, i.e. "he who had died" and to his present condition as he emerges from the tomb, i.e. "bound."

Assignment

A Story from the Second Apology of Justin Martyr (A.D. 157)

Εὑρέθη ἀκοὴ ἐν τοῖς γράμμασιν Ἰουστίνου Μαρτύρος[1]
περὶ γυναικὸς καὶ τοῦ ἀνδρὸς αὐτῆς. καὶ αὕτη ἦν κακὴ καὶ
ἁμαρτωλός, θέλουσα ἀρέσκειν[2] ἑαυτῇ μόνον καὶ οὐ θεῷ.
ἀλλ᾽ εἰσελθούσης τῆς τοῦ εὐαγγελίου διδαχῆς εἰς τὴν
ψυχὴν αὐτῆς, ἐδέξατο τὴν σωτηρίαν τὴν ἠγορασμένην διὰ
Χριστοῦ. καὶ εὐθὺς νυκτὸς καὶ ἡμέρας ἐπείραζεν πεῖσαι
τὸν ἄνδρα αὐτῆς ἐπιστρέψαι ἀπὸ τῶν πονηρῶν ὁδῶν αὐτοῦ.
αὐτὸς δὲ μένων ἐν ἀπιστίᾳ, ἀπῆλθεν εἰς τὴν Ἀλεξάνδρειαν,[3]
κἀκεῖ ἐσκανδάλισεν τὴν γυναῖκα αὐτοῦ ἔργοις κακοῖς. καὶ
ὑπὲρ τοῦτο ἔλυσεν τοὺς τῆς φύσεως[4] νόμους. καὶ οὕτως
ἁμαρτάνοντος αὐτοῦ εἰς οὐρανὸν καὶ εἰς τὴν ψυχὴν ἑαυτοῦ,
ἦν ἐν τῇ ψυχῇ τῆς γυναικὸς αὐτοῦ χάρις καὶ εἰρήνη ὅτι
ἐδιδάσκετο περὶ δικαιοσύνης, βεβαπτισμένη ἐν τῷ ὀνόματι
Χριστοῦ.

καὶ νῦν διὰ τοῦτο ἤθελεν αὐτὴ λυθῆναι ἀπὸ τοῦ ἀνδρὸς
αὐτῆς. ἀλλ᾽ οἱ ἅγιοι περὶ αὐτὴν γινώσκοντες τὸ θέλημα
αὐτῆς ἔπεισαν αὐτήν, λέγοντες, Οὐχ ἁμαρτήσεις εἰς τὸν τοῦ
θεοῦ νόμον οὐδὲ εἰς τὸν ἄνδρα σου ἀποστρέφουσα ἀπ᾽ αὐτοῦ.
ἡμεῖς δὲ αὐτοὶ προσευξόμεθα τῷ θεῷ πιστεύοντες ὅτι ἄξει
ὁ θεὸς τὸν ἄνδρα σου εἰς ἐλπίδα μετανοίας. καὶ αὕτη
ἤκουσεν αὐτῶν καὶ ἔμενεν πιστὴ τῷ γάμῳ[5] ἐκεῖνο τὸ ἔτος.

ἀλλὰ γενομένου τοῦ ἀνδρὸς αὐτῆς πονηροῦ ἔτι πλέον,[6]
ἤρξατο ἡ γυνὴ λέγειν ἐν ἑαυτῇ, Ἰδοὺ οὐ γινώσκει τὸν θεὸν
οὗτος ὁ ἀνήρ μου οὐδὲ ἀκούει τὰς ἁγίας ἐντολὰς τοῦ εὐαγγελίου. οὐκέτι ἐστὶν ἐν ἐμοὶ μένειν μετ᾽ αὐτοῦ. διὰ
τοῦτο ἐχωρίσθη[7] ἀπ᾽ αὐτοῦ καὶ παρέλαβεν ῥεπούδιον.[8]

ἀκούσας οὖν ὁ ἀνὴρ αὐτῆς ὅτι ἐστὶν αὐτὴ ἀπολελυμένη
ἀπ᾽ αὐτοῦ καὶ ὅτι ἔμενεν ἐν τῇ κώμῃ αὐτῆς χαίρουσα μετὰ
τῶν Χριστιανῶν καὶ διδασκομένη ὑπ᾽ αὐτῶν τὸ εὐαγγέλιον,
ἐδίωξεν τὸν διδάξαντα αὐτήν. καὶ ἔπεισεν τὸν βασιλέα
βαλεῖν τὸν διδάσκαλον εἰς τὴν φυλακήν. κἀκεῖ ἔπαθεν
δώδεκα ἡμέρας. τότε ἐκέλευσεν ὁ βασιλεὺς ἀχθῆναι τὸν
μακάριον διδάσκαλον ἐκ τῆς φυλακῆς. καὶ οὕτως ἦν ὁ
διδάσκαλος ἡτοιμασμένος ἀποθανεῖν ὑπὲρ Χριστοῦ. καὶ
ἀγομένου αὐτοῦ εἰς θάνατον, ἤχθη ἄλλος ὀνόματι Λούκιος.

καὶ εἶπεν ὁ βασιλεὺς αὐτῷ, Σὺ καὶ εἶ Χριστιάνος; καὶ
ἀπεκρίθη, λέγων, Ἐγὼ εἰμι.   καὶ εὐθὺς ἐκέλευσεν ὁ
βασιλεὺς τοὺς αὐτοῦ στρατιώτας, καὶ Λούκιος, ὁ πεπιστευ-
κὼς εἰς Ἰησοῦν, ὁ μὴ ἔχων φόβον τοῦ βασιλέως ἐν τῇ
καρδίᾳ αὐτοῦ, ἤρθη ἀπὸ τοῦ οἴκου αὐτοῦ καὶ ἀπὸ τῶν φίλων
αὐτοῦ ἀποθανεῖν.   καὶ ὢν αὐτὸς πιστὸς εἰς θάνατον,
ἐδέξατο τὴν ἐπαγγελίαν τῆς ζωῆς σὺν τῷ Χριστῷ εἰς τοὺς
αἰῶνας.

---

[1] of Justin Martyr
[2] to please
[3] Alexandria (Egypt)
[4] of nature
[5] to the marriage
[6] more
[7] χωρίζω - to separate
[8] repudium (Latin) - bill of divorce

Chapter 13

1. ἀκάθαρτος, -ον[1]   - unclean (catharsis = purgation)
2. ἄν (post-positive)   - (particle, not to be translated separately)
3. ἀντί (with gen.)   - instead of, opposite, in exchange for (antibody, antidote)
4. ἅπτω   - I light, kindle
5. ἅπτομαι (with gen.) - I touch (haptometer - measures sense of touch), lay hold of
6. ἐάν (with subj.)   - if (ἐὰν μή - if not, unless, except)
7. εἰ (with ind.)   - if[2] (εἰ μή - if not, unless, except)
8. ἰδού (particle)   - see! behold! cf. εἶδον
9. ἵνα (with subj.)   - in order that
10. μαρτυρία, -ας, ἡ   - witness (martyr)
11. μνημεῖον, -ου, τό   - tomb (mnemonic)
12. ναός, -οῦ, ὁ   - sanctuary
13. οἰκία, -ας, ἡ   - house (same meaning as οἶκος)
14. ὅλος, -η, -ον   - whole, all (holocaust)
15. ὅπου (relative)   - where (relative), ὅπου ἐάν = wherever
16. ὅπως (with subj.)   - in order that
17. ὅταν (with subj.)   - whenever
18. πίνω   - I drink
19. πότε (interrogative)- when?
20. ποτέ (enclitic)   - at some time, at any time - compare accent with #19.
21. ποῦ (interrogative) - where?
22. πρό (prep. w/gen.)   - before (prologue)
23. πῶς (interrogative) - how? Used in direct and indirect questions
24. σάββατον, -ου, τό   - Sabbath, week (dat.pl. irregular - σάββασιν; plural may have singular meaning)
25. σημεῖον, -ου, τό   - sign (semeiology - the science of signs)
26. σοφία, -ας, ἡ   - wisdom (sophistication)
27. ὑποστρέφω   - I return
28. φαρισαῖος, -ου, ὁ   - Pharisee

[1] An adjective of two terminations only.

[2] Frequently εἰ functions as an interrogative particle.

IN THIS LESSON YOU WILL:

    . . . see the famous Trojan warship - the Sub-Junk (subjunctive mood),

    . . . learn the endings for the subjunctive,

    . . . become familiar with the different uses of the subjunctive mood,

    . . . discover several red flags for the subjunctive mood.

Foundational Concepts

Subjunctive Mood

In chapter one as you learned the parsing procedure - TVMPN, via Vera Verb - you associated Vera's mumu dress with the word "mood." The word "mood" tells us how something is said. You learned that the indicative mood is the mood of statements or affirmations. Now the subjunctive mood is before you.

The subjunctive mood is the probability mood. It is the mood of contingency, generally indicated by words such as "may," "might," or "should." It will normally follow words such as: ἵνα - in order that and ἐάν - if.

These and other words which you will meet are like red flags which indicate that a subjunctive follows.

Red Flag Words

ἵνα   - in order that
ὅπως   - in order that
ἐάν   - if
ἄν   - not translated
            separately
ὅταν   - whenever
ὅπου ἐάν - wherever
οὐ μή   - no (strong
            negation)
ἕως ἄν   - until

PRESENT SUBJUNCTIVE OF εἰμί

Singular		Plural	
1.	ὦ	(1)	ὦμεν
2.	ᾖς	(2)	ἦτε (same form as imperfect of εἰμί)
3.	ᾖ	(3)	ὦσι(ν)

Observations

1. The above forms are phonetically quite similar to the endings of the present active indicative. They contain, however, the <u>long vowels</u> - "η" and "ω" - instead of the short vowels "ε" and "o."

2. The subjunctive will generally be introduced by one of the red flag words. For instance "ἵνα ὦμεν" is translated: "in order that we may be."

Memory Aid

Observe the strange scene of <u>Amy</u>, <u>present</u> in hand, near the <u>sub-junk</u> (present subjunctive of εἰμί), in the <u>oasis</u> (ὦ, ἦς, ἦ) with an <u>omelete oozing</u> (ὦμεν, ἦτε, ὦσιν). The oasis and the oozing omelete are <u>elongated</u>, reminding you of the long vowels ("η" and "ω").

Subjunctive Forms

The picture will aid you to remember the subjunctive endings. You observe the same <u>elongated oasis</u> (-ω,-ης,-η) with the <u>omelete oozing</u> (-ωμεν,-ητε,-ωσιν). And steering the sub-junk is none other than <u>elongated Amethyst</u> (-ωμεθα, -ησθε, -ωνται). Amethyst will help you remember the M/P endings. The middle or middle/passive endings also contain the long vowels: "η" or "ω."

Note the following keys which will help you to parse subjunctive forms. Then observe the charts noting the exact correspondence with the present subjunctive of εἰμί.

Keys

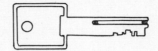

stem + ending = present λύ ω

stem + suffix + ending = first aorist λύ σ ω

stem + ϑ + ending = first aorist pass. λυ ϑ ῶ

stem (int.change) + ending = second βάλ ω
                                       aorist

PRESENT ACTIVE SUBJUNCTIVE OF λύω

	Singular		Plural
(1)	λύω	(1)	λύωμεν
(2)	λύῃς	(2)	λύητε
(3)	λύῃ	(3)	λύωσι(ν)

FIRST AORIST ACTIVE SUBJUNCTIVE OF λύω

	Singular		Plural
(1)	λύσω	(1)	λύσωμεν
(2)	λύσῃς	(2)	λύσητε
(3)	λύσῃ	(3)	λύσωσι(ν)

SECOND AORIST ACTIVE SUBJUNCTIVE OF βάλλω

	Singular		Plural
(1)	βάλω	(1)	βάλωμεν
(2)	βάλῃς	(2)	βάλητε
(3)	βάλῃ	(3)	βάλωσι(ν)

FIRST AORIST PASSIVE SUBJUNCTIVE OF λύω

	Singular		Plural
(1)	λυϑῶ	(1)	λυϑῶμεν
(2)	λυϑῇς	(2)	λυϑῆτε
(3)	λυϑῇ	(3)	λυϑῶσι(ν)

Now, note the keys below for the middle and middle/passive subjunctive endings. Then observe the charts and see the correspondence with the middle/passive indicative.

Keys

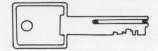

stem + endings = present λύ ωμαι
stem + suffix + endings = first aorist = λύ σ ωμαι

stem (internal change) + endings second aorist = βάλ ωμαι

PRESENT MIDDLE/PASSIVE SUBJUNCTIVE OF λύω

	Singular		Plural
(1)	λύ ωμαι	(1)	λυ ώμεθα
(2)	λύ ῃ	(2)	λύ ησθε
(3)	λύ ηται	(3)	λύ ωνται

FIRST AORIST MIDDLE SUBJUNCTIVE OF λύω

	Singular		Plural
(1)	λύσ ωμαι	(1)	λυσ ώμεθα
(2)	λύσ ῃ	(2)	λύσ ησθε
(3)	λύσ ηται	(3)	λύσ ωνται

SECOND AORIST MIDDLE SUBJUNCTIVE OF βάλλω

	Singular		Plural
(1)	βάλ ωμαι	(1)	βαλ ώμεθα
(2)	βάλ ῃ	(2)	βάλ ησθε
(3)	βάλ ηται	(3)	βάλ ωνται

Tense of the Subjunctive

The subjunctive occurs in the present tense and, much more frequently, in the aorist. The distinction between the two tenses lies not in their <u>time</u> of action but <u>kind</u> of action. If the tense is aorist, the action is decisive, if present, the action is durative.

Practice

It is very important to see the various keys that will help identify the tense of the subjunctive. Parse the following verbs and translate the various phrases:

1. ἵνα σώζω τὸν κόσμον.
2. ἐὰν δοξάσω ἐμαυτόν.
3. ἵνα βαπτισθῶμεν.
4. ἐὰν διδάσκητε τὰς ἀδελφάς.
5. ἐὰν εὐαγγελισώμεθα ὑμᾶς.
6. ἵνα γράψῃς.
7. ἐὰν εἰσέλθωσιν.
8. ἵνα σωθῶσιν.

KEY

1. PAS 1 S - in order that I may save the world.
2. 1AAS 1 S - if I should glorify myself
3. 1APS 1 P - in order that we might be baptized.
4. PAS 2 P - if you should teach the sisters.
5. 1A Dep S 1 P - if we should preach the gospel to you.
6. 1AAS 2 S - in order that you should write.
7. 2AAS 3 P - if they should enter.
8. 1APS 3 P - in order that they might be saved.

Use of the Subjunctive

You have just learned the endings for the subjunctive mood. Now you are to analyze the different uses of the subjunctive. It is used:

1. To express PURPOSE. The key words are ἵνα and ὅπως both translated by the words, "in order that."

   Example: 1 John 3:8 - ἐφανερώθη ὁ υἱὸς τοῦ θεοῦ ἵνα λύσῃ τὰ ἔργα τοῦ διαβόλου.

   The Son of God was manifested in order that he might destroy the works of the devil.

2. With CONDITIONAL sentences. The key word is ἐάν - "if." A sentence introduced by ἐάν expresses what may happen or what is expected to happen if the given condition is fulfilled.

    Example: John 13:35 - ἐν τούτῳ γνώσονται . . . ὅτι ἐμοὶ μαθηταί ἐστε, ἐὰν ἀγάπην ἔχητε ἐν ἀλλήλοις.

    In this they will know . . . that you are disciples to me if you have (present = continue to have) love among one another.

3. With INDEFINITE clauses. The words used are ἄν or ἐάν with things or persons. Though ἄν cannot be translated by itself it will be found with indefinite words like ὅπου, "where."

    ὅς ἐάν or ὅς ἄν = whoever
    ὅ ἐάν or ὅ ἄν = whatever
    ὅπου ἐάν or ὅπου ἄν = wherever

    Example: Luke 9:57 - ἀκολουθήσω σοι ὅπου ἐὰν ἀπέρχῃ.

    I will follow you wherever you (should) go.

4. To express TIME - temporal clause. The word used to introduce a temporal clause is ὅταν - "whenever."

    Example: Matthew 10:23 - ὅταν δὲ διώκωσιν ὑμᾶς ἐν τῇ πόλει(city) ταύτῃ, φεύγετε(flee) εἰς τὴν ἑτέραν.

    But whenever they persecute you in this city, flee (unto, into) the other (city).

5. As a NOUN CLAUSE introduced by ἵνα translated as "that."

    Example: John 15:8 - ἐν τούτῳ ἐδοξάσθη ὁ πατήρ μου, ἵνα καρπὸν πολὺν φέρητε.

    In this my father is glorified, that you bear much fruit.

    The aorist ἐδοξάσθη is not historical but gnomic, an accepted fact.

6. To express an EXHORTATION = HORTATORY Subjunctive. The subjunctive appears independently - without "red flags" - at the beginning of a clause in the first person plural and is to be rendered "let us."

    Example: Hebrews 13:13 - ἐξερχώμεθα πρὸς αὐτόν.
    Let us go forth to him.

7. To ask a DELIBERATIVE question = Deliberative subjunctive. This also appears without red flag words
   and will be found in the first person singular or
   plural.

   Example: 1 Corinthians 11:22 - τί (what) εἴπω ὑμῖν;
   What shall I say to you?

8. To give a PROHIBITION - subjunctive of prohibition.
   The subjunctive will appear in the second person
   singular or plural with the negative.

   Example: John 3:7 - μὴ θαυμάσῃς ὅτι εἶπόν σοι . . .
   Do not marvel that I said to you . . .

9. To give a strong NEGATION. The negatives οὐ and μή
   are sometimes found with an aorist subjunctive and
   together constitute a very strong negation.

   Example: Matthew 5:20 - οὐ μὴ εἰσέλθητε εἰς τὴν
   βασιλείαν τῶν οὐρανῶν.
   You shall not enter the kingdom of heaven.

Practice

Parse the verbs and translate:

1. ἐὰν εἴπωμεν ὅτι ἁμαρτίαν οὐκ ἔχομεν, . . . ἡ ἀλήθεια
   οὐκ ἔστιν ἐν ἡμῖν.
2. καὶ αὕτη ἐστὶν ἡ ἐντολὴ αὐτοῦ, ἵνα πιστεύσωμεν τῷ
   ὀνόματι τοῦ υἱοῦ αὐτοῦ Ἰησοῦ Χριστοῦ.
3. ἄγωμεν καὶ ἡμεῖς ἵνα ἀποθάνωμεν μετ᾽ αὐτοῦ.
4. Λάζαρος ἀπέθανεν, καὶ χαίρω δι᾽ ὑμᾶς, ἵνα πιστεύσητε,
   ὅτι οὐκ ἤμην ἐκεῖ.
5. ἐκηρύξαμεν τούτῳ τῷ λαῷ ἵνα δέξωνται τὴν ἀλήθειαν καὶ
   σωθῶσιν.
6. τὸν ἐρχόμενον πρὸς ἐμὲ οὐ μὴ ἐκβάλω ἔξω (out) - John
   6:37.

KEY

1. If we should say that we do not have sin, . . . the
   truth is not in us.
2. And this is his commandment, that (note: ἵνα is used
   here to introduce content) we should believe in the
   name of his son Jesus Christ, i.e. his command is
   that we should believe.
3. Let us also go in order that we may die with him.
4. Lazarus died, and I rejoice on account of you, in
   order that you may believe, because I was not there.
5. We preached to this people in order that they might
   receive the truth and be saved.
6. I will never cast out the one coming to me.

Conditional Sentences

Conditional sentences are the "if - then" sentences. Some use ἐάν with, the subjunctive, while others use εἰ and the indicative mood. Conditional sentences contain two parts:
1. The PROTASIS is the "if" clause.
2. The APODOSIS is the "then" clause.

There are basically four types of conditional sentences. Each contains an "if" clause that expresses:

1. A GENERAL CONDITION - ἐάν - "if" + the subjunctive.

John 11:40 - ἐὰν πιστεύσῃς ὄψῃ τὴν δόξαν τοῦ θεοῦ.

If you believe, you will see the glory of God.

A sentence introduced by ἐάν, and the subjunctive expresses what may happen or what is expected to happen if the given condition is fulfilled. "The subj. mode (mood) brings the expectation within the horizon of a lively hope in spite of the cloud of hovering doubt" (A.T. Robertson, A Grammar of the Greek New Testament in the Light of Historical Research, p. 1016).

Observe General Condish (general condition) who, with the A-On (ἐάν), steers the sub-junk (subjunctive).

2.   A TRUE CONDITION - εἰ - "if" + indicative.

<u>John 15:20</u> - εἰ ἐμὲ ἐδίωξαν, καὶ ὑμᾶς διώξουσιν.
If they persecuted me, they will also persecute you.

A sentence introduced by εἰ and the indicative may express something true or real. The above sentence assumes that Jesus was really persecuted.

The <u>Con-dish</u> (condition) is giving a lie detector (true) test to the <u>indicator</u> (indicative). He says, "<u>If</u> it <u>indicates</u> A (εἰ) - and it does -, it is <u>true</u>."

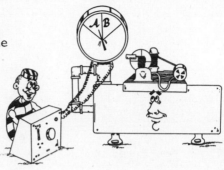

3.   A POSSIBLE CONDITION - εἰ - "if" + indicative

<u>II Timothy 2:13</u> - εἰ ἀπιστοῦμεν (disbelieve),ἐκεῖνος πιστὸς μένει.
If we disbelieve, that one remains faithful.

The sentence expresses a possibility only, with no indication that the condition is, or will be, factual or real.

Observe the <u>Con-dish</u> (condition) and <u>Pass-bull</u> (possible) watching the <u>indicator</u> (indicative). He says, "<u>If</u> it <u>indicates</u> <u>A</u> (εἰ) it is <u>Pass-bull</u>" (possible).

4. A CONTRARY TO FACT CONDITION - εἰ + past tense
(in both the "if" and "then" parts) + ἄν

John 5:46 - εἰ γὰρ ἐπιστεύετε Μωϋσεῖ, ἐπιστεύετε ἄν
ἐμοί.

For if you were believing in Moses, you would be
believing in me.

In the contrary to fact condition, a statement is
made which was not fulfilled. In the above sentence,
the Pharisees did not really believe Moses. Therefore,
they are unable to believe in Jesus.

Observe carefully: The A (εἰ) on (ἄν) the indicator
(indicative) passed (past tense) a contrary Con-dish
(contrary to fact condition).

Practice

Review again the four basic conditional sentences through the pictures. Analyze the type of condition in the following scriptures and translate.

1. Col. 2:20 - εἰ ἀπεθάνετε σὺν Χριστῷ . . .
2. 1 John 1:10 - ἐὰν εἴπωμεν ὅτι οὐχ ἡμαρτήκαμεν . . . ὁ λόγος αὐτοῦ οὐκ ἔστιν ἐν ἡμῖν.
3. John 11:32 - Κύριε, εἰ ἦς ὧδε, οὐκ ἄν μου ἀπέθανεν ὁ ἀδελφός.
4. 1 Cor. 1:16 - οὐκ οἶδα(know) εἰ . . . ἄλλον ἐβάπτισα.

KEY

1. <u>TRUE CONDITION</u> - If you died with Christ (which you did).
2. <u>GENERAL CONDITION</u> - If we should say that we have not sinned . . ., his word is not in us.
3. <u>CONTRARY TO FACT CONDITION</u> - Lord, if you had been here (which you were not) my brother would not have died (which he did).
4. <u>POSSIBLE CONDITION</u> - I do not know if I baptized . . . another.

Enrichment

John 20:31 is an important text since it expresses John's purpose in writing the gospel (observe ἵνα with the subjunctive). His purpose is two-fold, (ἵνα πιστεύητε or ἵνα πιστεύσητε), "that you may believe" and ἵνα ζωὴν ἔχητε . . ."that you may have life in his name." The Nestle text prints the first subjunctive as a present, ἵνα πιστεύητε, "that you may continue to believe," while the United Bible Society prints an aorist subjunctive, "that you may come to believe." There is strong evidence for both readings. You may want to return to the text of John 20 at a later time. At any rate, John's purpose is clear in that he lays stress on two basic concepts - faith and life.

Assignment

Ἰωσὴφ[1] καὶ οἱ ἀδελφοὶ αὐτοῦ (Part one)

ἐν τῷ πρώτῳ βιβλίῳ τῶν γραφῶν τῶν ἁγίων γέγραπται
ὅτι Ἰακὼβ[2] ἔμενεν ἐν τῇ γῇ Χανάαν[3] παρὰ τῷ μνημείῳ τῆς
Ῥαχήλ[4], τῆς γυναικὸς τοῦ Ἰακώβ.

ἦσαν δὲ τῷ Ἰακὼβ υἱοὶ δώδεκα, καὶ ὁ Ἰωσὴφ ἐν
αὐτοῖς καὶ ὁ νεώτερος[5] αὐτῶν Βενιαμίν[6]. καὶ διὰ τὴν
ἀγάπην τοῦ Ἰακὼβ εἰς τὸν Ἰωσήφ, ἡτοίμασεν αὐτῷ χιτῶνα[7]
καλόν. Ἰωσὴφ δὲ ἤνεγκεν μαρτυρίαν πονηρὰν πρὸς τὸν
πατέρα περὶ τῶν ἀδελφῶν. οἱ οὖν ἀδελφοὶ ἀκούσαντες
ταῦτα ἐσκανδαλίσαντο ἐν τῷ Ἰωσὴφ καὶ εἶπον κακὰ κατ'
αὐτοῦ. καὶ ἐν τῇ αὐτῇ ἡμέρᾳ νυκτὸς γενομένης ἀπεκαλύφθη
τῷ Ἰωσὴφ ἐπὶ κλίνης ὅτι αὐτὸς ἕξει ἐξουσίαν ἐπὶ τὸν
πατέρα καὶ τὴν μητέρα καὶ τοὺς ἀδελφοὺς αὐτοῦ. γενομένης
δὲ ἡμέρας καὶ συνελθόντων τοῦ πατρὸς αὐτοῦ καὶ τῶν
ἀδελφῶν, ἀπήγγελλεν τὰ ὀφθέντα αὐτῷ ἐν τῇ νυκτί. καὶ
εἶπεν ὁ πατὴρ αὐτοῦ, Ἐλευσόμεθα οὖν ἐγὼ καὶ ἡ μήτηρ σου
καὶ οἱ ἀδελφοί σου πίπτειν ἐπὶ τὴν γῆν πρὸς τοὺς πόδας
σου; θέλεις ἵνα ἄρχῃς ἡμῶν; ἀκούσαντες δὲ οἱ ἀδελφοὶ
τὴν ἀκοήν, συνήχθησαν ἐπὶ τὸ αὐτὸ[8] πρὸ τῆς οἰκίας
λέγοντες πρὸς ἑαυτούς, Ἕως πότε ἐσόμεθα μετ' αὐτοῦ;
ὅταν ἀπαγγέλλῃ τοῦτο πάλιν ἡμῖν, λύσωμεν αὐτόν.

καὶ ἐγένετο ὅτι ἐπορεύθησαν οἱ ἀδελφοὶ ἵνα φυλάξωσι
τὰ πρόβατα τοῦ πατρὸς ἐν Σύχεμ[9]. καὶ πορευθέντων αὐτῶν
καὶ γενομένης τῆς πρώτης ἡμέρας μετὰ τὸ σάββατον, ἠνέχθη
ὁ Ἰωσὴφ πρὸ τοῦ πατρὸς αὐτοῦ καὶ ἐπέμφθη ὅπως εὕρῃ τοὺς
ἀδελφοὺς αὐτοῦ καὶ ἴδῃ εἰ ἐν εἰρήνῃ εἰσίν, καὶ ὑποστρέψῃ
πρὸς τὸν πατέρα αὐτοῦ σὺν σημείῳ περὶ τῆς εἰρήνης
αὐτῶν.

καὶ ἐξῆλθεν Ἰωσὴφ ἐν τῇ ὁδῷ ἀντὶ Σύχεμ[9]. καὶ ἦν
ἐνδεδυμένος τὸν καλὸν χιτῶνα καὶ ὑποδήματα εἰς τοὺς πόδας
αὐτοῦ. καὶ ἰδοὺ ἔτρεχεν ὅπως ὑπακούσῃ τῇ ἐντολῇ τῇ
πιστευθείσῃ αὐτῷ ὑπὸ τοῦ πατρὸς αὐτοῦ. καὶ εὗρεν αὐτὸν
ἄνθρωπος ἐν τῷ ἀγρῷ καὶ εἶπεν αὐτῷ, Ποῦ πορεύῃ; καὶ
ἀπεκρίθη ὁ Ἰωσὴφ ὅτι, Ἐλήλυθα ἵνα εὕρω τοὺς ἀδελφούς
μου καὶ οὐ γινώσκω ποῦ εἰσιν. καὶ εἶπεν ὁ ἄνθρωπος,
Ἐγὼ εἶδον αὐτοὺς καὶ ἤκουσα αὐτῶν λεγόντων, Πορευθῶμεν

εἰς Δωθαΐμ[10]. καὶ εὐθὺς Ἰωσὴφ ἔδραμεν πρὸς Δωθαΐμ. καὶ
ἐγγίζοντα εἰς τὴν κώμην εἶδον αὐτὸν οἱ ἀδελφοὶ καὶ ἔλεγον
πρὸς ἑαυτούς, λέγοντες, Ἰδοὺ ὁ σοφὸς[11] ἔρχεται, ὁ
δεχόμενος σοφίαν ἐν τῇ νυκτὶ καθεύδων. ἀποκτείνωμεν
αὐτὸν καὶ βάλωμεν τὸ σῶμα αὐτοῦ εἰς τὴν ἔρημον. οὕτως ὁ
μὲν Ἰωσὴφ ἦλθεν πρὸς τοὺς ἀδελφοὺς μετὰ χαρᾶς, αὐτοὶ δὲ
ἁψάμενοι τοῦ Ἰωσὴφ ἐξέδυσαν[12] αὐτὸν τὸν χιτῶνα καὶ
ἔβαλον αὐτὸν εἰς λάκκον[13]. ἀλλὰ ἔσωσεν αὐτὸν ὁ Ῥούβην[14]
ἐκ τῶν χειρῶν αὐτῶν λέγων, Εἰ ἔστιν ὁ ἀδελφὸς ἡμῶν, πῶς
οὖν λέγετε, Ἀποκτείνωμεν αὐτόν; λέγων ταῦτα ἤλπιζεν
ἀγαγεῖν τὸν Ἰωσὴφ πρὸς τὸν πατέρα αὐτοῦ πάλιν.

καὶ ἐγένετο φαγόντων καὶ πιόντων τῶν λοιπῶν ἀδελφῶν
Ῥούβην[14] μὴ ὄντος μετ᾿ αὐτῶν, ἔκραξεν ὁ Ἰούδας[15], Ἐὰν
ἀποκτείνωμεν αὐτόν, ἐσόμεθα ἀκάθαρτοι εἰς τὸν αἰῶνα, ὅτι
ἀδελφὸς ἡμῶν καὶ σάρξ ἡμῶν ἐστιν. πέμψωμεν αὐτὸν εἰς
ἄλλην χώραν. ὑπήκουσαν δὲ Ἰούδᾳ. καὶ οὕτως τὸν ἀδελφὸν
αὐτῶν τὸν δίκαιον παρέδωκαν[16] ἀνθρώποις Μαδιηναίοις[17]
καὶ ἀντ᾿ αὐτοῦ ἐδέξαντο δῶρα. εἶτα οἱ Μαδιηναῖοι[17] οἱ μὴ
γινώσκοντες θεὸν ἤγαγον τὸν Ἰωσὴφ εἰς Αἴγυπτον.[18] οἱ δὲ
ἀδελφοὶ ἔλαβον τὸν χιτῶνα[7] τοῦ Ἰωσὴφ καὶ ἐμόλυναν[19]
αὐτὸν τῷ αἵματι θηρίου καὶ προσήνεγκον αὐτὸν πρὸς τὸν
πατέρα αὐτῶν, λέγοντες, Ἰδοὺ τοῦτον εὕρομεν. οὐ
γινώσκομεν εἰ χιτὼν τοῦ υἱοῦ σού ἐστιν ἢ[20] οὔ. καὶ
ἐγίνωσκεν ὁ Ἰακὼβ αὐτὸν καὶ εἶπεν, Χιτών ἐστιν τοῦ υἱοῦ
μου· θηρίον πονηρὸν ἔφαγεν αὐτόν. καὶ ἔκραξεν λέγων,
Οὐκ ὄψομαι αὐτὸν πάλιν ἐπὶ γῆς. ἐγὼ καταβήσομαι πρὸς
τὸν υἱόν μου εἰς ᾅδην[21].

ἰδοὺ τὸ κακὸν τὸ γενόμενον ἐν τῇ ψυχῇ τοῦ Ἰακώβ.
ἔπεμψεν μὲν τὸν Ἰωσὴφ ὑποστρέψαι πρὸς αὐτὸν σὺν σημείῳ
εἰρήνης τῶν αὐτοῦ υἱῶν. ὑπέστρεψαν δὲ οἱ υἱοί- οὐκ
Ἰωσὴφ - φέροντες τὸν χιτῶνα μεμολυμμένον[22] ἐν αἵματι,
σημεῖον τοῦ θανάτου Ἰωσήφ. εἰ οἱ ἀδελφοὶ ἔγνωκαν τὴν
ἀγάπην τοῦ πατρὸς αὐτῶν, οὐκ ἂν ἡμάρτηκαν εἰς τὸν ἀγαπητὸν υἱὸν αὐτοῦ.

---

[1]Joseph

[2]Jacob

[3]Canaan

[4]Rachel

[5]νεώτερος - youngest

[6]Benjamin

[7]tunic, coat

[8]ἐπὶ τὸ αὐτό - together

[9]Sichem, Shechem

[10]Dothan

[11]σοφός - wise

[12]ἐκδύω - strip off (opposite of ἐνδύω)

[13]λάκκος - pit, cistern

[14]Reuben

[15]Judah

[16]they handed over

[17]Midianites

[18]Αἴγυπτος - Egypt

[19]ἐμόλυναν - they stained

[20]ἤ - or

[21]ᾅδης - Hades

[22]μεμολυμμένον - stained

Chapter 14

1. ἄξιος, -ία, -ον — worthy (axiom)
2. ἀρέσκω (with dat.) — I please
3. γλῶσσα, -ης, ἡ — tongue (glossolalia)
4. δαιμονίζομαι — I am possessed by a demon
5. δεῖ — it is necessary (imperf.= ἔδει) (an impersonal verb which takes acc. & inf.)
6. δέκα (indeclinable) — ten (Decathlon, decalog)
7. εἰσπορεύομαι — I enter (πορεύομαι)
8. ἐκπορεύομαι — I go forth
9. ἐκτείνω — I stretch out (extend, tense)
10. ἔξεστιν — it is lawful (an impersonal verb which takes dat. & inf.)
11. ἐπιβάλλω — I put on, throw over, beat against (ballistic)
12. ἐπιγινώσκω — I recognize (gnostic)
13. ἐπιθυμία, -ας, ἡ — desire
14. ἐπιτρέπω (with dat.) — I permit
15. θυγάτηρ, -τρός, ἡ — daughter
16. Ἰορδάνης, -ου, ὁ — Jordan
17. ἰχθύς, -ύος, ὁ — fish (ichthyology)
18. μέλλω (with inf.) — I am about to
19. νέος, -α, -ον — new (neolithic, neophyte), young
20. οἶνος, -ου, ὁ — wine
21. ὀργή, -ῆς, ἡ — wrath, anger
22. πέραν (with gen.) — on the other side of, beyond
23. πλήρωμα, -ματος, τό — that which fills, fulness
24. ποταμός, -οῦ, ὁ — river (hippopotamus - "river horse")
25. σκεῦος, -ους, τό — vessel
26. σπέρμα, -ματος, τό — seed (sperm)
27. σπλαγχνίζομαι — I have pity, feel sympathy for (splanchnology deals with the viscera) - followed by ἐπί and acc.
28. ταράσσω — I trouble
29. τέλος, -ους, τό — end, goal (telescope, teleological)

30. τιμή, -ῆς, ἡ   - honor (<u>timocracy</u>, rulers mo-
                         tivated by love of honor)

31. τοιοῦτος, -αύτη,   - such
    -οῦτον

32. φυλή, -ῆς, ἡ   - tribe (<u>phylo</u>geny = racial
                         history)

. . . be re-introduced to Infant Ivy,

. . . review the endings of the infinitives, and

. . . become acquainted with new uses of the infinitives.

Foundational Concepts

As you see, Infant Ivy is a product of the union of verb and noun. The infinitive is a verbal noun, i.e. a noun with verbal qualities. But an infinitive is not declined. To parse an infinitive, you look for two things only - tense and voice. Observe Infant Ivy's <u>tense</u> tears and <u>voice</u> with electrical <u>AMP</u>s.

Analyze the following English sentences:

1. To <u>swim</u> is healthy.
2. The student came to the pier <u>to swim</u>.
3. As recreation, the student chose <u>to swim</u>.

In the first sentence the infinitive functions as a subject, in the second sentence as a purpose clause, and in the last sentence, as the direct object of the verb. Do you sense the noun qualities of the infinitive? For this reason it is called a verbal noun.

Forms of the Infinitive

You have seen the endings of the infinitives with their respective pictures in Chapters Four, Eight, and Nine. Now you will see the infinitives together.

PRESENT INFINITIVE

Lu is giving a <u>present</u> to <u>Infant Ivy</u> (present infinitive), standing in the <u>rain</u> (ειν) with an <u>S-tie</u> (εσθαι).

Active - λύ ειν - to loose
Middle/Passive - λύ εσθαι - to loose for oneself (M)
                        to be loosed (P)

SECOND AORIST INFINITIVE

Note βαλ the <u>arrowist</u> with his internal change and <u>two arrows</u> and little <u>Infant Ivy</u> (second aorist infinitive). They both appear to be rather wet. βαλ says, "I'm βαλ in the <u>rain</u> (ειν) with an <u>S-tie</u> (εσθαι), ain't I (ηναι)!" Compare this with the present infinitive.

Active - βαλ εῖν - to throw
Middle - βαλ έσθαι - to throw for oneself
Passive - γραφ ῆναι - to be written
(The change in the passive to the verb γράφω is made because βάλλω has a first aorist passive but γράφω, has a second aorist passive.)

FIRST AORIST INFINITIVE

Observe Lu the <u>arrowist</u> with <u>one arrow</u> and little <u>Infant Ivy</u> (first aorist infinitive). As they converse with each other under the "σ" sun, out jumps <u>Sy</u> who says, "I'm <u>Sy</u> (σαι) with a <u>Sash-tie</u> (σασθαι) <u>ain't I</u> (θῆναι)."

Active - λῦ σαι - to loose
Middle - λύ σασθαι - to loose for oneself
Passive - λυ θῆναι - to be loosed

PERFECT INFINITIVE

Observe Lu having his tie adjusted by <u>Infant Ivy</u>. Lu is looking into the <u>mirror</u> (reduplication) and the parrot (perfect) says, "<u>A nice tie</u> (-εναι, σθαι)."

Active - λε λυ κέναι - to have loosed
Middle/Passive - λε λύ σθαι - to have loosed for oneself (M)
 λε λύ σθαι - to have been loosed (P)

PRESENT INFINITIVE OF εἰμί

Amy with her present is being addressed by little Infant Ivy (present infinitive). He says, "Ain't I (εἶναι) Infant Ivy?" The infinitive of εἰμί is εἶναι - to be.

Before observing the use of the infinitive it will be helpful to understand the following principle:

The subject of an infinitive is found in the accusative case.

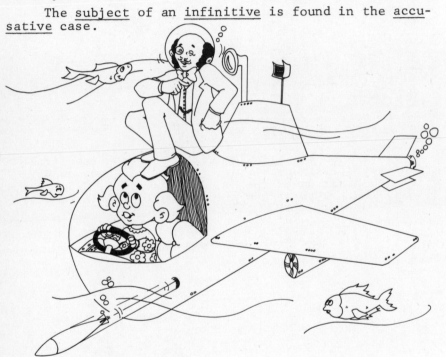

An easy way of remembering this is to see Infant Ivy and Armitage (Accusative) in the sub-jet. Observe the following examples:

δεῖ με ἀπελθεῖν
It is necessary for me to depart.

The subject of the infinitive is "με" and is found in the accusative case.

μετὰ τὸ ἐγερθῆναί με
After I have been raised.

διὰ τὸ εἶναι αὐτὸν ἐξ οἴκου . . . Δαυίδ.
Because he was out of the house of David.

214

Use of the Infinitive

You learned that an infinitive is a <u>verbal noun</u>. Therefore, it may be divided into the following categories:

1. As a <u>VERBAL</u> noun.
2. As a <u>verbal</u> <u>NOUN</u>.
3. As a complement to a verb. (Complementary infinitive)

I. The <u>Infinitive</u> <u>as</u> <u>a</u> <u>VERBAL</u> noun:

A. <u>PURPOSE</u> - The infinitive can express purpose in one of the following ways:

1. By following certain verbs.

   Matthew 5:17 - οὐκ ἦλθον καταλῦσαι (τὸν νόμον)
   I did not come to destroy (the law).

2. By following the preposition εἰς or πρὸς meaning "in order that."

   ἦλθον εἰς τὸ βλέπειν αὐτόν.
   I came (in order) to see him.

3. The preposition πρός and τό + infinitive = "so that," "in order to," "to."

   Acts 3:19 - πρὸς τὸ ἐξαλειφθῆναι ὑμῶν τὰς ἁμαρτίας (UBS = εἰς τὸ. . .).
   In order that your sins might be wiped out.

   The form ἐξαλειφθῆναι is first aorist passive infinitive of ἐξαλείφω - "to wipe out."

   The preposition πρός is a variant of εἰς.

215

Memory Aid

H. Armitage spins an <u>ace top</u> (εἰς τὸ) and a <u>pros-trate top</u> (πρὸς τὸ) in order to impress Infant Ivy's (infinitive) <u>porpoise</u> (purpose). Review the picture again seeing how both prepositions function with the accusative case and the infinitive to convey the idea of purpose.

B. The infinitive may also be used to express time (temporal).

1. πρὸ τοῦ + infinitive = "before."

πρὸ τοῦ με ἐλθεῖν.
Before I go.

Remember that the subject of an infinitive is found in the accusative case.

Memory Aid

<u>Gerard</u> (genitive) says to <u>Infant Ivy</u> (infin-itive) who is trying to hit the <u>clock</u> (temporal), "You will be a <u>pro, too</u> (πρὸ τοῦ) <u>before</u> long."

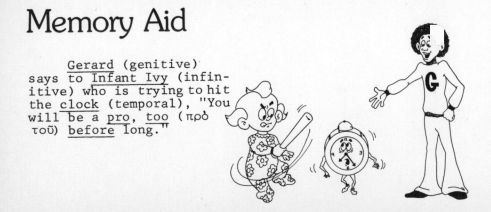

216

2. ἐν τῷ + infinitive = "while"

Matthew 13:4 - καὶ ἐν τῷ σπείρειν αὐτόν. And while he was sowing.

Memory Aid

While Demetrius (dative) pulls Infant Ivy (infinitive) in tow (ἐν τῷ) little Infant Ivy is fixing his clock (temporal).

3. μετὰ τό + infinitive = "after"

Matthew 26:32 - μετὰ τό ἐγερθῆναί με. After I have been raised.

Memory Aid

H. Armitage (accusative) spins a metal top (μετὰ τό) for Infant Ivy (infinitive) after he has fixed a clock (temporal).

C. The infinitive may be used in a causal clause.

διὰ τό + infinitive = "on account of," "because"

John 2:24 - διὰ τὸ αὐτὸν γινώσκειν πάντας. Because he knew all (persons).

Memory Aid

H. Armitage (accusative is resting against Infant Ivy's D-top (διὰ τό). This D-top is upon a ledger account with bee-gauze (because) wrapped around it. The word "gauze" will remind you of the causal use of the infinitive with διὰ τό.

D.   The infinitive may be used in a result clause.

ὥστε + infinitive = "so that," "with the result that"

1 Thess. 1:8 - ὥστε μὴ χρείαν ἔχειν ἡμᾶς λαλεῖν (to speak).
With the result that we have no need to speak.

Memory Aid

Observe the host (ὥστε) re-salt (result) Infant Ivy (infinitive).

218

II. The _infinitive_ as a verbal NOUN:

As a noun, the infinitive will be found as:

A. The Subject.

Phil. 1:21 - τὸ ἀποθανεῖν κέρδος (advantage)
To die is an advantage.

ἔξεστιν θεραπεύειν ἐν τῷ σαββάτῳ.
To heal on the Sabbath is lawful.

B. The Object.

Matthew 12:38 - Διδάσκαλε, θέλομεν ἀπὸ σοῦ σημεῖον ἰδεῖν.
Teacher, we wish to see a sign from you. The infinitive ἰδεῖν is the object of θέλομεν.

III. The complementary infinitive.

An infinitive may complement a verb, i.e. complete it. For example, if we hear someone say, "I am about to . . ." we normally ask the question, "What are you about to do?" The same is true for verbs such as "I begin" (ἄρχομαι) or "I wish" (θέλω). Normally, they will be complemented or completed by an infinitive.

Mark 10:47 - ἤρξατο κράζειν.
He began to cry out.

Matt. 16:21 - δεῖ αὐτὸν . . . ἀπελθεῖν.
It is necessary for him to depart.

John 12:21 - θέλομεν τὸν Ἰησοῦν ἰδεῖν.
We wish to see Jesus.

Thus, there are certain words which tell you that an infinitive will appear. Just as you learned red flags for the subjunctive mood (e.g. ἵνα - "in order that" and ἐάν - "if"), so you will learn that there are red flags for the infinitive. Observe each red flag and "get the feel" of the complementary infinitive that follows.

δεῖ	- it is necessary
ἔξεστιν	- it is lawful
μέλλω	- I am about to
ἄρχομαι	- I begin
συμφέρει	- It is profitable, expedient
ὀφείλω	- I ought to
δύναμαι	- I am able to
ζητέω	- I seek to

Practice

The following sentences will help you translate the infinitive. Parse each infinitive and be aware of the ways in which it functions. Also, remind yourself that Infant Ivy's sub-jet (subject) belongs to Armitage (acc.).

1. Matthew 22:3 - οὐκ ἤθελον ἐλθεῖν.
2. Luke 18:10 - Ἄνθρωποι δύο (two) ἀνέβησαν εἰς τὸ ἱερὸν προσεύξασθαι.
3. Matthew 17:4 - Κύριε, καλόν ἐστιν ἡμᾶς ὧδε εἶναι.
4. Matthew 16:27 - μέλλει ὁ υἱὸς τοῦ ἀνθρώπου ἔρχεσθαι.
5. Mark 6:2 - ἤρξατο διδάσκειν ἐν τῇ συναγωγῇ.
6. John 19:7 - ὀφέλει ἀποθανεῖν.
7. Luke 19:11 - διὰ τὸ ἐγγὺς εἶναι Ἰερουσαλὴμ αὐτόν.
8. Acts 19:21 - Μετὰ τὸ γενέσθαι με ἐκεῖ δεῖ με καὶ Ῥώμην ἰδεῖν.
9. Philippians 1:29 - ὑμῖν ἐχαρίσθη . . . οὐ μόνον τὸ εἰς αὐτὸν πιστεύειν ἀλλὰ καὶ τὸ ὑπὲρ αὐτοῦ πάσχειν.

KEY

1. They were not desiring to come.
2. Two men went up to the temple to pray.
3. Lord, it is good for us to be here.
4. The Son of Man is about to come.
5. He began to teach in the synagogue.
6. He ought to die.
7. Because he was near Jerusalem.
8. After I have been there, it is necessary for me to see Rome also.
9. To you it was given . . . not only to believe in him, but also to suffer on behalf of him.

Enrichment

Phil. 1:29 - ὑμῖν ἐχαρίσθη οὐ μόνον τὸ εἰς αὐτὸν πιστεύειν ἀλλὰ καὶ τὸ ὑπὲρ αὐτοῦ πάσχειν. "Not only was the act of believing in him freely given to you, but also the act of suffering on his behalf" (the translation is "wooden").

It may seem surprising, but the two infinitives (they are underlined) each with the neuter article τό, form the dual subject of the verb ἐχαρίσθη. Believing in him and suffering in his behalf are the twin gifts graciously bestowed on the Christians at Philippi. The infinitives are important but so are the prepositional phrases that come between the article and the infinitive. Not believing alone but believing in him, not just any suffering but suffering for him. The text may be an acid test for the church in any age.

Assignment

Ἰωσὴφ[1] καὶ οἱ ἀδελφοὶ αὐτοῦ - Part Two

Ἰωσὴφ δὲ ἤχθη εἰς Αἴγυπτον[2] κἀκεῖ μετὰ τὸ εἶναι ἐν φυλακῇ αὐτόν, ἄξιος ἄρχων ἐγένετο ἐπὶ τὴν γῆν ἀρέσκων τῷ θεῷ καὶ ἐν λόγῳ καὶ ἐν ἔργῳ. καὶ ἀπεκαλύφθη τῷ Ἰωσὴφ ὅτι ἔμελλεν λιμὸς[3] ἄρτου εἶναι. πρὸ δὲ τοῦ ἐλθεῖν τὰ ἔτη τοῦ λιμοῦ,[3] ἔλαβεν ὁ Ἰωσὴφ γυναῖκα καὶ δι' αὐτῆς ἔσχεν δύο υἱούς. μετὰ τοῦτο συνήγαγεν ὁ Ἰωσὴφ ὑπὲρ τοῦ λαοῦ σῖτον συναχθέντα ἐν τοῖς ἔτεσιν τοῖς καλοῖς, ὅτι ἐσπείροντο τὰ σπέρματα καὶ ἔφερεν ἡ γῆ σῖτον καὶ συνῆγεν ὁ Ἰωσὴφ τὸν σῖτον ὡς τὴν ἄμμον[4] τῆς θαλάσσης. εἶτα ἤρξατο ὁ λιμός.[3]

καὶ ἠκούσθη ἐν ταῖς φυλαῖς τῶν λαῶν πέραν τοῦ ποταμοῦ Ἰορδάνου ὅτι ἦν σῖτος ἐν Αἰγύπτῳ.[2] διὰ τοῦτο κατῆλθον καὶ εἰσεπορεύθησαν εἰς Αἴγυπτον εἰς τὸ ἀγοράσαι σῖτον φέροντες μετ' αὐτῶν σκεύη. καὶ ἤρχοντο[5] πρὸ τοῦ Ἰωσὴφ καὶ μετὰ τὸ ἀγοράσαι ὑπέστρεφον[5] πρὸς τὰς ἰδίας χώρας χαίροντες.

καὶ ἐν τῷ πληρώματι τῶν ἡμερῶν ἐκείνων οἱ δέκα ἀδελφοὶ τοῦ Ἰωσὴφ κατέβησαν καὶ ὤφθησαν αὐτῷ. καὶ Ἰωσὴφ μὲν ἐπεγίνωσκεν αὐτούς, αὐτοὶ δὲ οὐκ ἐπεγίνωσκον αὐτόν, καὶ ἔπεσον πρὸς τοὺς πόδας αὐτοῦ ἐν τιμῇ. καὶ ἐθαύμασεν Ἰωσὴφ καὶ ἔλεγεν ἐν ἑαυτῷ, ὅτι Τοῦτό ἐστιν τὸ ἀποκαλυφθέν μοι ἐν ἐκείνῃ τῇ νυκτὶ ἐν Χανάαν.[6]

εἶτα ἐν ὀργῇ ἐπείρασεν[7] Ἰωσὴφ αὐτούς, λέγων αὐτοῖς ἐν τῇ γλώσσῃ Αἰγύπτου δι' ἑρμηνευτοῦ,[8] Οὐκ ἐστὲ ἄξιοι ἀγοράσαι σῖτον, κατάσκοποι[9] γάρ ἐστε· εἰσήλθετε εἰς τὸ κατασκοπεῦσαι[10] τὴν χώραν ἡμῶν. οὐκ ἔξεστιν ὑμῖν κατάσκοποι εἶναι. ἀπεκρίθησαν αὐτῷ ἐν τῇ γλώσσῃ αὐτῶν, Οὔ, κύριε, οὐκ ἐσμὲν κατάσκοποι ἀλλὰ δώδεκα ἐσμὲν ἀδελφοί, υἱοὶ τοῦ αὐτοῦ ἀνδρὸς καὶ ὁ νεώτερος[11] μετὰ τοῦ πατρός, ὁ δὲ ἕτερος οὐκ ἔστιν. ἀπεκρίθη δὲ ὁ Ἰωσὴφ, λέγων, Δεῖ με πειράσαι τὰ ῥήματα ὑμῶν. καὶ ἐπέβαλεν τὰς χεῖρας αὐτοῦ τῷ Συμεών[12] τῷ ἀδελφῷ αὐτῶν καὶ ἤρθη ὁ Συμεὼν εἰς φυλακήν. εἶπεν οὖν αὐτοῖς Ἐὰν μὴ ἀγάγητε πρός με τὸν ἀδελφὸν ὑμῶν τὸν νεώτερον[11] οὐκ ὄψεσθε τὸ πρόσωπόν μου εἰς τὸν αἰῶνα, οὐδὲ ἀπολυθήσεται ἐκ τῆς φυλακῆς ὁ ἀδελφὸς ὑμῶν Συμεών.

καὶ ἐταράχθησαν καὶ ἕκαστος εἶπεν πρὸς τὸν ἀδελφὸν
αὐτοῦ λέγων, Ἰδοὺ ἐν ἁμαρτίᾳ ἡμεῖς ἐσμεν περὶ τοῦ
ἀδελφοῦ ἡμῶν Ἰωσήφ, ὅτι ἐπετρέψαμεν τοῖς Μαδιηναίοις[13]
ἀγοράσαι αὐτὸν ὡς δοῦλον καὶ ἡμεῖς οὐκ ἠκούσαμεν τὴν
φωνὴν αὐτοῦ ἐν τῷ κράζειν αὐτὸν ἡμῖν ἐκ τοῦ λάκκου.[14]
καὶ διὰ τὸ ἀκοῦσαι τὸν Ἰωσήφ τοιούτους τοὺς λόγους,
ἐταράχθη καὶ ἐσπλαγχνίσθη ἐπ' αὐτοὺς ἔχων ἐπιθυμίαν
ἅψασθαι τῶν χειρῶν αὐτῶν καὶ ἀποκαλύψαι αὐτοῖς ἑαυτόν.

Δεῖ δὲ νῦν ἡμᾶς ἰδεῖν τὸ τέλος τοῦ Ἰωσήφ καὶ πῶς
ἐγνώσθη τοῖς ἀδελφοῖς αὐτοῦ. μετὰ τὸ ἀγαγεῖν αὐτοὺς τὸν
Βενιαμὶν[15] τὸν νεώτερον[11] ἀδελφὸν εἰς Αἴγυπτον,[2] καὶ
συναχθέντων αὐτῶν ἐν τῇ οἰκίᾳ τοῦ Ἰωσήφ, ἔκλαιεν[16]
Ἰωσήφ πρὸ αὐτῶν λέγων, Ἐγώ εἰμι Ἰωσήφ· εἰ[17] ἐστιν ἔτι
εἰρήνη τῷ πατρί μου; καὶ ἐταράχθησαν καὶ ἤθελον ἀποκριθῆναι αὐτῷ ἀλλ' οὐκ εἶχον[18] λέγειν διὰ τὸ ταραχθῆναι τὰς
καρδίας αὐτῶν. ὁ δὲ Ἰωσήφ σπλαγχνισθεὶς εἶπεν, Ἐγώ
εἰμι Ἰωσήφ· οὐκ οὖν ὑμεῖς ἀπεστάλκατέ με ὧδε ἀλλ' ἡ[19]
ὁ θεός. ἀναβάντες εἰς Χαναὰν[6] εἰσελεύσεσθε πρὸς τὸν
πατέρα μου ἀπαγγέλλοντες αὐτῷ τὴν τιμὴν καὶ δόξαν μου.
καὶ ἀναλαβόντες οἴσετε αὐτὸν μεθ' ὑμῶν ἵνα μένῃ σὺν ἐμοὶ
καὶ χαίρῃ μεθ' ἡμῶν, φάγεται γὰρ μεθ' ἡμῶν τὸν ἄρτον τὸν
ἀπεσταλμένον ἡμῖν ὑπὸ τοῦ θεοῦ.

μετὰ ταῦτα ἐκτείνων τὴν χεῖρα ἥψατο αὐτῶν καὶ
ἔκλαιεν[16] ἐπὶ Βενιαμὶν καὶ ἐπὶ τοὺς ἄλλους ἀδελφούς. διὰ
τοῦτο τοῦ φόβου αὐτῶν ἀπελθόντος, ἔχαιρον οἱ ἀδελφοὶ
μετ' αὐτοῦ.

---

[1] Ἰωσήφ - Joseph   [2] Αἴγυπτος - Egypt
[3] λιμός - famine   [4] ἄμμος, ἡ - sand
[5] customary imperfects "would come," "would return"
[6] Χαναάν - Canaan   [7] πειράζω - put to the test
[8] ἑρμηνευτής - interpreter
[9] κατάσκοπος - spy   [10] κατασκοπεύω - to spy out
[11] νεώτερος - youngest   [12] Συμεών - Simeon (Gk. inde-
[13] Μαδιηναῖοι - Midianites   clinable)
[15] Βενιαμίν - Benjamin   [14] λάκκος - pit, cistern
[16] ἔκλαιεν - from κλαίω - weep (he began to weep)
[17] εἰ - interrog.
      part.   [18] εἶχον - imperfect of ἔχω -
[19] ἀλλ' ἡ - but, except   sometimes = "be able"

Chapter 15

1. ἀγαπάω — I love (ἀγάπη)
2. αἰτέω — I ask
3. ἀκολουθέω (takes dative case) — I follow (acolyte)
4. Γαλιλαῖος, -α, -ον — Galilean (Galilean)
5. γεννάω — I beget, become the father of
6. δοκέω — I think, suppose, 3rd person singular = "it seems" (docetism - says Christ only "seemed" to suffer)
7. ἐλεέω (foll. by acc. case) — I have mercy - Κύριε, ἐλέησον - Lord, have mercy!
8. ἐνώπιον (w/gen.) — before, in the sight of
9. ἔξω (w/gen.) — outside (exodus) - preposition or adverb
10. ἐπικαλέω — I name, call upon (compare καλέω)
11. ἐρωτάω — I ask, request
12. εὐλογέω — I bless (eulogy)
13. εὐχαριστέω (w.dat.) — I give thanks (eucharist)
14. ζάω — I live (zoology)
15. ζητέω — I seek
16. θεωρέω — I perceive (theory)
17. καλέω — I call (call)
18. λαλέω — I speak (glossolalia)
19. μαρτυρέω — I bear witness (martyr)
20. μετανοέω — I repent (compare μετάνοια)
21. μηδέ (cf. οὐδέ) — and not
22. μηκέτι (cf. οὐκέτι) — no longer
23. παραγίνομαι — I arrive (γίνομαι)
24. παρακαλέω — I invite, beseech, exhort (paraclete)
25. περιπατέω — I walk (peripatetic)
26. πληρόω — I fill, fulfill (compare πλήρωμα)
27. ποιέω — I make, do (poet)
28. προσκυνέω (usually foll. by dat. case) — I worship
29. σταυρόω — I crucify
30. τηρέω — I keep

31. τιμάω	I honor (compare τιμή)
32. ὑπάγω	- I go away (cf. ἄγω)
33. φανερόω	- I reveal, show (phanerosis = attaining of visibility, compare φανερός)
34. φιλέω	- I love (philharmonic)
35. φίλος, -η, -ον	- devoted, friend (philharmonic)
36. φοβέομαι[1]	- I am afraid, fear (phobia)
37. ὥσπερ	- just as (compare ὡς)

-----

[1]The verb φοβέομαι is sometimes followed by the negative μή "lest" with the subjunctive.

(1) Acts 27:17, φοβούμενοι . . . μὴ εἰς τὴν Σύρτιν ἐκπέσωσιν, "fearing . . . lest they should run aground on the Syrtis."

(2) Acts 5:26, ἐφοβοῦντο γάρ . . . μὴ λιθασθῶσιν, "For they were afraid . . . lest they be stoned."

It is possible, however, for μὴ to mean "lest" with other verbs. Compare Mark 13:36, μὴ ἐλθὼν . . . εὕρη ὑμᾶς καθεύδοντας, "Lest, when he comes . . . he find you sleeping."

IN THIS LESSON YOU WILL:

   . . . meet a new class of verbs called contract verbs,

   . . . learn how to parse and translate contract verbs.

Foundational Concepts

Contract Verbs

Previously when you learned verbs in the vocabulary, you found that all ended:
1. with a long vowel - λύω
2. with a diphthong - θεραπεύω, or
3. with a consonant - ἔχω

However, there is another class of verbs that end in short vowels, in "α," "ε," or "ο." As you pronounce them you will easily identify them because of a "hiccup" sound at the end of the stem. A few samples follow. Pronounce the forms, noting the hiccup sound.

ἀγαπάω I love	ποιέω I do, make	πληρόω I fill, fulfill
τιμάω I honor	λαλέω I speak	φανερόω I manifest

Did you notice that peculiar short sound before the personal ending? Each one of these verbs is a contract verb. Contract verbs end in a short "α," "ε," or "ο."

Before examining some peculiarities of the contract verbs, it may be helpful to try your hand at some parsing. Take a guess . . . an educated guess, of course, and then check yourself with the key.

T V M P N	Vocabulary Form	Translation

1. ἀγαπήσω
2. ἐποίησεν
3. πεπληρώκαμεν
4. ζήσομεν
5. λαλήσει
6. ἐφανερώθη

<u>KEY</u>

1. FAI 1 S - ἀγαπάω - I shall love
2. 1AAI 3 S - ποιέω - (S)he did, made
3. PfAI 1 P - πληρόω - We have filled, fulfilled
4. FAI 1 P - ζάω - We shall live
5. FAI 3 S - λαλέω - (S)he will speak
6. 1API 3 S - φανερόω - He, she, it was revealed

Lengthening

The tense indicators and personal endings all correspond with what you already know. One thing only is different. The short vowel at the end of the stem is lengthened before its tense suffix. Observe what happened in the first three examples:

1. The "α" in ἀγαπάω lengthened to η in ἀγαπήσω
2. The "ε" in ποιέω lengthened to η in ἐποίησεν.
3. The "ο" in πληρόω lengthened to ω in πεπληρώκαμεν.

The rules for lengthening follow the same rules as for the augment.

The principal parts of the three types of contract verbs are listed below. Note very carefully the lengthening of vowels before the tense suffix.

PRESENT	FUTURE	AOR.ACT.	PERF.ACT.	PERF.PASS.	AOR.PASS.
ἀγαπάω	ἀγαπήσω	ἠγάπησα	ἠγάπηκα	ἠγάπημαι	ἠγαπήθην
ποιέω	ποιήσω	ἐποίησα	πεποίηκα	πεποίημαι	ἐποιήθην
πληρόω	πληρώσω	ἐπλήρωσα	πεπλήρωκα	πεπλήρωμαι	ἐπληρώθην

226

Contraction

We have just observed the LENGTHENING of vowels before the tense suffix. Now we turn to the present and imperfect tenses. Since neither of these two tenses has a suffix, something else will happen, i.e. CONTRACTION. Thus, the final short vowels, "α," "ε," and "o," will CONTRACT with the vowels of the personal endings. They follow certain patterns or rules of contraction.

GENERAL.   Any α, ε, o, + ω = ω

Stem Vowel	+	Personal Ending Vowel	=	New Form
ἀγαπά	+	ω	=	ἀγαπῶ
ποιέ	+	ω	=	ποιῶ
πληρό	+	ω	=	πληρῶ

As you may observe, each one of the "new forms" is the PAI 1 S. Thus you will never see ἀγαπάω in the New Testament, only ἀγαπῶ. However, you will find ἀγαπάω listed in the Lexicon. You may be wondering, "Why am I learning ἀγαπάω when I will never see it that way in the New Testament?" Good question! The answer is that the "α" will merge into the personal endings according to a fixed pattern. You will see the new form and then be able to translate it correctly because you know its root form. Now, look at some more specific patterns. Fill in the column entitled "new form" and check yourself by the key.

SPECIAL.

Verbs with stems ending in "α."
1. α + o (υ) = ω
2. α + any other vowel or diphthong = α
    (iota retained as subscript except in infinitive)

Stem Vowel	+	Ending Vowel	=	New Form
ἀγαπά	+	ομεν	=	?
ἀγαπά	+	εις	=	?
ἀγαπά	+	ειν	=	?

KEY
ἀγαπῶμεν
ἀγαπᾷς
ἀγαπᾶν

Verbs with <u>stems</u> ending in "ε̲."   1. ε + ε(ι) = ει
                                          2. ε + ο(υ) = ου
                                          3. ε + η   = η

Stem Vowel	+	Ending Vowel	=	New Form
ποιέ	+	εις	=	?
ἐποίε	+	ον	=	?
ποιέ	+	η	=	?

KEY

ποιεῖς
ἐποίουν
ποιῇ

Verbs with <u>stems</u> ending in "ο̲." 1. ο + ε or ο(υ) = ου
                                         2. ο + η   = ω
                                         3. ο + ει, η   = οι
                                            Inf. -οῦν.

Stem Vowel	+	Ending Vowel	=	New Form
πληρό	+	ομεν	=	?
πληρό	+	εις	=	?

KEY

πληροῦμεν
πληροῖς

Now, you can put it all together by two simple keys:

LENGTHENING BEFORE TENSE SUFFIX
(All tenses but present and imperfect)

"ε̲" are being pulled into an "η,"
being stretched out before the "σ"
sun.

Also, an "o" is being stretched to "ω" before a sigma sun.

CONTRACTION IN PRESENT AND IMPERFECT

An "ε" is being pushed in with an ει and they are really squashed, and so an ει pops out.

One further clue that distinguishes the imperfect from the present is the augment. For example, if you were to see ἐκάλουν, you would first see the "ου" and note that this is a contraction. The augment points to the imperfect tense and you sense that the ending is either first singular or third plural, i.e. "ον."

Practice

With these two important clues in mind, parse the following forms and translate.

T	V	M	P	N	Vocabulary Form	Translation

1. πληροῦτε
2. ἀγαπήσομεν
3. ἐπληρώθημεν
4. ἐλάλουν
5. τοῦ ἀγαπῶντος
6. πεποίηκας
7. ἠγάπησαν
8. ποιοῦμεν

1. PAI 2 P   - πληρόω - you fill, fulfill
2. FAI 1 P   - ἀγαπάω - we shall love
3. API 1 P   - πληρόω - we were filled
4. 1AI 1S, 3P - λαλέω - I was speaking, they were
                        speaking
5. PAP MSG - ἀγαπάω - of the one who loves
6. Perf.AI 2 S - ποιέω - you have made
7. AAI 3 P   - ἀγαπάω - they loved
8. PAI 1 P   - ποιέω - we do, make

Enrichment

In John 16:26-27, Jesus says, ἐν ἐκείνῃ τῇ ἡμέρα ἐν τῷ ὀνόματί μου αἰτήσεσθε, καὶ οὐ λέγω ὑμῖν ὅτι ἐγὼ ἐρωτήσω τὸν πατέρα περὶ ὑμῶν. αὐτὸς γὰρ ὁ πατὴρ φιλεῖ ὑμᾶς ὅτι ὑμεῖς ἐμὲ πεφιλήκατε καὶ πεπιστεύκατε ὅτι ἐγὼ παρὰ τοῦ θεοῦ ἐξῆλθον.

Contract verbs meet us frequently in the Upper Room Discourse, e.g. αἰτέω, ἐρωτάω, φιλέω, and others. In the verses above, Jesus says, "You have loved me," (πεφιλή-κατε - perfect), and therefore, "you shall ask in my name," (αἰτήσεσθε ἐν τῷ ὀνόματί μου).   In the light of the enduring bond with him (πεφιλήκατε) and in view of his promise (αἰτήσεσθε), the disciples are assured of the enduring quality of the Father's love (φιλεῖ).   He continues to love you, says Jesus.

Assignment

Ἐν τῇ ἀρχῇ τῶν ἐσχάτων ἡμερῶν αὐτοῦ ἐπὶ τῆς γῆς,
Ἰησοῦς εἰσῆλθεν εἰς Ἱεροσόλυμα[1]. καὶ ἐν τῇ ὁδῷ ἠκολούθησαν αὐτῷ Ἰουδαῖοι καὶ Γαλιλαῖοι καὶ ἔκραξαν μετὰ
χαρᾶς, Εὐλογημένος ὁ ἐρχόμενος ἐν ὀνόματι κυρίου. ἀλλ'
ἐταράχθησαν οἱ Φαρισαῖοι. μαρτυροῦσιν δὲ αἱ γραφαὶ ὅτι
παραγενόμενος ἐκαθάρισεν ὁ Ἰησοῦς τὸ ἱερὸν ὅπου συνήχθησαν οἱ προσκυνοῦντες. ἦσαν δὲ Γαλιλαῖοι τῶν ἀναβαιν-
όντων ἵνα προσκυνήσωσιν. οὗτοι μετανοήσαντες προσῆλθον
τοῖς μαθηταῖς ζητοῦντες τὸν κύριον καὶ ἠρώτων αὐτοὺς
λέγοντες, Θέλομεν ἰδεῖν τὸν Ἰησοῦν. καὶ ἀκούσας Ἰησοῦς
ἀπεκρίθη αὐτοῖς· Ἐλήλυθεν ἡ ὥρα ἵνα δοξασθῇ ὁ υἱὸς τοῦ
ἀνθρώπου. βάπτισμα γὰρ ἔχω βαπτισθῆναι. ἐὰν μὴ τὸ
σπέρμα τοῦ σίτου πεσὸν εἰς τὴν γῆν ἀποθάνῃ, αὐτὸ μόνον
μένει· ἐὰν δὲ ἀποθάνῃ, καρπὸν φέρει. ἰδοὺ νῦν ὁ ἄρχων
τοῦ κόσμου τούτου ἐκβληθήσεται ἔξω. ἐστὶν ἔτι μικρὸς
χρόνος. ὁ περιπατῶν ἐν τῷ σκότει οὐ γινώσκει ποῦ ὑπάγει.
ἐὰν ἀκολουθῆτέ μοι, τιμήσει ὑμᾶς ὁ πατήρ. ὁ γὰρ πιστεύων
εἰς ἐμὲ πιστεύει εἰς τὸν πέμψαντά με, καὶ ὁ θεωρῶν ἐμὲ
θεωρεῖ τὸν πέμψαντά με. καὶ ἄλλοις τοιούτοις ῥήμασιν
ἐλάλησεν Ἰησοῦς πρὸς τοὺς ζητοῦντας ἀκολουθεῖν αὐτῷ καὶ
ἀρέσκειν τῷ πατρί.

μετὰ ταῦτα ἐπιγινώσκων Ἰησοῦς ὅτι αὐτὸς μέλλει
σταυρωθῆναι καὶ ἀποθανεῖν, μηκέτι ἔχων καιρὸν μετὰ τῶν
ἰδίων, ἐκάλεσεν αὐτοὺς πρὸς ἑαυτὸν ἵνα εὐλογήσῃ αὐτοὺς
καὶ φανερώσῃ τὴν ἀγάπην αὐτοῦ περὶ αὐτῶν. οὕτως γὰρ
γέγραπται ἐν τῇ μαρτυρίᾳ τοῦ εὐαγγελίου ὅτι Ἰησοῦς
ἀγαπήσας τοὺς ἰδίους τοὺς ἐν τῷ κόσμῳ, εἰς τέλος ἠγάπησεν
αὐτούς. καὶ διὰ τὸ ἀγαπῆσαι αὐτὸν αὐτούς, ἐφανέρωσεν
αὐτοῖς ὑπόδειγμα[2]. ἐγερθεὶς γὰρ ἐκ τοῦ δείπνου ἔβαλεν
ὕδωρ[3] εἰς σκεῦος καὶ ἤρξατο νίπτειν[4] τοὺς πόδας τῶν
μαθητῶν σπλαγχνισθεὶς ἐπ' αὐτούς. εἶτα ἐμαρτύρησεν
αὐτοῖς λέγων, Ἐγὼ ἐφανέρωσα ὑμῖν ὑπόδειγμα[2] ὅπως καθὼς
ἐγὼ ἐποίησα ὑμῖν καὶ ὑμεῖς ποιῆτε. ἤδη ὑμεῖς καθαροὶ

ἐστε διὰ τὸν λόγον ὃν[5] λελάληκα ὑμῖν. ἔτι μικρὸν[6] καὶ ὁ
κόσμος με οὐκέτι θεωρεῖ, ὑμεῖς δὲ θεωρεῖτέ με, ὅτι ἐγὼ
ζῶ, καὶ ὑμεῖς ζήσετε. ὑμεῖς φίλοι μού ἐστε ἐὰν ποιῆτε
τὰς ἐντολάς μου. καὶ αὕτη ἐστὶν ἡ ἐντολή μου ἵνα[7]
ἀγαπᾶτε ἀλλήλους καθὼς ἠγάπησα ὑμᾶς.

εἶτα μετὰ ταῦτα ἐδίδαξεν αὐτοὺς περὶ τοῦ πατρός,
λέγων, Τὰ ῥήματα ἃ[8] λέγω ὑμῖν, ἀπ' ἐμαυτοῦ οὐ λαλῶ, ὁ δὲ
πατὴρ ὁ ἐν ἐμοὶ μένων ποιεῖ τὰ ἔργα αὐτοῦ. ὁ ἔχων τὰς
ἐντολάς μου καὶ τηρῶν αὐτάς, ἐκεῖνός ἐστιν ὁ ἀγαπῶν με·
ὁ δὲ ἀγαπῶν με, ἀγαπηθήσεται ὑπὸ τοῦ πατρός μου, κἀγὼ
ἀγαπήσω αὐτὸν καὶ φανερώσω αὐτῷ ἐμαυτόν. ἐν ἐκείνῃ τῇ
ἡμέρᾳ αἰτήσεσθε ἐν τῷ ὀνόματί μου, καὶ οὐ λέγω ὑμῖν ὅτι
ἐρωτήσω τὸν πατέρα περὶ ὑμῶν. αὐτὸς γὰρ ὁ πατὴρ φιλεῖ
ὑμᾶς ὅτι ὑμεῖς ἐμὲ πεφιλήκατε καὶ πεπιστεύκατε ὅτι ἐγὼ
παρὰ τοῦ θεοῦ ἐξῆλθον. καὶ νῦν ἐκπορεύσομαι πρὸς τὸν
πατέρα.

λοιπόν,[9] ἐνώπιον τῶν μαθητῶν ἐδίδαξεν Ἰησοῦς πάλιν
μαρτυρῶν τῷ πνεύματι τῷ ἁγίῳ. ὥσπερ γὰρ ἐλάλησέν ποτε
ὅτι δεῖ τὸν Φαρισαῖον, Νικόδημον[10] γεννηθῆναι ἐκ τοῦ
πνεύματος, οὕτως νῦν ἐφανέρωσεν αὐτοῖς ὅτι ὁ παράκλητός[11]
ἐστιν τὸ πνεῦμα, λέγων, Ἐὰν μὴ ἀπέλθω, ὁ παράκλητος[11]
οὐκ ἐλεύσεται πρὸς ὑμᾶς. ὅταν δὲ ἔλθῃ ἐκεῖνος, οὐ λαλήσει
ἀφ' ἑαυτοῦ. λήμψεται γὰρ τὰ περὶ ἐμοῦ καὶ ἀποκαλύψει
αὐτὰ πρὸς ὑμᾶς. ἐλάλησεν δὲ τοῦτο ὅτι ἐδόκουν οἱ μαθηταὶ
ὅτι μέλλει Ἰησοῦς μένειν μετ' αὐτῶν εἰς τὸν αἰῶνα.

εἶτα πληρώσας τὴν διδαχὴν αὐτοῦ καὶ ἐλεήσας τοὺς
μαθητὰς ἐν ταῖς χρείαις αὐτῶν, προσηύξατο εὐχαριστῶν τῷ
πατρὶ λέγων, Πάτερ, ἐλήλυθεν ἡ ὥρα· ἐρωτῶ ἵνα δοξάσῃς
σου τὸν υἱόν, εἰς τὸ τιμῆσαι αὐτόν σε. ἐφανέρωσά σου τὸ
ὄνομα τοῖς μαθηταῖς μου, καὶ νῦν ἐρωτῶ περὶ αὐτῶν. οὐκ
εἰσὶν ἐκ τοῦ κόσμου καθὼς ἐγὼ οὐκ εἰμὶ ἐκ τοῦ κόσμου.
οὐκ ἐρωτῶ ἵνα αἴρῃς αὐτοὺς ἐκ τοῦ κόσμου ἀλλ' ἵνα
τηρήσῃς αὐτοὺς ἐκ τοῦ πονηροῦ. οὐ περὶ τούτων δὲ ἐρωτῶ
μόνον, ἀλλὰ καὶ περὶ τῶν πιστευόντων διὰ τοῦ λόγου αὐτῶν
εἰς ἐμέ, ἵνα καὶ αὐτοὶ ἐν ἡμῖν ὦσιν, ἵνα ὁ κόσμος
πιστεύσῃ ὅτι σύ με ἀπέσταλκας.

---

1. Ἱεροσόλυμα - Jerusalem

^{2}ὑπόδειγμα - pattern, example

^{3}ὕδωρ - water

^{4}νίπτω - wash

^{5}ὅν - which (relative pronoun)

^{6}ἔτι μικρόν - yet a little while, soon

^{7}The conjunction ἵνα introduces here the content of the commandment. Thus ἵνα may sometimes function like ὅτι.

^{8}ἅ - which (relative pronoun)

^{9}λοιπόν - finally

^{10}Νικόδημος - Nicodemus

^{11}παράκλητος - "paraclete," counselor (one called alongside to help)

Chapter 16

1. ἀληθής, -ές   - true (compare ἀλήθεια)
2. ἄφεσις, -έσεως, ἡ - forgiveness
3. βασιλεύς, -έως, ὁ - king (<u>basilica</u>)
4. γραμματεύς, -έως, ὁ - scribe (<u>grammatical</u>)
5. δύναμις, -μεως, ἡ - power (<u>dynamo</u>)
6. δύο   - two (<u>duet</u>)
7. εἰ μή   - if not (see ἐὰν μή), unless, except
8. εἷς, μία, ἕν   - one (<u>hen</u>otheism). Compare Eph. 4:5.
9. ἐπιστολή, -ῆς, ἡ - epistle, letter (<u>epistle</u>)
10. εὐθέως   - immediately (like εὐθύς)
11. ἱερεύς, -ρέως, ὁ - priest (<u>hier</u>archy)
12. κρίσις, -σεως, ἡ - judgment (<u>critic</u>)
13. μέγας, μεγάλη, μέγα - great (<u>mega</u>phone, <u>mega</u>lomania)
14. μηδείς, μηδεμία, μηδέν (with other than the indicative) - no one, nothing
15. οὐδείς, οὐδεμία, οὐδέν - no one, nothing
16. ὀφείλω   - I owe, ought
17. πᾶς, πᾶσα, πᾶν - every, each, all (<u>pan</u>theism)
18. πέντε (indecl.) - five (<u>Pent</u>ateuch = consisting of five books)
19. πίστις, -τεως, ἡ - faith (<u>pist</u>ic = relating to faith). cf. πιστεύω
20. πλῆθος, -ους, τό - multitude (plethora)
21. πλήρης, -ες - full (compare πλήρωμα)
22. πόλις, -λεως, ἡ - city (metro<u>polis</u>)
23. πολύς, πολλή, πολύ - much, many (<u>poly</u>gon). cf. the articular plural οἱ πολλοί = "hoi polloi"
24. στόμα, -ματος, τό - mouth (<u>stoma</u>titis)
25. τέσσαρες (m.f.), τέσσαρα (n.) - four (Dia<u>tessaron</u>)
26. τρεῖς (m.f.), τρία (n.) - three (trio)
27. ὕδωρ, ὕδατος, τό - water (<u>hyd</u>rant)
28. φῶς, φωτός, τό - light (<u>phot</u>ography)

29. χωρίς (adverbial   - without
    prep. with gen.)

IN THIS LESSON YOU WILL:

. . . be introduced to liquid verbs,

. . . become familiar with some miscellaneous nouns,
adjectives, and numerals.

Foundational Concepts

Liquid Lemonary

In the last lesson, you were introduced to contract verbs, verbs
whose stems end in short "α," "ε," or
"o." Now you meet another class of
verbs called LIQUID VERBS. These
verbs have stems which end in the
consonants "λ, μ, ν, or ρ." The above
picture of Sir Liquid LeMoNaRy will
help you remember the four letters.

Some examples are:

αἴρω
I take up, away

κρίνω
I judge

βάλλω
I throw

ἀγγέλλω
I proclaim

μένω
I remain, continue

ἐκτείνω
I extend

Professor Oddity

The professor informs us that these liquid verbs have one peculiarity. They will reject the "σ" suffix found in the future and aorist tenses. The four vowels "λ, μ, ν, or ρ" just will not be found with a "σ" following. For example:

βαλῶ - I shall throw - from βάλλω
ἤγειρα - I raised up - from ἐγείρω

The "σ" suffix has been an important key for you in identifying either the future or aorist tense. Now, for these verbs, that key is removed. You, therefore, may ask, "How can I identify a future or aorist liquid verb?" The answer is as follows:

When the "σ" is <u>rejected</u> it will generally leave behind either:
1. a stem change, and/or
2. an "α" in the first aorist active and middle.

We now turn to some more examples:

FUTURE ACTIVE INDICATIVE OF μένω

	Singular			Plural	
1.	μενῶ	- I shall remain	(1) μενοῦμεν	- We shall remain
2.	μενεῖς	- You will remain	(2) μενεῖτε	- You will remain
3.	μενεῖ	- She will remain He will remain	(3) μενοῦσι	- They will remain

Observations

1. The "σ" is rejected.

2. The circumflex accent and change of endings are ways by which the future forms are distinguished from the present.

FIRST AORIST ACTIVE INDICATIVE OF μένω

1. ἔμεινα –   (1) ἐμείναμεν –
   I remained   We remained
2. ἔμεινας –   (2) ἐμείνατε –
   You remained   You remained
3. ἔμεινε(ν) –   (3) ἔμειναν –
   She remained   They remained
   He remained

Observations

1. The "σ" is rejected.

2. An internal change appears

3. The characteristic "α" of the first aorist remains.

Common Liquid Verbs

Below is a chart of the principal parts of some of the more common liquid verbs in the New Testament. The blank spaces indicate the principal parts which do not occur in the New Testament. Look at each verb carefully, noting the absence of the "σ" in the future and aorist. Observe also the circumflex accents, the internal changes, and in the aorist, the presence of the "α."

PRESENT	FUTURE	AORIST	PERF.ACT.	PERF.PASS.	AOR.PASS.
announce					
ἀγγέλλω	ἀγγελῶ	ἤγγειλα			ἠγγέλην
lift up					
αἴρω	ἀρῶ	ἦρα	ἦρκα	ἦρμαι	ἤρθην
throw					
βάλλω	βαλῶ	ἔβαλον	βέβληκα	βέβλημαι	ἐβλήθην
raise					
ἐγείρω	ἐγερῶ	ἤγειρα		ἐγήγερμαι	ἠγέρθην
extend					
ἐκτείνω	ἐκτενῶ	ἐξέτεινα			
judge					
κρίνω	κρινῶ	ἔκρινα	κέκρικα	κέκριμαι	ἐκρίθην
remain					
μένω	μενῶ	ἔμεινα	μεμένηκα		
send					
στέλλω	στελῶ	ἔστειλα	ἔσταλκα	ἔσταλμαι	ἐστάλην

238

Memory Aid

Here we see Sir Liquid Lemonary watering his lemons at night. He is not seen with the "σ" sun. Observe his binoculars and arrows (future and aorist tenses). As you can see the "α" is maintained and the reaction to the rejection of the "σ" is usually an ax-sent (accent) or an internal change. (cf. Sir Liquid's portly figure).

Practice

Parse and translate the following. Note the circumflex accents, the internal changes, and the "α" of the aorist.

1. ἐγερεῖ ἡμᾶς σὺν Ἰησοῦ.
2. ἀποστελεῖ ὁ υἱὸς τοῦ ἀνθρώπου τοὺς ἀγγέλους αὐτοῦ.
3. ἦραν τὸν κύριον ἐκ τοῦ μνημείου.
4. μενεῖτε ἐν τῷ πατρί.
5. ἀποστελῶ εἰς αὐτοὺς προφήτας καὶ ἀποστόλους.
6. καὶ εὐθὺς ἄρας τὸν κράββατον (pallet) ἐξῆλθεν.
7. ὁ ἐγείρας τὸν Ἰησοῦν ἐγερεῖ τοὺς ἀδελφοὺς αὐτοῦ.

KEY

1. FAI 3 S - He will raise us up with Jesus.
2. FAI 3 S - The Son of man will send forth his angels.
3. AAI 3 P - They took away the Lord out of the tomb.
4. FAI 2 P - You will remain in the Father.
5. FAI 1 S - I will send to them prophets and apostles.
6. AAP MSN - And immediately having taken up the pallet, he went forth.
7. ἐγείρας - AAP MSN - The one who raised up Jesus will
   ἐγερεῖ - FAI 3 S -   raise up his brothers.

	Singular				Plural		
	Masc.	Fem.	Neut.		Masc.	Fem.	Neut.
N	πᾶς	πᾶσα	πᾶν	N	πάντες	πᾶσαι	πάντα
G	παντός	πάσης	παντός	G	πάντων	πασῶν	πάντων
D	παντί	πάσῃ	παντί	D	πᾶσι(ν)	πάσαις	πᾶσι(ν)
A	πάντα	πᾶσαν	πᾶν	A	πάντας	πάσας	πάντα

Memory Aid

    This picture will help you remember the endings for the masculine, feminine, and neuter forms. <u>All pas pass</u> a <u>pan</u> (πᾶς, πᾶσα, πᾶν) to <u>each</u> one. What a find!

Observations

1. The declension pattern is 3 - 1 - 3 (masc. - fem. - neut.).

2. The word πᾶς may be used without the article. Thus, πᾶσα πόλις means "every city." With the article, it may be found either in the attributive or the predicate position.

   πᾶσα ἡ πόλις = the entire city, or
   ἡ πᾶσα πόλις = the entire city

THE DECLENSION OF πολύς - "MUCH, MANY"

	Singular				Plural		
	Masc.	Fem.	Neut.		Masc.	Fem.	Neut.
N	πολύς	πολλή	πολύ	N	πολλοί	πολλαί	πολλά
G	πολλοῦ	πολλῆς	πολλοῦ	G	πολλῶν	πολλῶν	πολλῶν
D	πολλῷ	πολλῇ	πολλῷ	D	πολλοῖς	πολλαῖς	πολλοῖς
A	πολύν	πολλήν	πολύ	A	πολλούς	πολλάς	πολλά

Memory Aid

Observe Paul and his fate with the marbles. <u>Paul</u> loses <u>much</u>, yes, even <u>many</u> marbles to Polly. Note the connection with the nominative forms.

Observation

The pattern is very much like the article: 2 - 1 - 2 with the exception of the masculine and neuter nominative and accusative forms.

THE DECLENSION OF μέγας

	Singular				Plural		
	Masc.	Fem.	Neut.		Masc.	Fem.	Neut.
N	μέγας	μεγάλη	μέγα	N	μεγάλοι	μεγάλαι	μεγάλα
G	μεγάλου	μεγάλης	μεγάλου	G	μεγάλων	μεγάλων	μεγάλων
D	μεγάλῳ	μεγάλη	μεγάλῳ	D	μεγάλοις	μεγάλαις	μεγάλοις
A	μέγαν	μεγάλην	μέγα	A	μεγάλους	μεγάλας	μεγάλα

Memory Aid

Now notice the pattern of
endings for the word μέγας
"great." The picture of
the famous craftsman will
help you to remember the
nominative endings. He
says, "I make a leg
(μεγάλη) that is great."

Observation

The declension pattern is very similar to the article: 2 - 1 - 2. The exceptions are the same as for
πολύς, i.e. the nominative and accusative masculine
and neuter forms.

Professor Oddity

The professor wants you to
know another pattern for the
third declension nouns. It will
be helpful to become familiar
with all third declension patterns.

	Singular	Plural		Singular	Plural
N	βασιλεύς	βασιλεῖς	N	πίστις	πίστεις
G	βασιλέως	βασιλέων	G	πίστεως	πίστεων
D	βασιλεῖ	βασιλεῦσι(ν)	D	πίστει	πίστεσι(ν)
A	βασιλέα	βασιλεῖς	A	πίστιν	πίστεις

And now, the professor informs us of another irregularity - a third declension adjective with only two sets of endings. It is the common adjective ἀληθής, "true."

	Masc./Fem.	Neuter		Masc./Fem.	Neut.
N	ἀληθής	ἀληθές	N	ἀληθεῖς	ἀληθῆ
G	ἀληθοῦς	ἀληθοῦς	G	ἀληθῶν	ἀληθῶν
D	ἀληθεῖ	ἀληθεῖ	D	ἀληθέσι(ν)	ἀληθέσι(ν)
A	ἀληθῆ	ἀληθές	A	ἀληθεῖς	ἀληθῆ

Numeral Memory Aids

Observe the endings and study the memory picture.

One

To state the obvious, we only have singular endings for the numeral "one."

	Masc.	Fem.	Neut.
N	εἷς	μία	ἕν
G	ἑνός	μιᾶς	ἑνός
D	ἑνί	μιᾷ	ἑνί
A	ἕνα	μίαν	ἕν

I gave <u>one ace</u> (εἷς) to <u>my</u> (μία) <u>hen</u> (ἕν).

Two

δύο = two. This numeral is indeclinable except for a dative form δυσίν. A duet (δύο) is sung by <u>two</u> people.

Three

	Masc./Fem.	Neut.
N	τρεῖς	τρία
G	τριῶν	τριῶν
D	τρισί(ν)	τρισί(ν)
A	τρεῖς	τρία

A <u>tricycle</u> (τρεῖς) has
<u>three</u> wheels.

Four

	Masc./Fem.	Neut.
N	τέσσαρες	τέσσαρα
G	τεσσάρων	τεσσάρων
D	τέσσαρσι(ν)	τέσσαρσι(ν)
A	τέσσαρας	τέσσαρα

The scientist says - "I
<u>test our S</u> (τέσσαρες)
<u>four</u> ways."

Five - Two Hundred

The numbers 5 - 200 are indeclinable, i.e. πέντε (five) το διακόσιοι
(two hundred).

Enrichment

As Paul writes to the "Ephesian" Christians, he proclaims the unique oneness of their faith urging the Christians to appropriate what God has given to them. Observe in Ephesians 4 the number of times the word "one" is used and note all three genders. "Giving diligence to keep the unity of the Spirit in the bond of peace," is the reading of Ephesians 4:3.

In Ephesians 4:4-6, the Greek text reads, ἓν σῶμα καὶ ἓν πνεῦμα, καθὼς καὶ ἐκλήθητε ἐν μιᾷ ἐλπίδι τῆς κλήσεως ὑμῶν· εἷς κύριος, μία πίστις, ἓν βάπτισμα· εἷς θεὸς καὶ πατὴρ πάντων, ὁ ἐπὶ πάντων καὶ διὰ πάντων καὶ ἐν πᾶσιν. The very essence of Christian faith is unity, undergirded always by the One God who permeates and fills all that is. Thus, when believers understand that basic unity is found in God, the author of unity, they have, thereby, the strongest motive for guarding the unity of the church.

The text of John 15:10 reads, ἐὰν τὰς ἐντολάς μου τηρήσητε, μενεῖτε ἐν τῇ ἀγάπῃ μου, καθὼς ἐγὼ τὰς ἐντολὰς τοῦ πατρός μου τετήρηκα καὶ μένω αὐτοῦ ἐν τῇ ἀγάπῃ --- "If you keep my commandments, you will abide in my love, just as I have kept my Father's commandments and I abide in His love."

The pattern of Jesus for his servants is clear: He has kept (τετήρηκα - perf. of τηρέω) the Father's word. He continues to abide (μένω - present) in his love. And, he adds, if you keep (ἐὰν τηρήσητε - aor.subj. of τηρέω) my word, you shall abide (μενεῖτε - fut.ind. of μένω) in my love. The contrast between "if you keep" and "I have kept" and between "you will abide" and "I am abiding" is clear. The text clearly suggests that Jesus offers the incentive of his own example as the pattern for the disciple to follow.

Assignment

οἱ τέσσαρες λεπροί[1] ἐν ᾿Ισραήλ[2]

Γέγραφεν γραμματεὺς ἐν ἐπιστολῇ σοφίας ὅτι καρδία βασιλέως ἐν τῇ χειρὶ θεοῦ ὥσπερ ὁ ποταμὸς ὕδατος - ἐπιστρέφει αὐτὴν ὅπου θέλει.

διὰ τοῦτο οὐκ ἔστιν δύναμις εἰ μὴ ἡ δύναμις θεοῦ οὐδὲ κρίσις χωρὶς αὐτοῦ. ἐκπορεύεται γὰρ ἄφεσις τῶν ἁμαρτιῶν παρὰ τοῦ ἑνὸς θεοῦ τοῦ ἀληθοῦς καὶ πάλιν παρὰ τοῦ αὐτοῦ θεοῦ δέχονται γένη καὶ ἔθνη ἄρτους ταῖς χρείαις τοῦ σώματος ἵνα ἐν παντὶ τόπῳ ζήσωσιν καὶ δοξάσωσιν τὸν ποιήσαντα αὐτούς.

καὶ οὕτως ἐγένετο ἐν ταῖς ἡμέραις τῶν βασιλέων ᾿Ισραὴλ καὶ ᾿Ιουδαίας ὅτι ἐν μιᾷ τῶν πόλεων οὐκ ἦν ἄρτος. καὶ πλήρης φόβου ἦν πᾶσα ἡ πόλις καὶ ἔκραξεν τὸ πλῆθος πρὸς τοὺς ἱερεῖς καὶ τὸν βασιλέα σὺν ἐπιθυμίᾳ πολλῇ αἰτοῦντες ἵνα εὕρωσιν οἶνον καὶ ἄρτους ὅτι μέγας ἦν ὁ λιμός.[3] καὶ οὐδεὶς ἀπεκρίνατο αὐτοῖς, οὐδεὶς εἰ μὴ ᾿Ελισαῖος[4] ὁ προφήτης. ᾿Ελισαῖος γὰρ ἀπήγγειλεν ὅτι Μετ᾿ ὀλίγας ἡμέρας, θεὸς ἀποστελεῖ ὑμῖν καὶ ἄρτους καὶ οἶνον.

ἐν τῷ καιρῷ ἐκείνῳ ἦσαν τέσσαρες ἄνδρες λεπροί[1] ζῶντες ἔξω τῆς πόλεως καὶ διὰ τὸ εἶναι αὐτοὺς λεπρούς,[1] οὐδεὶς ποτε ἤγγισεν αὐτοῖς οὐδὲ ἥψατο αὐτῶν. καὶ εἶπον ἄλλος πρὸς ἄλλον,[5] Τί[6] σοι δοκεῖ; ἐὰν μείνωμεν ὧδε οὐ ζήσομεν· ἐὰν εἴπωμεν Εἰσέλθωμεν εἰς τὴν πόλιν, οὐχ εὑρήσομεν ἄρτον ἐκεῖ καὶ ἀποθανούμεθα ἐκεῖ. δεῦτε[7] πορευώμεθα καὶ πέσωμεν πρὸς τοὺς στρατιώτας Συρίας[8] τοὺς συναχθέντας ἐπὶ τὴν πόλιν. ἐὰν δέξωνται ἡμᾶς, ζήσομεν, καὶ ἐὰν μὴ δέξωνται ἡμᾶς ἀλλ᾿ ἀποκτείνωσι ἡμᾶς, ἀποθανούμεθα μόνον. ἐφοβοῦντο γὰρ μὴ[9] μείναντες ἔξω τῆς πόλεως ἀποθάνωσι.

καὶ εὐθέως ἐγερθέντες ἦλθον πρὸς τὰς σκηνὰς[10] τῶν ἐχθρῶν, καὶ ἰδοὺ οὐκ ἔστιν στρατιώτης ἐκεῖ οὐδείς. ὁ γὰρ κύριος πεποίηκεν τοὺς στρατιώτας Συρίας[8] φωνὴν ἀκοῦσαι, φωνὴν δυνάμεως μεγάλης, φωνὴν ἵππου,[11] φωνὴν ἁρμάτων,[12] καὶ ἔφυγον εἰς τὴν ἑαυτῶν χώραν φοβούμενοι πολλά. καὶ

οἱ τέσσαρες λεπροὶ θαυμάζοντες εἰσῆλθον εἰς μίαν σκηνήν,[10]
εἶτα εἰς ἑτέραν καὶ εὗρον παλαιοὺς ἄρτους καὶ οἶνον
πολύν. καὶ εὐθὺς ἔφαγον καὶ ἔπιον μηδενὸς θεωροῦντος
αὐτούς. καὶ ἔλαβον πολλὰ ἱμάτια καὶ ἦραν αὐτὰ εἰς τὸν
ἀγρὸν καὶ κατέκρυψαν[13] αὐτά.

πρὸ δὲ τοῦ γενέσθαι τὸ τῆς ἡμέρας φῶς, ἐλάλησαν οἱ
τέσσαρες λεπροὶ πρὸς ἀλλήλους λέγοντες, Οὐκ ἔξεστιν ἡμῖν
μεῖναι ὧδε. οὐχ οὕτως ὀφείλομεν ποιῆσαι, αὕτη γάρ ἐστιν
ἡμέρα χαρᾶς καὶ ἐλπίδος. καὶ νῦν, δεῦρο,[14] μὴ μείνωμεν
ὧδε ἀλλ' ἐξέλθωμεν καὶ ἀπαγγείλωμεν τὴν καλὴν ἀκοὴν πρὸς
τὴν οἰκίαν τοῦ βασιλέως. τοῦ γὰρ κυρίου ἡ γῆ καὶ τὸ
πλήρωμα αὐτῆς, καὶ εἰσῆλθον καὶ ἀπήγγειλαν πᾶσιν ἐν τῇ
πόλει.

ἀκούσας οὖν τοῦτο ἀπέστειλεν ὁ βασιλεὺς πέντε γραμματεῖς εἰς τὸ πειρᾶσαι τὸ ῥῆμα τῶν τεσσάρων λεπρῶν περὶ
τοῦ γεγονότος ἐν ταῖς σκηναῖς[10] τῶν τῆς Συρίας στρατιωτῶν. ἐπιστρέψαντες δὲ ἀπήγγειλαν οἱ γραμματεῖς ὅτι
λελαλήκασι οἱ ἀκάθαρτοι λεπροὶ ἀκοὴν ἀληθῆ.

διὰ τοῦτο εὐχαρίστησεν ὁ λαὸς τῷ θεῷ καὶ χωρὶς
φόβου ἐκπορευθέντες εὗρον ὅτι οὐκ ἔστιν στρατιώτης ἐν
ταῖς σκηναῖς[10] οὐδείς. καὶ ἔμειναν ἐκεῖ μηκέτι φοβούμενοι ἀλλ' ἐσθίοντες καὶ πίνοντες κατὰ τὴν ἐπαγγελίαν
τὴν ἐξελθοῦσαν ἀπὸ τοῦ στόματος τοῦ Ἐλισαίου,[4] τοῦ
προφήτου τοῦ πλήρους πίστεως καὶ τῆς τοῦ θεοῦ σοφίας.

---

[1]λεπροί - lepers   [11]ἵππος - cavalry(collective)
[2]Ἰσραήλ - Israel   [12]ἅρματα - chariotry
[3]λιμός - famine   [13]κατακρύπτω - hide
[4]Ἐλισαῖος - Elisha   [14]δεῦρο - come
[5]ἄλλος πρὸς ἄλλον - one to another
[6]Τί - what
[7]δεῦτε - come!
[8]Συρία - Syria
[9]μή - lest
[10]σκηνή - tent

Chapter 17

1. αἰώνιος, -ον[1]   - eternal (eon)
2. ἀληθῶς   - verily, truly (compare ἀλήθεια)
3. ἀμήν   - amen (amen)
4. ἄρα   - then, as a result
5. ἀρχιερεύς, -έως, ὁ - high priest (hierarchy) - compare ἱερεύς
6. ἀσπάζομαι   - I greet
7. ἄχρι, ἄχρις (with gen.) - until
8. δεξιός, -ά, -όν   - right (dexterity), i.e. right hand
9. διό   - therefore
10. ἔμπροσθεν (w/gen.)- in front of (compare ἐν - πρός)
11. ἤ   - or, than
12. θρόνος, -ου, ὁ   - throne (throne)
13. καθίζω   - I sit, cause to sit ("ex cathedra")
14. κακῶς   - evilly (compare κακός)
15. καλῶς   - beautifully (kaleidoscope), well (compare καλός)
16. κρατέω   - I seize, grasp (democracy)
17. λοιπόν   - finally
18. Λουκᾶς, -ᾶ, ὁ   - Luke (Luke)
19. Μαρία, -ας, ἡ   - Mary (Mary)
20. μέσος, -η, -ον   - middle, midst (Mesopotamia) ἐν μέσῳ = in the midst
21. νικάω   - I conquer
22. ὀπίσω (w. gen.)   - after
23. ὅς, ἥ, ὅ   - who, which
24. ὅσος, -η, -ον   - as great, as far, as many
25. ὅστις, ἥτις, ὅτι[2] - whoever, whatever[3]
26. οὖς, ὠτός, τό   - ear (otoscope - for examination of the ear)
27. οὔτε   - not
28. πολλά   - much (compare πολύς)
29. πρεσβύτερος, -α,-ον- older, elder (presbyter)
30. πῦρ, πυρός, τό   - fire (pyre)

31. τε (enclitic)   - and

32. τίς, τί   - who? which?

33. τις, τι (enclitic)- someone, something, anyone, anything

34. τρίτος, -η, -ον   - third (trio)

35. ὑπάρχω   - I exist, am, am present. The verb - like εἰμί - may take a predicate noun or a predicate adjective.

36. φωνέω   - I call (phonetic). Comp. φωνή

---

[1]An adjective of two terminations.

[2]ὅστις = ὅσ + τις, ἥτις = ἥ + τις, ὅτι = ὅ + τι

[3]Sometimes equivalent in meaning to ὅς, ἥ, ὅ.

. . . learn three new types of pronouns, and

. . . be introduced to the adverb.

Foundational Concepts

Interrogative and Indefinite Pronouns

Below you will see the forms for two new but very common types of pronouns:

Interrogative - As you can surmise, an interrogative pronoun asks a question.

Who?   (masc. & fem.)
What?   (neut.)
Why?   (neut.)

Indefinite - obviously the term means in-definite, not definite, either a person or thing that is not clearly specified.

Someone, a certain one, any (masc. & fem.)
Something, a certain thing, any (neut.)

250

(S) Singular

	M & F Int. "who"	N. Int. "what, why"	M & F Ind. "Someone, any certain one"	N. Ind. "Something, a certain thing"
N	τίς	τί	τις	τι
G	τίνος	τίνος	τινός	τινός
D	τίνι	τίνι	τινί	τινί
A	τίνα	τί	τινά	τι

(P) Plural

N	τίνες	τίνα	τινές	τινά
G	τίνων	τίνων	τινῶν	τινῶν
D	τίσι (ν)	τίσι (ν)	τισί (ν)	τισί (ν)
A	τίνας	τίνα	τινάς	τινά

Observations

1. The forms for the two pronouns follow the third declension and correspond to each other respectively.

2. The accent marks the difference between the two. The interrogative pronoun always has an acute over the first syllable (never grave): the indefinite pronoun is an enclitic and loses its accent. (cf. the appendix.)

3. Each of the pronouns may be used either alone or with a noun.

Memory Aid

Observe <u>Polly</u> standing by the Silly Bull with the <u>question mark</u> over his head (interrogative pronoun). The first silly bull says, "Who (masc. and fem.) put <u>what</u> (neut.) in τίς τί and <u>why</u> (neut.)?" Do you see <u>this tea</u> (τίς τί) pot? The <u>ax</u> with <u>fur</u> on the silly bull will remind you of the accent on the first syllable.

The second silly bull with an <u>ax</u> and <u>second hand</u> (accent on the second syllable) is <u>indefinite</u>. Thus, it is enclosed by dotted lines. To the question of bull #1, bull #2 replies, "I saw <u>someone</u> put <u>something</u> in <u>this tea</u> (τις τι). Examine the picture carefully with its various parts.

Practice

Observe the picture once more and translate the following sentences taken from Scripture.

1. John 12:34 - τίς ἐστιν οὗτος ὁ υἱὸς τοῦ ἀνθρώπου;
2. John 8:53 - τίνα σεαυτὸν ποιεῖς;
3. Rom. 6:21 - τίνα καρπὸν εἴχετε τότε;
4. John 10:20 - τί αὐτοῦ ἀκούετε;
5. 3 John 9 - ἔγραψά τι τῇ ἐκκλησίᾳ.
6. Acts 17:4 - καί τινες ἐξ αὐτῶν ἐπείσθησαν.
7. Luke 10:38 - γυνὴ δέ τις ὀνόματι Μάρθα ὑπεδέξατο αὐτόν,
8. John 6:28 - Τί ποιῶμεν ἵνα ἐργαζώμεθα τὰ ἔργα τοῦ θεοῦ; (Deliberative subjunctive)
9. John 12:27 - καὶ τί εἴπω; Πάτερ, σῶσόν με ἐκ τῆς ὥρας ταύτης; (Deliberative subjunctive)

KEY

1. Who is this Son of man?
2. Whom do you make yourself?
3. What fruit were you having at that time?
4. Why are you listening to him?
5. I wrote something to the church.
6. And some of them were persuaded.
7. And a certain woman by name Martha welcomed him.
8. What shall we do that we may work the works of God?
9. And what shall I say? (Shall I say) Father, save me out of this hour?

Relative Pronouns

The relative pronouns are the words, "who" and "which." They <u>relate</u> one part of a sentence to another.

I saw the tree <u>which</u> the lightning struck.

The pronoun "which" relates the second clause back to the tree. The declension of the relative pronoun is as follows:

	Singular				Plural		
	Masc.	Fem.	Neut.		Masc.	Fem.	Neut.
N	ὅς	ἥ	ὅ	(N)	οἵ	αἵ	ἅ
G	οὗ	ἧς	οὗ	(G)	ὧν	ὧν	ὧν
D	ᾧ	ᾗ	ᾧ	(D)	οἷς	αἷς	οἷς
A	ὅν	ἥν	ὅ	(A)	οὕς	ἅς	ἅ

Observations

1. Note the close parallel to the article, though the relative pronoun has no "τ."

2. Each relative pronoun has a rough breathing and an accent.

3. A relative pronoun will agree in gender and number with its antecedent, not necessarily in case (cf. lesson five).

Memory Aid

Polly's relative is Uncle Harry Hoo (who) who always eats sandwiches (which). The relative pronouns are who and which. As Uncle Hoo eats a sandwich he knocks the "τ" out of Art Icicle (article). All that remains is a vowel or dipthong with a rough breathing. Art appears to be beside himself. Look again at the declension of the relative pronoun above.

Indefinite Relative Clauses

The particles ἄν or ἐάν (red flags of the subjunctive) may be added to the relative pronoun, and will always be accompanied by the subjunctive mood.

ὃς ἐάν (or ὃς ἄν) = whoever
ὃ ἐάν (or ὃ ἄν) = whatever (thing)
ἃ ἐάν (or ἃ ἄν) = whatever (things)

Practice

1. John 4:50 - ἐπίστευσεν ὁ ἄνθρωπος τῷ λόγῳ ὃν εἶπεν
αὐτῷ ὁ Ἰησοῦς.
2. 1 Cor. 6:19 - τὸ σῶμα ὑμῶν ναὸς τοῦ ἐν ὑμῖν ἁγίου
πνεύματός ἐστιν, οὗ ἔχετε ἀπὸ θεοῦ.
3. 1 Cor. 15:10 - εἰμὶ ὃ εἰμι
4. 1 John 1:3 - ὃ ἑωράκαμεν καὶ ἀκηκόαμεν, ἀπαγγέλλομεν
καὶ ὑμῖν,
5. 1 John 2:7 - ἡ ἐντολή . . . ἐστιν ὁ λόγος ὃν ἠκούσατε.
6. 1 John 1:5 - καὶ ἔστιν αὕτη ἡ ἀγγελία ἣν ἀκηκόαμεν
ἀπ' αὐτοῦ.
7. Mark 3:35 - ὃς ἂν ποιήσῃ τὸ θέλημα τοῦ θεοῦ, οὗτος
ἀδελφός μου καὶ ἀδελφὴ καὶ μήτηρ ἐστίν.
8. 1 John 3:22 - ὃ ἐὰν αἰτῶμεν λαμβάνομεν ἀπ' αὐτοῦ.
9. Luke 9:57 - ἀκολουθήσω σοι ὅπου ἐὰν ἀπέρχῃ.

1. The man believed the word which Jesus spoke to him.
2. Your body is a sanctuary of the Holy Spirit who is in you, whom you have from God.
3. I am what I am.
4. That which we have seen and heard, we are announcing also to you.
5. The commandment is the word which you heard.
6. And this is the message which we have heard from him.
7. Whoever does the will of God, this one is my brother, and sister, and mother.
8. Whatever we ask we receive from him.
9. I will follow you wherever you go.

Adverbs

The two important forms of the adverb are:

1. The ending "ως" added to the stem of an adjective.

Adjective		Adverb	
καλός	= good	καλῶς	= well
ἀληθής	= true	ἀληθῶς	= truly
κακός	= evil	κακῶς	= evilly

2. The neuter adjective in the accusative case (singular or plural).

Adjective		Adverb	
λοιπός	= remaining	λοιπόν	= finally
πολύς	= much, many	πολλά	= much, often

Phil. 3:1 - τὸ λοιπόν, ἀδελφοί μου, χαίρετε ἐν κυρίῳ.

Practice

1. ἐάν τις ἀγαπᾷ τὸν κόσμον, οὐκ ἔστιν ἡ ἀγάπη τοῦ πατρὸς ἐν αὐτῷ.
2. τί θέλετε;
3. ἐὰν μή τις γεννηθῇ ἄνωθεν . . . (from above)
4. ἐάν τι αἰτώμεθα κατὰ τὸ θέλημα αὐτοῦ, ἀκούει ἡμῶν.
5. εἴδομέν τινα ἐν τῷ ὀνόματί σου ἐκβάλλοντα δαιμόνια.
6. ἔξεστι καλῶς ποιεῖν τοῖς σάββασι.

1. If anyone loves the world, the love of the Father is not in him.
2. What do you wish?
3. Unless someone should be born from above . . .
4. If we ask anything according to his will, he hears us.
5. We saw someone casting out demons in your name.
6. It is lawful to do well on the Sabbath.

Enrichment

The indefinite relative clause (ὃς ἐάν, ὃ ἐάν) occurs in many ways in the NT. One of the most striking uses is its emphasis on the grace of God and discipleship.

1. πᾶς ὃς ἂν ἐπικαλέσηται τὸ ὄνομα κυρίου σωθήσεται.
   Acts 2:21 - Whoever calls on the name of the Lord will be saved. SALVATION

2. ὃ ἐὰν αἰτῶμεν λαμβάνομεν ἀπ' αὐτοῦ ὅτι τὰς ἐντολὰς αὐτοῦ τηροῦμεν.
   1 John 3:22 - Whatever we ask we receive from him because we keep his commandments.
   PRAYER AND OBEDIENCE

3. ὃς ἂν ποιήσῃ τὸ θέλημα τοῦ θεοῦ, οὗτος ἀδελφός μου καὶ ἀδελφὴ καὶ μήτηρ ἐστίν.
   Mark 3:35 - Whoever does the will of God, this one is my brother and sister and mother.
   THE WILL OF GOD

Assignment

ἡ μετάνοια τοῦ Κορνηλίου[1] καὶ τοῦ Πέτρου[2]

Καλῶς γέγραφεν Λουκᾶς[3] περὶ τῆς ἀρχῆς τῆς πίστεως
ἐν τῷ κόσμῳ καθίζοντος Ἡρῴδου[4] ἐπὶ τοῦ θρόνου καὶ Ἄννα[5]
ὄντος ἀρχιερέως ἐν Ἱεροσόλυμα.

Ἀνὴρ ἦν τις ἐν Καισαρείᾳ[6] ὀνόματι Κορνήλιος[1] ἑκα-
τοντάρχης[7] καὶ φοβούμενος τὸν θεὸν σὺν παντὶ τῷ οἴκῳ
αὐτοῦ, καὶ προσευχόμενος πολλὰ τῷ θεῷ διὰ παντός.[8] καὶ
ὤφθη ἄγγελος τοῦ θεοῦ αὐτῷ εἰσελθὼν πρὸς αὐτὸν καὶ λέγων,
Κορνήλιε. καὶ θεωρῶν αὐτὸν ἐφοβήθη Κορνήλιος φόβον μέγαν
καὶ εἶπεν αὐτῷ, Τί ἐστιν, κύριε; εἶπεν δὲ αὐτῷ, Ἀναβέ-
βηκαν οἱ λόγοι τῆς καρδίας σου εἰς μνημόσυνον[9] ἔμπροσθεν
τοῦ θεοῦ. διὸ ἀποστελεῖς ἄνδρας εἰς Ἰόππην[10] μεταπέμ-
ψασθαι[11] Σίμωνά τινα ὃς ἐπικαλεῖται Πέτρος καὶ σὺ δέξῃ
αὐτὸν εἰς τὸν οἶκόν σου εἰς τὸ ἀκοῦσαί σε τὸν λόγον τῆς
ἀληθείας ἀπ᾽ αὐτοῦ. ὃς γὰρ ἂν δέξηται τὸν λόγον, δέχεται τὴν ζωήν.

καὶ ὑπαγαγόντος τοῦ ἀγγέλου, φωνήσας δύο τῶν δούλων
αὐτοῦ καὶ νέον στρατιώτην ἐλάλησεν Κορνήλιος αὐτοῖς πᾶν
τὸ γεγονός, καὶ ἀπέστειλεν αὐτοὺς εἰς Ἰόππην. καὶ
ἐγγιζόντων τῶν τριῶν τῇ πόλει ἀνέβη Πέτρος ἐπὶ τὸ δῶμα[12]
προσεύξασθαι. καὶ ἐγένετο ἐπ᾽ αὐτὸν ἔκστασις[13] καὶ ἔχων
ἐπιθυμίαν φαγεῖν ἐδόκει τὸν οὐρανὸν βλέπειν ἀνεῳγμένον
καὶ σκεῦός τι καταβαῖνον ἐν ᾧ ὑπῆρχεν πολλὰ θηρία τοῦ
ἀγροῦ καὶ πολλὰ πετεινὰ τοῦ οὐρανοῦ. ἐγένετο οὖν φωνὴ
πρὸς αὐτόν, Ἐγερθείς, Πέτρε, ἀποκτενεῖς καὶ φάγῃ. καὶ
εἶπεν Μηδαμῶς,[14] κύριε, οὐκ ἔξεστίν μοι τοῦτο ποιῆσαι
ὅτι ἀληθῶς οὐχ ἡψάμην ποτὲ ἀκαθάρτου τινός. καὶ φωνὴ
πάλιν πρὸς αὐτόν, Ὅσα ὁ θεὸς ἐκαθάρισεν, οὐ καλέσεις
ἀκάθαρτα. καὶ εὐθὺς ἀνελήμφθη τὸ σκεῦος εἰς τὸν οὐρανόν.

καὶ κατῆλθεν Πέτρος ἀπὸ τοῦ δώματος[12] θαυμάζων ἐπὶ
πᾶσιν οἷς ἑώρακεν καὶ ἀκήκοεν. καὶ εὐθέως παρεγένοντο
οἱ τρεῖς ἄνδρες οἱ ἀπεσταλμένοι ὑπὸ Κορνηλίου ζητοῦντες
Πέτρον. ἄρα Πέτρος ἀσπασάμενος αὐτοὺς καὶ κρατήσας τῆς
δεξιᾶς ἑκάστου ἐδέξατο αὐτοὺς εἰς τὸν οἶκον. καὶ εἰσελ-
θόντες καὶ καθίσαντες ἀπήγγειλαν τῷ Πέτρῳ καὶ τοῖς

πρεσβυτέροις τοῖς συναχθεῖσι ἐκεῖ πάντα ἃ γεγόνασι τῷ
Κορηλίῳ. καὶ ἀπεκρίθη Πέτρος λέγων, Ἀκολουθήσωμεν
ὀπίσω τούτων τῶν ἀνδρῶν καὶ ζητήσωμεν Κορνήλιον καὶ
ἀκούσωμεν τὴν ἀκοὴν ἀπὸ τοῦ στόματος ἑαυτοῦ.

καὶ τῇ τρίτῃ ἡμέρᾳ ἐθεώρει Κορνήλιος αὐτοὺς παραγιν-
ομένους. καὶ δραμὼν[15] εἰς τὸν Πέτρον ἔπεσεν πρὸς τοὺς
πόδας αὐτοῦ ἐν τιμῇ. ὁ δὲ Πέτρος κρατήσας τῆς δεξιᾶς
ἤγειρεν αὐτὸν λέγων, Οὔτε γινώσκεις οὔτε θεωρεῖς ὅτι ἐγὼ
αὐτὸς ἄνθρωπός εἰμι; καὶ εἰσέρχεται καὶ εὐρίσκει πολλοὺς
συνεληλυθότας καὶ λέγει Κορνήλιος, Πρὸ τεσσάρων ἡμερῶν[16]
ἤμην προσευχόμενος. καὶ τοῦτο ἐν τῷ ὀφθῆναί μοι ἄγγελον
τοῦ θεοῦ καὶ ἠρώτησεν ἵνα πέμψω εἰς Ἰόππην καὶ καλέσω
Σίμωνά τινα ὃς ἐπικαλεῖται Πέτρος εἰς τὸ ἀκοῦσαί με ἀπ᾽
αὐτοῦ λόγους σωτηρίας.

διὸ μετεπεμψάμην[11] σε. σύ τε καλῶς ἐποίησας παραγενόμενος ἐν μέσῳ ἡμῶν. νῦν οὖν πάντες ἡμεῖς ἔμπροσθεν
τοῦ θεοῦ ἐσμεν ἀκοῦσαι πάντα τὰ λαληθέντα σοι ὑπὸ τοῦ
θεοῦ.

ἀνοίξας δὲ Πέτρος αὐτοῦ τὸ στόμα, τοῦ λόγου ἅψαντος
πῦρ ἐν τῇ καρδίᾳ αὐτοῦ, εἶπεν, Ἀληθῶς ὑμεῖς γινώσκετε
τὸ γενόμενον ῥῆμα ἐν ὅλῃ τῇ Ἰουδαίᾳ ἀρξάμενος ἀπὸ τῆς
Γαλιλαίας μετὰ τὸ βάπτισμα ὃ ἐκήρυξεν Ἰωάννης. ἔχρισεν[17]
ὁ θεὸς Ἰησοῦν τὸν ἀπὸ τῆς Ναζαρὲθ[18] πνεύματι ἁγίῳ καὶ
μεγάλῃ δυνάμει ὃς διῆλθεν τὴν γῆν ἡμῶν θεραπεύων τοὺς
κακῶς ἔχοντας[19] καὶ πάντας τοὺς δαιμονισθέντας, ποιῶν
δὲ ἄλλα καλὰ ὅτι ὁ θεὸς ἦν μετ᾽ αὐτοῦ. καὶ ἔκριναν
αὐτὸν οἱ ἱερεῖς καὶ οἱ ἄρχοντες ἄξιον τοῦ θανάτου. ἀλλὰ
μετὰ τὸ σταυρωθῆναι αὐτὸν τρίτῃ ἡμέρᾳ ἤγειρεν ὁ θεὸς
αὐτὸν ἐκ τῶν νεκρῶν ποιήσας αὐτὸν κεφαλὴν ὑπὲρ πάντα.
καὶ δι᾽ αὐτοῦ φιλεῖ τὸν κόσμον ὁ θεὸς καὶ νικᾷ τὸν
πονηρὸν καὶ ἀπαίρει ἀπιστίαν. ὅσοι ἂν πιστεύσωσι εἰς
αὐτὸν λαμβάνουσι ζωὴν αἰώνιον καὶ εἰς κρίσιν οὐκ εἰσ-
ελεύσονται. τούτῳ πάντες οἱ προφῆται μαρτυροῦσιν,
ἄφεσιν ἁμαρτιῶν λαβεῖν διὰ τοῦ ὀνόματος αὐτοῦ πάντα τὸν
πιστεύοντα εἰς αὐτόν. καὶ ἰδοὺ ἀληθῆ τὰ τῶν προφητῶν
γράμματα.

λοιπόν, ἔτι ἀπαγγέλλοντος τοῦ Πέτρου τὰς ἐπαγγελίας
ταύτας, ἔπεσεν τὸ πνεῦμα τὸ ἅγιον ἐπὶ πάντας τοὺς ἀκού-
οντας τὸν λόγον. καὶ ἀπεκρίθη Πέτρος λέγων, Δεῖ τούτους

βαπτισθῆναι ὕδατι οἵτινες ἐγεννήθησαν ἐκ θεοῦ ὡς καὶ ἡμεῖς. καὶ εἶπον οἱ ἐν τῇ οἰκίᾳ, ᾽Αμήν.

ἰδοὺ ἡ μετάνοια τοῦ Κορνηλίου καὶ τοῦ Πέτρου. ὁ μὲν εὗρεν Χριστόν, ὁ δὲ ἐν Χριστῷ εὗρεν ἀδελφόν.

---

[1]Κορνήλιος - Cornelius
[2]Πέτρος - Peter
[3]Λουκᾶς - Luke
[4]῾Ηρῴδης - Herod
[5]῎Αννας - Annas
[6]Καισαρεία - Caesarea
[7]ἑκατοντάρχης - centurion
[8]διὰ παντός - continually
[9]μνημόσυνον - memorial offering
[10]᾽Ιόππη - Joppa
[11]μεταπέμπομαι - summon
[12]δῶμα - roof
[13]ἔκστασις - ecstasy, trance
[14]μηδαμῶς - by no means, "no way"
[15]δραμών - from τρέχω
[16]πρὸ τεσσάρων ἡμερῶν = four days ago
[17]χρίω - anoint
[18]Ναζαρέθ - Nazareth
[19]κακῶς ἔχειν - to be sick

Chapter 18

1. ἀγγελία, -ας, ἡ — message (cf. ἄγγελος)
2. ἀνάστασις, -εως, ἡ - resurrection
3. ἅπας, -ασα, -αν — all, every (cf. πᾶς) (panoply)
4. ἄρτι — now
5. ἀσθενέω — I am weak, sick (asthenic)
6. βλασφημέω — I blaspheme (blaspheme)
7. βούλομαι — I wish, want
8. γενεά, -ᾶς, ἡ — race, generation (cf. γένος)
9. δεύτερος, -α, -ον — second (Deuteronomy)
10. δέω — I bind (cf. δεῖ)
11. διάβολος, -ον — slanderous, Devil (diabolical)
12. διακονέω (w/dat.) — I serve (deacon)
13. διάκονος, -ου, ὁ, ἡ - servant (deacon)
14. δικαιόω — I justify (cf. δίκαιος)
15. ἐπάγω — I bring on (cf. ἄγω)
16. ἐπιθυμέω — I desire
17. ἐργάζομαι — I work, accomplish (cf. ἔργον)
18. θλῖψις, -εως, ἡ — tribulation, affliction
19. κατοικέω — I live, dwell (cf. οἶκος)
20. κλαίω — I weep
21. λογίζομαι — I think, consider (cf. λόγος)
22. μέρος, -ους, τό — part (polymerous)
23. μισέω — I hate (misanthrope)
24. οἰκοδομέω — I build, restore (cf. οἶκος)
25. οἰκουμένη, -ης, ἡ - inhabited earth, world
26. οἷος, -α, -ον — of what sort
27. οὐαί (foll. by dat. - Woe! Alas! (woe)
    or acc. case)
28. οὐχί — not (a stronger form of the negative οὐ)
29. πάντοτε — always (cf. πᾶς)
30. παρουσία, -ας, ἡ — presence, coming (Parousia)
31. περισσεύω — I have in abundance, I cause to abound, overflow
32. πλανάω — I deceive, wander (planet)

33. πράσσω   - I practice (pragmatic)

34. πρίν (conj.)   - before (foll. by acc and inf.
                          or by ἢ ἄν and aor. subj.)

35. προσευχή, -ῆς, ἡ   - prayer, place of prayer (cf.
                          προσεύχομαι)

36. πύλη, -ης, ἡ   - gate

37. σήμερον (indecl.) - today (cf. ἡμέρα)

IN THIS LESSON YOU WILL:

    . . . Meet a strange figure, the Imp-pear (Imperative mood),

    . . . see Lu as he desires to loose the optimistic octopus (optative mood),

    . . . observe the negatives οὐ and μή with questions and strong denials.

Foundational Concepts

      You will recall from Lesson One, that the word <u>mood</u> tells us <u>how</u> something is said. Previously, you have studied the indicative and subjunctive moods.

1. Indicative = statements of fact

2. Subjunctive = probability

Now, observe the imperative and optative moods, the other moods of the Greek verb.

Imperative Mood

The imperative mood is the mood of command.

LOOSE!

Singular

2. λῦε   loose   2. βάλε   throw
3. λυέτω let him loose,   3. βαλέτω let him throw,
        let her loose   let her throw

Plural

2. λύετε loose   2. βάλετε throw
3. λυέτωσαν let them loose 3. βαλέτωσαν let them throw

Observations

1. The imperative only appears in the second and third persons.

2. The present imperative is formed by:

   a. stem, and
   b. endings.

3. The second aorist is composed of:

   a. stem with internal change, and
   b. endings.

4. The difference in meaning between the present and aorist imperative is in type of action (continuous action vs. point action).

5. The second personal plural of the present imperative has the same form as the second person plural indicative. Context will help you decide between the two.

Memory Aids

Lu grasps the present while issuing a command to the Imp-pear "Loose" (= untie) the present (present active imperative). The Imp-pear tugs at Lu's present, while he sits on . . . a . . . a toe (-ε, -ετω), while he ate in Tucson (-ετε, -ετωσαν).

βαλ with his two arrows gives another command to the Imp-pear. The command is "Throw" the arrow (second aorist active imperative). Again note βαλ's heavy pouch (internal change). Imp-pear again is on. . . a toe (-ε, -ετω) while he ate in Tucson (-ετε, -ετωσαν).

PRESENT MIDDLE/PASSIVE IMPERATIVE OF λύω

	Singular		Plural
2.	λύου	2.	λύεσθε
	loose for yourself (M)		loose for yourselves (M)
	be loosed (P)		be loosed (P)
3.	λυέσθω	3.	λυέσθωσαν
	let him loose for himself (M)		let them loose for
	let her loose for herself (M)		themselves (M)
	let him be loosed (P)		let them be loosed (P)
	let her be loosed (P)		

SECOND AORIST MIDDLE IMPERATIVE OF βάλλω

	Singular		Plural
2.	βαλοῦ	2.	βάλεσθε
	throw for yourself		throw for yourselves
3.	βαλέσθω	3.	βαλέσθωσαν
	let him throw for himself		let them throw for them-
	let her throw for herself		selves

Memory Aid

Lu holds the present and he issues a command to the Imp-pear, "be loosed" (present middle/passive imperative). Observe the condition of both λυ and βαλ. They both glue an S-toe (-ου, -εσθω) while βαλ asks Lu, "Is the S-toast on (-εσθε, -εσθωσαν) for yourself?"

<u>FIRST AORIST ACTIVE IMPERATIVE OF λύω</u>

	Singular		Plural
2.	λῦσον	2.	λύσατε
	loose		loose
3.	λυσάτω	3.	λυσάτωσαν
	let him loose, let her loose		let them loose

Observation

Note the presence of the tense suffix "σ" and the characteristic "σα" of the first aorist.

Memory Aid

Lu grasps his <u>one arrow</u> while he tells the <u>Imp-pear</u> "<u>Loose</u>" the <u>arrow</u> (first aorist active imperative). Observe the "σ" sun (tense suffix) and note the Imp-pear <u>on a toe</u> (-σον, -σαιω) while he <u>ate</u> in <u>Tucson</u> (-σατε,-σατωσαν).

<u>FIRST AORIST MIDDLE IMPERATIVE OF λύω</u>

	Singular		Plural
2.	λῦσαι	2.	λύσασθε
	loose for yourself		loose for yourselves
3.	λυσάσθω	3.	λυσάσθωσαν
	let him loose for himself, let her loose for herself		let them loose for themselves

Observation

Note the presence of the tense suffix "σ" and the "σα" of the first aorist.

Memory Aid

Lu with <u>one arrow</u> gives a command to the <u>Imp-pear</u>, "<u>Loose for your-self</u>" your metal (first aorist middle impera-tive). Note the "σ" sun. Overhearing this command is <u>Sy</u> with an <u>S-toe</u> (-σαι, -σασθω) who says to Lu, "<u>Is the S-toast on</u>? (-σασθε, -σασθωσαν).

FIRST AORIST PASSIVE IMPERATIVE

	Singular		Plural
2.	λύθητι	2.	λύθητε
	be loosed		be loosed
3.	λυθήτω	3.	λυθήτωσαν
	let him be loosed		let them be loosed
	let her be loosed		

Observation

Note the presence of the θη, the characteristic mark of the first aorist passive.

Memory Aid

Lu with <u>one arrow</u> gave the command to the <u>Imp-pear</u>, "<u>be loosed</u>"(first aorist passive impera-tive). The <u>Imp-pear</u> was passive and could not do a thing about his predicament. Lu stood with a young lady named <u>Theta Eta</u> (θη). They both drank <u>tea</u>, contemplating Imp-pear's <u>toe</u> (-τι, -τω) and also they <u>ate</u> in <u>Tucson</u> (-τε, -τωσαν).

Memory Aid

Amy with her present says about the Imp-pear, "Let it be my present!" (present imperative of εἰμί). Observe her S-toe (ἔστω). Refer to the appendix for other less common forms of the imperative of εἰμί.

LET IT BE MY PRESENT!

3. ἔστω - let him be, let her be

Practice

Before applying the endings, review in your mind the various pictures and their corresponding meanings. When the endings are familiar, parse the following imperatives and translate the sentences (the imperative forms are underlined):

1. Matt. 7:1 - μὴ κρίνετε ἵνα μὴ κριθῆτε. The negative of the imperative is formed with μὴ.
2. 1 John 3:13 - μὴ θαυμάζετε, ἀδελφοί, εἰ μισεῖ (μισέω = I hate) ὑμᾶς ὁ κόσμος.
3. ὁ ἔχων ὦτα ἀκούειν, ἀκουέτω.
4. πορεύθητι πρὸς τὸν λαὸν τοῦτον.
5. John 1:39 - ἔρχεσθε καὶ ὄψεσθε.
6. John 2:19 - λύσατε τὸν ναὸν τοῦτον καὶ ἐν τρισὶν ἡμέραις ἐγερῶ αὐτόν.
7. Matt. 28:7 - εἴπατε τοῖς μαθηταῖς αὐτοῦ ὅτι ἠγέρθη.
8. Matt. 8:32 - καὶ εἶπεν αὐτοῖς, ὑπάγετε.
9. John 17:11 - Πάτερ ἅγιε, τήρησον αὐτοὺς ἐν τῷ ὀνόματί σου.
10. Matt. 6:10 - γενηθήτω το θέλημά σου.

KEY

1. P A Imper. 2P - Do not judge in order that you may not be judged.
2. P A Imper. 2P - Do not marvel brothers, if the world hates you.
3. P A Imper. 3S - The one who has ears to hear, let him hear.
4. A D Imper. 2S - Go to this people.
5. P D Imper. 2P - Come and you will see.
6. A A Imper. 2P - Destroy this temple and in three days, I will raise it up.
7. A A Imper. 2P - Say to his disciples that he arose.
8. P A Imper. 2P - And he said to them, "Depart."
9. A A Imper. 2S - Holy Father, keep them in your name.
10. A D Imper. 3S - Let your will come about.

The Optative Mood

The optative mood is the mood of remote possibility. The substitute word for optative is the <u>optimistic octopus</u>. Since the optative only occurs 67 times in the New Testament, it calls for an abbreviated treatment only. We will learn only the four most important forms, leaving the rest for reference.

Below you will find the endings for the optative mood, and memory aids to help you learn the third person singular. The underlined forms are important to learn since the majority of New Testament optatives occur in the third person singular.

<u>PRESENT ACTIVE OPTATIVE OF λύω</u>

	Singular		Plural
1.	λύοιμι	(1)	λύοιμεν
2.	λύοις	(2)	λύοιτε
3.	<u>λύοι</u>	(3)	λύοιεν

Memory Aid

Lu, with a <u>present</u>, <u>may</u> <u>loose</u> the <u>optimistic octopus</u> (present active optative). He intends to do this with a big can of <u>oil</u> (-οι) in the right places.

PRESENT OPTATIVE OF εἰμί

	Singular		Plural
1.	εἴην	(1)	εἴημεν
2.	εἴης	(2)	εἴητε
3.	εἴη	(3)	εἴησαν

Memory Aid

Amy, with her present, may be in prison with the optimistic octopus (present optative of εἰμί). She is delivered to prison by AA (εἴη), two little bodyguards.

FIRST AORIST ACTIVE OPTATIVE OF λύω

	Singular		Plural
1.	λύσαιμι	(1)	λύσαιμεν
2.	λύσαις	(2)	λύσαιτε
3.	λύσαι	(3)	λύσαιεν

Memory Aid

Lu, with his one arrow, may loose the optimistic octopus (first aorist active optative). His friend Sy (-σαι) wishes to aid in the endeavor.

Singular	Plural
1. γενοίμην	(1) γενοίμεθα
2. γένοιο	(2) γένοισθε
3. γένοιτο	(3) γένοιντο

Memory Aid

The kin of mine (γίνομαι) is another can of oil (γένοιτο). Notice the octopus with 2 arrows (2 aorist optative). The one can of oil says, "May it never be!" (μὴ γένοιτο = "may it never be," a common use of the second aorist middle optative of γίνομαι).

The Use of the Optative

Now that we are familiar with the four most common forms of the optative, it will be important for us to study a few sentences, observing the use of the optative. It expresses:

1. WISH - Romans 7:7 - ὁ νόμος ἁμαρτία; μὴ γένοιτο.
   Is the law sin? May it never be!

2. DELIBERATION - Luke 3:15 - They were wondering
   μήποτε αὐτὸς εἴη ὁ χριστός, if he might be the Christ.

3. A CONDITION - 1 Peter 3:14 - εἰ καὶ πάσχοιτε διὰ
   δικαιοσύνην, μακάριοι.
   Even if you should suffer on account of righteousness, (you are) blessed.

Additional Information

<u>QUESTIONS WITH οὐ AND μή</u>

1. <u>οὐ</u> + QUESTION expects a POSITIVE answer.

   1 Cor. 9:1 - οὐκ εἰμὶ ἀπόστολος; οὐχὶ Ἰησοῦν τὸν
   κύριον ἡμῶν ἑώρακα;
   Am I not an apostle? Have I not seen
   Jesus our Lord?

   Both the first and second questions expect a positive
   answer. YES, I am an apostle. YES, I have seen the
   Lord. And, Paul would add, my apostleship is based
   on my experience with the risen Lord.

2. <u>μή</u> + QUESTION expects a NEGATIVE answer.

   1 Cor. 1:13 - μὴ Παῦλος ἐσταυρώθη ὑπὲρ ὑμῶν;
   Was Paul crucified for you? "NO, of
   course not," is the expected answer.

<u>USE OF οὐ μή IN STRONG DENIALS</u>

The words οὐ μή are found both with the aorist subjunctive and future indicative to express a very strong
denial.

Matt. 5:20 - οὐ μὴ εἰσέλθητε εἰς τὴν βασιλείαν τῶν οὐρανῶν.
You shall never enter the kingdom of heaven

Matt. 16:22 - οὐ μὴ ἔσται σοι τοῦτο.
This shall never be to you.

Enrichment

The imperative mood aids our understanding of the letter to the "Ephesians." In the first three chapters, the <u>imperative</u> appears only once (2:11), because at the outset, the writer desires to highlight the grace of God that unites Jew and Gentile in one body in Christ. The <u>indicative</u> mood pre-eminently, can do just that. In contrast, chapters 4-6 contain some 38 <u>imperatives</u> which point us to the disciplined life that flows forth from the grace of God portrayed in Chapters 1-3. A few of the imperatives found in chapters 4-6 are as follows:

1. λαλεῖτε ἀλήθειαν - speak truth (4:25)
2. γίνεσθε . . . μιμηταί τοῦ θεοῦ - become imitators of God (5:1).
3. περιπατεῖτε ἐν ἀγάπῃ - walk in love (5:2)
4. βλέπετε - take heed (5:15)
5. πληροῦσθε ἐν πνεύματι - be continually filled with the Spirit (5:18)
6. ἀναλάβετε τὴν πανοπλίαν τοῦ θεοῦ - take up the panoply of God (6:13)

Assignment

<u>Παῦλος καὶ Σιλᾶς[1] ἐν Φιλίπποις[2]</u>

Ἐστί τις ἀκοὴ ἐν ταῖς τοῦ Λουκᾶ γραφαῖς περὶ καινῆς ἀρχῆς τοῦ εὐαγγελίου ἐν μέσῳ τῶν ἐθνῶν τῶν κατοικούντων Ἑλλάδα.[3] καὶ οὕτως ἐγένετο ὅτι ἐκηρύχθη ἡ τῆς ἀναστάσεως ἀγγελία ἐν Φιλίπποις[2]. γέγραπται γὰρ ὅτι ἀπῆλθον ἀπὸ τῆς Ἀντιοχείας[4] Παῦλος καὶ διάκονος δεύτερος ὀνόματι Σιλᾶς, καὶ αὐτοὶ κατέβησαν εἰς τὰς πόλεις Δέρβην[5] καὶ Λύστραν[6] ὅπου εὑρέθη μαθητής τις ὀνόματι Τιμόθεος.[7] καὶ ὁ Τιμόθεος οὗτος ἦν υἱὸς γυναικὸς Ἰουδαίας πιστῆς, πατρὸς δὲ Ἕλληνος.[8] καὶ Τιμόθεος ἐμαρτυρεῖτο καλῶς ὑπὸ πάντων τῶν ἀδελφῶν. τοῦτον ἐπεθύμησεν Παῦλος ἐπιθυμίᾳ μεγάλῃ σὺν αὐτῷ ἐξελθεῖν. οὕτως διῆλθον οἱ τρεῖς, Παῦλος καὶ Σιλᾶς καὶ Τιμόθεος, μίαν χώραν καὶ ἄλλην ἄχρι τῆς Τρῳάδος[9] παρὰ τῇ θαλάσσῃ.

οὕτως παραγενομένων ἐκεῖ καὶ ζητούντων αὐτῶν γινώσκειν ὅ τι δεῖ πρᾶξαι αὐτούς, ὤφθη Παύλῳ νυκτὸς καθεύδοντι ἐπὶ κλίνης φῶς ὥσπερ ἀπὸ τοῦ οὐρανοῦ καὶ ἀνὴρ Μακεδών[10] τις κρατῶν τῆς δεξιᾶς καὶ παρακαλῶν αὐτὸν καὶ λέγων, Διέλθετε εἰς Μακεδονίαν[11] καὶ διακονήσατε τῷ κυρίῳ ἐν μέσῳ ἡμῶν.

καὶ εὐθέως πρὶν γενέσθαι τὴν ἡμέραν ἐβούλετο Παῦλος εὐαγγελίσασθαι τὰ μέρη πέραν τῆς θαλάσσης, λέγων πρὸς τοὺς μετ᾽ αὐτοῦ ἀδελφούς, Ἡμᾶς δεῖ ἐργάζεσθαι ἐν Μακεδονίᾳ[11] τὰ ἔργα τοῦ ἀποστείλαντος ἡμᾶς. Ἔλθετε μετ᾽ ἐμοῦ καὶ διακονήσωμεν τῷ κυρίῳ ἐκεῖ μαρτυροῦντες τῇ ἀναστάσει τοῦ Ἰησοῦ καὶ οἰκοδομοῦντες ἐκκλησίαν εἰς τὴν τοῦ θεοῦ δόξαν.

καὶ γενομένης τῆς ἡμέρας ἠρώτησαν εἰ εὕροιεν[12] πλοῖον πρὸς Μακεδονίαν, καὶ εὑρόντες καὶ ἐμβάντες εἰς αὐτὸ διῆλθον τὴν θάλασσαν ἄχρι Φιλίππων[2] ἥ ἐστιν πρώτη[13] Μακεδονίας πόλις. καὶ ἦσαν ἐν τῷ τόπῳ ἐκείνῳ μένοντες ἡμέρας τινάς.

τῇ δὲ ἡμέρᾳ τῶν σαββάτων ἐξῆλθον ἔξω τῆς πύλης τῆς πόλεως παρὰ ποταμὸν ὅπου ἐλογίζοντο προσευχήν τινα εἶναι. καὶ Παῦλος καθίσας ἐβούλετο λαλῆσαι ταῖς συνελθούσαις

γυναιξίν. καὶ κηρύσσοντος αὐτοῦ τὸν λόγον, γυνή τις
ὀνόματι Λυδία[14] ἤκουεν τὴν ἀγγελίαν τῆς ἀναστάσεως καὶ ὁ
κύριος ἤνοιξεν τὴν καρδίαν αὐτῆς. αὕτη δὲ κλαίουσα διὰ
τὰς ἁμαρτίας αὐτῆς καὶ περισσεύουσα ἐν τῇ ἐπιθυμίᾳ αὐτῆς
πάντοτε τὸν λόγον ἀκοῦσαι, δικαιωθεῖσα τῇ χάριτι καὶ
βαπτισθεῖσα ὑπὸ Παύλου παρεκάλεσεν τοὺς ἀποστόλους,
λέγουσα, Μὴ ἀπέλθητε ἀφ' ἡμῶν ἀλλ' εἰ κεκρίκατέ με ἀξίαν
καὶ πιστὴν τῷ κυρίῳ σήμερον, εἰσέλθετε ἄρτι εἰς τὸν οἶκόν
μου καὶ οἰκοδομήσατε ἡμᾶς ἐν τῇ ἁγίᾳ πίστει. καὶ εἰσῆλθον καὶ ἀληθῶς ἐκεῖ ἐν τῇ οἰκίᾳ Λυδίας,[14] ἐνίκησεν ὁ
λόγος τοῦ κυρίου τὸν διάβολον ἐκεῖνον τὸν βλασφημοῦντα
τὸ τοῦ Χριστοῦ ὄνομα καὶ πλανῶντα πάντοτε τοὺς μὴ πιστεύ-
οντας. ἀλλὰ ἐχάρησαν οἱ ἀπόστολοι σὺν ἁπάσῃ τῇ οἰκίᾳ
Λυδίας διὰ τὴν πίστιν καὶ ἐλπίδα ἐν ψυχῇ Λυδίας καὶ ἐν
ψυχαῖς τῶν υἱῶν καὶ θυγατέρων ὧν αὐτὴ γεγέννηκεν. οὔπω
γὰρ ἦν φανερὸν τί ἔμελλεν γενέσθαι.

καὶ ἐγένετο πορευομένων αὐτῶν εἰς τὴν προσευχήν,
ἤγγισεν γυνὴ νέα δαιμονιζομένη καὶ αὐτὴ ἐποίει πολλὴν
ἐργασίαν[15] τοῖς κυρίοις αὐτῆς λαλοῦσα κακῷ πνεύματι
ῥήματα ὅμοια ῥήμασιν προφήτου. καὶ ἐβλασφήμει τὴν ὁδὸν
τῆς σωτηρίας ἣν ἐκήρυσσεν ὁ Παῦλος καὶ ἠκολούθει ὀπίσω
Παύλου καὶ Σιλᾶ κακῶς, ποιοῦσα μεγάλην θλῖψιν ἐν ταῖς
ψυχαῖς αὐτῶν.

λοιπόν, θεωρῶν αὐτὴν ὡς πράσσουσαν πολλὰ κακὰ καὶ
ἀσθενηθεὶς διὰ τῆς παρουσίας[16] αὐτῆς μετ' αὐτῶν διὰ παντός, Παῦλος ἐπιστρέψας τῷ δαιμονίῳ τῷ πονηρῷ εἶπεν,
Κελεύω σοι ἐν ὀνόματι Ἰησοῦ Χριστοῦ ἐξελθεῖν ἀπ' αὐτῆς
καὶ μὴ ἐπιστρέψαις[17] πρὸς αὐτὴν πάλιν εἰς τὸν αἰῶνα. καὶ
ἐξῆλθεν τὸ δαιμόνιον τῇ ὥρᾳ ἐκείνῃ.

ἰδόντες δὲ οἱ κύριοι αὐτῆς ὅτι, ἐξελθόντος τοῦ
δαιμονίου, ἐξῆλθεν καὶ ἡ ἐλπὶς τῆς ἐργασίας[15] αὐτῶν,
ἐβλασφήμουν τὸν τοῦ θεοῦ λόγον καὶ ἐμίσουν τὸν Παῦλον
διὰ τὸ σημεῖον ὃ ἠργάσατο. καὶ ἔκραζον λέγοντες, Οὐαὶ
ἡμῖν, μὴ μέλλομεν οὖν ἐπιτρέψαι τοιούτοις ζῆν; ἄρα
ἐξέτειναν τὰς χεῖρας καὶ προσενεγκόντες Παῦλον καὶ Σιλᾶν
εἰς τὴν ἀγορὰν ἔπεισαν τοὺς ἄρχοντας βαλεῖν τοὺς δύο
ἀποστόλους εἰς φυλακήν. κἀκεῖ ἔμειναν οἱ ἀπόστολοι
δεδεμένοι τοῖς ποσὶ καὶ ταῖς χερσὶν αὐτῶν, πάσχοντες
θλῖψιν μεγάλην.

274

καὶ ἰδοὺ ἐν μέσῳ νυκτός,δοξαζόντων τῶν δύο διακόνων
τὸν θεὸν καὶ προσευχομένων αὐτῷ,ἠνεώχθησαν αἱ τῆς φυλακῆς
θύραι καὶ ἅπαντες οἱ δεδεμένοι ἀπελύθησαν. καὶ ἐφοβήθη
ὁ δεσμοφύλαξ[18] πολλά. καὶ ὡς ἔμελλεν ἀποκτεῖναι ἑαυτόν,
Παῦλος ἐκτείνας τὴν χεῖρα ἥψατο αὐτοῦ λέγων, Μὴ πράξῃς
τι σεαυτῷ. οὐχὶ πάντες ἡμεῖς ὑπάρχομεν ἔτι ὧδε; μὴ δια-
κονήσεις τῷ διαβόλῳ ἀποκτείνων σεαυτόν; μὴ γένοιτο.
αἰτήσας δὲ φῶτα καὶ ἀψάμενος τῶν χειρῶν τῶν δύο ἀποστόλων
ἐκέκραξεν ὁ δεσμοφύλαξ[18] φωνῇ μεγάλῃ λέγων, Κύριοι, τί
με δεῖ ποιεῖν ἵνα σωθῶ; οἱ δὲ εἶπον, Πίστευσον ἐπὶ τὸν
κύριον Ἰησοῦν καὶ σωθήσῃ σὺ καὶ ὁ οἶκός σου. καὶ
ἐλάλησαν αὐτῷ τὸν λόγον τοῦ θεοῦ σὺν πᾶσιν τοῖς ἐν τῇ
οἰκίᾳ αὐτοῦ.

καὶ ἐν ἐκείνῃ τῇ ὥρᾳ τῆς νυκτὸς ἐβαπτίσθη ὁ δεσμοφύλαξ[18] ὑπὸ Παύλου καὶ ἤνεγκεν τοὺς ἀποστόλους εἰς τὸν
ἴδιον οἶκον κἀκεῖ ἔφαγον καὶ ἔπιον ἐπὶ τὸ αὐτὸ[19] χαίροντες ἐν τῇ δυνάμει τοῦ εὐαγγελίου καὶ ἐν τῇ ζωῇ τῇ καινῇ
ἐν Χριστῷ Ἰησοῦ.

διὸ νῦν, ἀδελφοὶ καὶ ἀδελφαί, τοῦτο τὸ μυστήριον
λογίζεσθε οἷα γενεὰ τῶν πιστευόντων ἐγενήθη ἐν Μακεδονίᾳ.
τοῦτο γάρ ἐστιν τὸ μυστήριον ὅτι μετὰ τοιαύτην θλῖψιν ἐν
ταῖς ψυχαῖς τῶν ἐν Φιλίπποις τῶν πιστευσάντων, ἐγένετο
ἀγαπητὴ ἡ ἐκκλησία τῶν Φιλίππων τῷ Παύλῳ παρὰ[20] πάσας
τὰς ἐκκλησίας ἐν τῇ οἰκουμένῃ. εἴρηταί ποτε ὑπὸ τοῦ
ἀποστόλου ὅτι Εἰ ἡ ῥίζα ἁγία, καὶ οἱ κλάδοι. οἳ ἔχουσιν
ὦτα ἀκούειν ἀκουέτωσαν.

---

[1]Σιλᾶς - Silas
[2]Φίλιπποι - Philippi
[3]Ἑλλάς, -άδος - Greece
[4]Ἀντιοχεία - Antioch
[5]Δέρβη - Derbe
[6]Λύστρα - Lystra
[7]Τιμόθεος - Timothy
[8]Ἕλλην, -ηνος - Greek
[9]Τρῳάς, -άδος - Troas
[10]Μακεδών, -όνος - Macedonian
[11]Μακεδονία - Macedonia

[12] εὕροιεν - 2nd aorist active optative

[13] πρώτη - foremost

[14] Λυδία - Lydia

[15] ἐργασία - profit, gain

[16] παρουσία - presence (here), usually "coming, advent" referring to Jesus' return

[17] ἐπιστρέψαις - 1st aorist active optative

[18] δεσμοφύλαξ - jailer

[19] ἐπὶ τὸ αὐτό - together (cf. Acts 1:15; 2:1, 47; 4:26; 1 Corinthians 11:20)

[20] παρά - with the accusative sometimes means "more than" (cf. Luke 13:2,4)

276

Chapter 19

Vocabulary

1. ἀποδίδωμι — I give back, give away (apodosis)
2. ἀρνέομαι — I deny, refuse
3. ἀστήρ, -έρος, ὁ — star (asterisk, astral)
4. διαθήκη, -ης, ἡ — covenant, decree (thesis)
5. διακονία, -ας, ἡ — service (deacon), (cf. διακονέω)
6. διατίθημι — I make a covenant, decree
7. δίδωμι — I give
8. δυνατός, -ή, -όν — powerful (cf. δύναμις)
9. ἐπιτίθημι — I put upon, lay upon (epithet)
10. ἐπιτιμάω — I rebuke
11. ἥλιος, -ου, ὁ — sun (heliocentric)
12. καυχάομαι — I boast
13. μάρτυς, μάρτυρος, ὁ — witness (martyr), (cf. μαρτυρέω, μαρτυρία)
14. μέλος, -ους, τό — member (melody)
15. μήτε — and not
16. παραδίδωμι — I hand over
17. παρατίθημι — I place before
18. περιτομή, -ῆς, ἡ — circumcision
19. Πέτρος, -ου, ὁ — Peter
20. πόθεν — from where, whence
21. ποτήριον, -ου, τό — cup (poterium, "pot")
22. προάγω — I go before, go forward, bring forth
23. προστίθημι — I add to (prosthetic)
    προστίθημι γράφειν — I write again
    προστίθημι λαλεῖν — I speak again
24. πτωχός, -ή, -όν — poor
25. Σαμάρεια, -ας, ἡ — Samaria (Samaria)
26. σελήνη, -ης, ἡ — moon (selenite = moon rock)
27. σταυρός, -οῦ, ὁ — cross (cf. σταυρόω)
28. τίθημι — I put, place, lay down (thesis)
29. ὑπομονή, -ῆς, ἡ — patience
30. ὑποτάσσω — I subject, subject myself (hypotactic). The verb takes the acc. of the thing that is subjected, the dat of the person to whom it is subjected.

IN THIS LESSON YOU WILL:

    . . . be introduced to a new class of verbs called "μι" verbs,

    . . . meet the principal parts of γινώσκω,

    . . . find a further use of μέν and δέ, and

    . . . gain additional insight into the relation between the aorist participle and the main verb.

Foundational Concepts

Up to this point you have studied verbs whose vocabulary forms end in "ω" (active) or "ομαι" (deponent). There is one further class of verbs called "μι" verbs. The first person singular of these verbs ends in "μι" as in:

δίδωμι = I give
τίθημι = I set, put, place

The differences between the "μι" verbs and "ω" or "ομαι" verbs are largely confined to the present and second aorist systems. Observe very carefully the principal parts of δίδωμι(stem δω or δο) and τίθημι (stem θε or θη).

Pres.Act.	Fut.Act.	Aor.Act.Mid.	Per.Act.	Per.M/P	Aor.Pas.
δίδωμι	δώσω	ἔδωκα(1 Aor.) ἐδόμην(2 Aor.Mid.)	δέδωκα	δέδομαι	ἐδόθην
τίθημι	θήσω	ἔθηκα(1 Aor.) ἐθέμην(2 Aor.Mid.)	τέθεικα	τέθειμαι	ἐτέθην

Observations

1. The "μι" verbs are similar to the "ω" verbs in all the principal parts except the present and aorist.

2. The aorist has the "κ," but the perfect has both the reduplication and the "κ."

3. The only place where the "ι" occurs is in the first principal part which includes both the present and imperfect tenses. THIS IS VERY IMPORTANT. The following keys will help to narrow down the search for the correct tense of a "μι" verb.

REDUPLICATION WITH "ι" OCCURS ONLY IN THE PRESENT SYSTEM

1. REDUPLICATION WITH "ι" WITHOUT AUGMENT (i.e.- δίδωμι, τίθημι) = PRESENT TENSE

2. REDUPLICATION WITH "ι" WITH AUGMENT (i.e.- ἐδίδουν, ἐτίθην) = IMPERFECT TENSE

Memory Aid

Me sees I (ι) in the mirror (reduplication) with a present (present system).

Observe the following charts and their corresponding memory aids. As you do, note very carefully the above principle as it applies to the verb δίδωμι.

PRESENT ACTIVE INDICATIVE OF δίδωμι

	Singular	Plural
1.	δίδωμι	(1) δίδομεν
2.	δίδως	(2) δίδοτε
3.	δίδωσι (ν)	(3) διδόασι (ν)

Present Active Infinitive = διδόναι

Observation

The stem of the "μι" verb in the singular has the long vowel "ω" while the plural contains the short "o."

Memory Aid

I give a present which is a ditto of me to the indicator (present active indicative of δίδωμι). The indicator looks into the mirror (reduplication). Note the "ι" in the mirror. The observers of this transaction are Missi(n) (-μι, -ς, -σι(ν)) and men teasing (-μεν, -τε, -ασι(ν)).

PRESENT MIDDLE/PASSIVE INDICATIVE OF δίδωμι

	Singular		Plural
1.	δίδομαι	(1)	διδόμεθα
2.	δίδοσαι	(2)	δίδοσθε
3.	δίδοται	(3)	δίδονται

Present M/P Infinitive = δίδοσθαι

IMPERFECT ACTIVE INDICATIVE OF δίδωμι

	Singular		Plural
1.	ἐδίδουν	(1)	ἐδίδομεν
2.	ἐδίδους	(2)	ἐδίδοτε
3.	ἐδίδου	(3)	ἐδίδοσαν

Memory Aid

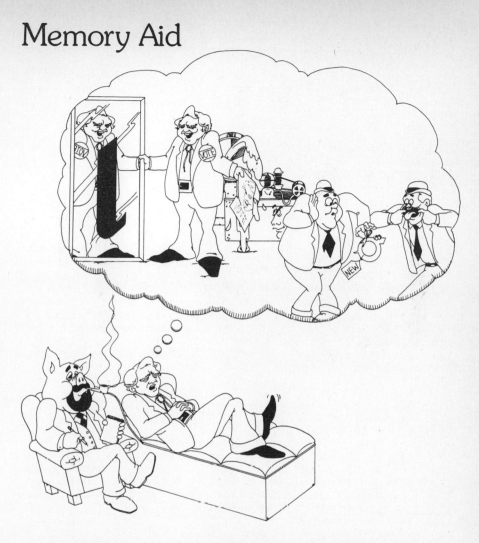

    I was giving an imperfect <u>ditto of me</u> to the <u>indicator</u> (imperfect active indicative of δίδωμι). Observe the <u>mirror</u> with "ι" (reduplication). The man on the couch confers with the psychiatrist P. Hogman (prefixed augment). Observing this scenario are a <u>new</u> "σ" that cost <u>nothing</u> (-ν, -σ, --), and some <u>men teasing</u> (-μεν, -τε, --σαν).

IMPERFECT MIDDLE/PASSIVE INDICATIVE OF δίδωμι

	Singular		Plural
1.	ἐδιδόμην	(1)	ἐδιδόμεθα
2.	ἐδίδοσο	(2)	ἐδίδοσθε
3.	ἐδίδοτο	(3)	ἐδίδοντο

SECOND AORIST MIDDLE INDICATIVE OF δίδωμι

	Singular		Plural
1.	ἐδόμην	(1)	ἐδόμεθα
2.	ἔδου	(2)	ἔδοσθε
3.	ἔδοτο	(3)	ἔδοντο

Other forms of δίδωμι

Aorist Active Infinitive = δοῦναι

The present subjunctive has an accented "ω" through-out (διδῶ, διδῷς . . .) while the aorist subjunctive omits the "δι" (δῶ, δῷς . . .). The present participle has the forms διδούς, διδοῦσα, διδόν, while the aorist participle omits the "δι" (δούς, δοῦσα, δόν).

τίθημι = I set, put, place

Review the KEYS for the "μι" verbs, and the pictures which helped you learn the endings for the present and imperfect active indicative forms of δίδωμι. Now observe the application to the important "μι" verb τίθημι.

PRESENT ACTIVE INDICATIVE OF τίθημι

	Singular		Plural
1.	τίθημι	(1)	τίθεμεν
2.	τίθης	(2)	τίθετε
3.	τίθησι(ν)	(3)	τιθέασι(ν)

PRESENT MIDDLE/PASSIVE INDICATIVE OF τίθημι

	Singular		Plural
1.	τίθεμαι	(1)	τιθέμεθα
2.	τίθεσαι	(2)	τίθεσθε
3.	τίθεται	(3)	τίθενται

IMPERFECT ACTIVE INDICATIVE OF τίθημι

	Singular		Plural
1.	ἐτίθην	(1)	ἐτίθεμεν
2.	ἐτίθεις	(2)	ἐτίθετε
3.	ἐτίθει	(3)	ἐτίθεσαν or
			ἐτίθουν

IMPERFECT MIDDLE/PASSIVE INDICATIVE OF τίθημι

	Singular		Plural
1.	ἐτιθέμην	(1)	ἐτιθέμεθα
2.	ἐτίθεσο	(2)	ἐτίθεσθε
3.	ἐτίθετο	(3)	ἐτίθεντο

Other forms of τίθημι

The present subjunctive is regular in form, irregular in accent (τιθῶ, τιθῇς . . .) while the aorist subjunctive omits the "τι" (θῶ, θῇς . . .).
The present participle has the forms τιθείς, τιθεῖσα, τιθέν while the aorist participle omits the "τι" (θείς, θεῖσα, θέν).
Present active infinitive = τιθέναι
Aorist active infinitive = θεῖναι

Practice

Parse the "μι" verbs and translate the following sentences.

1. ἵνα διδῶ
2. ἵνα δῶ
3. θέλω δοῦναι
4. ὑμῖν δέδοται γνῶναι (to know) τὰ μυστήρια τῆς βασιλείας.
5. ἐγὼ τίθημι τὴν ψυχήν μου.
6. ἵνα τις τὴν ψυχὴν αὐτοῦ θῇ.
7. ἐπέθηκαν αὐτοῖς τὰς χεῖρας καὶ ἔλαβον πνεῦμα ἅγιον.
8. παραδίδοται ὁ υἱὸς τοῦ ἀνθρώπου εἰς τὰς χεῖρας τῶν ἁμαρτωλῶν.
9. ἐδίδομεν

1. P A S 1S - δίδωμι - in order that I might give.
2. A A S 1S - δίδωμι - in order that I might give.
3. A A Inf. - δίδωμι - I desire to give.
4. Perf. P I 3S - δίδωμι - To you it has been given to know the mysteries of the kingdom.
5. P A I 1S - τίθημι - I lay down my life.
6. A A S 3S - τίθημι - In order that someone might lay down his life.
7. A A I 3P - ἐπιτίθημι - They placed their hands on them and they received the Holy Spirit.
8. P P I 3S - παραδίδωμι - The son of man is being handed over into the hands of sinners.
9. I A I 1P - δίδωμι - We were giving.

Professor Oddity

The principal parts of γινώσκω are listed. Since this verb occurs often in the NT, you need to become familiar with these principal parts. Some of the forms have been seen in the vocabulary pictures.

Pres.Act.	Fut.Dep.	Aor.Act.	Perf.Act.	Perf.M/P	Aor.Pass.
γινώσκω	γνώσομαι	ἔγνων	ἔγνωκα	ἔγνωσμαι	ἐγνώσθην

The second aorist forms are quite unique in that all - except the participle - contain the stem "γνω."

Indicative - ἔγνων - (first person singular)
Subjunctive - γνῶ - (first person singular)
Infinitive - γνῶναι -
Imperative - γνῶθι - (second person singular)

The aorist active participle, however, has the following forms: γνούς (gen. γνόντος), γνοῦσα, γνόν. For complete paradigms of the second aorist see the appendix.

Additional Information

Further uses of the particles μέν and δέ

You have often seen these two words as introducing two contrasting clauses. For example, Matt. 3:11 reads:

ἐγὼ μὲν ὑμᾶς βαπτίζω ἐν ὕδατι . . .
On the one hand, I baptize you in water . . .

ὁ δὲ . . . ἐρχόμενος . . . ὑμᾶς βαπτίσει ἐν πνεύματι ἁγίῳ.
But, on the other hand, he who is coming will baptize you in the Holy Spirit.

Quite often, however, the particles appear separately. Thus ὁ δὲ . . . may mean, "But he . . .," οἱ δὲ . . . "But they," or "And they."

Mark 16:6 - ὁ δὲ λέγει αὐταῖς,
           But he said to them . . .

Mark 8:5 - οἱ δὲ εἶπαν Ἑπτά.
           And they said, "Seven."

Moreover, the particle μέν quite often marks the beginning of a new section or a return to a main theme, combined with οὖν (common usages in Acts).

Acts 1:6 - Οἱ μὲν οὖν συνελθόντες . . .
           They, therefore, when they had come
           together . . .

Acts 8:4 - Οἱ μὲν οὖν διασπαρέντες . . .
           They, therefore, who had been scat-
           tered . . .

Enrichment

In John 15:16, we read the words of Jesus, ἔθηκα ὑμᾶς ἵνα . . . καρπὸν φέρητε . . . ἵνα ὅ τι ἂν αἰτήσητε τὸν πατέρα ἐν τῷ ὀνόματί μου δῷ ὑμῖν, "I appointed you that you should . . . bear fruit . . . in order that whatever you ask the Father in my name he may give (it) to you."

The text combines uniquely the verbs τίθημι and δίδωμι. Jesus says, ἔθηκα ὑμᾶς, "I appointed you," but the Father gives you (δῷ ὑμῖν) your requests in my name. That is to say, the disciples derive their appointment from Jesus (τίθημι), but are dependent on the Father for what he gives (δίδωμι) since he supplies their needs in the ministry.

1 Cor. 11:23f. Ἐγὼ γὰρ παρέλαβον ἀπὸ τοῦ κυρίου, ὃ καὶ <u>παρέδωκα</u> ὑμῖν, ὅτι ὁ κύριος Ἰησοῦς ἐν τῇ νυκτὶ ᾗ παρεδίδετο ἔλαβεν ἄρτον καὶ εὐχαριστήσας ἔκλασεν (broke) καὶ εἶπεν, Τοῦτό μού ἐστιν τὸ σῶμα τὸ ὑπὲρ ὑμῶν.

The text is well-known and enables us to see two important functions of the verb παραδίδωμι.

<u>First</u>, παραδίδωμι (παρέδωκα = first aorist) - in its first occurrence in the verse - is the twin term of παραλαμβάνω (παρέλαβον = first aorist) to indicate that tradition concerning Jesus is received and handed on faithfully to the Christian community.

<u>Second</u>, παραδίδωμι (παρεδίδετο = imperfect passive) - in its second occurrence in the verse - indicates "handing over" in the sense of betrayal. The imperfect tense points to the on-going treachery of Judas during that fateful night.

Assignment

ὁ θάνατος τοῦ Πολυκάρπου[1]

Μετὰ τὸ ἀποθανεῖν τοὺς ἀποστόλους καὶ ἐν ταῖς τῆς μεγάλης θλίψεως ἡμέραις, ἐπέμφθη ἐπιστολὴ ταῖς ἐκκλησίαις ἐν τῇ οἰκουμένῃ παρατιθεῖσα τοῖς πιστεύουσιν ἀκοὴν ἀληθῆ περὶ τῶν ἐσχάτων ἡμερῶν Πολυκάρπου τοῦ μακαρίου διδασκάλου τῶν ἁγίων. καὶ εἰς ἣν ἂν ἐκκλησίαν εἰσέλθῃ ἡ ἀκοή, ἐθαύμασαν οἱ ἀκούσαντες καὶ ἐχάρησαν. ἀληθῶς καλοῦσι πᾶσαι γενεαὶ Πολύκαρπον "Μακάριος" ὅτι πειραζόμενος ἀρνήσασθαι τὸν κύριον ἔδωκεν μαρτυρίαν πιστὴν καὶ ἔπιεν τὸ ποτήριον τῆς τοῦ Χριστοῦ θλίψεως. ἀληθῶς οὐδὲ ἐν κρυπτῷ οὐδὲ φανερῶς ἐλάλησεν κακόν τι, πάντοτε περισσεύων ἐν χάριτι θεοῦ. διὸ καὶ ἐκαυχήσατο ἐν τῷ σταυρῷ μόνον καὶ διὰ τῶν μελῶν τοῦ σώματος αὐτοῦ ἐτίμησεν τὸ τοῦ κυρίου ὄνομα.

οὕτως ἐγένετο ὅτι ἐπετέθη θλῖψις ἐπὶ τοὺς ἁγίους ὁμοία τῇ θλίψει τῇ κατὰ τῆς ἐκκλησίας ἐν Ἱεροσόλυμα[2] ἐν τῷ πεμφθῆναι Πέτρον καὶ Ἰωάννην εἰς Σαμάρειαν. καὶ ἀπέθανον πολλοὶ μαθηταί -- καὶ πτωχοὶ καὶ δυνατοί, ἕκαστος αὐτῶν μαρτυρῶν τῷ Χριστῷ ὑποτασσόμενος τῷ θελήματι αὐτοῦ. καὶ διὰ τοῦτο ἔκραζεν πᾶν τὸ πλῆθος τῶν ἐθνῶν κατὰ τῶν ἁγίων ὡς δαιμονιζόμενοι λέγοντες, Αἶρε τοὺς ἀθέους[3]. ζητείσθω Πολύκαρπος.

καὶ μὲν Πολύκαρπος ἀκούσας οὐκ ἐταράχθη, ἀλλ' ἐπεθύμει ἐν τῇ πόλει μένειν. οἱ δὲ πολλοὶ ἔπεισαν αὐτὸν ἀπελθεῖν ἀπὸ ἐκείνου τοῦ τόπου. ἐξελθὼν οὖν ἔμεινεν ἐν μικρᾷ οἰκίᾳ ἔγγυς τῆς πύλης τῆς πόλεως. καὶ προσευχομένου αὐτοῦ ἀπεκαλύφθη αὐτῷ νυκτὸς ὅτι μέλλει ἀποθανεῖν πυρί.

καὶ προσέθεντο οἱ φίλοι αὐτοῦ μεταβῆναι[4] αὐτὸν ἐκ δευτέρου[5] εἰς ἕτερον οἶκον, ἀλλ' οὐκ ἦν δυνατὸν φυγεῖν αὐτὸν ἀπὸ τῶν διωκόντων αὐτόν. γέγραφεν Λουκᾶς ἐν τῷ εὐαγγελίῳ ὅτι θλίψεις καὶ σημεῖα προάγουσιν τῆς τοῦ Ἰησοῦ παρουσίας, λέγων Ἔσονται σημεῖα ἐν ἡλίῳ καὶ σελήνῃ καὶ ἄστρασι τοῦ οὐρανοῦ ἀλλ' ἐπὶ γῆς θλῖψις καὶ φόβος. Πολύκαρπος δὲ γινώσκων θλῖψιν καὶ φόβον, οὐκ ἔσχεν σημεῖον εἰ μὴ τὸ σημεῖον τοῦ θανάτου αὐτοῦ πυρί.

οὕτως οἱ στρατιῶται παρεγένοντο εἰς τὴν οἰκίαν καὶ εὗρον τὸν μακάριον διδάσκαλον. καὶ εὐθὺς αὐτὸς ἐπιγινώσκων τὸ αὐτοῦ τέλος εἶναι ἔγγυς ἔλεγεν ὑπομονῇ μεγάλη, Τὸ θέλημα τοῦ θεοῦ γενέσθω. καὶ ὡς ἤμελλον οἱ στρατιῶται ἐπιβαλεῖν τῷ Πολυκάρπῳ τὰς χεῖρας ἠσπάσατο αὐτοὺς καὶ ἐκέλευσεν παρατεθῆναι αὐτοῖς φαγεῖν καὶ πιεῖν ἐν ἐκείνη τῇ ὥρα ὅσον ἂν βούλωνται. εἶτα ἠτήσατο αὐτοὺς ἵνα δῶσιν αὐτῷ ὥραν πρὸς τὸ προσεύξασθαι. καὶ ἐπιτρεψάντων αὐτῶν, προσηύξατο Πολύκαρπος ἐπὶ δύο ὥρας πλήρης ὢν χάριτος θεοῦ· διὰ τοῦτο ἐξεπλήσσετο πολλοὶ τῶν ἀκουόντων καὶ μετενόησάν τινες αὐτῶν. καὶ ἐν τῇ προσευχῇ αὐτοῦ ἠρώτα ἵνα δῷ ὁ θεὸς ὁ δυνατὸς σωτηρίαν τοῖς πᾶσι, μικροῖς τε καὶ μεγάλοις, καὶ ἐπιθῇ τὸ πνεῦμα αὐτοῦ ἐφ᾽ ἅπασαν τὴν κατὰ τὴν οἰκουμένην ἐκκλησίαν. ἄρα παρεκάλεσεν πάντας τοὺς ἁγίους.

λοιπόν, τῆς ὥρας ἐλθούσης, κρατήσαντες Πολύκαρπον καὶ ἀγαγόντες αὐτὸν ἐκ τοῦ οἴκου ἤγγισαν τῇ πύλῃ τῆς πόλεως. πρὸ δὲ τοῦ παραγενέσθαι αὐτοὺς, ἔπειθεν Πολύκαρπον ὁ εἰρήναρχος[6] καὶ ὁ πατὴρ αὐτοῦ λέγοντες, Τί γάρ, Πολύκαρπε, κακόν ἐστιν εἰπεῖν· Κύριος Καῖσαρ;[7] καὶ ἀποκριθεὶς εἶπεν ὁ Πολύκαρπος, Οὐ μέλλω ποιεῖν ὃ κελεύετέ με. οὕτως οὐκ ἠρνήσατο τὴν διαθήκην ἣν διέθηκεν αὐτῷ ὁ Ἰησοῦς διὰ τοῦ σταυροῦ αὐτοῦ.

νῦν οὖν εἰσεπορεύθη εἰς τὸ στάδιον[8] Πολύκαρπος ὁ ἀληθὴς μάρτυς καὶ ὁ ἀγαπητὸς μαθητὴς καὶ πιστὸς διδάσκαλος. εὐθὺς δὲ ἀνέβη φωνὴ μεγάλη ἀπὸ τοῦ πλήθους τοῦ ἀνόμου[9] -- καὶ τῶν τῆς περιτομῆς καὶ τῶν ἐθνῶν -- λέγοντες κακῶς, Πολύκαρπος εἴληπται. τυφλοὶ οὖν ὄντες ἐμίσουν αὐτόν, πλανηθέντες ποτὲ ὑπὸ τοῦ διαβόλου. εἶτα εἶπεν ὁ εἰρήναρχος[6] πάλιν. Ὅταν σὺ εἴπῃς, Κύριος Καῖσαρ,[7] εὐθέως ἀπολύσω σε. ἀπεκρίνατο δὲ Πολύκαρπος, Ἕως ἄρτι οὐκ ἐποίησεν πονηρόν μοι ὁ Χριστὸς οὐδέν· πῶς βλασφημήσω τὸν βασιλέα μου τὸν σώσαντά με;

λέγων δὲ ταῦτα ἤθελεν ἀρέσαι τῷ κυρίῳ αὐτοῦ. ἄρα ἐγένετο ἡτοιμασμένος ἀποδοῦναι τὸ ὀφειλόμενον τῷ Χριστῷ τῷ δόντι ζωὴν πρὸς αὐτὸν χωρὶς ἔργων καὶ τῷ θεμένῳ αὐτὸν εἰς διακονίαν.

εἶτα ἔδησαν Πολύκαρπον πρὸς δένδρον μικρὸν ἐν μέσῳ
τοῦ σταδίου[8] καὶ ἡτοιμάσθη τὸ πῦρ. ἀλλὰ πρὸ τοῦ ἅψαι
αὐτοὺς τὸ πῦρ, προσηύξατο ὁ Πολύκαρπος λέγων,

Κύριε, ὁ θεός, ὁ τοῦ ἀγαπητοῦ υἱοῦ σου Ἰησοῦ
Χριστοῦ πατήρ, δι᾽ οὗ τὴν περὶ σοῦ ἀλήθειαν εἰλήφαμεν, ὁ
θεὸς ἀγγέλων καὶ δυνάμεων καὶ πάσης τῆς οἰκουμένης παντός
τε τοῦ γένους τῶν δικαίων, οἳ ζῶσιν ἐνώπιόν σου, εὐλογῶ
σε ὅτι ἐποίησάς με ἄξιον τῆς ἡμέρας καὶ ὥρας ταύτης τοῦ
λαβεῖν μέρος ἐν ἀριθμῷ[10] τῶν μαρτύρων ἐν τῷ ποτηρίῳ τοῦ
Χριστοῦ σου εἰς ἀνάστασιν ζωῆς αἰωνίου ψυχῆς τε καὶ
σώματος ἐν ἀφθαρσίᾳ[11] πνεύματος ἁγίου· ἐν οἷς[12]
δεχθείην[13] ἐνώπιόν σου σήμερον καθὼς προητοίμασας[14] καὶ
προεφανέρωσας[15] καὶ ἐπλήρωσας, ὁ ἀληθῆς θεός. διὰ τοῦτο
καὶ περὶ πάντων σὲ εὐλογῶ, σὲ δοξάζω διὰ τοῦ αἰωνίου
ἀρχιερέως Ἰησοῦ Χριστοῦ, ἀγαπητοῦ σου υἱοῦ, δι᾽ οὗ σοὶ
σὺν αὐτῷ καὶ πνεύματι ἁγίῳ δόξα καὶ νῦν καὶ εἰς τοὺς
μέλλοντας αἰῶνας. ἀμήν.

ἀναπέμψαντος[16] δὲ αὐτοῦ τὸ Ἀμὴν τῷ θεῷ καὶ πληρώ-
σαντος τὴν προσευχήν, οἱ τοῦ πυρὸς ἄνθρωποι ἦψαν τὸ πῦρ.
καὶ οὕτως ἀπέθανεν ὁ ἅγιος μάρτυς ὁ ἀγαπήσας οὐ λόγῳ
οὐδὲ γλώσσῃ ἀλλὰ ἐν ἔργῳ καὶ ἀληθείᾳ. παρέθετο τὸ πνεῦμα
αὐτοῦ εἰς τὰς χεῖρας Χριστοῦ παραδεδομένος ὑπὸ τῶν
ἀδελφῶν τῇ χάριτι τοῦ θεοῦ πόθεν ἐδόθη αὐτῷ ἡ καινὴ ζωὴ
ἐν Χριστῷ. ἆρα ἐνίκησεν τὸν διάβολον. ἀληθῶς ἀπήγγειλεν
ἡ ἐπιστολὴ τὸν θάνατον ιοῦ Πολυκάρπου. ἀλλὰ λοιπόν,
ἀπαγγέλλει καὶ ἡ ἐπιστολὴ ὅτι διὰ τῆς μαρτυρίας τῆς
δοθείσης ἐν τῷ τοῦ Πολυκάρπου θανάτῳ, οὐκέτι οἱ ἐχθροὶ
ἐδίωκον τὴν ἐκκλησίαν ἀλλὰ εὐλόγει ὁ θεὸς τοὺς πιστεύ-
οντας διδοὺς αὐτοῖς εἰρήνην μεγάλην.

---

[1] Πολύκαρπος - Polycarp

[2] Ἱεροσόλυμα - Jerusalem

[3] ἄθεοι - godless (a term used by pagans against
Christians)

[4] μεταβαίνω - move, change residence ("And his
friends transferred him again, a second time, unto
another house."

[5] ἐκ δευτέρου - a second time

[6] εἰρήναρχος - chief of police

[7] Καῖσαρ - Caesar

[8] στάδιον - stadium

[9] ἄνομος - lawless

[10] ἀριθμός - number

[11] ἀφθαρσία - incorruptibility

[12] ἐν οἷς - The relative pronoun refers to τῶν μαρτύρων

[13] δεχθείην - 1st aorist passive optative of δέχομαι

[14] πρό + ἐτοιμάζω

[15] πρό + φανερόω

[16] ἀνά "up" + πέμπω

Chapter 20

Vocabulary

1. ἀληθινός, -ή, -όν - true (cf. ἀλήθεια)
2. ἄνεμος, -ου, ὁ - wind (<u>anemo</u>meter - instrument for measuring the force of wind)
3. ἀνίστημι - I raise up, rise (comp. ἀνάστασις)
4. ἀπόλλυμι - I destroy, perish (Apollyon)
5. ἀφίημι - I forgive, leave, allow (cf. ἀφεσις)
6. γαμέω - I marry (mono<u>gamy</u>)
7. γέ(enclitic) - at least, even, indeed
8. γνῶσις, -εως, ἡ - knowledge (gnostic, dia<u>gnostic</u>, cf. γινώσκω)
9. δείκνυμι - I show (cf. <u>deic</u>tic - "proving, pointing," para<u>digm</u>)
10. δύναμαι - I am able (compare δύναμις)
11. ἐξίστημι - I amaze, am amazed
12. ἐπεί - since, because
13. ἐπερωτάω - I ask (compare ἐρωτάω)
14. ἡγέομαι - I consider, lead (<u>hege</u>mony)
15. ἵστημι - I place, stand
16. κάθημαι - I sit (compare καθίζω)
17. κλέπτης, -ου, ὁ - thief (<u>klepto</u>maniac)
18. ναί - yes, certainly
19. οἶδα - I know
20. παραγγέλλω (often foll. by dat. case) - I command, instruct
21. παρρησία, -ας, ἡ - boldness
22. πλήν - nevertheless, only, except
23. ποῖος, -α, -ον - of what kind
24. συνείδησις, -εως, ἡ - conscience (syneidesis)
25. φαίνω - I shine, appear (<u>pheno</u>menon)
26. φημί - I say (pro<u>phet</u>)
27. ὥστε - so that (cf. ὡς). Sometimes it is followed by the accusative and the infinitive

IN THIS LESSON YOU WILL:

. . . become acquainted with additional "μι" verbs,

. . . meet two common but irregular verbs (οἶδα and δύναμαι), and

. . . become familiar with the pluperfect tense.

Foundational Concepts

In the previous lesson on the "μι" verbs you saw a very helpful principle which will aid you in determining their tense.

REDUPLICATION WITH "ι" OCCURS ONLY IN THE PRESENT SYSTEM

1. Reduplication with "ι" without augment = Present Tense
2. Reduplication with "ι" with augment = Imperfect Tense

ME SEES I!

You also learned the endings for the present and imperfect active indicative of the verb δίδωμι which will apply to the other "μι" verbs. Observe the following principal parts of ἵστημι.

ἵστημι - I make to stand, stand up

Pres.Act.	Fut.Act.	Aor.Act.	Perf.Act.	Perf.M/P	Aor.Pass.
ἵστημι	στήσω	ἔστησα (1 Aor.) ἔστην (2 Aor.)	ἕστηκα		ἐστάθην

Observations

1. The stem is στη or στα.

2. The "ι" is unique to the present tense, though there is no reduplication.

3. The verb may be transitive, namely it may take a direct object, or it may be intransitive.

   Matt. 25:33 - στήσει τὰ μὲν πρόβατα ἐκ δεξιῶν αὐτοῦ.
   And he will cause the sheep to stand (transitive) on his right.

   Luke 24:36 - αὐτὸς ἔστη ἐν μέσῳ αὐτῶν.
   He himself stood (intransitive) in their midst.

ἀφίημι - I forgive, allow, leave

Pres.Act.	Fut.Act.	Aor.Act.	Perf.Act.	Perf.M/P	Aor.Pass.
ἀφίημι	ἀφήσω	ἀφῆκα		ἀφεῖμαι	ἀφέθην

Observations

1. The verb was originally a compound verb from ἀπό + ἵημι.

2. The stem is ἀφιε (pres.) or ἀφε (aor.).

3. The "ι" occurs in the present tense only (compare ἵστημι).

PRESENT ACTIVE INDICATIVE OF ἀφίημι

	Singular		Plural
1.	ἀφίημι	(1)	ἀφίεμεν or ἀφίομεν
2.	ἀφεῖς	(2)	ἀφίετε
3.	ἀφίησι(ν)	(3)	ἀφίουσι(ν)

A few important forms of ἀφίημι appear below. They are not intended for memorization, but familiarity. Observe the similarities with the endings you already know.

AORIST ACTIVE INDICATIVE OF ἀφίημι

	Singular		Plural
1.	ἀφῆκα	(1)	ἀφήκαμεν
2.	ἀφῆκας	(2)	ἀφήκατε
3.	ἀφῆκεν	(3)	ἀφῆκαν

AORIST ACTIVE IMPERATIVE

	Singular		Plural
2.	ἄφες	(2)	ἄφετε
3.	ἀφέτων	(3)	ἀφέτωσαν

<u>Present Active Infinitive</u> = ἀφιέναι
<u>Second Aorist Active Infinitive</u> = ἀφεῖναι
<u>Present Active Subjunctive</u> = ἀφιῶ
<u>Second Aorist Active Subjunctive</u> = ἀφῶ
<u>Present Active Participle</u> = ἀφιείς   ἀφιεῖσα   ἀφιέν
<u>Second Aorist Active Participle</u> = ἀφείς   ἀφεῖσα   ἀφέν

Forms of ἵστημι

PRESENT ACTIVE INDICATIVE

	Singular		Plural
1.	ἵστημι	(1)	ἵσταμεν
2.	ἵστης	(2)	ἵστατε
3.	ἵστησι(ν)	(3)	ἵστασι(ν)

Infinitive = ἱστάναι

PRESENT MIDDLE/PASSIVE INDICATIVE

	Singular
1.	ἵσταμαι	(1)	ἱστάμεθα
2.	ἵστασαι	(2)	ἵστασθε
3.	ἵσταται	(3)	ἵστανται

Infinitive = ἵστασθαι

IMPERFECT ACTIVE INDICATIVE

	Singular		Plural
1.	ἵστην	(1)	ἵσταμεν
2.	ἵστης	(2)	ἵστατε
3.	ἵστη	(3)	ἵστασαν

IMPERFECT MIDDLE/PASSIVE INDICATIVE

	Singular		Plural
1.	ἱστάμην	(1)	ἱστάμεθα
2.	ἵστασο	(2)	ἵστασθε
3.	ἵστατο	(3)	ἵσταντο

294

Practice

The following sentences will give you some practice with
the "μι" verbs, ἵστημι and ἀφίημι

1. Mark 9:36 - καὶ λαβὼν παιδίον ἔστησεν αὐτὸ ἐν μέσῳ
             αὐτῶνλ.
2. Matt. 12:26 - πῶς οὖν σταθήσεται ἡ βασιλεία αὐτοῦ;

3. Acts 7:33 - ὁ γὰρ τόπος ἐφ᾽ ᾧ ἕστηκας γῆ ἁγία ἐστίν.

4. 1 John 1:9 - πιστός ἐστιν καὶ δίκαιος ἵνα ἀφῇ ἡμῖν
             τὰς ἁμαρτίας.

KEY

1. And having taken a small child he stood him in their
   midst.
2. How then shall his kingdom stand?
3. For the place upon which you stand is holy ground.
4. He is faithful and righteous so that he forgives us
   (our) sins.

ἀπόλλυμι - I destroy, lose (active)
          I perish (middle)

     Observe the various principal parts of ἀπόλλυμι .
Become familiar with the forms, noting the differences
between the active and middle voices. Compare the forms
with the other "μι" verbs.

Pres. Act.	Fut. Act.	Aor. Act.	Perf. Act.
ἀπόλλυμι	ἀπολῶ ἀπολέσω	ἀπώλεσα	ἀπολώλεκα

Pres. Mid.	Fut. Mid.	Aor. Mid.	Perf. Act.
ἀπόλλυμαι	ἀπολοῦμαι	ἀπωλόμην ("I perished")	ἀπόλωλα ("I am lost")

δείκνυμι - I show, point out

     The verb δείκνυμι keeps the stem δείκνυ in all forms
of the present system. In other tenses it follows the
pattern of the "ω" verbs. Observe the following principal
parts.

Pres.Act.	Fut.Act.	Aor.Act.	Perf.Act.	Perf.M/P	Aor.Pass.
δείκνυμι	δείξω	ἔδειξα			ἐδείχθην

δύναμαι - I am able

The vast majority of the forms of δύναμαι occur in the present tense. Normally it will be followed by a complementary infinitive.

PRESENT DEPONENT INDICATIVE OF δύναμαι

	Singular	Plural
1.	δύναμαι	δυνάμεθα
2.	δύνασαι or δύνῃ	δύνασθε
3.	δύναται	δύνανται

Pres.Act.	Fut.Act.	Aor.Act.	Perf.Act.	Perf.M/P	Aor.Pass.
δύναμαι	δυνήσομαι				ἠδυνήθην

Practice

1. καὶ προσελθόντες ἤγειραν αὐτὸν λέγοντες, Κύριε, σῶσον, ἀπολλύμεθα.
2. Ἀπὸ τότε ἤρξατο ὁ Ἰησοῦς δεικνύειν τοῖς μαθηταῖς αὐτοῦ ὅτι δεῖ αὐτὸν εἰς Ἱεροσόλυμα ἀπελθεῖν.
3. καὶ εἶπεν αὐτῷ Ναθαναήλ, Ἐκ Ναζαρὲτ δύναταί τι ἀγαθὸν εἶναι;
4. ἔδειξεν αὐτῷ πάσας τὰς βασιλείας τῆς οἰκουμένης.
5. ὃς γὰρ ἐὰν θέλῃ τὴν ψυχὴν αὐτοῦ σῶσαι, ἀπολέσει αὐτήν.

Key

1. And having approached, they raised him up saying, Lord, save (us), we are perishing.
2. From then, Jesus began to point out to his disciples that it is necessary for him to depart for Jerusalem.
3. And Nathanael said to him, "Is anything good able to be (to come) from Nazareth?"
4. He showed to him all the kingdoms of the inhabited world.
5. For whoever desires to save his life will lose it.

οἶδα - I know, perceive

The common verb οἶδα has the same stem as the second aorist form εἶδον, I saw, but οἶδα is a second perfect and is always translated by the PRESENT tense. As you observe, the endings are identical with the perfect active indicative of γράφω.

Second Perfect of οἶδα with Present Meaning

	Singular		Plural
1.	οἶδα	, I know	οἴδαμεν
2.	οἶδας		οἴδατε
3.	οἶδεν		οἴδασι(ν)

Infinitive = εἰδέναι

PERFECT PARTICIPLE OF οἶδα

Singular			Plural		
M	**F**	**N**	**M**	**F**	**N**
εἰδώς	εἰδυῖα	εἰδός	εἰδότες	εἰδυῖαι	εἰδότα
εἰδότος	εἰδυίας	εἰδότος	εἰδότων	εἰδυιῶν	εἰδότων
εἰδότι	εἰδυίᾳ	εἰδότι	εἰδόσι(ν)	εἰδυίαις	εἰδόσι(ν)
εἰδότα	εἰδυῖαν	εἰδός	εἰδότας	εἰδυίας	εἰδότα

Pluperfect Tense

In the perfect tense, the results extend into the present, "I have loosed." However, in the pluperfect tense, the results of a past action extend to a point in the past, "I had loosed."

The FIRST PLUPERFECT (Past Perfect) of λύω

	Singular			Plural
1.	ἐλελύκειν	1.		ἐλελύκειμεν
	I had loosed			We had loosed
2.	ἐλελύκεις	2.		ἐλελύκειτε
	You had loosed			You had loosed
3.	ἐλελύκει	3.		ἐλελύκεισαν
	He had loosed			They had loosed
	She had loosed			

Observations

1. The First Pluperfect is composed of:

   a. Augment (sometimes omitted),
   b. reduplication,
   c. stem,
   d. "κ" suffix,
   e. personal endings (note the similarity of endings to the perfect active indicative).

2. The second pluperfect (e.g. ᾔδειν from οἶδα) has no kappa. The pluperfect of οἶδα has imperfect meaning while οἶδα itself has present meaning.

Practice

Now translate the following Scriptures which will illustrate for you the various "μι" verbs, the verb οἶδα and the pluperfect tense.

1. πῶς δύναται ἄνθρωπος γεννηθῆναι;
2. ἄφες ἡμῖν τα ὀφειλήματα (debts) ἡμῶν, ὡς καὶ ἡμεῖς ἀφήκαμεν τοῖς ὀφειλέταις (debtors) ἡμῶν.
3. Ἐὰν γὰρ ἀφῆτε τοῖς ἀνθρώποις τὰ παραπτώματα (trans- gressions) αὐτῶν, ἀφήσει καὶ ὑμῖν ὁ πατὴρ ὑμῶν.
4. πέπεισμαι γὰρ ὅτι οὔτε θάνατος οὔτε ζωὴ . . . οὔτε ἐνεστῶτα (things present - from ἐνίστημι) οὔτε μέλλοντα . . . δυνήσεται ἡμᾶς χωρίσαι (to separate) ἀπὸ τῆς ἀγάπης τοῦ θεοῦ.
5. οἱ δὲ εὐθέως ἀφέντες τὸ πλοῖον καὶ τὸν πατέρα αὐτῶν ἠκολούθησαν αὐτῷ.
6. Ῥαββί, οἴδαμεν ὅτι ἀπὸ θεοῦ ἐλήλυθας διδάσκαλος.
7. οὔπω ἐληλύθει πρὸς αὐτοὺς Ἰησοῦς.

KEY

1. How is a man able to be born?
2. Forgive us our debts as we also forgave our debtors.
3. For if you forgive men their transgressions, your Father will forgive you also.
4. For I am persuaded that neither death, nor life . . . nor things present, nor things to come . . . will be able to separate us from the love of God.
5. And they, immediately after leaving the boat, and their father, followed him.
6. Rabbi, we know that you have come from God (as) a teacher.
7. Jesus had not yet come to them.

Enrichment

The earliest extant text of Paul's letters, Papyrus 46 (late second or early third century), has a unique reading in 1 Cor. 8:2-3. Its text appears below in comparison with the United Bible Society text. A translation of each column is provided.

Papyrus 46

v.2 - εἴ τις δοκεῖ ἐγνωκέ-
ναι, οὔπω ἔγνω καθὼς δεῖ
γνῶναι·

v.3 - εἰ δέ τις ἀγαπᾷ, οὗτος
ἔγνωσται.

Translation

v.2 - If anyone seems to have acquired knowledge, he does not yet know even as it is necessary (for him) to know.

v.3 - But if anyone loves, this one is known.

UBS Text

v.2 - εἴ τις δοκεῖ ἐγνωκέ-
ναι τι, οὔπω ἔγνω καθὼς
δεῖ γνῶναι·

v.3 - εἰ δέ τις ἀγαπᾷ τὸν
θεόν, οὗτος ἔγνωσται ὑπ᾽
αὐτοῦ.

Translation

v.2 - If anyone seems to have known anything, he does not yet know even as it is necessary (for him) to know.

v.3 - But if anyone loves God, this one is known by him.

Except for the second part of v.2, Papyrus 46 has a shorter reading than does the UBS text. Papyrus 46 may indeed reflect the original reading. In it, Paul contrasts the one who imagines that he has acquired knowledge with the one who loves, and whose love, in turn, is known (ἔγνωσται) or recognized (i.e. by others). His love is sacrificial. He will forego eating food offered to idols if his act, in any way, will injure anyone in the body of Christ. The context is clear, e.g. 1 Cor. 8:11-13. Paul urges not a love for God but a love for brothers and sisters in the church of God (cf. 1 Cor. 1:2). Thus, Papyrus 46 has a strong claim to originality in 1 Cor. 8:2-3.

ΠΑΡΘΕΝΟΝ ΚΑΛΩС ΠΟΙΗСΕΙ ΩСΤΕ ΚΑΙ
Ο ΓΑΜΙΖΩΝ ΤΗΝ ΠΑΡΘΕΝΟΝ ΑΥΤΟΥ
ΚΑΛΩС ΠΟΙΗСΕΙ ΚΑΙ Ο ΜΗ ΓΑΜΙΖΩΝ
ΚΡΙССΟΝ ΠΟΙΗСΕΙ ΓΥΝΗ ΔΕΔΕΤΑΙ
ΕΦ ΟСΟΝ ΧΡΟΝΟΝ ΖΗ Ο ΑΝΗΡ ΑΥΤΗС
ΕΑΝ ΔΕ ΚΟΙΜΗΘΗ Ο ΑΝΗΡ ΕΛΕΥΘΕΡΑ
ЕСΤΙΝ Ω ΘΕΛΕΙ ΓΑΜΗΘΗΝΑΙ ΜΟΝΟΝ
ΕΝ ΚΩ ΜΑΚΑΡΙΑ ДΕ ΕСΤΙΝ ΕΑΝ ΟΥΤΩС
ΜΕΙΝΗ ΚΑΤΑ ΤΗΝ ΕΜΗΝ ΓΝΩΜΗΝ
ΔΟΚΩ ΔΕ ΚΑΓΩ ΠΝΑ ΘΥ ΕΧΕΙΝ ΠΕΡΙ
ΔΕ ΤΩΝ ΕΙΔΩΛΟΘΥΤΩΝ ΟΙДΑΜΕΝ ΟΤΙ
ΠΑΝΤΕС ΓΝΩСΙΝ ΕΧΟΜΕΝ Η ΓΝΩСΙС
ΦΥСΙΟΙ Η ДΕ ΑΓΑΠΗ ΟΙΚΟДΟΜΕΙ
ΕΙ ΤΙС ΔΟΚΕΙ ΕΓΝΩΚΕΝΑΙ ΟΥΠΩ ΕΓΝΩ
ΚΑΘΩС ΔΕΙ ΓΝΩΝΑΙ ΕΙ ДΕ ΤΙС ΑΓΑΠΑ
ΟΥΤΟС ΕΓΝΩСΤΑΙ ΠΕΡΙ ΤΗС ΒΡΩСΕΩС
ΟΥΝ ΤΩΝ ΕΙΔΩΛΟΘΥΤΩΝ ΟΙДΑΜΕΝ
ΟΤΙ ΟΥДΕΝ ΕΙΔΩΛΟΝ ΕΝ ΚΟСΜΩ
ΚΑΙ ΟΤΙ ΟΥДΕΙС ΘС ΕΙ ΜΗ ΕΙС ΚΑΙ ΓΑΡ
ΕΙ ΠΕΡ ΕΙСΙΝ ΛΕΓΟΜΕΝΟΙ ΘΕΟΙ ΕΙΤΕ
ΕΝ ΟΥΡΑΝΩ ΕΙΤΕ ΕΠΙ ΓΗС ΩСΠΕΡ
ΠΟΛΛΟΙ ΕΙСΙΝ ΘΕΟΙ ΚΑΙ ΚΥΡΙΟΙ ΠΟΛΛΟΙ
ΗΜΙΝ ΕΙС ΘС ΚΑΙ ΟΠΡ ΕΞ ΟΥ ΤΑ
ΠΑΝΤΑ ΚΑΙ ΗΜΕΙС ΕΙС ΑΥΤΟΝ ΚΑΙ
ΕΙС ΚС ΙΗС ΧΡС ΔΙ ΟΥ ΤΑ ΠΑΝΤΑ
ΗΜΕΙС ΔΙ ΑΥΤΟΥ ΑΛΛ

1 Corinthians 7:37-8:7
(Papyrus 46)

Assignment

ἡ συνείδησις τοῦ προφήτου Ἰωνᾶ[1]

καὶ ἐγένετο λόγος κυρίου πρὸς Ἰωνᾶν λέγων,
Ἀνάστηθι[2] καὶ πορεύθητι εἰς Νινευὴ[3] τὴν πόλιν τὴν
μεγάλην καὶ κήρυξον ἐν αὐτῇ, ὅτι ἀνέβη ἡ κραυγὴ[4] τῆς
ἀδικίας αὐτῆς πρός με.

καὶ ἀνέστη Ἰωνᾶς τοῦ φυγεῖν εἰς θαρσὶς[5] ἐκ προσώπου
κυρίου ὥσπερ φεύγει κλέπτης ἀπὸ τοῦ φωτὸς τοῦ ἡλίου. καὶ
κατέβη εἰς Ἰόππην[6] ὅπου εὗρεν πλοῖον πορευόμενον εἰς
θαρσίς,[5] καὶ ἔδωκεν τὸ ναῦλον[7] αὐτοῦ καὶ ἐνέβη εἰς αὐτὸ
εἰς τὸ φυγεῖν ἐκ προσώπου κυρίου. καὶ ἦσαν πολλοὶ ἐν τῷ
πλοίῳ μετ᾽ αὐτοῦ καὶ ἐν τῷ διελθεῖν αὐτοὺς διὰ τῆς
θαλάσσης, ἐγένετο τὸ σκότος τῆς νυκτὸς ὥστε μὴ δύνασθαι
αὐτοὺς ἰδεῖν μήτε σελήνην μήτε ἀστέρας. καὶ ἤγειρεν ὁ
κύριος ἄνεμον δυνατὸν καὶ ἐπέβαλλεν κλύδων[8] μέγας εἰς τὸ
πλοῖον ὥστε φοβεῖσθαι πάντας ὅτι ἔμελλεν τὸ πλοῖον ἀπολ-
έσθαι. διὸ ἔκραζον, ἕκαστος πρὸς τὸν θεὸν αὐτοῦ, διὰ τὸ
ταραχθῆναι αὐτοὺς τῷ κλύδωνι.[8] καὶ ἤρξαντο ἐκβαλεῖν
σκεύη πολλὰ εἰς τὴν θάλασσαν, ἴσχυσεν γὰρ ὁ ἄνεμος ἀντ᾽
αὐτῶν. ἀλλὰ Ἰωνᾶς κατέβη εἰς τὴν κοίλην[9] τοῦ πλοίου
κἀκεῖ ἐκάθευδεν καὶ ἔρρεγχεν.[10]

καὶ προσῆλθεν πρὸς αὐτὸν ὁ πρωρεὺς[11] καὶ εἶπεν αὐτῷ,
Διάκονε τοῦ θεοῦ, τί σὺ ῥέγχεις[10]; ἀπολλύμεθα· ἄνάστα[2]
καὶ ἐπικαλοῦ τὸν θεόν σου ὅπως σώσῃ ἡμᾶς καὶ μὴ ἀπολ-
ώμεθα. καὶ ἐλάλει ἕκαστος πρὸς ἕτερον, Τίς δύναται
στῆναι ἔμπροσθεν τῆς τοῦ θεοῦ δυνάμεως; δεῦτε,[12] βάλωμεν
κλήρους[13] καὶ ἐπιγνῶμεν τὸν ἄνδρα τὸν ἄγοντα ἡμᾶς εἰς
θάνατον. καὶ ἔβαλον κλήρους[13] καὶ ἔπεσεν ὁ κλῆρος ἐπὶ
Ἰωνᾶν. εἶτα ἐπηρώτησαν αὐτόν, Ἀπάγγειλον ἡμῖν, Τίς εἶ,
καὶ ἀπὸ τίνος χώρας ἔρχῃ, καὶ τί κακὸν πεποίηκας; μὴ
ἀρνήσῃ ἀποκριθῆναι ἡμῖν. ὁ δὲ ἀποκριθεὶς εἶπεν, Δοῦλος
κυρίου ἐγώ εἰμι καὶ τῷ κυρίῳ τῷ ἀληθινῷ θεῷ τοῦ οὐρανοῦ
ἐγὼ προσκυνῶ, φεύγων νῦν ἐκ προσώπου κυρίου. καὶ ἐπηρώ-
των αὐτὸν λέγοντες, Δεῖξον ἡμῖν τί σοι ποιήσωμεν ὅτι
οὗτος ὁ κλύδων[8] ἐστὶν ἐφ᾽ ἡμᾶς. καὶ εἶπεν Ἰωνᾶς πρὸς
αὐτούς, Ἄραντες βάλετέ με εἰς τὴν θάλασσαν, ἐπεὶ οἶδα
ὅτι δι᾽ ἐμὲ ὁ κλύδων[8] ὁ μέγας οὗτος ἐφ᾽ ὑμᾶς ἐστιν.

πλὴν ἐπείραζον οἱ ἄνδρες τοῦ ἐπιστρέψαι τὸ πλοῖον πρὸς τὴν γῆν, καὶ οὐκ ἠδύναντο ὅτι ἡ θάλασσα ταρασσομένη ἀνίστατο ἐπ᾽ αὐτούς.

λοιπόν, ἐκέκραξαν μεγάλῃ φωνῇ λέγοντες, Οὐαὶ ἡμῖν, μὴ ἀπολλύμεθα διὰ τὴν ψυχὴν τοῦ ἀνθρώπου τούτου; μὴ γένοιτο, κύριε, μὴ ἐπιθῇς ἐφ᾽ ἡμᾶς αἷμα δίκαιον. τί ποιήσωμεν; καὶ ἦραν τὸν Ἰωνᾶν καὶ ἐξέβαλον αὐτὸν εἰς τὴν θάλασσαν. καὶ εὐθὺς ἔστη ἡ θάλασσα μηκέτι ταρασσομένη, ὥστε φοβηθῆναι τοὺς ἄνδρας φόβῳ μεγάλῳ τὸν κύριον καὶ προσήνεγκον θυσίαν τῷ κυρίῳ καὶ προσηύξαντο πολλά, ὅτι ἐξέστησαν πάντες ἐπὶ τῷ γεγονότι.

ἀλλὰ πρὶν ἢ ἂν ἐκβληθῇ Ἰωνᾶς εἰς τὴν θάλασσαν παρήγγειλεν κύριος θεὸς ἰχθύι μεγάλῳ καταπιεῖν[14] τὸν Ἰωνᾶν· καὶ ἦν Ἰωνᾶς ἐν τῷ ἰχθύι τρεῖς ἡμέρας καὶ τρεῖς νυκτάς, καὶ προσηύξατο Ἰωνᾶς πρὸς κύριον ἐν μέσῳ τοῦ ἰχθύος.

εἶτα παρήγγειλεν ὁ κύριος τῷ ἰχθύι καὶ ἐξέβαλεν τὸν Ἰωνᾶν ἐπὶ τὴν γῆν.

καὶ ἐγένετο λόγος κυρίου πρὸς Ἰωνᾶν ἐκ δευτέρου[15] λέγων, Ἀνάστηθι[2] καὶ πορεύθητι εἰς Νινευὴ καὶ κήρυξον ἐν αὐτῇ ὃ ἐγὼ ἐλάλησα πρός σε. καὶ ἀνέστη Ἰωνᾶς καὶ πορευθεὶς ἤγγισεν τῇ Νινευή, καθὼς ἐλάλησεν κύριος. καὶ παρρησίᾳ ἤρξατο εἰσέρχεσθαι εἰς τὴν πόλιν καὶ ἐκήρυξεν λέγων, Ἔτι τρεῖς ἡμέραι καὶ Νινευὴ ἀπολεῖται. καὶ ἐπίστευσαν οἱ ἄνδρες τῆς Νινευὴ τῷ θεῷ καὶ μετενόησαν καὶ ἐνήστευσαν καὶ ἐνεδύσαντο σάκκους[16] ἀπὸ μεγάλου αὐτῶν ἕως μικροῦ αὐτῶν. καὶ ἤγγισεν ὁ λόγος πρὸς τὸν βασιλέα τῆς Νινευή, καὶ ἰδοὺ ἀνέστη ἀπὸ τοῦ θρόνου αὐτοῦ καὶ ἐνεδύσατο σάκκους[16] καὶ ἐκάθισεν ἐπὶ γῆς καὶ εἶπεν τῷ λαῷ, Κλαίωμεν ἐπὶ τὰς ἁμαρτίας ἡμῶν· πᾶς ζητείτω τὸν θεὸν Ἰσραήλ· μηδεὶς γαμησάτω μηδὲ ποιησάτω δεῖπνον ὑπὲρ τῶν φίλων αὐτοῦ. ἐπιθῶμεν σάκκους καὶ ἐπὶ πάντα θηρία καὶ μὴ φαγέτω θηρίον τὸν χόρτον μηδὲ πιέτω ὕδωρ. τίς οἶδεν εἰ μετανοήσει ὁ θεὸς καὶ ἀποστρέψει ἐξ ὀργῆς αὐτοῦ καὶ οὐ μὴ ἀπολόμεθα. καὶ οὕτως ἦν μετάνοια μεγάλη ἐν Νινευὴ οἷα οὐ γέγονεν ἀπ᾽ ἀρχῆς κόσμου ἕως τοῦ ἄρτι. εἶδεν οὖν ὁ θεὸς τὰ ἔργα αὐτῶν, ὅτι ἀπέστρεψαν ἀπὸ τῶν ὁδῶν αὐτῶν τῶν πονηρῶν καὶ μετενόησεν ὁ θεὸς ἐπὶ τῷ κακῷ

ᾧ ἐλάλησεν τοῦ ποιῆσαι αὐτοῖς καὶ οὐκ ἐποίησεν αὐτὸ ἀλλ'
ἀφῆκεν αὐτοῖς.

καὶ διὰ τοῦτο Ἰωνᾶς ἀφεὶς[17] ἐξῆλθεν ἔξω καὶ ἐκάθητο
ἐπὶ γῆν ἐγγὺς τῶν πυλῶν τῆς πόλεως. ἐκεῖ γε ἐλυπήθη καὶ
προσηύχετο τῷ κυρίῳ λέγων, Ναί, κύριε, οὐχὶ ἐλογιζόμην
ταῦτα ἐν τῇ ἀρχῇ ἔτι ὢν ἐν τῇ γῇ μου; οὕτως διακονήσας
σοι καλῶς ἡγησάμην ἐμαυτὸν δίκαιον τοῦ φυγεῖν εἰς θαρσὶς[5]
ὅτι ἔγνων ὅτι σὺ ὁ ἐλεῶν καὶ ὁ ἔχων ἐξουσίαν ἀφιέναι τὰς
ἁμαρτίας τούτων τῶν ἐθνῶν. καὶ νῦν, Δυνατὲ κύριε, λαβὲ
τὴν ψυχήν μου ἀπ' ἐμοῦ ὅτι καλόν μοι τὸ ἀποθανεῖν με ἢ ζῆν.

ὁ δὲ θεὸς ἀπεκρίθη ἐπιτιμῶν αὐτῷ καὶ λέγων, Οὐχὶ
δεῖ ἐλεῆσαί με καὶ σῶσαι πόλιν ἐν ᾗ κατοικοῦσι πολλοὶ
μετανοοῦντες ἀπὸ τῆς ἀδικίας, καὶ πόλιν ἔχουσαν θηρία
πολλά;

---

[1] Ἰωνᾶς - Jonah

[2] 2nd aorist active imperative, 2nd Sing. of ἀνίστημι.
The 2nd aor. act. imperative 2nd sing. actually shows
two forms - ἀνάστηθι and ἀνάστα.

[3] Νινευή - Nineveh (indecl.)

[4] κραυγή - cry (cf. κράζω)

[5] θαρσίς - Tarshish

[6] Ἰόππη - Joppa

[7] ναῦλον, τό - fare (for passage)

[8] κλύδων - ωνος - wave

[9] κοίλη - hollow, hold

[10] ῥέγχω - snore

[11] πρωρεύς - look-out man (at the bow of ship)

[12] δεῦτε - come! (imperatival particle)

[13] κλῆρος - lot

[14] καταπίνω - swallow down

[15] ἐκ δευτέρου - a second time

[16] σάκκος - sackcloth

[17] ἀφείς - after leaving (2 Aor. Act. Participle).
Compare ἀφῆκεν "he forgave" in the previous sentence -
from the same verb ἀφίημι.

Chapter 21

Vocabulary

1. ἀδικία, -ας, ἡ   - injustice, unrighteousness (compare δίκαιος)

2. ἀποστρέφω   - I turn away, reject (apostrophe). (compare ὑποστρέφω)

3. βαστάζω   - I bear, carry

4. ἐκεῖθεν   - from there (cf. ἐκεῖ and ἐκεῖνος)

5. ἔλεος, -ους, τό   - mercy, pity (cf. ἐλεέω)

6. ἐμός, ἐμή, ἐμόν (adj.)   - my, mine (cf. ἐμοῦ)

7. ἐορτή, -ῆς, ἡ   - feast

8. ἥκω   - I have come

9. ἡμέτερος, -α, -ον   - our (cf. ἡμεῖς). An adj.

10. θυσία, -ας, ἡ   - sacrifice

11. ἰάομαι   - I heal (pediatrics)

12. ἰσχυρός, -ά, -όν   - strong (cf. ἰσχύω)

13. καταργέω   - I make ineffective, nullify

14. κρίμα, -ατος, τό   - judgment, decree (critic). (cf. κρίνω)

15. λυπέω   - I grieve

16. μᾶλλον   - more, rather

17. μάχαιρα, -ης, ἡ   - sword ("machete")

18. μείζων, μεῖζον   - greater ("mezzanine")

19. μέχρι (with gen.)   - until

20. μισθός, -οῦ, ὁ   - pay, reward

21. ὀμνύω   - I swear, take an oath. (Aorist = ὤμοσα)

22. ὁμοίως   - likewise (cf. ὅμοιος)

23. παράκλησις, -εως, ἡ   - encouragement, appeal (Paraclete cf. παρακαλέω)

24. παρέρχομαι   - I pass by (cf. ἔρχομαι)

25. πάσχα, τό (indecl.)   - Passover (paschal)

26. πλείων, πλεῖον   - more (pleonasm)

27. πλούσιος, -ία, -ιον   - rich (plutocrat)

28. πόσος, -η, -ον   - how great, how much (posology - study of dosage)

29. προσκαλέομαι   - I call to myself (cf. καλέω), summon

30. προφητεύω   - I prophesy (prophet).

31. σός, σή, σόν (adj.) - your, yours (cf. σοῦ)

32. συνίημι   - I understand

33. σωτήρ, -ῆρος, ὁ   - savior (soteriology).
                                  (cf. σωτηρία)

34. τελέω   - I finish, complete (teleologi-
                                  cal). (cf. τέλος)

35. ὑμέτερος, -α, -ον - your (cf. ὑμεῖς). An adj.

36. φρονέω   - I think (phrenology)

37. χήρα, -ας, ἡ   - widow

IN THIS LESSON YOU WILL:

> . . . see the possessive adjectives, and

> . . . become acquainted with the comparative and
> superlative adjectives.

Foundational Concepts

Possessive Adjectives

The possessive adjective shows possession, irrespective of the case in which it is found. Normally the personal pronoun shows possession in the genitive case only (= the possessive pronoun). But the possessive adjective may occur in any case and generally gives greater emphasis than does the possessive pronoun.

Nominative Singular

M	F	N
ἐμός	ἐμή	ἐμόν
"my"	"my"	"my"
σός	σή	σόν
"your"	"your"	"your"

Nominative Plural

M	F	N
ἡμέτερος	ἡμετέρα	ἡμέτερον
"our"	"our"	"our"
ὑμέτερος	ὑμετέρα	ὑμέτερον
"your"	"your"	"your"

Observations

1. Note the declension patterns: 2-1-2.

2. To help you remember these forms, relate:
    ἐμός to ἐμοῦ   ἡμέτερος to ἡμεῖς
    σός to σοῦ   ὑμέτερος to ὑμεῖς

306

Practice

Translate the following Scriptures and observe the emphatic use of the possessive adjectives.

1. αὕτη οὖν ἡ χαρὰ ἡ ἐμὴ πεπλήρωται.
2. ἆρον (liquid verb) τὸ σὸν καὶ ὕπαγε.
3. ἡ κοινωνία ἡ ἡμετέρα μετὰ τοῦ πατρός.
4. ὑμετέρα ἐστὶν ἡ βασιλεία τοῦ θεοῦ.

KEY

1. Therefore this <u>my</u> joy has been fulfilled.
2. Take what is <u>yours</u> and go.
3. <u>Our</u> fellowship (is) with the Father.
4. The kingdom of God is <u>yours</u>.

Comparative and Superlative Adjectives

The word "small" is a simple adjective, "smaller" is a comparative adjective, and "smallest" a superlative adjective.

Comparative adjectives express a relationship, and, in English, they are generally followed by the word "than." This train is faster than that car. Greek comparative adjectives are normally formed by adding -τερος -α -ον to the adjective stem while the superlative adjectives are formed by adding -τατος, -η, -ον to the stem. Observe the following examples.

Simple Adjective	Comparative Adjective	Superlative Adj.
ἰσχυρός "strong"	ἰσχυρότερος "stronger"	ἰσχυρότατος "strongest"
μικρός "small"	μικρότερος "smaller"	----[1] "smallest"
περισσός "abundant"	περισσότερος "more abundant"	----[1] "most abundant"

[1]The comparatives μικρότερος and περισσότερος have no superlatives in Greek corresponding to "smallest" and "most abundant" in English. New Testament usage shows that the comparative form functions either as comparative or superlative.

Memory Aid

Observe A.D. Detective (Adjective). In his left hand he holds a <u>comb-pear</u> (comparative), a pear that is combing itself. The little hairs cry out, "Don't <u>tear us</u>! (-τερος). The comparative adjectives are formed with -τερος. In his right hand he holds a super (superlative) <u>potato</u> (-τατος). The superlative adjectives are formed with -τατος, -τάτη, -τατον.

DON'T TEAR US!

DECLENSION OF μικρότερος "SMALLER" (The "normal" pattern)

Singular

	Masc.	Fem.	Neut.
N	μικρότερος	μικροτέρα	μικρότερον
G	μικροτέρου	μικροτέρας	μικρότερου
D	μικροτέρῳ	μικροτέρᾳ	μικρότερῳ
A	μικρότερον	μικροτέραν	μικρότερα

Plural

	Masc.	Fem.	Neut.
N	μικρότεροι	μικρότεραι	μικρότερα
G	μικροτέρων	μικροτέρων	μικροτέρων
D	μικροτέροις	μικροτέραις	μικροτέροις
A	μικροτέρους	μικροτέρας	μικρότερα

DECLENSION OF μείζων "GREATER" (An "Irregular" pattern)

	Singular			Plural	
	Masc./Fem.	Neut.		Masc./Fem.	Neut.
N	μείζων	μεῖζον	(N)	μείζονες	μείζονα
G	μείζονος	μεῖζονος	(G)	μειζόνων	μειζόνων
D	μείζονι	μεῖζονι	(D)	μείζοσι(ν)	μείζοσι(ν)
A	μείζονα	μεῖζον	(A)	μείζονας	μείζονα

In the statement, "He is greater," an implicit question is raised. Who is he greater than? In Greek, the second member of the comparison is introduced in one of two ways:

1. By the particle ἤ "than" before the second member of the comparison. (See practice sentence #4 below), or

2. By placing the second member in the genitive case. (See sentences #1-3 below.)

Practice

Translate the following Scriptures:

1. Matthew 11:11 - ὁ δὲ μικρότερος ἐν τῇ βασιλείᾳ τῶν οὐρανῶν μείζων αὐτοῦ ἐστιν.
2. John 14:12 - μείζονα τούτων ποιήσει·
3. Mark 1:7 - Ἔρχεται ὁ ἰσχυρότερός μου ὀπίσω μου.
4. 1 John 4:4 - μείζων ἐστὶν ὁ ἐν ὑμῖν ἤ ὁ ἐν τῷ κόσμῳ.

KEY

1. But the least in the kingdom of heaven is greater than he.
2. He will do greater things than these.
3. The one who is stronger than I comes after me.
4. He who is in you is greater than he who is in the world.

Comparative and Superlative Adverbs

Just as adjectives modify nouns, adverbs modify verbs, adjectives, and other adverbs. For example, "slowly, quickly, abundantly" are adverbs. Comparative adverbs in Greek are formed from the neuter singular accusative of comparative adjectives.

Practice

1. 1 Cor. 15:10 - ἀλλὰ περισσότερον αὐτῶν πάντων
ἐκοπίασα (toiled).
2. Luke 9:48 - ὁ γὰρ μικρότερος ἐν πᾶσιν ὑμῖν ὑπάρχων,
οὗτός ἐστιν μέγας.
3. Mark 12:31 - μείζων τούτων ἄλλη ἐντολὴ οὐκ ἔστιν.

4. Luke 16:10 - ὁ πιστὸς ἐν ἐλαχίστῳ καὶ ἐν πολλῷ
πιστός ἐστιν.

KEY

1. But I toiled more abundantly than all of them.
2. For the one who is smallest among all of you, this
one is great.
3. There is no other commandment greater than these.
4. The one faithful in (what is) least is also faithful
in much.

Enrichment

From the lesson on comparative and superlative adjectives, you have met the forms μικρότερος ("smaller"),
comparative of μικρός, and ἐλάχιστος ("smallest" or
"least"), used as the superlative of μικρός. In Eph. 3:
8, a very unusual form of ἐλάχιστος occurs. The text
reads, ἐμοὶ τῷ ἐλαχιστοτέρῳ πάντων ἁγίων ἐδόθη ἡ χάρις
αὕτη, "To me, the one who is less than the least of all
the saints this grace was given." The underlined form
is nothing less than a superlative strengthened by a comparative ending! The form is unusual, but possible, for
comparable forms do exist in the ancient Greek dialects.
The form before us, however, may well be Paul's own
creation. It means that the one who calls himself the
"first" (πρῶτος) of sinners (1 Tim. 1:15), and the
"least of the apostles" (ὁ ἐλάχιστος τῶν ἀποστόλων -
1 Cor. 15:9), now offers us another amazing confession,
"less than the least of all saints." In view of the
richness of the grace of Christ, made known to Paul,
grace which unites Jew and Gentile in one body (Eph. 3:
6-7), Paul stands in complete awe and wonder. That is
to say, "less than the least" issues not from self-
effacing piety but from frank amazement at the grace
of God.

Assignment

Γέγραπται ὅτι ἐγενήθη Ἰωσαίας βασιλεὺς ἀντὶ τοῦ
πατρὸς αὐτοῦ καὶ ἦρξεν ἔτη πολλὰ ἐν Ἰεροσόλυμα[2]. καὶ
ἐποίησεν πάντοτε τὸ δίκαιον ἐνώπιον τοῦ κυρίου, ἀποστρέφων
ἀδικίαν ἀπὸ τῆς γῆς καὶ περιπατῶν ἐν ταῖς ὁδοῖς Δαυιδ[3]
τοῦ πατρὸς αὐτοῦ. ὢν παιδίον μικρότερον πάντων τῶν
ἀρχόντων τῶν πρὸ αὐτοῦ, οὐκ ἠσθένησεν ἐν πίστει ἀλλὰ
ἴσχυσεν ἐν τῷ κυρίῳ. ἐζήτησεν γὰρ τὸν κύριον καὶ ἤρξατο
τὸν Ἰούδαν[4] καθαρίσαι καὶ τὴν Ἰεροσόλυμα -- οὐ τῇ
μαχαίρῃ ἀλλὰ πίστει -- ἀπὸ τῶν θεῶν τῶν ἐν τοῖς ἔθνεσιν.

καὶ Ἰωσαίας ἐξίστατο ἐπὶ πᾶσιν τοῖς κακοῖς τοῖς
πρασσομένοις ἐν τῷ ἱερῷ, καὶ ἐλύπει ἐπὶ τῇ τῶν χηρῶν
θλίψει. καὶ οὕτως ἐγένετο, μετὰ τὸ ἄρξαι τὸν νέον
βασιλέα δέκα ἔτη ὅτι ἐφρόνει τὴν τοῦ θεοῦ δικαιοσύνην
καὶ τὴν ἀδικίαν τῆς πόλεως καὶ χώρας. καὶ ἐλογίζετο ἐν
ἑαυτῷ λέγων· Πλείονές εἰσιν αἱ ἡμέτεραι ἁμαρτίαι τῶν
ἁμαρτιῶν τῶν πατέρων ἡμῶν ὥστε μηκέτι ἡμᾶς δύνασθαι ἆραι
τὰς κεφαλὰς ἡμῶν. ὁμοίως κατηργήθησαν αἱ θυσίαι καὶ
ἑορταὶ ἡμῶν, ὅτι ἡμεῖς ἠγαπήσαμεν μᾶλλον ἑαυτοὺς ἢ τὸν
ἡμέτερον θεόν, καὶ οὐκ εὐχαριστήσαμεν τῷ θεῷ τῷ πιστῷ
ὑπὲρ τοῦ ἐλέους αὐτοῦ. καὶ νῦν ἀληθῶς καταβήσεται τὰ
κρίματα αὐτοῦ ἐπὶ τὴν γενεὰν ἡμῶν καὶ ἀπολέσει ἡμᾶς καὶ
τὰ ἡμέτερα ὑπάρχοντα[5] καὶ βαστάσομεν τὰς ἀδικίας ἡμῶν
εἰς τὸν αἰῶνα. Τί ποιήσωμεν ἵνα ἰάσηται ὁ ἐλεῶν τὴν γῆν
ἡμῶν καὶ δῷ ἡμῖν τὴν γνῶσιν τῆς ἀφέσεως καὶ παρακλήσεως
αὐτοῦ ἧς χρείαν ἔχομεν;

διὸ ὤμοσεν ὁ βασιλεὺς παρρησίᾳ κατὰ τοῦ ἀληθινοῦ καὶ
ζῶντος θεοῦ ὅτι οἰκοδομηθήσεται ἡ διακονία τοῦ ἱεροῦ καὶ
ἁγιασθήσεται καὶ ὅτι αὐτὸς συνάξει ἀγαθοὺς λίθους καὶ
ξύλα[6] καλὰ καὶ τὰ ἄλλα εἰς τὸ τελεσθῆναι τὸν ναὸν ἵνα
αὐτὸς ἀποδῷ δόξαν τῷ θεῷ. εἶτα ἤρξαντο ὁ λαὸς φέρειν
δῶρα πολλὰ τῷ ναῷ.

καὶ οὕτως ἐγένετο ἐν ἐκείνῳ τῷ χρόνῳ ὅτι ἀπέστειλεν
ὁ Ἰωσαίας τὸν Σαπφὰν[7] γραμματέα οἴκου κυρίου πρὸς
Χελκίαν[8] τὸν ἀρχιερέα ἵνα συναγάγωσι τὸ ἀργύριον[9] τὸ

δοθὲν ὑπὸ τοῦ λαοῦ ἐν τῷ ἱερῷ, καὶ εἶπεν· Δοθήτω ὁ
μισθὸς τοῖς ἐργαζομένοις τὸ ἔργον ἐν οἴκῳ κυρίου καὶ
τελεσάτωσαν τὸ ἔργον καλῶς. διὸ πολλοὶ ἔδωκαν -- καὶ
πλούσιοι καὶ πτωχοί -- τῷ ἔργῳ. καὶ ἐγένετο ἐν τῷ φέρειν
αὐτοὺς τὸ ἀργύριον ἐκ τοῦ ἱεροῦ, εὗρεν Χελκίας βιβλίον
νόμου κυρίου. καὶ ἔδωκεν Χελκίας τὸ βιβλίον τῷ Σαπφὰν,
καὶ παρήγγειλεν αὐτῷ δεῖξαι τὸ βιβλίον τῷ βασιλεῖ. καὶ
ἐκεῖθεν ἤνεγκε ὁ Σαπφὰν τὸ βιβλίον πρὸς τὸν βασιλέα καὶ
εἰσελθὼν πρὸς τὸν βασιλέα καὶ ἀσπασάμενος αὐτὸν ἀπέδωκεν
πρῶτον τῷ βασιλεῖ λόγον[10] λέγων, Οὗτός ἐστιν ὁ λόγος[10]
παντὸς τοῦ ἀργυρίου[9] τοῦ δοθέντος τοῖς ἐργασαμένοις τὸ
ἔργον ἐν οἴκῳ τοῦ κυρίου. καὶ προσέθετο Σαπφὰν λαλεῖν
λέγων, Ἄφες μοι, βασιλεῦ,[11] ἵνα ἀναγνῶ ἐκ τοῦ βιβλίου
τοῦ νόμου ὃ εὑρήκαμεν ἐν τῷ οἴκῳ τοῦ κυρίου, καὶ ἀκουσάτω
ὁ βασιλεὺς τοὺς λόγους τούτους ἐπεὶ ἰσχυροὶ καὶ δυνατοὶ
καὶ ἀληθινοί εἰσιν.

καὶ τοῦ Σαπφὰν ἀναγινώσκοντος, ἐλυπήθη ἡ καρδία τοῦ
βασιλέως πολλὰ καὶ οἱ περὶ αὐτόν, καὶ ἔφη, Πόση ἐστὶν ἡ
ἁμαρτία ἡ ἐμή· ἀμὴν αὕτη ἐστὶν μείζων τοῦ ἀφεθῆναί με.
φοβούμενος δὲ φόβον μέγαν ἔπεμψεν πρὸς τὴν προφῆτιν[12]
Ὀλδάν,[13] θυγατέρα ἀληθῆ τοῦ νόμου, καὶ ἰδοὺ αὕτη κατῴκει
ἐν Ἱεροσόλυμα καὶ δέδοται αὐτῇ λόγος σοφίας καὶ γνώσεως.
καὶ αὐτὴ συνιεῖσα τὴν τοῦ βασιλέως μετάνοιαν εἶπεν·
Τάδε[14] λέγει κύριος, Ἰδοὺ ἐγὼ ἐπάγω κακὰ ἐπὶ τὸν τόπον
τοῦτον καὶ ἐπὶ τοὺς ταύτην τὴν γῆν κατοικοῦντας, πάντας
τοὺς λόγους οὓς ἀνέγνωκεν ὁ βασιλεύς. διὰ δὲ τὸ μετα-
νοῆσαί σε, οὐκ ὄψονται οἱ σοὶ ὀφθαλμοὶ τὴν κρίσιν ἣν ἐγώ
εἰμι ἐπάγω ἐπὶ τὸν τόπον τοῦτον.

ἀκούσας δὲ ταῦτα τὰ ῥήματα ἀπὸ τῆς προφήτιδος[12],
Ἰωσαίας οὐκ ἠρνήσατο ὑπακοῦσαι αὐτοῖς ἀλλὰ προσεκαλέσατο
πάντα τὸν λαὸν ἀπὸ μικροῦ μεχρὶ μεγάλου συνάγων αὐτοὺς
περὶ αὐτόν. καὶ ἔστη ὁ βασιλεὺς ἔμπροσθεν τοῦ ναοῦ καὶ
διέθετο διαθήκην ἐπιθυμῶν τοῦ πορευθῆναι ἐνώπιον κυρίου
τοῦ φυλάσσειν τὰς ἐντολὰς αὐτοῦ ἐν ὅλῃ καρδίᾳ καὶ ψυχῇ
ὥστε ποιεῖν αὐτὸν τοὺς λόγους τῆς διαθήκης τοὺς γεγραμ-
μένους ἐν τῷ νόμῳ. καὶ ἔστησεν ὁ βασιλεὺς τὸν λαὸν
καὶ ἐστῶτες ὤμοσαν πάντες κατὰ τοῦ ζῶντος θεοῦ ἵνα

περιπατήσωσι ἐν ἀληθέσιν ὁδοῖς καὶ τηρήσωσι τὴν διαθήκην
τοῦ κυρίου τοῦ θεοῦ τῶν πατέρων αὐτῶν.

ἐν τῷ ἔτει ἐκείνῳ ἀπέστειλεν Ἰωσαίας ἀγγελίαν παντὶ
τῷ λαῷ καὶ ἔφη, Ἰδοὺ ἥκει ἡ ὥρα ἵνα δῶμεν τιμὴν τῷ θεῷ·
ἐπιστρέψατε πρὸς τὸν κύριον καὶ ἔλθετε εἰς Ἰεροσόλυμα,
ποιήσατε τὴν ἑορτὴν τοῦ πάσχα τῷ κυρίῳ τῷ θεῷ ὑμῶν καθὼς
γέγραπται ἐν βιβλίῳ τῆς διαθήκης. "Προσενέγκατε θυσίαν
τοῦ προβάτου τοῦ μικροῦ" ὅτι -- καθὼς λέγει ἡ γραφή --
προάξει ὑμῶν ὁ κύριος καὶ ἔσται ὁ σωτὴρ ὑμῶν. παρελεύ-
σεται τὴν θύραν τὴν ὑμετέραν, καὶ οὐκ ἀφήσει τὸν
ἀπολλύονα[15] εἰσελθεῖν εἰς τὰς οἰκίας ὑμῶν τοῦ ἀπολέσαι
ὑμᾶς. διὸ ἐν τῇ ἡμέρᾳ ἐκείνῃ εὐλόγησεν ὁ θεὸς τὰς φυλὰς
τοῦ γένους Ἰσραὴλ σπλαγχνισθεὶς ἐπ' αὐτοὺς διὰ τὴν
μετάνοιαν καὶ τὴν ὑπομονὴν τοῦ Ἰωσαία.

ἀληθῶς συνῆκεν Ἰωσαίας τὸν τοῦ κυρίου λόγον καὶ
ὑπήκουσεν αὐτῷ. ὁμοίως οὐκ ἠσθένησεν ἐν παρρησίᾳ ἀλλ'
ἠκολούθησεν μᾶλλον τοῖς προφητεύουσιν ἐν τῷ ὀνόματι τοῦ
θεοῦ, διακονήσας τῷ θεῷ καλῶς. διὰ τοῦτο εἴρηται ἐν τοῖς
βιβλίοις τῶν βασιλειῶν ὅτι ὅμοιος αὐτῷ οὐκ ἐγεννήθη
ἔμπροσθεν αὐτοῦ βασιλεύς, ὃς ἐπέστρεψε πρὸς τὸν κύριον
ἐν ὅλῃ καρδίᾳ αὐτοῦ κατὰ πάντα τὸν νόμον Μωϋσέως[16], καὶ
ἕως ἄρτι οὐκ ἀνέστη μετ' αὐτὸν ὅμοιος αὐτῷ.

---

[1] Ἰωσαίας - Josiah

[2] Ἰεροσόλυμα - Jerusalem (indeclinable)

[3] Δαυίδ - David (indeclinable)

[4] Ἰούδας - Judah

[5] ὑπάρχοντα - "possessions" (neut. pl. participle)

[6] ξύλα - wood

[7] Σαπφάν - Shaphan (indeclinable)

[8] Χελκίας - Hilkiah

[9] ἀργύριον - silver

[10] λόγος - "account" (financial)

[11] βασιλεῦ - vocative of βασιλεύς

[12] προφῆτις, -τιδος ἡ - prophetess (cf. Luke 2:36; Rev. 2:20)

[13] Ὀλδᾶς - Oldah (= Huldah)

[14] Τάδε - thus

[15] Ἀπολλύων, -ονος - destroyer, "Apollyon" (Rev. 9:11)

[16] Μωϋσῆς, -σέως - Moses

313

Appendix

Accents

Brief Summary on accents[1]

(a) The accent on verb forms is <u>recessive</u>, normally
the acute ('). It normally appears over the ante-
penult if the ultima is short, over the penult if
the ultima is long.

(b) The accent on noun forms - as far as possible - is
<u>stationary</u>, either the acute or circumflex (˜).

(c) Accents appear only over a vowel or over the
second vowel of a diphthong.

Detailed rules on accents

(a) <u>The circumflex</u> (˜)

   (1) Occurs only on the penult or ultima.
   (2) Occurs only over a long vowel or diphthong.
   (3) Cannot be found on the penult if the ultima
      is long.
   (4) Is found over a long penult when the ultima
      is short - if the penult is to have an accent.
   (5) Occurs over the ultima of nouns and adjectives
      -- genitive and dative (singular and plural)
      -- if the ultima is to be accented.

(b) <u>The acute</u> (')

   (1) Is the only accent that can be placed in any
      of the three possible positions -- over the
      ante-penult, the penult, or the ultima.
   (2) Occurs only over the ante-penult if the ultima
      is short and the ante-penult is to be accented.
   (3) May occur over short or long vowels and diph-
      thongs.
   (4) Normally changes to the grave (`) when it
      occurs over the ultima that is followed by
      another word without intervening punctuation.

(c) <u>The grave</u> (`)

   (1) Only occurs on the ultima.
   (2) Normally occurs when the ultima bears an acute
      accent followed by another word without inter-
      vening punctuation.

---

[1]Originally accents indicated the rise (acute) or fall
(circumflex) or the ordinary pitch (grave) of the voice
in pronunciation. For the modern student, accents serve
(a) to show the syllable to be stressed, and (b) to distinguish between the meaning of certain words which are
written the same but have different accents.

Enclitics

Rules for Enclitics

An enclitic may consist of one syllable, e.g. μου, μοι, με, σου, σοι, σε or of two, e.g. εἰμί, ἐστί, ἐσμέν, ἐστέ, εἰσί (εἶ - 2nd sing. is not an enclitic).

a. It yields its accent to the preceding word, the accent appearing as an acute (never grave) on the ultima. Examples: ὁ ἀπόστολός μου, my apostle; ἀπόστολός ἐστι, he is an apostle; ὁ δοῦλός σου, your servant; δοῦλός ἐστι, he is a servant.

b. If the ultima of the preceding word is already accented, the accent of the enclitic simply disappears. Examples: ὁ υἱός μου, my son; τοῦ υἱοῦ μου, of my son; υἱός ἐστι, he is a son. Note: neither the acute nor the circumflex changes to a grave.

c. If the preceding word has an acute on the penult, the accent of a two-syllable enclitic is retained (λόγος ἐστίν, it is a word) while the accent of the one-syllable enclitic disappears (ὁ λόγος μου, my word).

Paradigms

I. Declension of the article ὁ, ἡ, τό "the"

	Singular				Plural		
	Masc.	Fem.	Neut.		Masc.	Fem.	Neut.
N	ὁ	ἡ	τό	(N)	οἱ	αἱ	τά
G	τοῦ	τῆς	τοῦ	(G)	τῶν	τῶν	τῶν
D	τῷ	τῇ	τῷ	(D)	τοῖς	ταῖς	τοῖς
A	τόν	τήν	τό	(A)	τούς	τάς	τά

II. Paradigms of Nouns and Adjectives

A. First Declension Nouns

ὥρα, ἡ - hour   δόξα, ἡ - glory   γραφή, ἡ - writing

Feminine

	Singular				Plural		
NV	ὥρα	δόξα	γραφή	(NV)	ὧραι	δόξαι	γραφαί
G	ὥρας	δόξης	γραφῆς	(G)	ὡρῶν	δοξῶν	γραφῶν
D	ὥρᾳ	δόξῃ	γραφῇ	(D)	ὥραις	δόξαις	γραφαῖς
A	ὥραν	δόξαν	γραφήν	(A)	ὥρας	δόξας	γραφάς

προφήτης, ὁ - prophet

Masculine

	Singular		Plural
N	προφήτης	(NV)	προφῆται
G	προφήτου	(G)	προφητῶν
D	προφήτῃ	(D)	προφήταις
A	προφήτην	(A)	προφήτας
V	προφῆτα		

B. Second Declension Nouns

λόγος, ὁ - word   ὁδός, ἡ - way   δῶρον, τό - gift

	Masculine				Feminine				Neuter		
	Sing.		Plur.		Sing.		Plur.		Sing.		Plur.
N	λόγος	NV	λόγοι	N	ὁδός	NV	ὁδοί	NAV	δῶρον	NAV	δῶρα
G	λόγου	G	λόγων	G	ὁδοῦ	G	ὁδῶν	G	δώρου	G	δώρων
D	λόγῳ	D	λόγοις	D	ὁδῷ	D	ὁδοῖς	D	δώρῳ	D	δώροις
A	λόγον	A	λόγους	A	ὁδόν	A	ὁδούς				
V	λόγε			V	ὁδέ						

C. First and Second Declension Adjectives

1. ἀγαθός - good

	Singular				Plural		
	Masc.	Fem.	Neut.		Masc.	Fem.	Neut.
N	ἀγαθός	ἀγαθή	ἀγαθόν	(NV)	ἀγαθοί	ἀγαθαί	ἀγαθά
G	ἀγαθοῦ	ἀγαθῆς	ἀγαθοῦ	(G)	ἀγαθῶν	ἀγαθῶν	ἀγαθῶν
D	ἀγαθῷ	ἀγαθῇ	ἀγαθῷ	(D)	ἀγαθοῖς	ἀγαθαῖς	ἀγαθοῖς
A	ἀγαθόν	ἀγαθήν	ἀγαθόν	(A)	ἀγαθούς	ἀγαθάς	ἀγαθά
V	ἀγαθέ	ἀγαθή	ἀγαθόν				

2. μικρός - small

	Singular				Plural		
	Masc.	Fem.	Neut.		Masc.	Fem.	Neut.
N	μικρός	μικρά	μικρόν	(NV)	μικροί	μικραί	μικρά
G	μικροῦ	μικρᾶς	μικροῦ	(G)	μικρῶν	μικρῶν	μικρῶν
D	μικρῷ	μικρᾷ	μικρῷ	(D)	μικροῖς	μικραῖς	μικροῖς
A	μικρόν	μικράν	μικρόν	(A)	μικρούς	μικράς	μικρά
V	μικρέ	μικρά	μικρόν				

3. πολύς (irregular) - much

	Singular				Plural		
	Masc.	Fem.	Neut.		Masc.	Fem.	Neut.
N	πολύς	πολλή	πολύ	(N)	πολλοί	πολλαί	πολλά
G	πολλοῦ	πολλῆς	πολλοῦ	(G)	πολλῶν	πολλῶν	πολλῶν
D	πολλῷ	πολλῇ	πολλῷ	(D)	πολλοῖς	πολλαῖς	πολλοῖς
A	πολύν	πολλήν	πολύ	(A)	πολλούς	πολλάς	πολλά

4. μέγας (irregular) - great

	Singular				Plural		
	Masc.	Fem.	Neut.		Masc.	Fem.	Neut.
N	μέγας	μεγάλη	μέγα	(NV)	μεγάλοι	μεγάλαι	μεγάλα
G	μεγάλου	μεγάλης	μεγάλου	(G)	μεγάλων	μεγάλων	μεγάλων
D	μεγάλῳ	μεγάλη	μεγάλῳ	(D)	μεγάλοις	μεγάλαις	μεγάλοις
A	μέγαν	μεγάλην	μέγα	(A)	μεγάλους	μεγάλας	μεγάλα
V	μεγάλε	μεγάλη	μέγα				

D. Third Declension Nouns

1. ἄρχων, ὁ - ruler   2. σάρξ, ἡ - flesh

	Singular		Plural		Singular		Plural
NV	ἄρχων	NV	ἄρχοντες	NV	σάρξ	NV	σάρκες
G	ἄρχοντος	G	ἀρχόντων	G	σαρκός	G	σαρκῶν
D	ἄρχοντι	D	ἄρχουσι(ν)	D	σαρκί	D	σαρξί(ν)
A	ἄρχοντα	A	ἄρχοντας	A	σάρκα	A	σάρκας

3. γυνή, ἡ - woman   4. ῥῆμα, τό - word

	Singular		Plural		Singular		Plural
N	γυνή	(NV)	γυναῖκες	NAV	ῥῆμα	(NAV)	ῥήματα
G	γυναικός	(G)	γυναικῶν	G	ῥήματος	(G)	ῥημάτων
D	γυναικί	(D)	γυναιξί(ν)	D	ῥήματι	(D)	ῥήμασι(ν)
A	γυναῖκα	(A)	γυναῖκας				
V	γύναι						

5. ἔθνος, τό - nation   6. βασιλεύς, ὁ - king

	Singular		Plural		Singular		Plural
NAV	ἔθνος	NAV	ἔθνη	N	βασιλεύς	(NV)	βασιλεῖς
G	ἔθνους	G	ἐθνῶν	G	βασιλέως	(G)	βασιλέων
D	ἔθνει	D	ἔθνεσι(ν)	D	βασιλεῖ	(D)	βασιλεῦσι(ν)
				A	βασιλέα	(A)	βασιλεῖς
				V	βασιλεῦ		

7. πατήρ, ὁ - father   8. πίστις, ἡ - faith

	Singular		Plural		Singular		Plural
N	πατήρ	(NV)	πατέρες	N	πίστις	(NV)	πίστεις
G	πατρός	(G)	πατέρων	G	πίστεως	(G)	πίστεων
D	πατρί	(D)	πατράσι(ν)	D	πίστει	(D)	πίστεσι(ν)
A	πατέρα	(A)	πατέρας	A	πίστιν	(A)	πίστεις
V	πάτερ			V	πίστι		

E. Other Third Declension Forms

1. πᾶς - every, all

	Masc.	Fem.	Neut.		Masc.	Fem.	Neut.
N	πᾶς	πᾶσα	πᾶν	(N)	πάντες	πᾶσαι	πάντα
G	παντός	πάσης	παντός	(G)	πάντων	πασῶν	πάντων
D	παντί	πάσῃ	παντί	(D)	πᾶσι(ν)	πάσαις	πᾶσι(ν)
A	πάντα	πᾶσαν	πᾶν	(A)	πάντας	πάσας	πάντα

2. εἷς - one

	Masc.	Fem.	Neut.
N	εἷς	μία	ἕν
G	ἑνός	μιᾶς	ἑνός
D	ἑνί	μιᾷ	ἑνί
A	ἕνα	μίαν	ἕν

3. τρεῖς - three

	Masc./Fem.	Neut.
N	τρεῖς	τρία
G	τριῶν	τριῶν
D	τρισί(ν)	τρισί(ν)
A	τρεῖς	τρία

4. ἀληθής - true

	Singular		Plural	
	Masc./Fem.	Neut.	Masc./Fem.	Neut.
N	ἀληθής	ἀληθές	(NV) ἀληθεῖς	ἀληθῆ
G	ἀληθοῦς	ἀληθοῦς	(G) ἀληθῶν	ἀληθῶν
D	ἀληθεῖ	ἀληθεῖ	(D) ἀληθέσι(ν)	ἀληθέσι(ν)
A	ἀληθῆ	ἀληθές	(A) ἀληθεῖς	ἀληθῆ
V	ἀληθές			

III. Declension of Pronouns

A. Personal Pronouns

ἐγώ - I σύ - you αὐτός - he αὐτή - she αὐτό - it

Singular

N	ἐγώ	σύ	αὐτός	αὐτή	αὐτό
G	ἐμοῦ(μου)	σοῦ	αὐτοῦ	αὐτῆς	αὐτοῦ
D	ἐμοί(μοι)	σοί	αὐτῷ	αὐτῇ	αὐτῷ
A	ἐμέ(με)	σέ	αὐτόν	αὐτήν	αὐτό

Plural

N	ἡμεῖς	ὑμεῖς	αὐτοί	αὐταί	αὐτά
G	ἡμῶν	ὑμῶν	αὐτῶν	αὐτῶν	αὐτῶν
D	ἡμῖν	ὑμῖν	αὐτοῖς	αὐταῖς	αὐτοῖς
A	ἡμᾶς	ὑμᾶς	αὐτούς	αὐτάς	αὐτά

B. Demonstrative Pronoun, οὗτος - this

	Singular				Plural		
	Masc.	Fem.	Neut.		Masc.	Fem.	Neut.
N	οὗτος	αὕτη	τοῦτο	(N)	οὗτοι	αὗται	ταῦτα
G	τούτου	ταύτης	τούτου	(G)	τούτων	τούτων	τούτων
D	τούτῳ	ταύτῃ	τούτῳ	(D)	τούτοις	ταύταις	τούτοις
A	τοῦτον	ταύτην	τοῦτο	(A)	τούτους	ταύτας	ταῦτα

C. Reflexive Pronoun

1. ἐμαυτοῦ, -ῆς - of myself   2. σεαυτοῦ, -ῆς - of yourself

	Singular			Plural	
	Masculine	Feminine		Masculine	Feminine
G	ἐμαυτοῦ	ἐμαυτῆς	(G)	ἑαυτῶν	ἑαυτῶν
D	ἐμαυτῷ	ἐμαυτῇ	(D)	ἑαυτοῖς	ἑαυταῖς
A	ἐμαυτόν	ἐμαυτήν	(A)	ἑαυτούς	ἑαυτάς

	Singular			Plural	
	Masculine	Feminine		Masculine	Feminine
G	σεαυτοῦ	σεαυτῆς	(G)	ἑαυτῶν	ἑαυτῶν
D	σεαυτῷ	σεαυτῇ	(D)	ἑαυτοῖς	ἑαυταῖς
A	σεαυτόν	σεαυτήν	(A)	ἑαυτούς	ἑαυτάς

3. ἑαυτοῦ, -ῆς, -οῦ - of himself, herself, itself

	Singular			Plural		
	Masc.	Fem.	Neut.	Masc.	Fem.	Neut.
G	ἑαυτοῦ	ἑαυτῆς	ἑαυτοῦ	(G)ἑαυτῶν	ἑαυτῶν	ἑαυτῶν
D	ἑαυτῷ	ἑαυτῇ	ἑαυτῷ	(D)ἑαυτοῖς	ἑαυταῖς	ἑαυτοῖς
A	ἑαυτόν	ἑαυτήν	ἑαυτό	(A)ἑαυτούς	ἑαυτάς	ἑαυτά

D. Relative Pronoun, ὅς, ἥ, ὅ - who, which, what

	Singular			Plural		
	Masc.	Fem.	Neut.	Masc.	Fem.	Neut.
N	ὅς	ἥ	ὅ	(N)	οἵ	αἵ	ἅ
G	οὗ	ἧς	οὗ	(G)	ὧν	ὧν	ὧν
D	ᾧ	ᾗ	ᾧ	(D)	οἷς	αἷς	οἷς
A	ὅν	ἥν	ὅ	(A)	οὕς	ἅς	ἅ

E. Interrogative Pronoun, τίς τί, - who?which?what?

	Singular			Plural	
	Masc./Fem.	Neut.		Masc./Fem.	Neut.
N	τίς	τί	(N)	τίνες	τίνα
G	τίνος	τίνος	(G)	τίνων	τίνων
D	τίνι	τίνι	(D)	τίσι(ν)	τίσι(ν)
A	τίνα	τί	(A)	τίνας	τίνα

IV. Some Common Positive, Comparative, and Superlative Adjectives

Positive	Comparative	Superlative
ἀγαθός - good	κρείσσων - better κρείττων βελτίων	κράτιστος - best
κακός - bad	ἥσσων - worse ἥττων χείρων	
μέγας - great	μείζων - greater μειζότερος	μέγιστος - greatest
μικρός - small	μικρότερος - smaller ἐλάσσων ἐλάττων	ἐλάχιστος - least
πολύς - much	πλείων - more πλέων	πλεῖστος - most

V. Paradigms of Verbs

A. Synopsis of λύω[1]

Principal Parts

λύω	λύσω	ἔλυσα	λέλυκα	λέλυμαι	ἐλύθην
I loose	I shall loose	I loosed	I have loosed	I have been loosed	I was loosed

---

[1]1st singular of indicatives and subjunctives, 2nd singular of imperatives, all infinitives, nominative singular masculine of participles.

319

Tense:

<u>Present Future Aorist Perf.Act. Perf.Pass Aor.Pass.</u>

Indicative

Act.	λύω	λύσω	ἔλυσα	λέλυκα		
Mid.	λύομαι	λύσομαι	ἐλυσάμην		λέλυμαι	
Pass.	λύομαι	λυθήσομαι			λέλυμαι	ἐλύθην

Subjunctive

Act.	λύω		λύσω			
Mid.	λύωμαι		λύσωμαι			
Pass.	λύωμαι					λυθῶ

Imperative

Act.	λῦε (2nd sg.)	λῦσον
Mid.	λύου (2nd sg.)	λῦσαι
Pass.	λύου (2nd sg.)	λύθητι

Infinitive

Act.	λύειν	λῦσαι	λελυκέναι		
Mid.	λύεσθαι	λύσασθαι		λελύσθαι	
Pass.	λύεσθαι			λελύσθαι	λυθῆναι

Participle

Act.	λύων	λύσας	λελυκώς		
Mid.	λυόμενος	λυσάμενος		λελυμένος	
Pass.	λυόμενος			λελυμένος	λυθείς

B. <u>The Regular Verb λύω - I loose</u>

(Principal parts - λύω, λύσω, ἔλυσα, λέλυκα,
λέλυμαι, ἐλύθην)

1. Present and Imperfect Tenses of λύω (1st
    principal part)

Indicative

Singular

Pres.Act.	Pres.Mid/Pass.	Imper.Act.	Imper.Mid/Pass.
1. λύω	λύομαι	ἔλυον	ἐλυόμην
2. λύεις	λύῃ	ἔλυες	ἐλύου
3. λύει	λύεται	ἔλυε(ν)	ἐλύετο

Plural

Pres.Act.	Pres.Mid/Pass.	Imper.Act.	Imper.Mid/Pass.
1. λύομεν	λυόμεθα	ἐλύομεν	ἐλυόμεθα
2. λύετε	λύεσθε	ἐλύετε	ἐλύεσθε
3. λύουσι(ν)	λύονται	ἔλυον	ἐλύοντο

Subjunctive

Present Active		Present Mid./Pass.	
Singular	Plural	Singular	Plural
1. λύω	λύωμεν	λύωμαι	λυώμεθα
2. λύῃς	λύητε	λύῃ	λύησθε
3. λύῃ	λύωσι(ν)	λύηται	λύωνται

Imperative

Present Active		Present Mid./Pass.	
Singular	Plural	Singular	Plural
2. λῦε	λύετε	λύου	λύεσθε
3. λυέτω	λυέτωσαν	λυέσθω	λυέσθωσαν

Infinitive		Participle	
Active	Mid./Pass.	Active	Mid./Pass.
λύειν	λύεσθαι	Masc. λύων	λυόμενος
		Fem. λύουσα	λυομένη
		Neut. λῦον	λυόμενον

2. Future Active and Middle Based on λύσω (2nd principal part)

Indicative

Future Active		Future Middle	
Singular	Plural	Singular	Plural
1. λύσω	λύσομεν	1. λύσομαι	λυσόμεθα
2. λύσεις	λύσετε	2. λύσῃ	λύσεσθε
3. λύσει	λύσουσι(ν)	3. λύσεται	λύσονται

3. First Aorist Active and Middle Based on ἔλυσα (3rd principal part)

Indicative

First Aorist Active		First Aorist Middle	
Singular	Plural	Singular	Plural
1. ἔλυσα	ἐλύσαμεν	1. ἐλυσάμην	ἐλυσάμεθα
2. ἔλυσας	ἐλύσατε	2. ἐλύσω	ἐλύσασθε
3. ἔλυσε(ν)	ἔλυσαν	3. ἐλύσατο	ἐλύσαντο

Subjunctive

Active		Middle	
Singular	Plural	Singular	Plural
1. λύσω	λύσωμεν	1. λύσωμαι	λυσώμεθα
2. λύσῃς	λύσητε	2. λύσῃ	λύσησθε
3. λύσῃ	λύσωσι(ν)	3. λύσηται	λύσωνται

Imperative

Active		Middle	
Singular	Plural	Singular	Plural
2. λῦσον	λύσατε	2. λῦσαι	λύσασθε
3. λυσάτω	λυσάτωσαν	3. λυσάσθω	λυσάσθωσαν

Infinitive		Participle	
Active	Middle	Active	Middle
λῦσαι	λύσασθαι	Masc. λύσας	λυσάμενος
		Fem. λύσασα	λυσαμένη
		Neut. λῦσαν	λυσάμενον

4. Perfect Active   5. Pluperfect Active

Both are based on λέλυκα (4th principlar part).

Indicative Active		Indicative Active	
Singular	Plural	Singular	Plural
1. λέλυκα	λελύκαμεν	1. ἐλελύκειν	ἐλελύκειμεν
2. λέλυκας	λελύκατε	2. ἐλελύκεις	ἐλελύκειτε
3. λέλυκε(ν)	λελύκασι(ν)	3. ἐλελύκει	ἐλελύκεισαν
	λέλυκαν		

Infinitive Active	Participle Active		
λελυκέναι	Masc.	Fem.	Neut.
	λελυκώς	λελυκυῖα	λελυκός

6. Perfect Middle/Passive based on λέλυμαι (5th principal part).

Indicative Middle/Passive		Infinitive Middle/Passive
Singular	Plural	λελύσθαι
1. λέλυμαι	λελύμεθα	
2. λέλυσαι	λέλυσθε	
3. λέλυται	λέλυνται	

Participle Middle/Passive

Masc.	Fem.	Neut.
λελυμένος	λελυμένη	λελυμένον

7. First Aorist Passive and Future Passive Based on ἐλύθην (6th principal part).

Indicative Aorist Passive		Future Passive	
Singular	Plural	Singular	Plural
1. ἐλύθην	ἐλύθημεν	1. λυθήσομαι	λυθησόμεθα
2. ἐλύθης	ἐλύθητε	2. λυθήσῃ	λυθήσεσθε
3. ἐλύθη	ἐλύθησαν	3. λυθήσεται	λυθήσονται

Subjunctive Aorist Passive		Imperative Aorist Passive	
Singular	Plural	Singular	Plural
1. λυθῶ	λυθῶμεν	2. λύθητι	λύθητε
2. λυθῇς	λυθῆτε	3. λυθήτω	λυθήτωσαν
3. λυθῇ	λυθῶσι (ν)		

Infinitive Aorist Passive	Participle Aorist Passive		
λυθῆναι	Masc.	Fem.	Neut.
	λυθείς	λυθεῖσα	λυθέν

C. Verbs with Second Aorist and/or Second Perfect Forms

1. The verb ἔρχομαι - I come

Second Aor. Act. Indicative		Second Aor. Act. Subjunctive	
Singular	Plural	Singular	Plural
1. ἦλθον	ἤλθομεν	1. ἔλθω	ἔλθωμεν
2. ἦλθες	ἤλθετε	2. ἔλθῃς	ἔλθητε
3. ἦλθε (ν)	ἦλθον	3. ἔλθῃ	ἔλθωσι(ν)

Second Aor. Act. Imperative		Second Aor. Act. Infinitive
Singular	Plural	ἐλθεῖν
2. ἐλθέ	ἐλθέτε	
3. ἐλθέτω	ἐλθέτωσαν	Second Aorist Active Part.

ἐλθών	ἐλθοῦσα	ἐλθόν

2. The verb βάλλω - I throw

Second Aor. Act. Indicative		Second Aor. Mid. Indicative	
Singular	Plural	Singular	Plural
1. ἔβαλον	ἐβάλομεν	1. ἐβαλόμην	ἐβαλόμεθα
2. ἔβαλες	ἐβάλετε	2. ἐβάλου	ἐβάλεσθε
3. ἔβαλε (ν)	ἔβαλον	3. ἐβάλετο	ἐβάλοντο

Second Aor. Act. Subjunctive   Second Aor. Mid. Subjunctive

	Singular	Plural		Singular	Plural
1.	βάλω	βάλωμεν	1.	βάλωμαι	βαλώμεθα
2.	βάλῃς	βάλητε	2.	βάλῃ	βάλησθε
3.	βάλῃ	βάλωσι(ν)	3.	βάληται	βάλωνται

Second Aor. Act. Imperative   Second Aor. Mid. Imperative

	Singular	Plural		Singular	Plural
2.	βάλε	βάλετε	2.	βαλοῦ	βάλεσθε
3.	βαλέτω	βαλέτωσαν	3.	βαλέσθω	βαλέσθωσαν

Second Aor. Act. Infinitive   Second Aor. Mid. Infinitive

βαλεῖν   βαλέσθαι

Second Aor. Act. Participle   Second Aor. Mid. Participle

βαλών   βαλοῦσα   βαλόν   βαλόμενος βαλομένη βαλόμενον

D.   Contract Verbs

   1. The Present Active and Imperfect Active of
       ἀγαπάω - I love.

Present Active Indicative   Imperfect Active Indicative

	Singular	Plural		Singular	Plural
1.	ἀγαπῶ	ἀγαπῶμεν	1.	ἠγάπων	ἠγαπῶμεν
2.	ἀγαπᾷς	ἀγαπᾶτε	2.	ἠγάπας	ἠγαπᾶτε
3.	ἀγαπᾷ	ἀγαπῶσι(ν)	3.	ἠγάπα	ἠγάπων

   2. The Present Active and Imperfect Active of
       ποιέω - I make

Present Active Indicative   Imperfect Active Indicative

	Singular	Plural		Singular	Plural
1.	ποιῶ	ποιοῦμεν	1.	ἐποίουν	ἐποιοῦμεν
2.	ποιεῖς	ποιεῖτε	2.	ἐποίεις	ἐποιεῖτε
3.	ποιεῖ	ποιοῦσι(ν)	3.	ἐποίει	ἐποίουν

   3. The Present Active and Imperfect Active of
       πληρόω - I fulfill

Present Active Indicative   Imperfect Active Indicative

	Singular	Plural		Singular	Plural
1.	πληρῶ	πληροῦμεν	1.	ἐπλήρουν	ἐπληροῦμεν
2.	πληροῖς	πληροῦτε	2.	ἐπλήρους	ἐπληροῦτε
3.	πληροῖ	πληροῦσι(ν)	3.	ἐπλήρου	ἐπλήρουν

E.   Liquid Verbs

   1. The Future Indicative Active and Middle of
       μένω - I remain

Future Active Indicative   Future Middle Indicative

	Singular	Plural		Singular	Plural
1.	μενῶ	μενοῦμεν	1.	μενοῦμαι	μενούμεθα
2.	μενεῖς	μενεῖτε	2.	μενῇ	μενεῖσθε
3.	μενεῖ	μενοῦσι(ν)	3.	μενεῖται	μενοῦνται

   2. The First Aorist Active and Middle of μένω

First Aorist Act. Indicative   First Aorist Mid Indic.

	Singular	Plural		Singular	Plural
1.	ἔμεινα	ἐμείναμεν	1.	ἐμεινάμην	ἐμεινάμεθα
2.	ἔμεινας	ἐμείνατε	2.	ἐμείνω	ἐμείνασθε
3.	ἔμεινε(ν)	ἔμειναν	3.	ἐμείνατο	ἐμείναντο

F. -μι Verbs
    1. The verb δίδωμι - I give (principal parts -
        δίδωμι, δώσω, ἔδωκα, δέδωκα, δέδομαι,
        ἐδόθην)

Present Indicative Active

Singular	Plural
1. δίδωμι	δίδομεν
2. δίδως	δίδοτε
3. δίδωσι(ν)	διδόασι(ν)

Present Ind. Mid./Pass.

Singular	Plural
1. δίδομαι	διδόμεθα
2. δίδοσαι	δίδοσθε
3. δίδοται	δίδονται

Present Active Subjunctive

Singular	Plural
1. διδῶ	διδῶμεν
2. διδῷς	διδῶτε
3. διδῷ	διδῶσι(ν)

Present Active Imperative

Singular	Plural
2. δίδου	δίδοτε
3. διδότω	διδότωσαν

Imperfect Active Indicative

Singular	Plural
1. ἐδίδουν	ἐδίδομεν
2. ἐδίδους	ἐδίδοτε
3. ἐδίδου	ἐδίδοσαν

Imperfect Mid./Pass. Ind.

Singular	Plural
1. ἐδιδόμην	ἐδιδόμεθα
2. ἐδίδοσο	ἐδίδοσθε
3. ἐδίδοτο	ἐδίδοντο

Present Active Infinitive
διδόναι

Present Mid./Pass. Inf.
δίδοσθαι

Present Active Participle
διδούς διδοῦσα διδόν

Present Mid./Pass. Part.
διδόμενος, -η, -ον

Aorist Active Indicative

Singular	Plural
1. ἔδωκα	ἐδώκαμεν
2. ἔδωκας	ἐδώκατε
3. ἔδωκε(ν)	ἔδωκαν

Aorist Middle Indicative

Singular	Plural
1. ἐδόμην	ἐδόμεθα
2. ἔδου	ἔδοσθε
3. ἔδοτο,-ετο	ἔδοντο

Aorist Active Subjunctive

Singular	Plural
1. δῶ	δῶμεν
2. δῷς	δῶτε
3. δῷ	δῶσι(ν)

Aorist Middle Subjunctive

Singular	Plural
1. δῶμαι	δώμεθα
2. δῷ	δῶσθε
3. δῶται	δῶνται

Aorist Active Infinitive
δοῦναι

Aorist Middle Infinitive
δόσθαι

Aorist Active Participle
δούς δοῦσα δόν

Aorist Middle Participle
δόμενος, -η, -ον

Aorist Active Imperative

Singular	Plural
2. δός	δότε
3. δότω	δότωσαν

Aorist Middle Imperative

Singular	Plural
2. δοῦ	δόσθε
3. δόσθω	δόσθωσαν

    2. The verb ἀφίημι - I forgive (principal parts,
        ἀφίημι, ἀφήσω, ἀφῆκα, ---, ἀφεῖμαι, ἀφέθην)

Present Active Indicative

Singular	Plural
1. ἀφίημι	ἀφίεμεν
2. ἀφεῖς	ἀφίετε
3. ἀφίησι	ἀφίεσαν

Present Active Subjunctive

Singular	Plural
1. ἀφιῶ	ἀφιῶμεν
2. ἀφιῇς	ἀφιῆτε
3. ἀφιῇ	ἀφιῶσι(ν)

Present Active Infinitive	Present Active Participle
ἀφιέναι	ἀφιείς ἀφιεῖσα ἀφιέν

Present Mid./Pass. Indic.		Present Mid./Pass. Subjunc.	
Singular	Plural	Singular	Plural
1. ἀφίεμαι	ἀφιέμεθα	1. ἀφιῶμαι	ἀφιώμεθα
2. ἀφίεσαι	ἀφίεσθε	2. ἀφιῇ	ἀφιῆσθε
3. ἀφίεται	ἀφίενται	3. ἀφιῆται	ἀφιῶνται

Aorist Active Indicative		Aorist Active Subjunctive	
Singular	Plural	Singular	Plural
1. ἀφῆκα	ἀφήκαμεν	1. ἀφῶ	ἀφῶμεν
2. ἀφῆκας	ἀφήκατε	2. ἀφῇς	ἀφῆτε
3. ἀφῆκε(ν)	ἀφῆκαν	3. ἀφῇ	ἀφῶσι(ν)

Aorist Active Infinitive	Aorist Active Participle
ἀφεῖναι	ἀφείς ἀφεῖσα ἀφέν

Aorist Active Imperative	
Singular	Plural
2. ἀφές	ἄφετε
3. ἀφέτω	ἀφέτωσαν

3. The verb τίθημι - I place (principal parts - τίθημι, θήσω, ἔθηκα, τέθεικα, τέθειμαι, ἐτέθην)

Present Active Indicative		Present Mid./Pass. Indic.	
Singular	Plural	Singular	Plural
1. τίθημι	τίθεμεν	1. τίθεμαι	τιθέμεθα
2. τίθης	τίθετε	2. τίθεσαι	τίθεσθε
3. τίθησι(ν)	τιθέασι(ν)	3. τίθεται	τίθενται

Present Active Subjunctive		Present Mid./Pass. Subj.	
Singular	Plural	Singular	Plural
1. τιθῶ	τιθῶμεν	1. τιθῶμαι	τιθώμεθα
2. τιθῇς	τιθῆτε	2. τιθῇ	τιθῆσθε
3. τιθῇ	τιθῶσι(ν)	3. τιθῆται	τιθῶνται

Present Active Infinitive	Present Mid./Pass. Infin.
τιθέναι	τίθεσθαι

Present Active Participle	Present Mid./Pass. Part.
τιθείς τιθεῖσα τιθέν	τιθέμενος, -η,-ον

Present Active Imperative		Present Mid./Pass Imper.	
Singular	Plural	Singular	Plural
2. τίθει	τίθετε	2. τίθεσο	τίθεσθε
3. τιθέτω	τιθέτωσαν	3. τιθέσθω	τιθέσθωσαν

Imperfect Active Indicative		Imperfect Mid./Pass. Ind.	
Singular	Plural	Singular	Plural
1. ἐτίθην	ἐτίθεμεν	1. ἐτιθέμην	ἐτιθέμεθα
2. ἐτίθεις	ἐτίθετε	2. ἐτίθεσο	ἐτίθεσθε
3. ἐτίθει	ἐτίθεσαν, ἐτίθουν	3. ἐτίθετο	ἐτίθεντο

Aorist Active Indicative		Aorist Middle Indicative	
Singular	Plural	Singular	Plural
1. ἔθηκα	ἐθήκαμεν	1. ἐθέμην	ἐθέμεθα
2. ἔθηκας	ἐθήκατε	2. ἔθου	ἔθεσθε
3. ἔθηκε(ν)	ἔθηκαν	3. ἔθετο	ἔθεντο

Aorist Active Subjunctive

	Singular	Plural
1.	θῶ	θῶμεν
2.	θῇς	θῆτε
3.	θῇ	θῶσι(ν)

Aorist Middle Subjunctive

	Singular	Plural
1.	θῶμαι	θώμεθα
2.	θῇ	θῆσθε
3.	θῆται	θῶνται

Aorist Active Infinitive

θεῖναι

Aorist Middle Infinitive

θέσθαι

Aorist Active Participle

θείς,   θεῖσα,   θέν

Aorist Middle Participle

θέμενος, -η, -ον

Aorist Active Imperative

	Singular	Plural
2.	θές	θέτε
3.	θέτω	θέτωσαν

Aorist Middle Imperative

	Singular	Plural
2.	θοῦ	θέσθε
3.	θέσθω	θέσθωσαν

4. The verb ἵστημι - I stand (principal parts - ἵστημι, στήσω, ἔστησα (1 aor.), ἔστην(2 aor.), ἔστηκα, ---, ἐστάθην)

Present Active Indicative

	Singular	Plural
1.	ἵστημι	ἵσταμεν
2.	ἵστης	ἵστατε
3.	ἵστησι(ν)	ἵστασι(ν)

Present Mid./Pass. Indic.

	Singular	Plural
1.	ἵσταμαι	ἱστάμεθα
2.	ἵστασαι	ἵστασθε
3.	ἵσταται	ἵστανται

Present Active Subjunctive

	Singular	Plural
1.	ἱστῶ	ἱστῶμεν
2.	ἱστῇς	ἱστῆτε
3.	ἱστῇ	ἱστῶσι(ν)

Present Mid./Pass. Subj.

	Singular	Plural
1.	ἱστῶμαι	ἱστώμεθα
2.	ἱστῇ	ἱστῆσθε
3.	ἱστῆται	ἱστῶνται

Present Active Infinitive

ἱστάναι

Present Mid./Pass. Infin.

ἵστασθαι

Present Active Participle

ἱστάς   ἱστᾶσα   ἱστάν

Present Mid./Pass. Part.

ἱστάμενος, -η, -ον

Present Active Imperative

	Singular	Plural
2.	ἵστη	ἵστατε
3.	ἱστάτω	ἱστάτωσαν

Present Mid./Pass Imper.

	Singular	Plural
2.	ἵστασο	ἵστασθε
3.	ἱστάσθω	ἱστάσθωσαν

Imperfect Active Indicative

	Singular	Plural
1.	ἵστην	ἵσταμεν
2.	ἵστης	ἵστατε
3.	ἵστη	ἵστασαν

Imperfect Mid./Pass. Ind.

	Singular	Plural
1.	ἱστάμην	ἱστάμεθα
2.	ἵστασο	ἵστασθε
3.	ἵστατο	ἵσταντο

First Aor. Act. Indicative

	Singular	Plural
1.	ἔστησα	ἐστήσαμεν
2.	ἔστησας	ἐστήσατε
3.	ἔστησε(ν)	ἔστησαν

Second Aor. Act. Indicative

	Singular	Plural
1.	ἔστην	ἔστημεν
2.	ἔστης	ἔστητε
3.	ἔστη	ἔστησαν

Second Aor. Act. Subjunctive

	Singular	Plural
1.	στῶ	στῶμεν
2.	στῇς	στῆτε
3.	στῇ	στῶσι(ν)

Second Aor. Act. Imperative

	Singular	Plural
2.	στῆθι	στῆτε
3.	στήτω	στήτωσαν

First Aor. Act. Infinitive

στῆσαι

Second Aor. Act. Infinitive

στῆναι

First Aor. Act. Participle

στήσας   στήσασα   στῆσαν

Second Aor. Act. Participle

στάς   στᾶσα   στάν

First Aor. Act. Imperative

Singular	Plural
2. στῆσον	στήσατε
3. στησάτω	στησάτωσαν

Pluperfect Act. Indicative

	Singular	Plural
1.	εἰστήκειν	εἰστήκειμεν
2.	εἰστήκεις	εἰστήκειτε
3.	εἰστήκει	εἰστήκεισαν

5.   The verb οἶδα - I know

Perfect Active Indicative

	Singular	Plural
1.	οἶδα	οἴδαμεν
2.	οἶδας	οἴδατε
3.	οἶδε(ν)	οἴδασι(ν)

Pluperfect Active Indic.

	Singular	Plural
1.	ᾔδειν	ᾔδειμεν
2.	ᾔδεις	ᾔδειτε
3.	ᾔδει	ᾔδεισαν

Perfect Active Subjunctive

	Singular	Plural
1.	εἰδῶ	εἰδῶμεν
2.	εἰδῇς	εἰδῆτε
3.	εἰδῇ	εἰδῶσι(ν)

Perfect Active Imperative

	Singular	Plural
2.	ἴσθι	ἴστε
3.	ἴστω	ἴστωσαν

Perfect Active Infinitive

εἰδέναι

Perfect Active Participle

εἰδώς   εἰδυῖα   εἰδός

6.   The verb γινώσκω - I know

Second Aor. Act. Indicative

	Singular	Plural
1.	ἔγνων	ἔγνωμεν
2.	ἔγνως	ἔγνωτε
3.	ἔγνω	ἔγνωσαν

Second Aor. Active Subj.

	Singular	Plural
1.	γνῶ	γνῶμεν
2.	γνῷς	γνῶτε
3.	γνῷ	γνῶσι(ν)

Second Aor. Act. Infinitive

γνῶναι

Second Aor. Act. Participle

γνούς   γνοῦσα   γνόν

Second Aor. Act. Imperative

Singular	Plural
2. γνῶθι	γνῶτε
3. γνώτω	γνώτωσαν

7.   The verb εἰμί - I am

Pres. Ind.

Sing.	Pl.
1.εἰμί	ἐσμέν
2.εἶ	ἐστέ
3.ἐστί(ν)	εἰσί(ν)

Imp. Ind.

	Sing.	Pl.
1.	ἤμην	ἤμεν
2.	ἦς	ἦτε
3.	ἦν	ἦσαν

Future Ind.

	Sing.	Pl.
1.	ἔσομαι	ἐσόμεθα
2.	ἔσῃ	ἔσεσθε
3.	ἔσται	ἔσονται

Pres. Subj.

	Sing.	Pl.
1.	ὦ	ὦμεν
2.	ᾖς	ἦτε
3.	ᾖ	ὦσι(ν)

Pres. Imp.

	Sing.	Pl.
2.	ἴσθι	ἔστε
3.	ἔστω	ἔστωσαν

Pres. Part.

Singular	
Masc.	ὤν
Fem.	οὖσα
Neut.	ὄν

Present Infinitive

εἶναι

Future Infinitive

ἔσεσθαι

Vocabulary

With respect to the verbs, all principal parts which occur in the New Testament are listed. Irregular verb forms are listed alphabetically, followed by the first principal part in parentheses.

ἀγαθός, -ή, -όν - good
ἀγαπάω, ἀγαπήσω, ἠγάπησα, ἠγάπηκα, ἠγάπημαι, ἠγαπήθην - I love
ἀγάπη, -ης, ἡ - love
ἀγαπητός, -ή, -όν - beloved
ἀγγελία, -ας, ἡ - message
ἄγγελος, -ου, ὁ - angel, messenger
ἁγιάζω, --, ἡγίασα, --, ἡγίασμαι, ἡγιάσθην - I consecrate, sanctify
ἅγιος, -α, -ον - holy (οἱ ἅγιοι = the saints)
ἀγορά, -ᾶς, ἡ - market place
ἀγοράζω, --, ἠγόρασα, ἠγόρακα, ἠγόρασμαι, ἠγοράσθην - I buy
ἀγρός, -οῦ, ὁ - field
ἄγω, ἄξω, ἤγαγον, --, ἦγμαι, ἤχθην - I lead, bring, go
ἀδελφή, -ῆς, ἡ - sister
ἀδελφός, -οῦ, ὁ - brother
ἀδικία, -ας, ἡ - injustice, unrighteousness
αἷμα, -ματος, τό - blood
αἴρω, ἀρῶ, ἦρα, ἦρκα, ἦρμαι, ἤρθην - I take up, take away, lift up
αἰτέω, αἰτήσω ᾔτησα, ᾔτηκα, --, ᾐτήθην - I ask
αἰών, -ῶνος, ὁ - age (εἰς τὸν αἰῶνα - forever)
αἰώνιος, -ον - eternal
ἀκάθαρτος, -ον - unclean
ἀκοή, -ῆς, ἡ - report
ἀκολουθέω, ἀκολουθήσω, ἠκολούθησα, ἠκολούθηκα - I follow (takes dative)
ἀκούω, ἀκούσω, ἤκουσα, ἀκήκοα, --, ἠκούσθην - I hear
ἀλήθεια, -ας, ἡ - truth
ἀληθής, -ές - true
ἀληθινός, -ή, -όν - true
ἀληθῶς - verily, truly
ἀλλά - but, indeed
ἀλλήλων, -οις, -ους - of one another, . . .
ἄλλος -η, -ο - other, another
ἁμαρτάνω, ἁμαρτήσω, ἡμάρτησα or ἥμαρτον, ἡμάρτηκα, --, -- - I sin
ἁμαρτία, -ας, ἡ - sin
ἁμαρτωλός, -όν - sinner, sinful
ἀμήν - amen
ἄν - particle (not translated)
ἀναβαίνω, -βήσομαι, -έβην, -βέβηκα - I go up
ἀναβλέπω - I look up, regain sight
ἀναγινώσκω - I read
ἀναλαμβάνω - I take up
ἀνάστασις, -εως, ἡ - resurrection
ἄνεμος, -ου, ὁ - wind
ἀνήρ, ἀνδρός, ὁ - man, husband
ἄνθρωπος, -ου, ὁ - man
ἀνίστημι - I raise up, rise
ἀνοίγω, ἀνοίξω, ἀνέῳξα or ἤνοιξα or ἠνέῳξα, ἀνέῳγα, ἀνέῳγμαι or ἠνέῳγμαι
    or ἤνοιγμαι, ἀνεῴχθην or ἠνοίχθην or ἠνεῴχθην - I open
ἀντί (with gen.) - instead of, opposite
ἄξιος, -ία, -ον - worthy
ἀπαγγέλλω, -αγγελῶ, -ήγγειλα, --, --, -ηγγέλην - I announce, proclaim
ἀπαίρω - I take away
ἅπας, -ασα, -αν - all
ἀπέθανον (ἀποθνήσκω)
ἀπέρχομαι - I go away, depart, leave
ἀπέστειλα (ἀποστέλλω)
ἀπιστία, -ας, ἡ - unbelief
ἀπό (with gen.) - from
ἀποδίδωμι - I give back, give away
ἀποθνήσκω, -θανοῦμαι, -έθανον, -- - I die
ἀποκαλύπτω, -καλύψω, -εκάλυψα, --, --, -εκαλύφθην - I reveal
ἀποκρίνομαι, --, ἀπεκρινάμην, --, --, ἀπεκρίθη - I answer
ἀποκτείνω or ἀποκτέννω, -κτενῶ, -έκτεινα, --, --, -εκτάνθην - I kill
ἀπόλλυμι, -λέσω or -λῶ, ἀπώλεσα (1 aor.), ἀπωλόμην (2 aor.), ἀπολώλεκα
    (1st perf.), ἀπόλωλα (2nd perf.) - I destroy, perish
ἀπολύω - I release, send away
ἀποστέλλω, -στελῶ, -έστειλα, -έσταλκα, -έσταλμαι, -εστάλην - I send

ἀπόστολος, -ου, ὁ - apostle
ἀποστρέφω, -στρέψω, -έστρεψα, --, -έστραμμαι, ἀπεστράφην - I turn away,
    reject
ἅπτομαι - I touch, lay hold of (followed by gen.)
ἅπτω, --, ἧψα, -- - I light, kindle
ἅρα - then, as a result
ἀρέσκω, ἀρέσω, ἤρεσα, -- - I please (with dative)
ἀρνέσμαι, ἀρνήσομαι, ἠρνησάμην, ἤρνημαι, -- - I deny, refuse
ἄρτι - now
ἄρτος, -ου, ὁ - bread, loaf
ἀρχή, -ῆς, ἡ - beginning
ἀρχιερεύς, -έως, ὁ - high priest
ἄρχομαι - I begin
ἄρχω, ἄρξω, ἦρξα - I rule over (followed by gen.)
ἄρχων, -οντος, ὁ - ruler
ἀρῶ (αἴρω)
ἀσθενέω, --, ἠσθένησα, -- - I am weak, sick
ἀσπάζομαι, --, ἠσπασάμην, -- - I greet
ἀστήρ, -έρος, ὁ - star
αὐτός,-ή, -ό - self, same, he, she, it
ἄφεσις, -έσεως, ἡ - forgiveness
ἀφίημι, ἀφήσω, ἀφῆκα, --, ἀφεῖμαι, ἀφέθην - I forgive, leave, allow
ἄχρι, ἄχρις (with gen.) - until
βάλλω, βαλῶ, ἔβαλον, βέβληκα, βέβλημαι, ἐβλήθην - I throw
βαπτίζω, βαπτίσω, ἐβάπτισα, --, βεβάπτισμαι, ἐβαπτίσθην - I baptize
βάπτισμα, -ματος, τό - baptism
βασιλεία, -ας, ἡ - kingdom
βασιλεύς, -έως, ὁ - king
βαστάζω, βαστάσω, ἐβάστασα, -- - I bear, carry
βήσομαι (βαίνω) (see ἀναβαίνω)
βιβλίον, -ου, τό - book
βλασφημέω, --, ἐβλασφήμησα, --, --, ἐβλασφημήθην - I blaspheme
βλέπω, βλέψω, ἔβλεψα, -- - I see
βούλομαι, --, --, --, --, ἐβουλήθην - I wish, want
Γαλιλαία, -ας, ἡ - Galilee
Γαλιλαῖος, -α, -ον - Galilean
γαμέω, --, ἔγημα or ἐγάμησα, --, --, ἐγαμήθην - I marry, enter matrimony
γάρ - for (conj.)
γε (enclitic) - at least, even, indeed, yet
γέγονα (γίνομαι)
γενεά, -ᾶς, ἡ - race, generation
γενήσομαι (γίνομαι)
γεννάω, γεννήσω, ἐγέννησα, γεγέννηκα, γεγέννημαι, ἐγεννήθην - I beget
γένος, -ους, τό - race, nation
γῆ, γῆς, ἡ - earth, land
γίνομαι, γενήσομαι, ἐγενόμην, γέγονα, γεγένημαι, ἐγενήθην - I become
γινώσκω, γνώσομαι, ἔγνων, ἔγνωκα, ἔγνωσμαι, ἐγνώσθην - I know
γλῶσσα, ης, ἡ - tongue
γνῶσις, -εως, ἡ - knowledge
γνώσομαι (γινώσκω)
γράμμα, -ματος, τό - letter, writing
γραμματεύς, -έως, ὁ - scribe
γραφή, -ῆς, ἡ - writing, scripture
γράφω, γράψω, ἔγραψα, γέγραφα, γέγραμμαι, ἐγράφην - I write
γυνή, γυναικός, ἡ - woman, wife
δαιμονίζομαι, --, --, --, --, (δαιμονισθείς) - I am possessed by a demon
δαιμόνιον, -ου, τό - demon
δέ - and, but
δεῖ - it is necessary (impersonal verb, followed by acc. and inf.)
δείκνυμι, δείξω, ἔδειξα, --, δέδειγμαι, ἐδείχθην - I show
δεῖπνον, -ου, τό - supper
δέκα - ten (indeclinable)
δένδρον, -ου, τό - tree
δεξιός, -ά, -όν - right
δεύτερος, -α, -ον - second
δέχομαι, δέξομαι, ἐδεξάμην, --, δέδεγμαι - I receive, welcome
δέω, --, ἔδησα, δέδεκα, δέδεμαι, ἐδέθην - I bind
διά (with gen.) - through
διά (with acc.) - on account of
διάβολος, -ον - slanderous, Devil
διαθήκη, -ης, ἡ - covenant, decree
διακονέω, διακονήσω, διηκόνησα, --, --, διηκονήθην - I serve (followed
    by dat.)
διακονία, -ας, ἡ - service
διάκονος, -ου, ὁ, ἡ - servant
διὰ τί - why?
διατίθημι - I make a covenant, decree (foll. by dat. or πρός and acc.)

διδάσκαλος, -ου, ὁ - teacher
διδάσκω, διδάξω, ἐδίδαξα, --, --, ἐδιδάχθην - I teach
διδαχή, -ῆς, ἡ - teaching
δίδωμι, δώσω, ἔδωκα, δέδωκα, δέδομαι, ἐδόθην - I give
διέρχομαι - I go through
δίκαιος, -α, -ον - righteous
δικαιοσύνη, -ης, ἡ - righteousness
δικαιόω, δικαιώσω, ἐδικαίωσα, --, δεδικαίωμαι, ἐδικαιώθην - I justify
διό - therefore
διώκω, διώξω, ἐδίωξα, δεδίωκα, δεδίωγμαι, ἐδιώχθην - I pursue, persecute
δοκέω, δόξω, ἔδοξα, -- - I think (3rd pers. sing. = it seems)
δόξα, -ης, ἡ - glory
δοξάζω, δοξάσω, ἐδόξασα, --, δεδόξασμαι, ἐδοξάσθην - I glorify
δοῦλος, -ου, ὁ - slave
δύναμαι, δυνήσομαι, --, --, --, ἐδυνήθην or ἠδυνήθην - I am able
δύναμις, -εως, ἡ - power
δυνατός, -ή, -όν - powerful
δύο - two(indeclinable except for a dat. δυσί)
δώδεκα - twelve (indeclinable)
δῶρον, -ου, τό - gift
ἐάν - if (with subj.)
ἐὰν μή - if not, unless (with subj.)
ἑαυτοῦ, -ῷ, -όν - himself (reflexive pronoun, masc.)
ἔβην (see ἀναβαίνω)
ἐβλήθην (βάλλω)
ἐγγίζω, ἐγγιῶ, ἤγγισα, ἤγγικα, -- - I come near, draw nigh
ἐγγύς (with gen. or dat.) - near
ἐγείρω, ἐγερῶ, ἤγειρα, --, ἐγήγερμαι, ἠγέρθην - I raise up
ἐγενήθην (γίνομαι)
ἐγενόμην (γίνομαι)
ἔγνωκα (γινώσκω)
ἔγνων (γινώσκω)
ἐγνώσθην (γινώσκω)
ἐγώ - I
ἔδραμον (τρέχω)
ἔθνος, -ους, τό - nation
εἰ - if (with indicative), frequently εἰ is used as an interrogative
    particle.
εἰ μή - if not, except, unless
εἶδον (ὁράω)
εἴληφα (λαμβάνω)
εἰμί, ἔσομαι, -- - I am (imperf.= ἤμην)
εἶναι - to be
εἶπον (λέγω)
εἴρηκα (λέγω)
εἰρήνη, -ης, ἡ - peace
εἰς (with acc.) - into, unto, against
εἷς, μία, ἕν - one
εἰσέρχομαι - I enter
εἰσπορεύομαι - I enter
εἶτα - then
ἐκ, ἐξ (with gen.) - out of
ἕκαστος, -η, -ον - each, every
ἐκβάλλω - I cast out
ἐκεῖ - there (adv.)
ἐκεῖθεν - from there
ἐκεῖνος, -η, -ο - that (demonstrative)
ἐκκλησία, -ας, ἡ - church
ἐκπλήσσομαι, --, --, --, --, ἐξεπλήγην - I am amazed
ἐκπορεύομαι - I go out, go forth
ἐκτείνω, ἐκτενῶ, ἐξέτεινα, -- - I stretch out
ἔλαβον (λαμβάνω)
ἐλεέω, ἐλεήσω, ἠλέησα, --, ἠλέημαι, ἠλεήθην - I have mercy on (followed
    by acc.)
ἔλεος, -ους, τό - mercy, pity
ἐλεύσομαι (ἔρχομαι)
ἐλήλυθα (ἔρχομαι)
ἐλήμφθην (λαμβάνω)
ἐλπίζω, ἐλπιῶ, ἤλπισα, ἤλπικα, -- - I hope
ἐλπίς, ἐλπίδος, ἡ - hope
ἐμαυτοῦ, -ῷ, -όν - myself (reflexive pronoun, masc.)
ἐμβαίνω, -βήσομαι, -έβην, -βέβηκα - I embark, step in
ἔμεινα (μένω)
ἐμός, ἐμή, ἐμόν - my, mine
ἔμπροσθεν (with gen.) - in front of
ἐν (with dat.) - in, with
ἐνδύω, --, ἐνέδυσα, -- (ἐνδεδυμένος) - I put on

ἐντολή, -ῆς, ἡ - commandment
ἐνώπιον (with gen.) - before, in the sight of
ἐξέρχομαι - I come forth
ἔξεστιν - it is lawful (impersonal verb, followed by dat. and inf.)
ἐξίστημι - I amaze, am amazed
ἐξουσία, -ας, ἡ - authority
ἔξω (with gen.) - outside
ἔξω (ἔχω)
ἑορτή, -ῆς, ἡ - feast
ἐπαγγελία, -ας, ἡ - promise
ἐπάγω - I bring on
ἔπαθον (πάσχω)
ἐπεί - since, because
ἐπερωτάω - I ask
ἔπεσον (πίπτω)
ἐπί (with gen.) - upon, in the time of, on
ἐπί (with dat.) - on, against, at
ἐπί (with acc.) - across, upon, against (ἐπί τὸ αὐτό - together)
ἐπιβάλλω - I put on, throw over, beat against
ἐπιγιώνσκω - I recognize
ἐπιθυμέω, ἐπιθυμήσω, ἐπεθύμησα, -- - I desire
ἐπιθυμία, -ας, ἡ - desire
ἐπικαλέω - I name, call upon
ἐπιστολή, -ῆς, ἡ - epistle, letter
ἐπιστρέφω, -στρέψω, -έστρεψα, --, --, -εστράφην - I turn, turn back
ἐπιτίθημι - I put on, lay upon
ἐπιτιμάω - I rebuke (followed by the dat.)
ἐπιτρέπω, ἐπιτρέψω, ἐπέτρεψα, --, --, ἐπετράφην - I permit (followed by dat.)
ἑπτά - seven (indeclinable)
ἐργάζομαι, --, ἠργασάμην or εἰργασάμην, -- - εἴργασμαι, -- - I work
ἔργον, -ου, τό - work
ἔρημος, -ου, ἡ - desert
ἔρχομαι, ἐλεύσομαι, ἦλθον, ἐλήλυθα, -- - I come, go
ἐρῶ (λέγω)
ἐρωτάω, ἐρωτήσω, ἠρώτησα, --, --, ἠρωτήθην - I ask, request
ἐσθίω, φάγομαι, ἔφαγον, -- - I eat
ἔσομαι (εἰμί)
ἔσχατος, -η, -ον - last
ἔσχον (ἔχω)
ἕτερος, -α, -ον - other, another
ἔτι - yet
ἑτοιμάζω, --, ἡτοίμασα, ἡτοίμακα, ἡτοίμασμαι, ἡτοιμάσθην - I prepare
ἔτος, -ους, τό - year
εὐαγγελίζομαι, --, εὐηγγελισάμην, --, εὐηγγέλισμαι, εὐηγγελίσθην -- - I announce good news, preach (the gospel) - active forms occur twice only in the N.T.
εὐαγγέλιον, -ου, τό - gospel
εὐθέως - immediately
εὐθύς - immediately
εὐλογέω, εὐλογήσω, εὐλόγησα, εὐλόγηκα, εὐλόγημαι, εὐλογήθην - I bless
εὕρηκα (εὑρίσκω)
εὑρήσω (εὑρίσκω)
εὑρίσκω, εὑρήσω, εὗρον, εὕρηκα, --, εὑρέθην - I find
εὗρον (εὑρίσκω)
εὐχαριστέω, --, εὐχαρίστησα, --, --, εὐχαριστήθην, -- - I give thanks (followed by dat. case)
ἔφαγον (ἐσθίω)
ἐχθρός, -οῦ, ὁ - enemy
ἔχω, ἕξω, ἔσχον, ἔσχηκα, -- - I have, hold
ἑώρακα (ὁράω)
ἕως - until, as far as (followed by gen.)
ζάω, ζήσω (ζήσομαι), ἔζησα, -- - I live
ζητέω, ζητήσω, ἐζήτησα, -- - I seek
ζωή, -ῆς, ἡ - life
ἤ - or, than
ἡγέομαι, --, ἡγησάμην, -- - ἥγημαι, -- - I consider, lead
ἡγέρθην (ἐγείρω)
ᾔδειν (οἶδα)
ἤδη - already
ἠθέλησα (θέλω)
ἥκω, ἥξω, ἦξα, ἧκα, -- - I have come
ἦλθον (ἔρχομαι)
ἥλιος, -ου, ὁ - sun
ἡμέρα, -ας, ἡ - day
ἡμέτερος, -α, -ον - our
ἤνεγκα (φέρω)

ἠνέχθην (φέρω)
ἦρα (αἴρω)
θάλασσα, -ης, ἡ - sea
θάνατος, -ου, ὁ - death
θαυμάζω, θαυμάσομαι, ἐθαύμασα, --, --, ἐθαυμάσθην - I marvel, wonder (at)
θέλημα, -ματος, τό - will
θέλω, θελήσω, ἠθέλησα, -- - I wish, desire
θεός, -οῦ, ὁ - God
θεραπεύω, θεραπεύσω, ἐθεράπευσα, --, τεθεράπευμαι, ἐθεραπεύθην - I heal
θερισμός, -οῦ, ὁ - harvest
θεωρέω, θεωρήσω, ἐθεώρησα, -- - I perceive
θηρίον, -ου, τό - beast
θλῖψις, -εως, ἡ - tribulation, affliction
θνήσκω - I die (only in perf. τέθνηκα)
θρόνος, -ου, ὁ - throne
θυγάτηρ, -τρός, ἡ - daughter
θύρα, -ας, ἡ - door
θυσία, -ας, ἡ - sacrifice
ἰάομαι, --, ἰασάμην, --, ἰαμαι, ἰάθην - I heal
ἴδιος, -α, -ον - one's own
ἰδού (particle) - see! behold!
ἰερεύς, -ρέως, ὁ - priest
ἰερόν, -οῦ, τό - temple
'Ιησοῦς, -οῦ, -οῦν, ὁ - Jesus (gen.,dat., and voc. have the same form
ἰκανός, -ή, -όν - sufficient, fit, worthy
ἰμάτιον, -ου, τό - garment
ἴνα - in order that (with subj.)
'Ιορδάνης, -ου, ὁ - Jordan
'Ιουδαία, -ας, ἡ - Judea, Judean
'Ιουδαῖος, -ου, ὁ - Jew
ἰσχυρός, -ά, -όν - strong
ἴστημι, στήσω, ἔστην (2 aor.), ἔστησα (1st aor.), ἔστηκα, --, ἐστάθην -
    I place, stand
ἰσχύω, ἰσχύσω, ἴσχυσα, -- - I am strong, can, be able
ἰχθύς, -ύος, ὁ - fish
'Ιωάννης, -ου, ὁ - John
κἀγώ = καὶ ἐγώ
καθαρίζω, καθαριῶ, ἐκαθάρισα, --, κεκαθάρισμαι, ἐκαθαρίσθην - I cleanse
καθαρός, -ά, -όν - clean
καθεύδω, -- - I sleep
κάθημαι, καθήσομαι, -- - I sit
καθίζω, καθίσω or καθιῶ, ἐκάθισα, κεκάθικα, -- - I sit, cause to sit
καθώς - as, just as
καί - and, even, also, both (καί . . . καί = both . . . and)
καινός, -ή, -όν - new
καιρός, -οῦ, ὁ - time, opportunity
κἀκεῖ = καὶ ἐκεῖ - and there (crasis)
κακός, -ή, -όν - evil
κακῶς - evilly
καλέω, καλέσω, ἐκάλεσα, κέκληκα, κέκλημαι, ἐκλήθην - I call
καλός, -ή, -όν - good, beautiful
καλῶς - beautifully, well
καρδία, -ας, ἡ - heart
καρπός, -οῦ, ὁ - fruit
κατά (with gen.) - against, down upon
κατά (with acc.) - according to, in, throughout
καταβαίνω, -βήσομαι, -έβην, -βέβηκα - I go down
καταργέω, -αργήσω, -ήργησα, -ήργηκα, -ήργημαι, -ηργήθην - I make inef-
    fective, nullify
κατέρχομαι - I come down
κατοικέω, -οικήσω, -ῴκησα, -- - I live, dwell
καυχάομαι, καυχήσομαι, ἐκαυχησάμην, --, κεκαύχημαι, -- - I boast
κελεύω, --, ἐκέλευσα, -- - I command
κεφαλή, -ῆς, ἡ - head
κηρύσσω, κηρύξω, ἐκήρυξα, --, --, ἐκηρύχθην, -- - I preach, proclaim
κλάδος, -ου, ὁ - branch
κλαίω, κλαύσω or κλαύσομαι, ἔκλαυσα, -- - I weep
κλέπτης, -ου, ὁ - thief
κλίνη, -ης, ἡ - bed
κόσμος, -ου, ὁ - world
κράζω, κράξω or κεκράξομαι, ἔκραξα or ἐκέκραξα, κέκραγα, -- - I cry out
κρατέω, κρατήσω, ἐκράτησα, κεκράτηκα, κεκράτημαι, -- - I seize, grasp
κρίμα, -ατος, τό - judgment, decree
κρίνω, κρινῶ, ἔκρινα, κέκρικα, κέκριμαι, ἐκρίθην - I judge
κρίσις, -σεως, ἡ - judgment
κρυπτός, -ή, όν - hidden, secret
κύριος, -ου, ὁ - lord, master

κώμη, -ης, ἡ - village
λαλέω, λαλήσω, ἐλάλησα, λελάληκα, λελάλημαι, ἐλαλήθην - I speak
λαμβάνω, λήμψομαι, ἔλαβον, εἴληφα, εἴλημμαι, ἐλήμφθην - I take, receive
λαός, -οῦ, ὁ - people
λέγω, ἐρῶ, εἶπον, εἴρηκα, εἴρημαι, ἐρρέθην or ἐρρήθην - I say
λήμψομαι (λαμβάνω)
λίθος, -ου, ὁ - stone
λογίζομαι, --, ἐλογισάμην, --, --, ἐλογίσθην - I think, consider
λόγος, -ου, ὁ - word
λοιπόν - finally
λοιπός, -οῦ, ὁ - remaining, rest
Λουκᾶς, -ᾶ, ὁ - Luke
λυπέω, --, ἐλύπησα, λελύπηκα, --, ἐλυπήθην - I grieve
λύω, λύσω, ἔλυσα, λέλυκα, λέλυμαι, ἐλύθην - I loose, destroy
μαθητής, -οῦ, ὁ - disciple
μακάριος, -α, -ον - blessed
μᾶλλον - more, rather
Μαρία, -ας, ἡ - Mary
μαρτυρέω, μαρτυρήσω, ἐμαρτύρησα, μεμαρτύρηκα, μεμαρτύρημαι, ἐμαρτυρήθην -
   I bear witness (followed by dat. or by περί with gen.)
μαρτυρία, -ας, ἡ - witness
μάρτυς, μάρτυρος, ὁ - witness
μάχαιρα, -ης, ἡ - sword
μέγας, μεγάλη, μέγα - great
μείζων, μεῖζον - greater
μέλλω, μελλήσω, -- I am about to (Imperfect = ἔμελλον, ἤμελλον)
μέλος, -ους, τό - member
μέν . . . δέ - on the one hand . . . on the other hand
μένω, μενῶ, ἔμεινα, μεμένηκα, -- - I remain
μέρος, -ους, τό - part
μέσος, -η, -ον - middle, midst
μετά (with gen.) - with
μετά (with acc.) - after
μετανοέω, μετανοήσω, μετενόησα, -- - I repent
μετάνοια, -ας, ἡ - repentance
μέχρι (with gen.) - until
μή - not (with other than indicative mood)
μηδέ - and not
μηδείς, μηδεμία, μηδέν - no one, nothing (with other than indicative)
μηκέτι - no longer
μήτε - and not
μήτηρ, μητρός, ἡ - mother
μικρόν - a little while
μικρός, -ά, -όν - small
μισέω, μισήσω, ἐμίσησα, μεμίσηκα, μεμίσημαι, -- - I hate
μισθός, -οῦ, ὁ - pay, reward
μνημεῖον, -ου, τό - tomb
μόνον - alone, only (adv.)
μόνος, -η, -ον - only (adj.)
μυστήριον, -ου, τό - mystery
ναί - yes, certainly
ναός, -οῦ, ὁ - sanctuary
νεκρός, -ά, -όν - dead
νέος, -α, -ον - new, young
νηστεύω, νηστεύσω, ἐνήστευσα, -- - I fast
νικάω, νικήσω, ἐνίκησα, νενίκηκα, --, (νικηθείς) - I conquer
νόμος, -ου, ὁ - law
νόσος, -ου, ἡ - disease
νῦν - now
νύξ, νυκτός, ἡ - night
ὁδός, -οῦ, ἡ - way, road, path
οἶδα (2nd perf. used as present), εἰδήσω or εἴσομαι, -- - I know
οἰκία, -ας, ἡ - house, home
οἰκοδομέω, οἰκοδομήσω, ᾠκοδόμησα, --, ᾠκοδόμημαι, ᾠκοδομήθην - I build,
   restore
οἶκος, -ου, ὁ - house, home
οἰκουμένη, -ης, ἡ - world, inhabited earth
οἶνος, -ου, ὁ - wine
οἷος, -α, -ον - of what sort
οἴσω (φέρω)
ὀλίγος, -η, -ον - few
ὅλος, -η, -ον - whole, all
ὀμνύω, --, ὤμοσα, -- - I swear, take an oath (foll. by acc. of pers. or thing)
ὅμοιος, -α, -ον - like, similar (with dat. of pers. or thing compared)
ὁμολογέω - I confess
ὁμοίως - likewise
ὄνομα, -ματος, τό - name

ὀπίσω (with gen.) - after
ὅπου - where (relative)
ὅπως - in order that (with subj.)
ὁράω, ὄψομαι, εἶδον, ἑώρακα or ἑόρακα, --, ὤφθην - I see (ὤφθην - "I
    appeared")
ὀργή, ῆς, ἡ - wrath, anger
ὅρος, -ους, τό - mountain
ὅς, ἥ, ὅ - who, which (relative pronoun)
ὅσος, -η, -ον - as great, as far, as many
ὅστις, ἥτις, ὅτι - whoever, whatever
ὅταν - whenever (with subjunctive)
ὅτε - when (particle)
ὅτι - because, that (conj.)
οὐ, οὐκ, οὐχ - not
οὐαί - Woe! Alas! (followed by dat. or acc.)
οὐδέ - and not
οὐδέ . . . οὐδέ - neither . . . nor
οὐδείς, οὐδεμία, οὐδέν - no one, nothing (with indicative)
οὐκέτι - no more
οὖν - therefore, then (post positive)
οὔπω - not yet
οὐρανός, -οῦ, ὁ - heaven
οὖς, ὠτός, τό - ear
οὔτε - not
οὗτος, αὕτη, τοῦτο - this
οὕτως - thus
οὐχί - not
ὀφείλω, --, (ὄφελον = "would that"), -- - I owe, ought
ὀφθαλμός, οῦ, ὁ - eye
ὄχλος, -ου, ὁ - crowd
ὄψομαι (ὁράω)
παιδίον, ου, τό - a small child
παλαιός, -ά, -όν - old
πάλιν - again
πάντοτε - always
παρά (with gen.) - from
παρά (with dat.) - near, in the presence of
παρά (with acc.) - along
παραβολή, ῆς, ἡ - parable
παραγγέλλω, --, -ήγγειλα, -- - I command, instruct
παραγίνομαι - I arrive
παράγω - I pass by
παραδίδωμι - I hand over
παρακαλέω - I invite, beseech, exhort
παράκλησις, -εως, ἡ - encouragement, appeal
παραλαμβάνω - I receive from, take along, take from
παρατίθημι - I place before
παρέχομαι - I pass by
παρουσία, -ας, ἡ - presence, coming
παρρησία, -ας, ἡ - boldness
πᾶς, πᾶσα, πᾶν - every, each
πάσχα, τό (indeclinable) - Passover
πάσχω, --, ἔπαθον, πέπονθα, -- - I suffer
πατήρ, πατρός, ὁ - father
πείθω, πείσω, ἔπεισα, πέποιθα, πέπεισμαι, ἐπείσθην - I persuade
πειράζω, --, ἐπείρασα, --, πεπείρασμαι, ἐπειράσθην - I tempt, try
πέμπω, πέμψω, ἔπεμψα, --, --, ἐπέμφθην - I send
πέντε - five (indeclinable)
πέπονθα (πάσχω)
πέραν - on the other side of, beyond (with gen.)
περί (with gen.) - concerning
περί (with acc.) - around
περιβλέπομαι - I look around
περιπατέω, -πατήσω, -επάτησα, -πεπάτηκα, -- - I walk
περισσεύω, περισσεύσω, ἐπερίσσευσα, --, --, (περισσευθήσομαι) - I have
    in abundance, I cause to abound, overflow
περιτομή, -ῆς, ἡ - circumcision
πετεινόν, -οῦ, τό - bird
Πέτρος, -ου, ὁ - Peter
πίνω, πίομαι, ἔπιον, πέπωκα, --, ἐπόθην - I drink
πίπτω, πεσοῦμαι, ἔπεσον, πέπτωκα, -- - I fall
πιστεύω, πιστεύσω, ἐπίστευσα, πεπίστευκα, πεπίστευμαι, ἐπιστεύθην - I
    believe (followed by dat. or by εἰς with acc.), entrust
πίστις, -εως, ἡ - faith
πιστός, -ή, -όν - faithful
πλανάω, πλανήσω, ἐπλάνησα, --, πεπλάνημαι, ἐπλανήθην - I deceive
πλείων, πλεῖον - more

334

πλῆθος, -ους, τό - multitude
πλήν - nevertheless, only, except
πλήρης, -ες - full
πληρόω, πληρώσω, ἐπλήρωσα, πεπλήρωκα, πεπλήρωμαι, ἐπληρώθην - I fill,
    fulfill
πλήρωμα, -ματος, τό - fullness
πλοῖον, -ου, τό - boat
πλούσιος, -ία, -ιον - rich
πνεῦμα, -ματος, τό - spirit
πόθεν - from where
ποιέω, ποιήσω, ἐποίησα, πεποίηκα, πεποίημαι, ἐποιήθην - I make, do
ποῖος, -α, -ον - of what kind
πόλις, -εως, ἡ - city
πολλά - much (adverb)
πολύς, πολλή, πολύ - much, many
πονηρός, -ά, -όν - evil
πορεύομαι, πορεύσομαι, --,--,πεπόρευμαι, ἐπορεύθην - I go
πόσος, -η, -ον - how great, how much
ποταμός, -οῦ, ὁ - river
πότε - when? (interrogative adj.)
ποτέ - at some time (enclitic particle)
ποτήριον, -ου, τό - cup
ποῦ - where? (interrogative)
πούς, ποδός, ὁ - foot
πράσσω, πράξω, ἔπραξα, πέπραχα, πέπραγμαι, -- - I practice
πρεσβύτερος, -α, -ον - older, elder
πρίν - before (conj. followed by acc. and inf. or by the aorist subj.)
πρό (with gen.) - before
προάγω - I go foward, bring forth, go before
πρόβατον, -ου, τό - sheep
πρός (with acc.) - toward, to
προσέρχομαι (with dat.) - I come to, approach
προσευχή, -ῆς, ἡ - prayer, place of prayer
προσεύχομαι, προσεύξομαι, προσηυξάμην, -- - I pray (with dat. of person
    to whom prayer is made)
προσκαλέομαι - I call to myself
προσκυνέω, προσκυνήσω, προσεκύνησα, -- - I worship (often followed by dat.)
προστίθημι - I add to
προσφέρω - I bring to, offer (foll. by acc. of thing or person brought
    and often by dat. of person or place to which something is brought)
πρόσωπον, -ου, τό - face
προφητεύω, προφητεύσω, ἐπροφήτευσα, -- - I prophesy
προφήτης, -ου, ὁ - prophet
πρῶτος, -η, -ον - first   (ἐν πρώτοις - at first, first, foremost)
πτωχός, -ή, -όν - poor
πύλη, -ης, ἡ - gate
πῦρ, πυρός, τό - fire
πῶς - how (interrogative). Used with direct or indirect questions
ῥῆμα, -ματος, τό - word
ῥίζα, -ης, ἡ - root
σάββατον, ου, τό - Sabbath, week
Σαμάρεια, -ας, ἡ - Samaria
σάρξ, σαρκός, ἡ - flesh
Σατανᾶς, -ᾶ, ὁ - Satan
σεαυτοῦ, -ῆς -- - yourself (reflexive pronoun)
σελήνη, -ης, ἡ - moon
σημεῖον, -ου, τό - sign
σήμερον - today (indeclinable)
Σίμων, -ωνος, ὁ - Simon
σῖτος, -ου, ὁ - wheat, grain
σκανδαλίζω, --, ἐσκανδάλισα, --, (ἐσκανδαλισμένος), ἐσκανδαλίσθην - I
    offend, cause to stumble (midd. with ἐν = "I take offense at")
σκεῦος, -ους, τό - vessel
σκότος, -ους, τό - darkness
σός, σή, σόν - your, yours
σοφία, -ας, ἡ - wisdom
σπείρω, --, ἔσπειρα, --, ἔσπαρμαι, ἐσπάρην - I sow (i.e. seed)
σπέρμα, -ματος, τό - seed
σπλαγχνίζομαι, --, --, --, --, ἐσπλαγχνίσθην - I have compassion (foll.
    by ἐπί and acc.)
σταυρός, -οῦ, ὁ - cross (noun)
σταυρόω, σταυρώσω, ἐσταύρωσα, --, ἐσταύρωμαι, ἐσταυρώθην - I crucify
στόμα, -ματος, τό - mouth
στρατιώτης, -ου, ὁ - soldier
σύν (with dat.) - with
συνάγω - I gather together
συναγωγή, -ῆς, ἡ - synagogue

συνείδησις, -εως, ἡ - conscience
συνέρχομαι - I come together
συνίημι, συνήσω, συνῆκα, -- - I understand
σώζω, σώσω, ἔσωσα, σέσωκα, σέσω(σ)μαι, ἐσώθην - I save
σῶμα, ματος, τό - body
σωτήρ, -ῆρος, ὁ - savior
σωτηρία, -ας, ἡ - salvation
ταράσσω, --, ἐτάραξα, --, τετάραγμαι, ἐταράχθην - I trouble
τε (enclitic) - and
τέθνηκα (θνήσκω)
τέκνον, -ου, τό - child
τελέω, --, ἐτέλεσα, τετέλεκα, τετέλεσμαι, ἐτελέσθην - I finish, complete
τέλος, -ους, τό - end, goal
τελώνης, -ου, ὁ - tax-collector
τέσσαρες (m.f.), τέσσαρα (n.) - four
τηρέω, τηρήσω, ἐτήρησα, τετήρηκα, τετήρημαι, ἐτηρήθην - I keep
τίθημι, θήσω, ἔθηκα, τέθεικα, τέθειμαι, ἐτέθην - I put, place, lay down
τιμάω, τιμήσω, ἐτίμησα, --, τετίμημαι, -- I honor
τιμή, -ῆς, ἡ - honor
τίς, τί - who, what or why (neut.)
τις, τι - someone, something
τοιοῦτος, αὕτη, -οῦτον (-οῦτο) - such
τόπος, -ου, ὁ - place
τότε - then
τρεῖς (m.f.), τρία (n.) - three
τρέχω, --, ἔδραμον, -- - I run
τρίτος, -η, -ον - third
τυφλός, -ή, -όν - blind
ὕδωρ, ὕδατος, τό - water
υἱός, -οῦ, ὁ - son
ὑμέτερος, -α, -ον - your
ὑπάγω - I go away
ὑπακούω - I obey (followed by the dat.)
ὑπάρχω, -- - I exist, am present
ὑπέρ (with gen.) - in behalf of
ὑπέρ (with acc.) - above, over, more than
ὑπό (with gen.) - by, by means of
ὑπό (with acc.) - under
ὑπόδημα, -ματος, τό - sandal
ὑπομονή, -ῆς, ἡ - patience, steadfastness
ὑποστρέφω, -στρέψω, -έστρεψα, --, --, ὑπεστράφην - I return, turn back
ὑποτάσσω, ---, -έταξα, --, -τέταγμαι, -ετάγην - I subject, subject myself
φάγομαι (ἐσθίω)
φαίνω, --, ἔφανα, --, --, ἐφάνην - I shine, appear
φανερός, -ά, -όν - visible
φανερόω, φανερώσω, ἐφανέρωσα, --, πεφανέρωμαι, ἐφανερώθην - I reveal,
    show
Φαρισαῖος, -ου, ὁ - Pharisee
φέρω, οἴσω, ἤνεγκα or ἤνεγκον, ἐνήνοχα, --, ἠνέχθην - I bring, carry
φεύγω, φεύξομαι, ἔφυγον, -- - I flee
φημί - I say (ἔφη - 3rd sing. of imperf. and 2nd aor.)
φιλέω, --, ἐφίλησα, πεφίληκα, -- - I love
φίλος, -η, -ον - devoted, friend
φοβέομαι, --, --, --, --, ἐφοβήθην - I am afraid, fear
φόβος, -ου, ὁ - fear
φρονέω, φρονήσω, ἐφρόνησα, -- - I think
φυλακή, -ῆς, ἡ - guard, watch, prison
φυλάσσω, φυλάξω, ἐφύλαξα, πεφύλαχα, --, ἐφυλάχθην - I guard
φυλή, -ῆς, ἡ - tribe
φωνέω, φωνήσω, ἐφώνησα, --, --, ἐφωνήθην - I call
φωνή, -ῆς, ἡ - voice
φῶς, φωτός, τό - light
χαίρω, χαρήσομαι, --, --, --, ἐχάρην - I rejoice
χαρά, -ᾶς, ἡ - joy
χαρίζομαι, χαρίσομαι, ἐχαρισάμην, --, κεχάρισμαι, ἐχαρίσθην - I give
    freely, forgive (with dat. of person to whom it is forgiven, acc. of
    whom or what is forgiven)
χάρις, χάριτος, ἡ - grace
χείρ, χειρός, ἡ - hand
χήρα, -ας, ἡ - widow
χόρτος, -ου, ὁ - grass
χρεία, -ας, ἡ - need
Χριστός, -οῦ, ὁ - Christ
χρίω - I anoint
χρόνος, -ου, ὁ - time
χώρα, -ας, ἡ - country
χωρίς (with gen.) - without

ψυχή, -ῆς, ἡ - soul, person, life
ὧδε - here
ὥρα, -ας, ἡ - hour
ὡς - as
ὥσπερ - just as
ὥστε - so that (sometimes followed by acc. and inf.)
ὤφθην (ὁράω)

Index of Subjects

References to Pages. A Complete
List of Topics is not attempted

A

Accent: signs of, 314; rules for accent of enclitics and proclitics, 315.
Active voice: 11.
Accusative case: double accusative, 186; meaning of, 20, 23; with the infinitive, 214; of time, 186.
Adjectives: declension of, 30; agreement with substantives, 31; attributive, 36; predicate, 36; comparative, 307-309; superlative, 309; used as substantives 36.
Adverbs: use of, 255, 309; forms of, 255, 309.
Agency: words expressing, 47; dative of, 48; with passive, 47.
Aktionsart: see tense.
Alphabet: original Greek, 5.
Anarthrous: attributive, 37; predicate, 37; participle, 155.
Aorist: meaning of, 99; indicative, 99; subjunctive, 197; aorist subjunctive with οὐ μή, 201; imperative, 265; optative, 269f., participle, 166, irregular verbs, 104; first and second aorist compared, 99.
Apodosis: see conditional sentences, 202.
Article: significance of, 31; agreement with substantives, 31; forms of, 31; position with attributives, 36.
Articular infinitive: 185,216.
Attributive: adjective, 36; participle, 152.

B

Breathings: 6; use with ρ, 137, 98.

C

Cases: number of, 21; syntax of, 20-21; nominative, 21; genitive, 22; dative, 22; accusative, 23; vocative, 23.
Complementary infinitive: 219.
Compound verbs: 45, 72.
Conditional sentences: general, 202; true, possible, 203; contrary to fact, 204.
Contraction: in verbs, 225,227; rules of, 227-228; principal parts of, 226.

D

Dative: form, 25; meaning, 22; of agency, 48; of respect, 97, 185; location, 185; time, 185.
Declension: first or α, 29; second or o, 25; third, 139; meaning of, 18-19; numerals, 243-244.
Deliberative subjunctive: 201, 252.
Demonstrative pronouns: forms of, 75; meaning, 74-75.
Deponent verbs: 48.
Diphthongs: 6.

E

Elision: 45.
Enclitics: 315.

F

First or α declension: 29.
Future: 84; forms, 84-85; meaning, 84-85; of liquid verbs, 237-238; irregular verbs, 88ff.

G

Gender: 19; agreement, 31.
Genitive: 22; form, 25; meaning of, 24; of time, 185; genitive absolute, 176-177; of article with infinitive, 185; of relationship, 185.

H

Historical present: 16, 40.
Hortatory: 200.